HarperCollins*Publishers*
1 London Bridge Street
London SE1 9GF

www.harpercollins.co.uk

First published by HarperCollins*Publishers* 2022

10 9 8 7 6 5 4 3 2 1

Text and photography © Good Housekeeping 2022

Project editor: Tracy Müller-King

Recipe writers: Meike Beck, Emma Franklin, Alice Shields,
Grace Evans, Georgie D'Arcy Coles, Lucy Jessop, Suzannah Butcher,
Elizabeth Fox, Sophie Austen-Smith, Monaz Dumasia,
Charlotte Watson, Madeline Burkitt, Gabriella English,
Zoe Garner, Olivia Spurrell

Photographers: Alex Luck, Mike English, Myles New,
Maja Smend, Kris Kirkham, Stuart West, Gareth Morgans,
William Davis, Kate Whitaker, Charlie Richards, Will Heap,
Adrian Lawrence, Tom Regester

A catalogue record of this book is available from the British Library
ISBN 978-0-00-848783-6

Printed and bound GPS Group

MIX
Paper from
responsible sources
FSC™ C007454

FSC
www.fsc.org

Good Housekeeping

COOKING *for* FRIENDS & FAMILY

THE ONLY RECIPES YOU WILL EVER NEED TO FEED YOUR NEAREST AND DEAREST

HarperCollins*Publishers*

Contents

Foreword by Gaby Huddart, Editor-in-Chief

Good Housekeeping readers often ask me what I enjoy most about my job, and one of the first things that comes to mind is that I'm lucky enough to taste all the fabulous recipes developed by our cookery team in the GH kitchens.

Once a month or so, we'll gather around a table laden with delicious dishes that our cookery director Meike Beck talks me through – much like a chef would do at a top restaurant – before we start to taste them. It's usually something of a culinary marathon as we sample small plates of around 20 dishes while trying to forget what season we're in. Let me explain: the cookery team work several months ahead so we're likely to be trying Easter lunch in December, a Christmas feast and mince pies in July and August, new barbecue dishes in very early spring, and getting our tastebuds stuck into Bonfire Night recipes in June!

Hand on heart, by the time the dishes are ready for me to try, they're already delicious. The only thing up for debate is whether we adjust the level of seasoning or spice, add a squeeze or two of lemon or lime juice, or perhaps tweak the portion sizes.

What's most fascinating to hear is the cookery team sharing their inspiration for each new recipe because they often talk of the family traditions that have gone into their thinking. For instance, Meike will tell me about her Dutch heritage and how she has a preference for savoury rather than sweet pancakes (such as the Fluffy Spinach Pancakes, page 21), while cookery writer Alice Shields keeps us entertained with the extraordinary number of potato dishes she learned to cook at her Lancashire mother's side (do try the Buttery Potato Stacks, page 362), and cookery editor Emma Franklin has a lot to say when it comes to Christmas! The thought of not serving turkey would bring her family out in a collective rash, she says, and the Dry-brined Turkey with Ultimate Get-ahead Gravy that we share in this collection (page 484) heroes two outstanding Essex ingredients that are central to their festivities: bronze turkey and sea salt.

What these examples show is that precious memories of those we hold dear are absolutely intertwined with the foods we serve and enjoy together. In my own home, my husband Mo is a barbecue obsessive, which means that no summer is properly underway until we have friends and family to visit, pop a few corks and fill the air with clouds of smoke, and the soundtrack is one of sizzling. 'Summer isn't summer without a barbecue,' is Mo's mantra! Two of the inevitable crowd-pleasers are Smokey Pulled Pork with Cola Barbecue Sauce (page 220) and Sticky Sausages (page 218); with the latter recipe, I'd always advise making three times the amount you think you'll need as I guarantee they'll all disappear. Also, thanks to the skill of our cookery team, sometimes even simple recipes can result in gasps of delight when served – the Cheesy Hedgehog Bread (page 150) is another one of my favourites as it's easy to make and is guaranteed to put smiles on the faces of those gathered around, waiting to tuck in.

It's no exaggeration to claim, I think, that preparing and sharing food is a vitally important way of showing friends and family that you care – indeed, that you love them and want to nurture them. During the Covid-19 pandemic lockdowns, those isolating received great comfort from meals brought to their doors by friends and neighbours. And when restrictions lifted, we were reminded of the true and unique joy that comes when we share food with those we love around a table. As family and friends reunited over bountiful barbecues and oven-fresh cakes, the importance – the necessity, even – of these celebrations was clear. Delicious meals bring us together and help to create memories to cherish.

As we've been working on this collection of our favourite recipes for sharing with family and friends, we have been celebrating our centenary at *Good Housekeeping*. This has involved us getting knee-deep into our archives and allowed us to take the long view of the importance of food throughout our history. Tastes have most definitely changed over the 10 decades we've been going, and I can promise you that we won't be bringing back some of our early recipes, such as Fillets of Beef with Bananas Garnished with Horseradish, or Cauliflower, Date and Banana Salad! But I can assure you that what hasn't faltered over the past 100 years is *Good Housekeeping*'s dedication to accuracy and commitment to quality. The reason that every recipe in GH is Triple Tested is because we want to ensure it's foolproof and will work every time.

To sign off, I'll share a quote from one my favourite philosophers, AA Milne's Winnie the Pooh, who asked 'What could be more important than a little something to eat?' For me, the only thing more important is sharing that 'little something to eat' with the people you love.

I hope you enjoy doing exactly that with the recipes in this book...

Gaby

Editor-in-chief, *Good Housekeeping*

Dietary Index

For those following a vegetarian, vegan, gluten-free or dairy-free diet, you'll find recipes throughout the cookbook where you see these symbols.

VN　Vegan recipes

GF　Gluten-free recipes

DF　Dairy-free recipes

V　Vegetarian recipes

- Check all packaging if following a specific diet, as brands vary.
- Not all cheese is vegetarian, although vegetarian cheeses (and dairy-free cheese suitable for a vegan diet) are widely available in supermarkets and health food stores. Always read the label and look out for the Vegetarian Society Approved symbol.
- Vegetable stock is not always vegan. Always check the label if you are following a special diet.
- Stock can contain gluten or dairy, so check the label if needed.
- Wine can contain animal protein, so check the label to ensure it is suitable for vegetarians or vegans.

The Measurements

OVEN TEMPERATURES

°C	Fan oven	Gas mark
110	90	¼
130	110	½
140	120	1
150	130	2
170	150	3
180	160	4
190	170	5
200	180	6
220	200	7
230	210	8
240	220	9

WEIGHTS

Metric	Imperial
15g	½oz
25g	1oz
40g	1½oz
50g	2oz
75g	3oz
100g	3½oz
125g	4oz
150g	5oz
175g	6oz
200g	7oz
225g	8oz
250g	9oz
275g	10oz
300g	11oz
350g	12oz
375g	13oz
400g	14oz
425g	15oz
450g	1lb
550g	1¼lb
700g	1½lb
900g	2lb
1.1kg	2½lb

VOLUMES

Metric	Imperial
5ml	1 tsp
15ml	1 tbsp
25ml	1fl oz
50ml	2fl oz
100ml	3½fl oz
125ml	4fl oz
150ml	5fl oz (¼ pint)
175ml	6fl oz
200ml	7fl oz
250ml	9fl oz
300ml	10fl oz (½ pint)
500ml	17fl oz
600ml	1 pint
900ml	1½ pints
1 litre	1¾ pints
2 litres	3½ pints

LENGTHS

Metric	Imperial
5mm	¼in
1cm	½in
2cm	¾in
2.5cm	1in
3cm	1¼in
4cm	1½in
5cm	2in
7.5cm	3in
10cm	4in
15cm	6in
18cm	7in
20.5cm	8in
23cm	9in
25.5cm	10in
28cm	11in
30.5cm	12in

ALWAYS REMEMBER

- Use one set of measurements – never mix metric and imperial.
- Ovens and grills must be preheated to the specified temperature before cooking.
- All spoon measures are for calibrated measuring spoons, and should be level, unless otherwise stated.
- Eggs are medium and free-range and butter is salted, unless otherwise stated.
- Always buy the best-quality meat you can afford.

1

Brunch

Curried Baked Beans

Scale this recipe up or down, or swap the
haricots for mixed beans, if you like.

1 onion, finely chopped
2 tsp olive oil
2 tbsp medium curry powder
2 x 400g tins haricot beans, drained and rinsed
2 x 400g tins chopped tomatoes
1 tsp caster sugar
4 medium eggs
4 tbsp mango chutney
4 slices sourdough bread, toasted
Large handful coriander, roughly chopped, to serve

1. Preheat the oven to 200°C (180°C fan) mark 6.
   In a large roasting tin, mix the onion, oil and
   curry powder. Roast for 15min, until the onion
   has started to soften. Stir through the beans,
   tomatoes, sugar and plenty of seasoning. Return
   to the oven for 30min, stirring occasionally, until
   the sauce is bubbling and has thickened slightly.

2. When the beans are nearly ready, poach the
   eggs. Bring a large, deep pan of water to the boil,
   then reduce to a simmer. Crack an egg into
   a ramekin or coffee cup, then neatly pour the
   egg into the simmering water. Working quickly,
   add a further 3 eggs in a similar fashion. Poach
   the eggs for 4min, or until the whites feel firm
   but the yolks remain soft. Lift the eggs out with
   a slotted spoon and drain on kitchen paper.

3. Spread the mango chutney over the toasted
   sourdough. Top each slice of toast with some
   beans, a poached egg and a sprinkling of
   coriander. Serve.

Hands-on time: 25min
Cooking time: about 45min
Serves 4

PER SERVING 405cals, 20g protein, 8g fat (2g saturates),
57g carbs (18g total sugars), 12g fibre

Speedy Mushrooms on Crumpets

This super-quick brunch doubles as a wonderful mid-week supper.

15g butter
1 small garlic clove, crushed
½ tsp dried thyme
125g mixed exotic mushrooms, ripped if large
1 medium egg
1 tbsp brandy (optional)
Large handful baby spinach
2 tbsp crème fraîche
2 crumpets, toasted

1. Bring a small deep pan of water to the boil. Melt the butter in a medium frying pan over a medium heat. Add the garlic and thyme to the frying pan and sizzle for 10sec, then turn up the heat to high and add the mushrooms. Fry until golden and any liquid in the pan has evaporated, about 5min.

2. Meanwhile, poach the egg. Reduce the water pan to a simmer and swirl to create a whirlpool. Crack the egg into a ramekin or coffee cup, then neatly pour the egg into the centre of the whirlpool. Poach for 4min, or until the white feels firm but the yolk remains soft when lifted out with a slotted spoon. Drain on kitchen paper.

3. Add the brandy, if using, to the mushrooms and bubble for 10sec. Stir in the spinach to wilt, followed by the crème fraîche. Check the seasoning. Serve the mushrooms on freshly toasted crumpets, topped with the poached egg and freshly ground black pepper.

Hands-on time: 15min
Cooking time: about 10min
Serves 1

PER SERVING 541cals, 17g protein, 30g fat
(17g saturates), 40g carbs (4g total sugars), 6g fibre

Harissa and Feta Shakshuka

The perfect no-fuss meal for weekend mornings and just as good for a relaxed supper, too.

1 tbsp olive oil
1 onion, finely chopped
2 mixed-colour peppers (we used green and red),
    de-seeded and finely chopped
2 garlic cloves, crushed
1 tbsp tomato purée
2 tbsp rose harissa
½ tsp ground cumin
2 x 400g tins cherry tomatoes
8 medium eggs
50g feta, crumbled
Large handful coriander, roughly chopped
Flatbreads, to serve (optional)

1. Heat the oil in a large frying pan or shallow
   casserole dish (that has a lid) over medium heat.
   Add the onion and cook for 5min, until softened.
   Stir in the peppers and cook for 10min.

2. Add the crushed garlic, tomato purée, harissa
   and cumin and cook for 2min. Stir in the tinned
   tomatoes and some seasoning and bubble for
   15min, until reduced.

3. Reduce the heat to low, make 8 wells in the
   tomato mixture and crack an egg into each well.
   Cover and cook for 10–13min, or until the egg
   whites are fully set but the yolks are still runny.

4. Sprinkle over the feta and coriander and serve
   with flatbreads, if you like.

Hands-on time: 25min
Cooking time: about 45min
Serves 4

PER SERVING (without flatbreads) 323cals, 21g protein,
19g fat (6g saturates), 14g carbs (13g total sugars), 5g fibre

Spicy Scrambled Tofu

A speedy recipe for brunch, lunch or dinner. Adjust the quantity of chilli to suit your heat preference.

3 tbsp vegetable oil
400g silken tofu, drained
1 red onion, finely chopped
1 red chilli, deseeded and finely sliced
4 tomatoes, roughly chopped
200g spinach
1 tbsp crispy chilli oil, plus extra to drizzle (optional)
4 large slices sourdough bread

1. Heat 1 tbsp vegetable oil in a large frying pan over high heat. Add the tofu and some seasoning. Fry, stirring to break up the tofu, for 2–3min, or until lightly golden and resembling scrambled eggs. Transfer to a plate.

2. Lower the heat to medium and add 1 tbsp more vegetable oil to the pan. Cook the onion for 10min, until softened. Add most of the fresh chilli and all the tomatoes and cook for 5min, until the tomatoes are starting to break down. Stir through the spinach to wilt.

3. Add the chilli oil, scrambled tofu and plenty of seasoning. Cook for 2min, to heat through.

4. Meanwhile, preheat a griddle pan over high heat. Brush the sourdough slices on both sides with the remaining 1 tbsp oil. Griddle for 2min per side, or until golden and charred. Serve the scrambled tofu on top of the griddled sourdough. Garnish with the remaining chilli and an extra drizzle of crispy chilli oil, if you like.

Hands-on time: 20min
Cooking time: about 20min
Serves 4

PER SERVING 386cals, 20g protein, 19g fat
(2g saturates), 31g carbs (8g total sugars), 7g fibre

Full English Traybake

An all-in-one version of the traditional English breakfast that's perfect for a family meal or when friends are staying.

450g baby new potatoes, halved
30g butter, melted
4 gluten-free pork sausages
4 gluten-free black pudding slices, about 225g
175g portabellini or chestnut mushrooms
250g cherry tomatoes on the vine
4 medium eggs
Small handful parsley, roughly chopped

1. Preheat the oven to 220°C (200°C fan) mark 7. On a large non-stick baking tray or ovenproof serving dish, toss the potatoes in the butter and some seasoning to coat. Add the sausages and roast for 15min.

2. Carefully remove from the oven. Add the black pudding and mushrooms, turning to mix in the buttery juices. Roast for another 15min.

3. Carefully remove the tray/dish from the oven. Lay the tomatoes on top, in 4 bunches. Make 4 small spaces in the tray/tin and crack an egg into each. Return to the oven for 8min, or until the egg whites are set. Scatter over parsley and some freshly ground black pepper and serve.

Hands-on time: 15min
Cooking time: about 40min
Serves 4

PER SERVING 585cals, 24g protein, 39g fat (15g saturates), 33g carbs (5g total sugars), 5g fibre

Peach Melba Breakfast Trifle

This recipe makes enough granola for the trifle, but you can easily make a double batch so you have some extra for weekday breakfasts.

FOR THE GRANOLA
100g gluten-free rolled jumbo oats
25g roasted chopped hazelnuts
½ tsp ground cinnamon
½ tsp ground ginger
25ml vegetable oil
50g apple sauce
15g runny honey
30g sultanas
5g freeze-dried raspberry pieces (optional)

FOR THE COMPOTE
300g fresh or frozen raspberries
50g caster sugar

FOR THE TRIFLE
1.2kg low-fat or full-fat Greek-style yogurt
2 x 410g tins peach slices in natural juices, drained

◆ **GET AHEAD**
Make the granola up to 1 week ahead. Once cool, store in an airtight container at room temperature. Assemble the trifle up to 30min ahead. Chill.

◆ **GH TIP**
For a sweeter trifle, reserve some of the juices from the peach tins and drizzle it over the yogurt layers.

1. Preheat the oven to 170°C (150°C fan) mark 3 and line a medium baking tray with baking parchment. For the granola, mix the oats, hazelnuts and spices in a medium bowl, until combined. Add the oil, apple sauce, honey and a pinch of salt and mix until well coated.

2. Spread the granola in an even layer on the lined tray and bake for 35min, turning once. Remove from the oven and stir through the sultanas and freeze-dried raspberry pieces, if using. Leave to cool completely.

3. Meanwhile, make the raspberry compote. In a medium pan over medium heat, cook the raspberries, sugar and 50ml water, squashing the raspberries with a wooden spoon, until mushy and pulped down, about 8min. Set aside to cool.

4. To assemble the trifle, spoon a third of the yogurt into a trifle dish or large glass bowl that holds roughly 2 litres. Drizzle over a third of the compote, then arrange a third of the peach slices on top and scatter over a third of the granola. Repeat the layering twice more, then serve.

Hands-on time: 30min, plus cooling
Cooking time: 35min
Serves 8

PER SERVING (with 2% fat Greek yogurt) 290cals, 18g protein, 8g fat (2g saturates), 34g carbs (26g total sugars), 34g fibre

Smokey Black Bean and Corn Fritters with Tomato Salsa

With a fresh salsa and Tex-Mex flavours, these spicy black-bean fritters are a lively start to the day. You could also serve them with a spiced yogurt instead of the poached eggs.

FOR THE SALSA
1 red onion, finely chopped
2 large tomatoes, roughly chopped
1 green chilli, deseeded and finely chopped
1 garlic clove, crushed
2 tsp white wine vinegar
Juice ½ lime
Small handful coriander, roughly chopped,
    plus extra to serve

FOR THE FRITTERS
175g self-raising flour
400g tin black beans, drained and rinsed
1 large carrot, peeled and coarsely grated
150g tinned or frozen sweetcorn
3 medium eggs, lightly beaten
½ tbsp chipotle chilli paste
1 tsp smoked paprika
1 garlic clove, crushed
1 tbsp vegetable oil

TO SERVE
4 poached eggs

1. Mix all the salsa ingredients with plenty of seasoning and set aside.

2. For the fritters, mix all the ingredients, except the oil, with plenty of seasoning in a large bowl, until combined. Heat ½ tbsp of the oil in a large non-stick frying pan over a medium heat. Working in batches, add large spoonfuls (about 2 heaped tbsp each) of the bean mixture to the pan, spreading each out a little with the back of the spoon.

3. Cook for 4–5min per side, until golden brown and cooked through. Repeat until you have used all the mixture (you should have 12 fritters), adding a little more oil as needed.

4. Divide the fritters between 4 plates, top each stack with a poached egg and garnish with coriander. Serve with the salsa.

Hands-on time: 10min
Cooking time: about 20min
Serves 4

PER SERVING 450cals, 22g protein, 13g fat
(3g saturates), 57g carbs (10g total sugars), 10g fibre

Peppered Mackerel Kedgeree

This delicious Anglo-Indian dish can be adapted to use any fish you like – try swapping the mackerel for hot smoked salmon for a luxurious twist.

1 tbsp vegetable oil
1 onion, finely chopped
15g fresh root ginger, peeled and finely grated
1½ tbsp mild curry powder
1 tsp turmeric
250g long grain rice
600ml hot vegetable stock
300g frozen leaf spinach
200g peppered mackerel fillets
4 medium eggs
Juice ½ lemon, plus wedges to serve
3 tbsp double cream

1. Heat the oil in a large, deep frying pan over a low heat and gently fry the onion with a large pinch of salt for 8–10min, until softened. Add the ginger, curry powder and turmeric and cook, stirring, for 2min. Stir in the rice and cook for 1min.

2. Add the stock, bring to the boil, then cover with a lid, reduce the heat and simmer gently for 10min, until the rice is just tender.

3. Meanwhile, defrost the spinach in a microwave or in a sieve in the sink by pouring over a kettleful of freshly boiled water. When defrosted and cool enough to handle, lift up the spinach and squeeze out all the excess moisture. Set aside until needed.

4. Flake the mackerel, discarding the skin. To poach the eggs, bring a large, deep pan of water to the boil, then reduce to a simmer. Crack an egg into a ramekin or coffee cup, then pour it into the simmering water. Working quickly, add the remaining 3 eggs. Poach for 4min, or until the whites feel firm but the yolks are soft. Lift the eggs out with a slotted spoon and drain on kitchen paper.

5. Gently stir the mackerel, spinach and lemon juice into the rice. Remove from the heat, then cover and rest for 2min, until warmed through. Divide among 4 shallow bowls, drizzle over the cream, top each bowl with a poached egg and serve with the lemon wedges to squeeze over.

Hands-on time: 35min
Cooking time: about 30min
Serves 4

PER SERVING 545cals, 23g protein, 24g fat (7g saturates), 56g carbs (5g total sugars), 5g fibre

Eggs Royale Bake

Combining the best of eggs Benedict and bread pudding, this savoury egg dish is a great way to feed a family. Swap the smoked salmon for slices of ham or wilted spinach, if you like.

6 English muffins
4 medium eggs
300ml whole milk
2 tsp Dijon mustard
200g smoked salmon, cut into strips
50g shop-bought hollandaise sauce
Small handful chives, finely chopped

1. Slice the muffins in half horizontally to make 12 circles. Arrange in a roughly 20 x 25cm ovenproof serving dish. In a jug, whisk the eggs, milk, mustard and plenty of seasoning. Pour over the muffins and leave to soak for 20min.

2. Preheat the oven to 170°C (150°C fan) mark 3. Once the muffins are soaked, tuck the salmon slices in the gaps between them. Cook for 30min, or until the custard is almost set.

3. Remove the dish from the oven, dollop over the hollandaise, then return to the oven for 10min, or until the custard is just set. Garnish with the chives and serve.

◆ GET AHEAD
Prepare up to end of step 1 up to 1 day ahead. Cover and chill. Complete recipe to serve.

Hands-on time: 15min, plus soaking
Cooking time: about 40min
Serves 6

PER SERVING 365cals, 23g protein, 16g fat (7g saturates), 32g carbs (4g total sugars), 2g fibre

Fluffy Spinach Pancakes

Swap the spinach for blanched kale or cavolo nero, if you prefer. Top the pancakes with bacon or a poached egg for a more substantial meal.

200g spinach
Handful mint, leaves picked
2 medium eggs
175ml milk
40g butter, melted, plus extra to fry
275g self-raising flour
1 tbsp baking powder
150g ricotta
100g pea shoots

1. Whizz the spinach, mint, eggs, milk, butter and plenty of seasoning in a blender until smooth. Add the flour and baking powder and whizz again (you may need to scrape down the sides once or twice, but the batter will come together). Set aside to rest for 5min.

2. Heat a large non-stick frying pan over a medium heat and brush with a little butter. Working in batches, add large spoonfuls of batter (about 3 tbsp each) to the pan, spacing apart. Cook for 1–2min, until bubbles appear on the surface, then flip and cook for another 2min until golden and cooked through. Remove to a plate, cover and keep warm. Cook the remaining pancakes, wiping the pan with kitchen paper and re-buttering between batches.

3. Divide the pancakes between 4 plates. Top with the ricotta, pea shoots and plenty of freshly ground black pepper. Serve.

Hands-on time: 10min, plus resting
Cooking time: about 10min
Serves 4

PER SERVING 448cals, 17g protein, 17g fat (9g saturates), 55g carbs (3g total sugars), 4g fibre

Rhubarb and Custard Brioche Bake

Tangy pink rhubarb balances the soft vanilla sweetness of this indulgent breakfast bake. It's best served warm from the oven, but leftovers are also delicious eaten cold the next day.

400g rhubarb, cut into 4cm pieces
125g caster sugar
Butter, to grease
300ml milk
200ml double cream
3 medium eggs
1 tbsp vanilla bean paste
400g brioche loaf, cut into 2cm-thick slices

◆ GH TIP
If you only have 1 large ovenproof serving dish, cook the rhubarb in it, then drain off the syrup and transfer the rhubarb to a plate before continuing.

1. Preheat the oven to 160°C (140°C fan) mark 3. Toss the rhubarb pieces with 75g of the sugar in an ovenproof dish, then arrange in a single layer. Cover with foil and bake for 15min. Remove from the oven, uncover and gently tip the dish from side to side, encouraging the syrup to coat any unmelted sugar.

2. Re-cover and return to the oven for 5min, until the rhubarb is just tender and all the sugar has melted. Carefully pour the pink syrup into a small bowl and set the bowl and dish aside.

3. Grease a roughly 2.6 litre ovenproof serving dish and arrange half the cooked rhubarb in the bottom. In a jug, whisk the milk, cream, eggs, vanilla and remaining 50g sugar. Cut the brioche slices in half diagonally and arrange them standing on their cut sides in the dish, on top of the rhubarb.

4. Dot over the remaining rhubarb, pour over the milk mixture, then cover loosely with foil and set aside to soak for 30min.

5. Reheat the oven (if needed) to 160°C (140°C fan) mark 3. Bake (covered) for 30–35min, or until the custard has just set (check in the middle between the slices). Remove from the oven and serve with the reserved syrup for spooning over.

Hands-on time: 25min, plus soaking
Cooking time: about 55min
Serves 8

PER SERVING 430cals, 9g protein, 24g fat (14g saturates), 44g carbs (24g total sugars), 2g fibre

Choc Chip Banana Bread Muffins

Banana bread gets a chocolatey upgrade in these delicious breakfast muffins. They keep really well as the banana helps them stay moist, and make a great lunchbox snack, too.

FOR THE TOPPING
25g butter
1 tbsp runny honey
40g rolled oats
40g skin-on almonds, chopped

FOR THE MUFFINS
3 medium, very ripe bananas (300g peeled weight)
200g light brown soft sugar
125ml sunflower oil
2 medium eggs
2 tbsp almond butter
2 tsp vanilla extract
200g plain flour
1 tsp bicarbonate of soda
50g dark chocolate chips

1. Preheat the oven to 180°C (160°C fan) mark 4 and line a 12-hole muffin tin with paper cases.

2. Make the topping. In a small pan over a low heat, melt the butter and honey. Remove the pan from the heat and stir in the oats, almonds and a pinch of salt. Set aside.

3. For the muffins, mash the bananas thoroughly in a medium bowl, then mix in the sugar, oil, eggs, almond butter and vanilla, until combined. Add the flour, bicarbonate of soda and chocolate chips and stir through.

4. Divide the batter evenly among the cases (they will be fairly full), then spoon over the topping. Bake for 25–30min, until well risen and browned on top. Remove to a wire rack to cool slightly (or completely) before serving.

◆ GET AHEAD
The cooled muffins will keep in an airtight container at room temperature for up to 1 week. To serve warm, reheat in an oven preheated to 180°C (160°C fan) mark 4 for 5min.

Hands-on time: 25min, plus cooling
Cooking time: about 35min
Makes 12 muffins

PER MUFFIN 305cals, 5g protein, 14g fat (3g saturates), 40g carbs (24g total sugars), 1g fibre

Apple, Clementine and Pecan Bircher

Prepare a bowl of this the night before so it's ready to grab from the fridge when people get up. By varying your milk and yogurt choices, you can adapt it to suit all diets and palates. We've made it without additional sweetness, but you can stir in some maple syrup, if you prefer.

FOR THE BIRCHER
150g gluten-free rolled oats
2 eating apples, coarsely grated
300ml milk or milk alternative (oat or rice), plus extra
    to loosen (optional)
Finely grated zest and juice 2 clementines
300g Greek-style yogurt or yogurt alternative (soya
    or coconut)
2 tbsp mixed seeds
40g dried cranberries, roughly chopped
¾–1 tsp mixed spice, to taste

TO SERVE
50g pomegranate seeds
40g pecans
2 clementines, peeled and opened into segments
Maple syrup, to drizzle (optional)

1. In a large non-metallic bowl, mix the Bircher ingredients well to combine. Cover, chill and leave to soak for at least 4hr or ideally overnight.

2. To serve, loosen the Bircher with a little milk or milk alternative, if you like. Spoon into bowls and sprinkle over the pomegranate seeds, pecans and clementine segments. Drizzle with a little maple syrup, if you like.

Hands-on time: 10min, plus (overnight) soaking
Serves 6

PER SERVING 327cals, 10g protein, 15g fat (6g saturates), 36g carbs (17g total sugars), 4g fibre

Cinnamon and Raisin Bagels

These authentic bagels take a little effort to make, but are well worth it. Try them as part of a brunch spread with cream cheese and fresh fruit.

FOR THE BAGELS
500g strong white flour
7g sachet fast-action dried yeast
2 tsp ground cinnamon
200g raisins
1 tbsp malt extract
1 tbsp honey
Oil, to grease

FOR THE POACHING LIQUID
2 tbsp malt extract
1 tbsp bicarbonate of soda

◆ TO STORE
Once cool, store in an airtight container at room temperature for up to 3 days.

1. To make the bagels, mix the flour, yeast, cinnamon and 1 tsp fine salt in a freestanding mixer fitted with a dough hook. Briefly mix in the raisins. In a jug, mix the malt extract, honey and 325ml tepid water. Pour into the flour bowl and knead for 5min, or until smooth and elastic. Cover the bowl and leave to rise in a warm place for 1hr, or until doubled in size.

2. Line 2 large baking sheets with lightly greased baking parchment, oil-side up. Divide the dough into 8 equal pieces, shaping each piece into a ball. Working with 1 ball at a time, poke a hole in the middle using your index finger, then poke your other index finger through the hole from the other side and roll your fingers around each other to make the hole gradually larger. Put on the lined sheet. Repeat with the remaining dough balls, spacing the bagels apart.

3. Cover the bagels with greased clingfilm (oil-side down). Leave to rise again in a warm place for 20min, or until visibly puffed.

4. Preheat the oven to 220°C (200°C fan) mark 7. For the poaching liquid, bring a large pan of water to the boil and stir in the malt extract. Reduce the heat to a gentle simmer and whisk in the bicarbonate of soda (it will foam up initially, but keep whisking until it subsides).

5. Gently lower in the bagels (in batches if needed). Cook for 2min, turning halfway through using a slotted spoon. Lift back on to the lined sheets and repeat the poaching process with the remaining bagels.

6. Bake in the oven for 17–20min, or until the bagels are deep golden brown. Transfer to a wire rack to cool completely. Serve.

Hands-on time: 45min, plus rising and cooling
Cooking time: about 25min
Makes 8 bagels

PER BAGEL 331cals, 7g protein, 1g fat (0g saturates), 72g carbs (24g total sugars), 3g fibre

Danish Cinnamon Twist

This sweet, soft pastry is similar to a cinnamon bun but has an added layer of crème pâtissière. The perfect sharing breakfast, it tastes as good as it looks!

FOR THE DOUGH
7 green cardamom pods
150ml whole milk
40g butter, plus extra to grease
1 tsp fast-action dried yeast
1 large egg yolk, plus whole egg, to glaze
275g plain flour, plus extra to dust
40g caster sugar

FOR THE CRÈME PÂTISSIÈRE
125ml whole milk
1 large egg yolk
½ tsp vanilla bean paste
1 tbsp caster sugar
½ tbsp plain flour
½ tbsp cornflour

FOR THE CINNAMON BUTTER
75g butter, softened
75g light brown soft sugar
1 tbsp ground cinnamon

FOR THE ICING
50g icing sugar, sifted

◆ **GH TIP**
For an even more indulgent treat, sprinkle some chocolate chips over the dough after you spread on the cinnamon butter in step 6.

Hands-on time: 1hr 30min, plus rising, cooling, chilling and setting
Cooking time: about 35min
Makes 1 twist/serves 8

PER SERVING 376cals, 7g protein, 16g fat
(9g saturates), 52g carbs (24g total sugars), 1g fibre

1. For the dough, use a pestle and mortar to bash the cardamom pods to break the husks. Pick out the black seeds and discard the husks, then grind the seeds until fine. Set aside. Heat the milk in a pan until hot, but not boiling. Take off the heat and stir in the butter to melt. Set aside to cool for 5min.

2. Stir the yeast into the milk mixture and leave for 5min until bubbly. Whisk in the egg yolk.

3. Using a freestanding mixer fitted with a dough hook, briefly mix the flour, ground cardamom, sugar and ½ tsp fine salt. Add the milk mixture, mix and knead for 5–10min, until the dough is elastic (it will be fairly wet). Cover and leave in a warm place to rise for 2hr, until visibly risen.

4. Meanwhile, make the crème pâtissière. Heat the milk in a small pan until hot but not boiling. In a heatproof bowl, whisk the egg yolk, vanilla and sugar until fully combined, then whisk in the flour and cornflour. Gradually whisk in the hot milk. Pour back into the pan and return to a medium heat. Cook for 2–3min, whisking constantly, until thickened and smooth. Scrape into a bowl and lay baking parchment or cling film on the surface to stop a skin forming. Cool and then chill.

5. For the cinnamon butter, mix the butter, light brown soft sugar and cinnamon in a medium bowl until combined. Set aside at room temperature until needed.

6. Line a large baking sheet with baking parchment. Punch down the dough in the bowl, then tip on to a lightly floured work surface. Roll out to a rough 26 x 33cm rectangle, with a long edge closest to you. Spread over the cinnamon butter, leaving a 1cm border. Then spread the crème pâtissière in a 10cm-wide strip lengthways along the centre of the dough.

7. Roll up the dough from the long edge closest to you and lift on to the lined baking sheet. Chill for 10min to firm up.

8. Using a pair of scissors, and starting 2cm in from one of the ends, make a diagonal snip halfway through the roll. Twist open the snipped section and lay to one side. Continue snipping diagonally at 2cm intervals, opening out the sections to alternate sides. Loosely cover with greased cling film (butter-side down) and leave to rise in a warm place for 45min, until puffed.

9. Preheat the oven to 200°C (180°C fan) mark 6. Brush the twist with beaten egg to glaze and bake for 20min, until golden. Leave to cool completely on the sheet.

10. For the icing, mix the icing sugar with just enough water to make a thick but drizzleable consistency. Drizzle the icing over the cooled twist and leave to set until ready to serve.

◆ GET AHEAD

The night before you want to bake the cinnamon twist, prepare to just before the end of step 8, but chill the twist instead of leaving it to rise. To serve, allow the pastry to come to room temperature for 45min, then uncover and complete the recipe.

Fluffy Ricotta Pancakes with Blueberry Compote

A classic combination — the lightest pancakes served with a bursting berry sauce. These pancakes freeze well, too.

FOR THE COMPOTE
250g blueberries
50g caster sugar
Finely grated zest and juice ½ lemon
1 tbsp cornflour

FOR THE PANCAKES
250g plain flour
1 tsp baking powder
¾ tsp bicarbonate of soda
50g caster sugar
175g ricotta cheese
150ml milk
3 medium eggs
Finely grated zest and juice ½ lemon
25g unsalted butter, to fry

◆ GET AHEAD
Once cool, pack the pancakes into a freezer-safe container, separating them with baking parchment. Freeze for up to 1 month. Make the blueberry compote up to 1 day ahead. Cool, cover and chill. To serve, reheat the frozen pancakes on a baking sheet in an oven preheated to 150°C (130°C fan) mark 2 for 12min. Gently rewarm the compote in a pan.

Hands-on time: 30min
Cooking time: about 30min
Makes 12 pancakes/serves 4

PER SERVING 498cals, 18g protein, 16g fat (9g saturates), 69g carbs (20g total sugars), 3g fibre

1. First, make the blueberry compote. In a medium pan over a low-medium heat, cook the blueberries, sugar, lemon zest and juice with 50ml water, stirring occasionally, until the blueberries are starting to burst.

2. Remove the pan from the heat. In a small bowl, mix the cornflour with 2 tbsp of the blueberry liquid, until smooth. Return the cornflour mixture to the pan. Bring back up to the boil and bubble for 1min, until thickened. Set aside until needed.

3. For the pancakes, whisk the flour, baking powder, bicarbonate of soda, sugar and a pinch of salt in a large bowl to combine. In a medium jug, whisk the ricotta, milk, eggs and lemon zest and juice, until smooth. Whisk the ricotta mixture into the flour bowl until just combined.

4. Heat a little of the butter in a large non-stick frying pan over a low-medium heat. Add about 1½–2 tbsp batter and spread to an 8–9cm circle with the back of a spoon. Add more pancakes to the pan, spacing them apart. Cook for 3–4min, or until the bases are golden and the tops are setting. Flip and cook for 2min more to cook through. Transfer to a plate, cover and keep warm. Repeat frying with the remaining batter to make 12 pancakes, adding a little more butter before each batch.

5. Serve the pancakes with the blueberry compote spooned over them.

Soups

Thai Green Curry Soup

Use shredded cooked chicken instead of a chicken breast, if you like, and adjust the amount of chilli to suit your taste.

2 tsp vegetable oil
2 spring onions, roughly chopped
1 carrot, peeled and finely chopped
½–1 green chilli, deseeded and finely chopped
2 tbsp Thai green curry paste
400ml chicken stock
200ml coconut milk
1 medium skinless chicken breast
50g basmati rice, well rinsed
100g sugar snap peas
Juice ½ lime, plus optional wedges to serve
Small handful coriander, roughly chopped

1. Heat the oil in a medium pan over a medium heat, then fry the spring onions, carrot and chilli for 5min, stirring occasionally, until the veg is softening. Stir through the curry paste and cook for 1min, until fragrant. Add the stock, coconut milk, chicken, rice and seasoning.

2. Bring to the boil and simmer for 15min, until the chicken is cooked through and the rice is almost tender. Lift the chicken on to a board and shred with 2 forks. Return to the pan with the sugar snap peas. Cook for 5min, until the peas are tender.

3. Stir through the lime juice and check the seasoning. Garnish with coriander and serve with extra lime wedges, if you like.

Hands-on time: 20min
Cooking time: about 30min
Serves 2

PER SERVING 431cals, 24g protein, 23g fat (16g saturates), 30g carbs (7g total sugars), 5g fibre

Chicken Katsu Noodle Soup

Using mayonnaise to help create the katsu chicken adds an extra layer of flavour to this delicious noodle soup.

FOR THE KATSU
1 small skinless chicken breast
40g panko breadcrumbs
1 tbsp mayonnaise

FOR THE SOUP
2 tsp vegetable oil, plus extra to shallow fry
1 carrot, halved lengthways and thinly sliced
4 spring onions, sliced
2 tsp medium curry powder
400ml hot chicken stock
100ml coconut milk
1 nest (50g) dried fine egg noodles (see GH Tip)
1–2 tsp soy sauce
Sesame seeds, to sprinkle (optional)

◆ GH TIP
Different brands of noodles vary in how much liquid they absorb – you may need to adjust the amount of stock.

1. Bash the chicken breast between 2 sheets of baking parchment or cling film with a rolling pin, to flatten to an even thickness. Put the breadcrumbs into a shallow bowl and season. Brush the chicken all over with the mayonnaise, then lay it in the breadcrumbs, pressing to coat it all over. Set aside while you make the soup.

2. Heat the oil in a medium pan and fry the carrot and most of the spring onions over a low heat for 3min, until slightly softened. Add the curry powder and fry, stirring, for 1min. Stir in the stock and coconut milk and simmer for 5min. Cover and keep warm.

3. Heat a shallow layer of oil in a small-medium non-stick frying pan over a medium heat. Cook the chicken for 4–5min per side, or until dark golden and cooked through. Remove to a plate lined with kitchen paper while you finish the soup.

4. Bring the soup to the boil, add the noodles and simmer for 3–5min, until just tender. Season to taste with soy sauce. Ladle the soup into a bowl, slice the chicken katsu and arrange it on top, then sprinkle over the reserved spring onions and sesame seeds, if using. Serve.

Hands-on time: 20min
Cooking time: about 25min
Serves 1

PER SERVING 752cals, 42g protein, 39g fat
(17g saturates), 7g carbs (1g total sugars), 1g fibre

Spinach and Broccoli Soup

Topped with a poached egg and croutons, this rich soup becomes a hearty meal.

FOR THE CROUTONS
4 thick slices sourdough bread, crusts removed,
    cut into cubes
1 tbsp olive oil

FOR THE SOUP
1 tbsp olive oil
1 onion, finely chopped
2 celery sticks, finely chopped
2 garlic cloves, crushed
1 litre vegetable stock
1 large broccoli head (about 350g)
250g spinach
100ml double cream
4 medium eggs
1 red chilli, deseeded and finely sliced

◆ GET AHEAD
This soup keeps well in the fridge (without
toppings) for up to 3 days. It does thicken a bit,
so loosen with more stock on reheating.

Hands-on time: 25min
Cooking time: about 25min
Serves 4

PER SERVING 353cals, 16g protein, 21g fat
(10g saturates), 21g carbs (8g total sugars), 7g fibre

1. Make the croutons. Preheat the oven to 200°C
   (180°C fan) mark 6. Toss the bread, oil and
   plenty of seasoning on a large baking tray.
   Cook for 10min, or until golden. Set aside.

2. Meanwhile, make the soup. Heat the oil in a
   large pan over a low heat and cook the onion for
   5min, until slightly softened. Add the celery and
   cook for 5min, then stir in the garlic. Cook for
   1min more, until aromatic.

3. Stir in the stock and bring to the boil. Roughly
   chop the broccoli (including the stalk) and add
   to the pan. Simmer for 10min, until the broccoli
   is tender. Stir through the spinach to wilt, then
   carefully blend until smooth. Stir through the
   cream and check the seasoning.

4. Meanwhile, poach the eggs. Bring a large, deep
   pan of water to the boil, then reduce to a simmer.
   Crack an egg into a ramekin or coffee cup,
   then neatly pour the egg into the simmering
   water. Working quickly, add a further 3 eggs in
   a similar fashion. Poach for 4min or until, when
   lifted out with a slotted spoon, the whites feel
   firm but the yolks remain soft. Once lifted out,
   drain the eggs on kitchen paper.

5. Ladle the soup into 4 bowls and top each with
   an egg, croutons and a sprinkling of chilli. Serve.

Roast Tomato and Chilli Soup

Roasted for extra flavour, with a chilli kick and chickpea 'croutons', this tomato soup is anything but ordinary.

2 red onions, roughly chopped
2 large carrots, roughly chopped
2 celery sticks, roughly chopped
600g ripe tomatoes, roughly chopped
4 red chillies, deseeded and roughly chopped
4 garlic cloves, unpeeled
2 tbsp tomato purée
1 tbsp olive oil
1 litre gluten-free vegetable stock
1 tsp caster sugar
2 tbsp double cream

FOR THE 'CROUTONS'
400g tin chickpeas, drained and rinsed
1 tbsp cornflour
2 tsp dried mixed herbs
1 tsp olive oil

◆ GET AHEAD
You can make the chickpea 'croutons' up to 2 days before you need them – store in an airtight container at room temperature.

1. Preheat the oven to 200°C (180°C fan) mark 6. In a large roasting tin, mix together the onions, carrots, celery, tomatoes, chillies, garlic, tomato purée, oil and plenty of seasoning. Roast for 55min, stirring halfway through, until all the vegetables are very tender.

2. Meanwhile, make the 'croutons'. Pat dry the chickpeas with kitchen paper, then tip into a small roasting tin and mix in the cornflour, mixed herbs, oil and plenty of seasoning. Cook in the oven alongside the veg for 40min, until crispy. Set aside.

3. When the vegetables are ready, gently press the garlic cloves out of their skins (discard the skins). Blend with the veg mixture, stock and sugar until smooth. Check the seasoning. Return to the pan to reheat. Stir through cream and ladle into 4 bowls. Sprinkle over the chickpea 'croutons' and serve.

Hands-on time: 20min
Cooking time: about 1hr
Serves 4

PER SERVING 282cals, 8g protein, 11g fat (3g saturates), 32g carbs (18g total sugars), 11g fibre

Crab, Harissa and Chickpea Soup

If using tinned crab, look for lump rather than shredded. For a fiery vegetable soup, omit the crab and use vegetable stock.

1 tbsp olive oil
1 onion, finely chopped
2 carrots, peeled and finely chopped
2 celery sticks, finely chopped
1 tsp ground cumin
1–2 tbsp harissa paste
4 tbsp tomato purée
850ml fish or vegetable stock
2 x 400g tins chickpeas, drained and rinsed
Juice ½ lemon
150g white crab meat, tinned or fresh

TO SERVE
Large handful parsley, roughly chopped
1 tbsp non-pareil capers
Toasted or griddled sourdough, to serve (optional)

1. Heat the oil in a large pan over a low heat and fry the onion for 5min, until softened. Add the carrots and celery and fry for 5min more, before stirring in the cumin, harissa, tomato purée and some seasoning. Fry for 1min, until aromatic.

2. Stir in the stock and bring to the boil. Add the chickpeas and simmer for 5min. Stir in the lemon juice and crab meat and check the seasoning.

3. Divide among 4 bowls and garnish with parsley and capers. Serve with toasted or griddled sourdough, if you like.

Hands-on time: 10min
Cooking time: about 20min
Serves 4

PER SERVING 285cals, 19g protein, 8g fat
(1g saturates), 28g carbs (8g total sugars), 11g fibre

Black-eyed Bean 'Taco' Soup

Fibre-rich black-eyed beans are a great source of protein and, along with the salsa topping, give this Mexican-style soup an authentic taste.

1 tbsp vegetable oil
1 onion, finely chopped
1 garlic clove, crushed
2 tsp ground cumin
1 tbsp chipotle chilli paste
1 tbsp tomato purée
3 x 400g tins black eyed beans, drained and rinsed
1 litre hot vegan vegetable stock
Juice 1 lime, plus wedges, to serve

FOR THE SALSA TOPPING
4 tbsp tinned sweetcorn, drained
½ ripe avocado, chopped
1 large ripe tomato, finely chopped
2 spring onions, thinly sliced

1. Heat the oil in a large pan over a low heat and fry the onion for 7–8min, stirring occasionally, until tender. Add the garlic, cumin, chilli paste and tomato purée and fry, stirring, for 1min. Stir through the beans and stock, bring to the boil and simmer for 10min.

2. Meanwhile, mix together the salsa ingredients and season.

3. Remove half the beans and liquid to a blender and whizz until smooth. Return to the pan with the unblended soup and season to taste with salt, pepper and lime juice.

4. Divide the soup between 4 bowls and top with the salsa. Serve.

◆ GH TIP
If you prefer, soak dried black-eyed beans and pre-cook them from scratch.

Hands-on time: 10min
Cooking time: about 20min
Serves 4

PER SERVING 333cals, 16g protein, 9g fat (1g saturates), 42g carbs (8g total sugars), 11g fibre

Pea, Ham and Watercress Soup with Stilton and Walnut Soda Bread

Soups are gloriously adaptable, and an excellent way to use up leftovers. This pea soup would also work well with cooked sprouts. Any leftover soda bread can be toasted the next day.

FOR THE SODA BREAD
200g wholemeal flour
150g plain flour, plus extra to dust
1½ tsp bicarbonate of soda
1 tsp sugar
125g Stilton (without rind), crumbled
60g walnuts, chopped
325g natural yogurt

FOR THE SOUP
1½ tbsp olive oil
1 onion, finely chopped
2 garlic cloves, crushed
700g frozen peas
600ml chicken or vegetable stock
100g watercress or rocket
100g crème fraîche
250g thick-cut ham, shredded, or ham hock

1. Preheat the oven to 190°C (170°C fan) mark 5 and line a baking sheet with baking parchment. For the bread, combine the flours, bicarbonate of soda, sugar, ½ tsp fine salt and freshly ground black pepper in a large bowl. Add the Stilton and walnuts and mix gently. Make a well in the centre and add the yogurt. Mix into to a shaggy dough.

2. Tip on to a lightly floured work surface and shape into a ball. Put on the lined baking sheet and flatten slightly. Cut a cross into the top, or press in a cross using a floured wooden spoon handle – you want to go at least halfway down into the dough. Bake for 35–40min, or until deeply golden and the base sounds hollow when tapped. Cool on a wire rack.

3. Meanwhile, make the soup. Heat 1 tbsp of the oil in a large pan over medium heat and fry the onion, covered with a lid, for 10min until softened. Add the garlic and fry for 1min. Stir in the peas, stock and some seasoning. Bring to the boil and simmer for a few minutes. Stir in the watercress or rocket, to wilt. Blend until smooth, then return to the pan and whisk in the crème fraîche and 150g of the ham. Check the seasoning.

4. To serve, heat the remaining ½ tbsp oil in a medium frying pan over a high heat. Add the remaining ham and fry until crisp, about 5min. Reheat the soup, if needed, and divide among 4 soup bowls. Top with the crispy ham and some freshly ground black pepper, then serve with the soda bread.

Hands-on time: 25min
Cooking time: about 45min, plus cooling
Serves 4

PER SERVING (with 1 slice of bread) 678cals, 38g protein, 30g fat (13g saturates), 57g carbs (17g total sugars), 15g fibre

Squash, Sage and Chestnut Soup

Butternut squash gives this autumnal soup a creamy edge and is easy to make ahead. For a vegan version, omit the goat's cheese or choose a vegan substitute.

FOR THE SOUP
1 tbsp olive oil
2 onions, roughly chopped
2 garlic cloves, crushed
800g skin-on butternut squash, deseeded and cut into
   2.5cm pieces (see GH Tip)
2 medium carrots, peeled and roughly chopped
180g pouch ready-cooked chestnuts
1.5 litres vegetable stock
2 sage sprigs

TO GARNISH
2 tsp olive oil
Small handful small sage leaves
100g goat's cheese log

◆ GET AHEAD
Make the soup up to 2 days ahead, then cool, cover and chill. Garnishes can be made up to 3hr ahead and stored at room temperature. To serve, reheat the soup in a pan until piping hot, check the seasoning and complete the recipe.

◆ GH TIP
For an extra garnish, rinse your butternut squash seeds and dry on kitchen paper. Heat 1 tsp oil in a small non-stick frying pan over a low heat, then add the seeds with a pinch of smoked paprika and salt. Fry gently until golden and crisp, about 10min. Leave to cool before sprinkling over the soup.

Hands-on time: 20min
Cooking time: about 45min
Serves 8

PER SERVING 190cals, 6g protein, 7g fat (3g saturates), 23g carbs (13g total sugars), 6g fibre

1. For the soup, heat the oil in a large pan over a low heat and cook the onions for 5min, until softened. Stir in the garlic, butternut squash, carrots and all but about 8 of the chestnuts. Cook for 5min. Pour in the stock and add the sage sprigs and plenty of seasoning.

2. Bring up to the boil and simmer for 20–25min, until the squash is completely tender. Working in batches, whizz until smooth. Check the seasoning and pour into a clean pan.

3. For the garnish, heat 1 tsp oil in a small frying pan over a medium heat. Meanwhile, chop the 8 reserved chestnuts. When the oil is hot, fry the chestnuts for a few minutes, until golden and crisp. Set aside on a plate. Add the remaining oil and fry the small sage leaves, until golden and crisp. Lift on to kitchen paper to drain.

4. To serve, reheat the soup and ladle into 8 soup bowls. Garnish with the fried chestnuts and sage leaves. Crumble over the goat's cheese and sprinkle over some freshly ground black pepper.

Cauliflower Soup with Gruyère Crisps

This rich, creamy soup looks elegant and sophisticated, but is a wonderfully no-fuss, make-ahead dish.

2 small (or 1 large) cauliflowers (about 1kg total)
60g unsalted butter
3 large echalion shallots, sliced
250ml whole milk
900ml gluten-free chicken or vegetable stock
¼ tsp ground white pepper
Grating of nutmeg
1 tbsp crème fraîche
1–2 tsp lemon juice
75g ready-cooked chestnuts, roughly chopped

FOR THE GRUYÈRE CRISPS
60g Gruyère, finely grated
1 tsp finely chopped rosemary

◆ GET AHEAD
Make the soup up to 2 days ahead. Cool, cover and chill. Reserve the cauliflower leaves for garnish wrapped in damp kitchen paper in a food bag in the fridge. Make the Gruyère crisps up to 3hr ahead and store at room temperature. To serve, reheat the soup until piping hot in a pan, thinning with extra water, if needed. Complete the recipe.

Hands-on time: 25min, plus cooling
Cooking time: about 40min
Serves 6

PER SERVING 254cals, 13g protein, 15g fat (9g saturates), 14g carbs (9g total sugars), 5g fibre

1. Trim the base off the cauliflower(s) and cut away the leaves, discarding the large, tough outer leaves, but reserving any tender inner leaves for garnish. Cut the cauliflower(s) into florets, discarding the core, then roughly chop.

2. Heat 40g of the butter in a large pan over a medium heat. Stir in the cauliflower, shallots and a good pinch of salt. Cover and fry gently for 10min, stirring occasionally, until softened.

3. Uncover and cook for a further 5min, until just taking on a little colour. Add the milk and simmer gently for 5min. Stir in the stock and simmer for another 5min. Set aside to cool for 10min. Blend with the white pepper, nutmeg, crème fraîche and lemon juice (to taste), until smooth. Check the seasoning and thin with extra stock, if needed. Return to a clean pan.

4. For the Gruyère crisps, preheat the oven to 200°C (180°C fan) mark 6 and line a large baking tray with baking parchment. Lightly mix the Gruyère and rosemary. Place in 6 heaped piles, spacing apart, on the prepared tray. Cook for 8min, or until bubbling and golden. Cool for 1min on the tray, then transfer to kitchen paper to soak up excess oil. Cool.

5. When ready to serve, heat the remaining butter in a small frying pan. Add the chestnuts and reserved cauliflower leaves, season, then fry for 3–4min, until golden. Reheat the soup, if needed, and divide among 6 bowls. Top with the chestnut garnish and serve with the Gruyère crisps.

Zesty Carrot and Lentil Soup

A simple and warming soup brought to life with orange zest and a swirl of harissa.

1 tbsp olive oil
1 onion, finely chopped
2 celery sticks, chopped
450g carrots, roughly chopped
200g red split lentils, rinsed under cold water
1.2 litres gluten-free vegan vegetable stock
Finely grated zest ½ orange

TO FINISH
1 tbsp rose harissa paste, to taste
100g plain dairy-free yogurt
Finely grated zest ½ orange

1. Heat the oil in a large pan over a medium heat and cook the onion and celery, stirring occasionally, for 10min, until softened. Add the carrots, lentils and plenty of seasoning and fry for 1min.

2. Stir in the stock and orange zest, bring to the boil, then simmer for 20min, until the lentils are mushy and the carrots tender. Blend until smooth, then return to the pan, if needed, to reheat. Check the seasoning.

3. To serve, marble the harissa through the dairy-free yogurt. Divide the soup among 4 bowls and swirl on the harissa yogurt. Serve scattered with some orange zest and a grinding of fresh black pepper.

Hands-on time: 15min
Cooking time: about 35min
Serves 4

PER SERVING 311cals, 15g protein, 6g fat (1g saturates), 43g carbs (16g total sugars), 11g fibre

Hearty Mussel Soup

Cream gives a luxurious feel to this herby soup of mussels and fresh vegetables.

1kg fresh mussels
1 tbsp olive oil
2 onions, finely chopped
1 leek, finely sliced
3 large carrots, diced
2 medium potatoes, cut into small cubes
2 garlic cloves, crushed
1 bay leaf
900ml gluten-free fish or vegetable stock
50ml double cream
2 tbsp chopped chives

1. Sort through the mussels (see GH Tip) and clean them, removing any barnacles and beards with a knife. Heat a large pan and add the mussels. Put on the lid and cook for 3–4min until the mussels open. Strain. Set aside a few mussels in their shells, then pick out the meat from the rest. Discard the empty shells and any mussels that haven't opened.

2. Heat the oil in a large pan and gently cook the onions, leek, carrots and potatoes for 10min until tender. Stir in the garlic and bay leaf and cook for 1min. Pour in the stock and bring to the boil.

3. Add the mussel meat and cream to the pan. Discard the bay leaf and check the seasoning. Divide among 4 warmed soup bowls, scatter over the chives and garnish with the reserved mussels in their shells.

◆ GH TIP
Keep fresh mussels in an open bag in the fridge, covered with damp kitchen paper. To clean, put in a colander under cold running water. The shells should be tightly closed (give them a sharp tap on a work surface if they aren't, and discard any that have broken shells or haven't closed after 30sec).

GF

Hands-on time: 25min
Cooking time: about 20min
Serves 4

PER SERVING 323cals, 17g protein, 13g fat (6g saturates), 32g carbs (12g total sugars), 8g fibre

Jerusalem Artichoke and Cider Soup

The sweet acidity of cider beautifully balances the earthy, nutty flavour of the Jerusalem artichokes in this unusual soup.

FOR THE SOUP
40g butter
1 onion, finely chopped
2 garlic cloves, crushed
1kg Jerusalem artichokes, peeled and roughly chopped
1 medium potato, peeled and roughly chopped
750ml vegetable stock
500ml cider
1 tsp ground white pepper
150ml double cream, plus extra, to garnish (optional)

FOR THE TOPPING
40g sourdough bread, cut or torn into small pieces
1 eating apple, cored and finely chopped
40g mature vegetarian Cheddar, finely grated
1 tsp olive oil

◆ GET AHEAD
Make the soup up to a day ahead, then cool, cover and chill. To serve, make the topping and gently reheat the soup in a pan.

1. Preheat the oven to 200°C (180°C fan) mark 6. To make the soup, melt the butter in a large pan over a medium heat. Add the onion and cook for 10min, stirring occasionally, until softened. Stir in the garlic, artichokes and potato. Cook for 10min, until the vegetables have started to soften. Add the stock and cider, bring to the boil and simmer for 15min, or until the vegetables are tender. Stir in some salt and pepper to taste.

2. Meanwhile, mix all the topping ingredients with some seasoning in a small roasting tin. Cook for 15min, stirring occasionally, until golden. Set aside until needed.

3. Cool the soup slightly before blending it until smooth (thin with extra stock if needed). Return to a clean pan, stir in the cream. Reheat if needed, then divide among 6 bowls. Garnish with a swirl of cream, if you like, and the topping, then serve.

Hands-on time: 25min, plus cooling
Cooking time: about 45min
Serves 6

PER SERVING 654cals, 23g protein, 44g fat
(13g saturates), 31g carbs (9g total sugars), 12g fibre

Tofu Satay Noodle Soup

This recipe works well with egg or rice noodles, but only rice noodles are (typically) vegan. If you want to use pre-cooked noodles, stir them into the coconut mixture with the carrots.

200g egg or rice noodles
275g firm tofu, cut into 2cm cubes
2 tbsp cornflour
1–2 tbsp vegetable oil
400ml tin coconut milk
2 medium carrots, shaved into ribbons with
　a vegetable peeler
4 tbsp peanut butter
1½ tbsp soy sauce
2 tbsp sweet chilli sauce
1 lime
3 spring onions, finely sliced
25g salted peanuts, roughly chopped
Large handful coriander, roughly chopped

1. Bring a large pan of water to the boil. Cook the noodles according to the packet instructions. Drain, then run under cold water to cool them down and drain again. Set aside.

2. Meanwhile, pat dry the cubed tofu with kitchen paper. Put the cornflour into a shallow bowl and season well with salt and pepper. Toss the tofu gently in the cornflour. Heat the oil in a large non-stick frying pan over a medium-high heat. Fry the tofu, carefully turning occasionally, until golden and crisp. Set aside.

3. Return the empty noodle pan to a medium heat, add the coconut milk and 400ml water, then bring to the boil. Add the carrot ribbons and cook for 2min, until just tender. In a separate bowl, mix the peanut butter, soy and sweet chilli sauces and the juice of ½ lime. Whisk into the coconut pan.

4. Stir the cooked noodles and most of the spring onions into the pan and check the seasoning. Divide among 4 bowls. Top with the fried tofu and garnish with peanuts, coriander and the remaining spring onions. Cut the remaining lime half into wedges and add a wedge to each bowl. Serve.

Hands-on time: 20min
Cooking time: 15min
Serves 4

PER SERVING 657cals, 22g protein, 37g fat
(18g saturates), 56g carbs (12g total sugars), 7g fibre

Tantanmen Pork Ramen

If you have time, marinate your soft-boiled eggs (see GH Tip) to add an extra flavour dimension to this restorative bowl.

4 medium eggs
1 litre carton fresh ramen broth
200ml chicken stock
Handful dried shiitake mushrooms
2 tbsp soy sauce
1 tbsp caster sugar
150g ramen or other flat dried noodles
150g beansprouts
4 baby pak choi, halved lengthways
2 tsp vegetable oil
250g pork mince
2 tbsp chilli bean sauce or sriracha hot sauce
2 spring onions, finely chopped, plus extra, sliced,
    to garnish

◆ GH TIP

For soy marinated eggs, heat 5 tbsp each soy sauce and water with 1 tbsp sugar in a small pan, stirring to dissolve the sugar. Cool, then put into a food bag with the peeled, soft-boiled eggs. Seal and chill for at least 4hr (or up to 2 days).

1. Bring a small pan of water to the boil. Add the eggs, then reduce the heat to low and simmer gently for 6min. Drain and put into a large bowl of cold water to stop the cooking. Peel, rinse and set aside (see GH Tip).

2. Combine the ramen broth and stock in a medium pan, add the mushrooms, bring to a gentle simmer, then reduce the heat to as low as possible and keep warm. In a small bowl, mix the soy sauce and sugar until dissolved, then set aside.

3. Cook the noodles in a large pan of salted water according to the packet instructions, adding the beansprouts for the final 30sec of cooking. Drain and rinse under cold water, then drain again. Divide among 4 deep bowls and top with baby pak choi.

4. Heat the oil in a frying pan over a high heat. Add the mince and fry for 3–4min until opaque, stirring to break up any lumps. Add the chilli bean sauce/sriracha and spring onions, then stir-fry for 3min.

5. Remove the hot broth from the heat and stir in the soy mixture. Top the noodle bowls with pork mince, then pour over the hot broth. Halve the eggs lengthways and add to the bowls. Garnish with spring onions and serve.

Hands-on time: 30min
Cooking time: about 20min
Serves 4

PER SERVING 404cals, 30g protein, 15g fat
(4g saturates), 34g carbs (8g total sugars), 4g fibre

Beef Pho

The strength of this Vietnamese classic is in its base broth. Authentically, the meat is either simmered with the broth for hours or added raw at the end, so the boiling broth lightly cooks it. Carrots are not traditional, but give extra texture.

1.5 litres fresh beef stock (don't use a stock cube)
1 cinnamon stick
5cm piece fresh root ginger, roughly chopped
1 star anise
1 red onion, roughly chopped
4 whole cloves
1 tbsp coriander seeds
Large handful coriander
1 sirloin steak (about 175g), excess fat removed
200g flat rice noodles
2 carrots, peeled into ribbons with a vegetable peeler
1 tbsp fish sauce

FOR THE GARNISH
2 spring onions, thinly sliced
1–2 bird's eye chillies, to taste, deseeded and sliced
Large handful Thai basil
Lime wedges, to serve

1. Put the stock into a large pan and add the cinnamon stick, ginger, star anise, onion, cloves and coriander seeds. Cut the stems from the coriander (reserve the leaves) and add to the stock. Bring to the boil and simmer for 30min to intensify the flavours.

2. Meanwhile, wrap the steak in cling film and freeze for 15min (this will make it easier to slice).

3. Bring a large pan of water to the boil and cook the noodles according to the pack instructions, adding the carrots for the final 2min of cooking. Drain and run under cold water to stop the cooking. Divide among 4 bowls.

4. When the stock is ready, taste and adjust the seasoning with the fish sauce. Slice the beef as thinly as you can (across the grain) and lay it on top of the noodles.

5. Strain the stock into a clean pan and bring back to the boil. Pour into the bowls (over the beef and noodles) and garnish with spring onions, chillies, coriander leaves and Thai basil. Serve with lime wedges.

Hands-on time: 15min, plus freezing
Cooking time: about 40min
Serves 4

PER SERVING 431cals, 50g protein, 5g fat
(1g saturates), 46g carbs (7g total sugars), 4g fibre

Spring Minestrone with Mint Pesto

In Italy, minestrone is made with any in-season veg — this spring version is packed with greens. New potatoes give the soup body, but you could use cooked rice or small pasta shapes, if you like.

1 tbsp olive oil
6 spring onions, roughly chopped
1 carrot, roughly chopped
200g baby new potatoes, cut into 5mm slices
1.25 litres vegetable stock
200g baby courgettes, trimmed and sliced
200g spring greens, finely shredded (woody stalks discarded)
200g peas, fresh or frozen
Large handful mint leaves

FOR THE MINT PESTO
1 garlic clove, crushed
25g pine nuts, toasted
25g mint leaves
15g Italian-style vegetarian hard cheese, grated, plus extra to sprinkle
75ml extra virgin olive oil

1. Heat the oil in a large pan over a medium heat and fry the spring onions for 2–3min, until softened. Add the carrot, potatoes and stock. Bring to the boil and simmer for 10min, until the potatoes are tender.

2. Meanwhile, whizz all the pesto ingredients and some seasoning in the small bowl of a food processor until almost, but not quite, smooth. Alternatively, bash the dry ingredients using a pestle and mortar before mixing in the oil.

3. Add the vegetables and mint to the pan and simmer for 5–7min, until tender. Divide among 4 bowls, then top each with a spoonful of pesto and a sprinkling of cheese and serve.

Hands-on time: 20min
Cooking time: about 25min
Serves 4

PER SERVING 372cals, 11g protein, 25g fat (4g saturates), 22g carbs (12g total sugars), 9g fibre

Smoked Haddock Sweetcorn Chowder

More commonly made with potatoes to give the soup body, our chowder uses rice for speed. Cooking the haddock in the same pan means all the lovely smokey flavours of the fish will infuse the soup.

½ tbsp vegetable oil
6 spring onions, chopped
1 tsp sweet smoked paprika
750ml gluten-free vegetable stock
2 skinless and boneless smoked haddock fillets
   (about 250g total)
250g pouch microwave long grain rice
300g tinned or frozen sweetcorn
75ml double cream

1. Heat the oil in a large pan over a medium heat. Add most of the spring onions and cook for a few minutes, until softened. Stir in the paprika and fry for 1min.

2. Pour in the stock and bring to a simmer. Add the haddock and simmer gently for 3–4min, or until the fish flakes easily when pressed. Using a slotted spoon, lift the haddock on to a plate.

3. Stir the rice and sweetcorn into the pan, breaking up any clumps of rice. Simmer for 3min. Meanwhile, flake the haddock into chunks.

4. Remove 4 ladlefuls (about 500ml) of the soup mixture to a large jug and whizz with a stick blender until smooth (or do this in a blender). Return to the pan along with the flaked haddock, cream and some seasoning. Heat through, then ladle into 4 bowls and top with the reserved spring onions and some extra freshly ground black pepper. Serve.

◆ GH TIP
For something a little different, you could replace the sweetcorn with fresh or frozen peas.

GF

Hands-on time: 5min
Cooking time: about 20min
Serves 4

PER SERVING 330cals, 15g protein, 15g fat (7g saturates), 31g carbs (9g total sugars), 4g fibre

3

Starters

Chargrilled Asparagus and Romesco Toasts

A pepper and tomato dip from Catalonia in Spain, Romesco combines sweet and smokey flavours to make it positively addictive. If you don't have a griddle pan, you can boil or steam the asparagus instead.

100g blanched almonds
300g flame-roasted red peppers from a jar (drained weight)
75g sun-dried tomatoes in oil (drained weight)
1½ tbsp sherry or red wine vinegar
1 tsp hot or sweet smoked paprika
2 garlic cloves, peeled
1 tbsp extra virgin olive oil, plus extra to drizzle and brush
300g fine asparagus spears, woody ends trimmed
Flaked sea salt, to sprinkle
6 long slices rustic bread

1. Toast the almonds in a dry frying pan over low heat for 4–6min, until golden. Tip into a food processor with the peppers, tomatoes, vinegar, paprika, 1 garlic clove, the oil and plenty of seasoning. Whizz to a chunky paste. Cover and set aside at room temperature.

2. Heat a griddle pan over a high heat. Griddle the asparagus, in batches if needed, for 7–8min, until charred but still firm (they will continue to soften on cooling). Remove to a plate, drizzle over some oil and sprinkle with a little flaked sea salt. Set aside until needed.

3. To serve, lightly brush the bread with oil on both sides. Griddle or toast under the grill for 1–2min per side (in batches if needed). Halve the remaining garlic clove and rub the cut sides over the hot toasts. Divide the toasts among 6 plates and spread a little Romesco sauce over each. Top with asparagus and serve with the remaining sauce on the side.

◆ GET AHEAD

Make the Romesco 1 day ahead, then cover and chill. Griddle the asparagus up to 2hr ahead, then cool, cover and keep at room temperature. To serve, allow the sauce to come up to room temperature for 1hr, then stir to recombine. Complete the recipe.

Hands-on time: 20min
Cooking time: about 25min
Serves 6

PER SERVING 318cals, 12g protein, 15g fat (2g saturates), 32g carbs (4g total sugars), 6g fibre

Grilled Herbed-butter Scallops

Served in scallop shells, this impressive starter is easy to prepare ahead and cooks in a matter of minutes.

---

18 scallops in their shells (see GH Tip)
150g butter, softened
2 small garlic cloves, crushed
6 tbsp capers, drained and roughly chopped
Juice 1 lemon
Small handful parsley, finely chopped
50g fresh white breadcrumbs
Lemon wedges, to serve

◆ GET AHEAD
Prepare and chill the scallops, and wash and boil the shells, up to 2hr ahead. Complete the recipe to serve. Make the herby butter and chill up to 3 days ahead.

◆ GH TIP
If you prefer, buy 18 large loose scallops and grill them in shallow ramekins rather than their shells.

1. To open a scallop, hold it in your hand with the flat shell on top and the hinge away from you. Insert a cutlery knife into the small opening near the hinge and twist it to release the shell. Gently run the knife along the inside of the curved shell to free the scallop. Open the shells completely and scrape the contents on to a board (reserve the curved shell). Pull off and discard anything surrounding the central scallop, including the coral roe (or keep the roe attached, if you prefer).

Repeat, preparing the remaining scallops and reserving 6 of the curved shells in total. Rinse the scallops thoroughly under cold running water for at least 5min. Drain well, then cover and chill until needed (up to 2hr).

2. Meanwhile, wash the 6 reserved shells in hot soapy water. Bring a large pan of water to the boil, add the cleaned shells and bubble for 5min to sterilise them. Drain and set aside to dry.

3. In the small bowl of a food processor, whizz the butter, garlic, capers, lemon juice, parsley and some seasoning until well combined. Alternatively, mix together in a bowl. Scrape on to a sheet of baking parchment, wrap into a sausage shape and chill until needed.

4. Preheat the grill to high. Pat dry the scallops with kitchen paper and put 3 into each shell. Arrange the shells on a baking tray. Slice the butter into 18 portions and put 1 on top of each scallop. Grill for 4min, or until the butter has melted slightly.

5. Carefully spread the butter around the scallops, then sprinkle over the breadcrumbs. Grill for 2min more, or until the scallops are cooked through and the breadcrumbs are golden. Serve with lemon wedges for squeezing over.

Hands-on time: 45min
Cooking time: about 12min
Serves 6

PER SERVING 316cals, 23g protein, 22g fat (13g saturates), 7g carbs (1g total sugars), 1g fibre

Warm Roasted Squash and Burrata Salad with Salsa Verde

A quick-to-assemble salad that's filled with warmth and freshness.

FOR THE SALAD
50g blanched hazelnuts
6 small balls vegetarian burrata
1 medium butternut squash (about 1.5kg), peeled, halved
  and deseeded
2 tbsp olive oil

FOR THE SALSA VERDE
6 tbsp extra virgin olive oil
1 tbsp red wine vinegar
2 tsp capers, finely chopped
1 small garlic clove, crushed
½ tsp caster sugar
Large handful flat-leaf parsley, finely chopped
Handful basil leaves, finely chopped
Handful mint leaves, finely chopped

◆ GET AHEAD
Toast the hazelnuts up to 4hr ahead. The salsa
verde is best made fresh, but can be made up
to 2hr ahead. Stir before serving.

◆ GH TIP
To make this vegan, roast small wedges of peeled
beetroot with the squash, and replace the burrata
with spoonfuls of dairy-free crème fraîche. Also
check your red wine vinegar is suitable.

Hands-on time: 25min
Cooking time: about 35min
Serves 6

PER SERVING 544cals, 20g protein, 39g fat
(15g saturates), 26g carbs (11g total sugars), 6g fibre

1. Preheat the oven to 180°C (160°C fan) mark 4.
   For the salad, put the nuts on a small baking tray,
   toast for 8min in the oven, or until golden, and
   set aside. Bring the burrata to room temperature
   for 30min.

2. Increase the oven temperature to 220°C (200°C
   fan) mark 7. Cut the squash into 1cm-wide
   wedges (either lengthways or widthways) and
   arrange in a single layer on a large baking tray.
   Drizzle with the olive oil, then season and roast
   for 25min, until tender and golden.

3. Meanwhile, make the salsa verde. Whizz the oil,
   red wine vinegar, capers, garlic, sugar and some
   seasoning in the small bowl of a food processor.
   Add the chopped herbs and whizz again
   until fairly smooth. Alternatively, finely chop
   everything by hand and mix together.

4. To assemble the salad, divide the squash among
   6 plates. Drain the burrata, then tear it into
   pieces and dot around the squash. Roughly chop
   the nuts and scatter over, then spoon over some
   of the salsa verde. Serve with the remaining
   salsa verde on the side.

Trout Pâté with Date and Caraway Soda Bread

Home-made bread and a zesty fish pâté will start a special lunch with a bang. Use whichever cooked smoked fish you prefer – try kippers, smoked mackerel or hot-smoked salmon.

FOR THE SODA BREAD
175g plain flour, plus extra to dust
175g wholemeal flour
100g jumbo rolled oats
1 tsp bicarbonate of soda
40g unsalted butter, chilled and cubed
5 pitted Medjool dates, roughly chopped
1½ tsp caraway seeds
350ml buttermilk

FOR THE PÂTÉ
175g crème fraîche
50g cream cheese
1½ tbsp hot horseradish sauce
1½ tbsp capers, rinsed, drained and chopped
Finely grated zest 1 lemon and juice ½ lemon
3 tbsp chopped dill
375g skinless hot-smoked trout fillets

◆ GET AHEAD
Soda bread is best eaten on the day it's baked, but it can be lightly toasted if made a day in advance. The pâté can be made 1 day ahead, covered and chilled. Allow it to come up to room temperature for 15min before serving.

1. Preheat the oven to 200°C (180°C fan) mark 6. For the soda bread, dust a baking sheet with a little plain flour. Mix both flours, the oats, bicarbonate of soda and 1 tsp fine salt in a large mixing bowl, then rub in the butter with your fingertips until combined.

2. Stir through the dates and 1 tsp caraway seeds. Make a well in the centre, pour in the buttermilk and mix to a soft dough with a wooden spoon. Tip on to a work surface and knead lightly with your hands. Bring to a rough round.

3. Put the dough on the prepared baking sheet. Dust the handle of the wooden spoon with a little flour and press it on to the top of the dough to make a cross. Scatter over the remaining caraway seeds and bake for 40–45min, until risen and golden. Transfer to a wire rack to cool completely.

4. For the pâté, mix the crème fraîche, cream cheese, horseradish sauce, capers, lemon zest and juice, most of the dill and some seasoning. Flake in the fish, then use a fork to mash together to a rough pâté. Spoon into 6 individual ramekins or one large serving dish and garnish with the remaining dill. Serve with the soda bread.

Hands-on time: 35min, plus cooling
Cooking time: about 45min
Serves 6

PER SERVING 620cals, 24g protein, 27g fat (15g saturates), 68g carbs (14g total sugars), 6g fibre

Crab and Ricotta Tartlets

These delicate tartlets come together quickly and are best served warm.

250g ricotta
125g crème fraîche
200g white crabmeat
4 spring onions, finely sliced, white and green
   parts separated
3 medium egg yolks
2 lemons
1 red chilli, deseeded and finely chopped
75g butter, melted
4 sheets filo pastry
Handful rocket, to serve (optional)

1. Preheat the oven to 180°C (160°C fan) mark 4. Mix the ricotta, crème fraîche, 150g of the crab, the white parts of the spring onions, egg yolks, the finely grated zest of 1½ lemons and the chilli. Season well. Mix the remaining crab with the green parts of the spring onions.

2. Brush 8 holes of a muffin tin with butter. Working with one filo sheet at a time, brush the top with butter, then lay it on top of another filo sheet. Brush again with butter, then cut into quarters. Press each quarter into a muffin hole, scrunching in the edges so they don't overhang too much. Repeat with the remaining filo sheets and butter.

3. Divide the ricotta mixture among the cases, then top with the crab and spring onion mixture. Cook for 25-30min, until the filo is golden and the filling is just set with a slight wobble.

4. Zest the remaining ½ lemon and scatter over the tartlets. Leave to set in the tin for 5min before removing carefully. Serve with rocket, if you like.

◆ GET AHEAD
Prepare to the end of step 1 up to 4hr ahead. Cover the filling and topping separately and chill. Complete the recipe to serve.

Hands-on time: 20min
Cooking time: about 30min, plus setting
Makes 8 tartlets

PER TARTLET 247cals, 10g protein, 20g fat
(12g saturates), 6g carbs (1g total sugars), 0g fibre

Melon and Chorizo Salad

A super-quick dish. If making for those avoiding gluten and dairy, make sure the chorizo you choose does not contain either.

1 cantaloupe melon
75ml balsamic vinegar
1 tbsp runny honey
75g chorizo, in one piece, skinned
1 tbsp oil
1 punnet cress, trimmed

1. Halve the melon, then spoon out and discard the seeds. Cut each half into 3 wedges, then cut the skin off each wedge. Chill until needed (or up to 2hr).

2. Put the balsamic vinegar and honey into a small pan and simmer gently for 5min until syrupy. Leave to cool (up to 2hr).

3. Cut the chorizo into small cubes. Heat the oil in a small frying pan and add the sausage cubes. Fry for 3min until the chorizo is golden and has given up some of its oil. Strain into a small bowl and set the oil aside. Set aside the chorizo or chill until needed (or up to 2hr).

4. To assemble, put a melon wedge on each of 6 small plates, then sprinkle over some of the fried chorizo and cress. Drizzle the chorizo oil and balsamic glaze over each plate and serve.

Hands-on time: 10min, plus chilling
Cooking time: about 10min
Serves 6

PER SERVING 60cals, 2g protein, 2g fat (<1g saturates), 7g carbs (7g total sugars), 1.5g fibre

Smoked Salmon and Mackerel Mousse Ring

Use your favourite smoked fish with the salmon to add interest to this retro-style starter.

500g smoked salmon slices
500g cream cheese
500g smoked mackerel
200g crème fraîche
Large handful parsley, finely chopped, plus extra to garnish
50g capers, rinsed and roughly chopped
Finely grated zest of 1½ lemons

◆ GET AHEAD
Make up to end of step 3 up to 1 day ahead. Cover and chill. Complete the recipe to serve.

1. Line a 1 litre ring mould with a couple of layers of cling film. Set aside 150g of the smoked salmon, then use the remaining salmon to line the prepared tin, overlapping the slices slightly.

2. Put the cream cheese into a large bowl and beat until smooth. Peel and discard the skin from the mackerel fillets. Flake the mackerel into the cream cheese and add the crème fraîche, parsley, capers and lemon zest. Stir to combine and check the seasoning.

3. Spoon the mixture into the salmon-lined tin and press down to level the surface. Cover the filling with the reserved smoked salmon. Wrap the whole mould in cling film and chill for at least 4hr, or overnight.

4. Take the mould out of the fridge 10min before serving. To serve, unwrap the outer layer of cling film, put a serving plate over the mould and invert. Peel off the cling film, garnish with parsley and black pepper and serve with Melba Toasts (see right).

Hands-on time: 20min, plus chilling
Serves 8

PER SERVING 458cals, 31g protein, 36g fat (14g saturates), 3g carbs (2g total sugars), 0g fibre

Melba Toasts

A simple, versatile alternative to crackers for pâtés, dips and cheese.

8 slices white bread

1. Preheat the grill to medium. Put 4 slices of bread on a baking sheet and toast until golden on both sides. Cut off the crusts, then use a serrated knife to cut each slice horizontally through its depth to make 8 very thin squares, each with one toasted side.

2. Repeat the toasting and slicing process with the remaining bread slices, then slice each square of bread in half diagonally.

3. Put the bread triangles back on to the baking sheet, un-toasted side up, and grill until golden (do this in batches if necessary). Leave to cool, then serve with the Smoked Salmon and Mackerel Mousse Ring opposite, or your favourite dip or cheese.

◆ GET AHEAD
Make up to 3hr ahead. Store in a bowl, unwrapped, at room temperature.

Hands-on time: 15min
Cooking time: 10min
Serves 8

PER SERVING 83cals, 3g protein, 0g fat (0g saturates), 16g carbs (1g total sugars), 1g fibre

Ham Hock Terrine with Cider Jelly

Buy the best-quality meat you can afford to allow the pork to shine in this impressive starter.

2.6kg gammon hocks (also called knuckles), check with your butcher that they are cured
500ml apple juice
4 bay leaves
1 onion, roughly chopped
Small handful thyme sprigs
1 tsp black peppercorns
Oil, to grease
Large handful parsley, finely chopped
2 tbsp wholegrain mustard
1 tbsp capers, rinsed
3 gelatine leaves
200ml cider

TO SERVE
Fruity chutney or onion marmalade
Caper berries (optional)
Melba Toasts (see recipe p63)

1. Put the gammon hocks into a large pan. Add the apple juice, bay leaves, onion, thyme and peppercorns, then add cold water to cover. Bring to the boil, then turn down the heat and simmer for 2hr 30min–3hr, topping up the water as needed, until the hocks are tender and the meat is falling from the bone. Leave the hocks to cool in the liquid for about 1hr, then lift out (reserve the liquid).

2. Strain the liquid through a fine sieve into a clean pan and boil fiercely to reduce to about 500ml. Set aside. Lightly oil a 900g loaf tin and line with a couple of layers of cling film, making sure there is plenty hanging over the sides (to make removal easier).

3. Remove and discard the skin from the hocks and finely shred the meat – you should have about 700g. Discard any fatty or sinewy bits.

4. Put the hock into a bowl and mix in the parsley, mustard and capers. Spoon into the tin, pressing down. Chill.

5. Put the gelatine into a pan and cover with the cider. Leave to soak for 5min, then heat gently to dissolve the gelatine. Take off the heat, add the reduced cooking liquid and check the seasoning.

6. Slowly pour the liquid into the tin, allowing it to seep in until it's just covering the meat (you may not need all of the liquid). Cover the tin with cling film (make sure it doesn't touch the liquid) and chill overnight.

7. To serve, unwrap the cling film and invert the terrine on to a serving platter or board. Lift off the tin and peel off the cling film. Spoon some chutney or onion marmalade on top and decorate with caper berries, if using. Serve with Melba Toasts (see previous page).

Hands-on time: 45min, plus cooling, soaking and (overnight) chilling
Cooking time: about 3hr 20min
Serves 8

PER SERVING (without chutney and toasts) 164cals, 17g protein, 7g fat (2g saturates), 7g carbs (7g total sugars), 0g fibre

Scandi Smorgasbord

Take inspiration from Scandinavia, where cold cured, smoked or cooked fish is served buffet style, with pickled vegetables and crispbreads for guests to assemble open-faced sandwiches themselves.

200g cooked beetroot, diced
3 sprigs dill, chopped
1½ tsp wholegrain mustard
100g each pickled onions and cornichons, drained
150g cooked crayfish tails or cooked prawns
125g smoked, peppered mackerel fillets, skinned
    and flaked
4 tbsp soured cream
200g sliced gravadlax
12 crispbreads or crackers

1. In a serving bowl, mix the beetroot with the dill and mustard. Put the pickled onions and cornichons into a separate small serving bowl. Put the crayfish or prawns and mackerel flakes into a medium serving bowl and the soured cream into a small serving bowl.

2. Lay the slices of gravadlax on a board. Let everyone help themselves at the table, spreading crispbreads with soured cream and topping with the fish and vegetables.

Hands-on time: 15min
Serves 4

PER SERVING 386cals, 27g protein, 19g fat
(5g saturates), 27g carbs (7g total sugars), 2g fibre

Potted Salmon and Prawns

Served with brown bread and a generous squeeze of lemon juice, these individually potted pâtés are a perennial favourite.

400g unsalted butter, chopped
500g hot-smoked salmon
200g cooked cold-water prawns (or a small prawn variety)
¼ tsp ground mace
¼ tsp cayenne pepper
Few dashes Worcestershire sauce
Brown bread and lemon wedges, to serve (optional)

1. Gently melt the butter, then set aside to settle for a minute. Carefully pour the clear melted butter into a jug, leaving the milky whey behind (discard this).

2. Peel the skin off the salmon and discard. Flake the fish into a medium bowl and add the prawns, mace, cayenne, Worcestershire sauce and some seasoning. Gently mix together (trying not to break up the salmon too much).

3. Divide the mixture among 8 ramekins or small Kilner jars and gently flatten to level.

4. Pour over the clarified butter, making sure the fish mixture is just covered. Tap the ramekins/jars down on the work surface to release any air bubbles, then cover and chill to set – about 3hr.

5. Allow the pots to soften at room temperature for 20–30min before serving alongside some brown bread and lemon wedges, if you like.

◆ GET AHEAD
Make the pots up to 2 days ahead and chill.
Complete the recipe to serve.

Hands-on time: 15min, plus chilling
Cooking time: 5min
Makes 8 pots

PER POT 511cals, 15g protein, 50g fat (8g saturates), 1g carbs (1g total sugars), 0g fibre

Asparagus Straws with Cheat's Hollandaise

These stylish canapés are super simple and equally delicious served hot or at room temperature. If you don't need the straws to be vegetarian you can use Parmesan instead.

6 sheets filo pastry
50g unsalted butter, melted
24 asparagus spears, at least 16cm long, woody ends trimmed
15g Italian-style vegetarian hard cheese, finely grated
Pinch cayenne pepper (optional)

FOR THE CHEAT'S HOLLANDAISE
125g butter, chopped
100g mayonnaise
1 tsp lemon juice

◆ GET AHEAD
Prepare to end of step 3 up to 1 day ahead. Cover and chill. Make the hollandaise up to 1 day ahead, then cover and chill. To serve, complete the recipe, gently warming the hollandaise in a pan to loosen.

◆ GH TIP
Use regular rather than fine asparagus spears, as these will hold their shape better during cooking.

Hands-on time: 25min, plus cooling
Cooking time: about 20min
Makes 24 asparagus straws

PER STRAW (with hollandaise) 110cals, 1g protein, 10g fat (4g saturates), 4g carbs (1g total sugars), 1g fibre

1. Preheat the oven to 200°C (180°C fan) mark 6. Line 2 baking sheets with baking parchment. Place a filo sheet on a board (keep the remaining filo covered with a damp tea towel). Brush with a little butter, then top with another filo sheet. Cut into quarters, then slice each rectangle in half diagonally to make 8 sloping triangles.

2. Working with one triangle at a time and the longest edge closest to you, place an asparagus spear vertically on the left of the long edge. Roll up tightly in the filo. Repeat with 7 more asparagus spears and arrange on a lined baking sheet, seam-side down.

3. Repeat the filo buttering, slicing and rolling process to make 24 asparagus straws. Brush the straws with a little more butter and sprinkle cheese and a pinch of cayenne, if using, over the pastry ends.

4. Cook for 15–18min until the pastry is crisp. Cool for 10min.

5. Meanwhile, make the cheat's hollandaise. Melt the butter in a small pan, remove from the heat and cool for a few minutes. In a medium bowl, gradually whisk the melted butter into the mayonnaise. Whisk in the lemon juice, then adjust the seasoning with lemon juice, salt and freshly ground black pepper. Serve with the asparagus straws.

Crunchy Crab Cakes with Pickled Veg

We've used a mixture of fresh brown and white crab meat to give these crab cakes a stronger flavour, but you can use all white, if you prefer.

FOR THE PICKLED VEG
4 baby courgettes
4 baby carrots (about 100g), trimmed and thinly sliced
100g radishes, trimmed, quartered and finely sliced – we used watermelon radishes
2 tbsp white wine vinegar
½ tbsp caster sugar

FOR THE DIP
75g mayonnaise
75g light crème fraîche
½ tsp sweet smoked paprika
1 tsp Dijon mustard
Finely grated zest ½ lemon
2 tsp non-pareil capers, drained and roughly chopped

FOR THE CRAB CAKES
100g fresh crab meat, mix of white and brown
150g ricotta
2–3 tsp chopped chives or tarragon, to taste
1 medium egg
90g panko breadcrumbs
2 tbsp vegetable oil

1. To make the pickled vegetables, finely slice the courgettes lengthways (or peel into ribbons using a Y-shaped vegetable peeler). Add to a bowl with the carrots and radishes, and mix through the vinegar, sugar and some seasoning. Set aside to lightly pickle.

2. Make the dip. In a small serving bowl, whisk the mayonnaise and crème fraîche until smooth. Add the remaining ingredients with some seasoning. Chill until needed.

3. For the crab cakes, mix together the crab, ricotta, chives/tarragon, egg, 50g of breadcrumbs and plenty of seasoning in a medium bowl. Allow to sit for 2min for the breadcrumbs to absorb some of the moisture. Meanwhile, sprinkle the remaining 40g breadcrumbs into a shallow bowl.

4. With damp hands, shape the crab mixture into 12 patties. Press lightly into the remaining breadcrumbs to coat.

5. Heat the oil in a large non-stick frying pan over a medium heat. Add the crab cakes and fry for 5–8min, turning once, or until golden and piping hot. Meanwhile, drain the pickled vegetables and empty into a serving bowl. Serve with the crab cakes and dip.

Hands-on time: 30min, plus sitting
Cooking time: about 10min
Serves 4

PER SERVING 406cals, 14g protein, 30g fat
(7g saturates), 20g carbs (7g total sugars), 2g fibre

Rainbow Vegetable Fritters

These colourful fritters are delicately spiced with cumin and coriander. Serve them on a platter for people to help themselves to their favourite flavour.

FOR THE RAITA
150g natural yogurt
½ cucumber, coarsely grated
Small handful mint, leaves picked and finely chopped
Small handful coriander, leaves picked and
    finely chopped

FOR THE FRITTERS
300g courgettes, trimmed
325g carrots, peeled
250g raw beetroot, washed and peeled
100g shredded kale (woody stems discarded)
4 large eggs
150g self-raising flour
2 tbsp milk
1 tsp ground cumin
1 tsp ground coriander
½ onion, finely chopped
Vegetable oil, to fry
2 lemons, cut into wedges, to serve

◆ GET AHEAD
Make the raita and cook the fritters up to 1 day ahead, then cool, cover and chill. To serve, preheat the oven to 220°C (200°C fan) mark 7, and reheat the fritters on a large baking tray for 8min, or until piping hot.

◆ GH TIP
A food processor with a wide shredding blade will make quick work of grating the veg.

Hands-on time: 1hr
Cooking time: about 35min
Serves 8

PER SERVING 201cals, 9g protein, 7g fat (1g saturates), 23g carbs (9g total sugars), 4g fibre

1. For the raita, mix together all the ingredients in a serving bowl with some seasoning. Cover and chill until ready to serve.

2. For the fritters, coarsely grate the courgettes, carrots and beetroot (see GH Tip) and put each in separate bowls.

3. Cook the kale in boiling water for 2min, drain, then run under cold water until cool. Drain again. Empty on to the centre of a clean tea towel and top with the grated courgette. Wrap up and firmly squeeze over the sink to remove all the excess liquid. Return to the courgette bowl.

4. In a large jug, whisk the eggs, flour, milk, spices and plenty of seasoning, until combined. Divide the chopped onion between the 3 veg bowls, followed by the batter, then mix each well.

5. Heat 1–2 tbsp oil in a large, non-stick frying pan over a medium heat. Cooking in batches, add spoonfuls of the courgette and kale batter to the pan, spreading each with the back of the spoon so they are 5–6cm across. Cook for 2–3min per side, or until golden. Transfer to a plate, cover and keep warm. Repeat until you have used all the batters (cook the carrot batter next, then the beetroot), adding a little more oil as needed.

6. Pile the fritters on a serving platter and serve with the raita and lemon wedges.

Spelt Flatbreads with Pickled Rhubarb

Try these topped flatbreads as a starter before a curry or tagine course, or even on their own with a green salad for a light lunch.

FOR THE FLATBREADS
200g white spelt flour, plus extra to dust
1 tsp fast-action dried yeast
2 tbsp olive oil

FOR THE PICKLED RHUBARB
175g rhubarb, trimmed
2 tbsp caster sugar
1 tbsp red wine vinegar

FOR THE HERBY OIL
50ml extra virgin olive oil
Small handful each coriander and parsley, finely chopped
    (see GH Tips)

FOR THE TOPPING
250g cream cheese
2 tbsp wholegrain mustard
4 cooked skinless chicken breasts, shredded
    (see GH Tips)

◆ GH TIPS
Swap the chicken for quartered 6-min boiled eggs, if you like, for a vegetarian version.

Use wild garlic for the herby oil, if you can get hold of it, instead of the soft herbs.

Hands-on time: 45min, plus rising and pickling
Cooking time: about 20min
Serves 4

PER SERVING 667cals, 45g protein, 31g fat
(12g saturates), 49g carbs (11g total sugars), 3g fibre

1. For the flatbreads, mix the flour, yeast, olive oil, ½ tsp salt and 100–125ml tepid water in a medium bowl to make a shaggy dough. Tip on to a lightly floured work surface and knead for 5min, until smooth and elastic. Return to the bowl, cover and leave to rise in a warm place for 30min, or until visibly puffed.

2. For the pickled rhubarb, use a Y-shaped vegetable peeler to shave the rhubarb into ribbons. Add to a bowl and mix in the sugar and vinegar. Set aside to lightly pickle.

3. For the herby oil, whizz all the ingredients with plenty of seasoning in the small bowl of a food processor until finely chopped. Thin with a little water, if needed, to get a drizzling consistency. Set aside.

4. Tip the dough on to a lightly floured work surface, divide into quarters and roll each piece into a rough 20.5cm circle. Heat a griddle pan over high heat. Cook the flatbreads one at a time, for 5min, turning halfway through, until golden and lightly charred.

5. For the topping, mix together the cream cheese, mustard and plenty of seasoning, then spread over the flatbreads. Top with the shredded chicken. Drain the pickled rhubarb and arrange on top of the chicken, then drizzle over the herby oil. Serve.

Salads

Fruity Feta and Mixed Grain Salad

Sweet fresh fruit is a welcome complement to the salty feta and almonds in this colourful, summery salad.

250g pouch cooked/microwaveable mixed grains
150g cherries, pitted and halved (see GH Tip)
2 nectarines, de-stoned and thickly sliced
4 spring onions, finely sliced
Large handful mint leaves
100g rocket
150g feta cubes, drained (or chop from a block)
Small handful roasted salted almonds, roughly chopped

FOR THE DRESSING
Juice 1 lemon
1 tbsp sherry vinegar
1 tbsp maple syrup
3 tbsp extra virgin olive oil

1. Warm the grains through according to the pack instructions. Meanwhile, whisk together all the dressing ingredients and some seasoning in a small bowl.

2. Empty the warmed grains into a large bowl, pour over half the dressing and toss to coat. Add the cherries, nectarines, spring onions, mint, rocket and feta. Pour over the remaining dressing and toss gently (with your hands is easiest).

3. Tip on to a large platter or divide among 4 plates, sprinkle over the almonds and serve.

◆ GH TIP
A cherry pitter will make speedy work of the salad prep, but you could use whole blueberries instead of cherries for ease.

Hands-on time: 10min
Cooking time: about 5min
Serves 4

PER SERVING 389cals, 13g protein, 22g fat (7g saturates), 32g carbs (13g total sugars), 6g fibre

Light Asian Chicken Salad

Warming and aromatic, this speedy Asian-style supper salad is sure to become a midweek favourite.

FOR THE SALAD
2 tbsp vegetable oil
200g choi sum, tat soi or pak choi, thickly shredded
100g sugar snap peas, sliced lengthways
200g cooked vermicelli rice noodles
3 medium skinless chicken breasts, cut into
    finger-sized strips
2 medium carrots, peeled and cut into matchsticks
Small handful each coriander and mint, roughly chopped
2 spring onions, thinly sliced
25g salted peanuts, roughly chopped

FOR THE DRESSING
1 tsp vegetable oil
5cm piece fresh root ginger, peeled and cut
    into matchsticks
2 garlic cloves, crushed
1-2 red chillies, halved, deseeded and thinly sliced
½ tbsp tamari
200ml light coconut milk
Juice ½ lime

◆ GH TIP
Next time, try with fried firm tofu cubes instead of the chicken.

1. For the salad, heat ½ tbsp of the oil in a large, deep non-stick frying pan over a medium heat and fry the choi sum/tat soi/pak choi and sugar snaps for 3–4min, stirring occasionally, until beginning to wilt. Empty into a large bowl.

2. Return the pan to the heat with ½ tbsp of the oil and cook the noodles for 2min, until piping hot. Add to the greens bowl.

3. Return the pan to the heat with the remaining oil and cook the chicken for 5min, until golden and cooked through. Add to the noodle bowl together with the carrots, most of the herbs and spring onions.

4. Return the pan to a low heat and make the dressing. Add the oil and stir in the ginger, garlic and most of the chilli. Fry for 1min, until aromatic, then mix in the tamari, coconut milk and lime juice and bring just to the boil.

5. Mix the dressing into the salad bowl and toss to coat. Check the seasoning. Divide among 4 bowls and garnish with the remaining herbs, spring onions and chilli, and the peanuts. Serve.

Hands-on time: 25min
Cooking time: about 15min
Serves 4

PER SERVING 360cals, 26g protein, 17g fat (5g saturates), 23g carbs (6g total sugars), 4g fibre

Vegan Caesar Salad

Savoury roast chickpeas and tofu replace chicken to add a protein hit to this vegan version of the popular green salad.

FOR THE CRISPY CHICKPEAS AND TOFU
3 tbsp cornflour
1 tsp smoked paprika
2 tbsp sesame oil
2 tbsp soy sauce
450g extra firm tofu, drained
400g tin chickpeas, drained and rinsed

FOR THE CROUTONS
1 ciabatta roll
1 tsp olive oil

FOR THE DRESSING
100g vegan mayo
1 garlic clove, crushed
1 tsp Dijon mustard
1 tsp soy sauce
1 tsp maple syrup
1 tbsp lemon juice
1 tbsp capers, roughly chopped

TO ASSEMBLE
2 romaine lettuces
20g vegan Italian-style hard cheese, grated or shaved

1. Preheat the oven to 240°C (220°C fan) mark 9. Line a large baking tray with baking parchment.

2. For the crispy chickpeas and tofu, mix the cornflour, smoked paprika, sesame oil, soy sauce and some seasoning in a large bowl. Cut the tofu into 1cm pieces, then pat dry with kitchen paper, pressing gently to squeeze out the excess moisture. Add to the bowl. Pat dry the chickpeas with kitchen paper, then add to the bowl and toss to coat. Tip on to the lined tray and spread to a single layer. Cook for 15–20min, or until beginning to crisp.

3. Meanwhile, tear the ciabatta into small chunks. Mix with the oil and some seasoning on a small baking tray, then add to the oven. Cook for 5min, until crisp.

4. Meanwhile, in a small jug, whisk the vegan mayo, garlic, mustard, soy, maple syrup, lemon juice and capers with some seasoning. Set aside.

5. To assemble, chop the lettuces and arrange on a platter. Top with the tofu and chickpeas, then drizzle over the dressing. Toss to coat, sprinkle over the vegan cheese and serve.

Hands-on time: 10min
Cooking time: about 20min
Serves 4

PER SERVING 476cals, 20g protein, 28g fat (4g saturates), 33g carbs (5g total sugars), 6g fibre

Warm Lamb Salad

Wondering what to do with leftover roast lamb? This salad is the perfect option.

FOR THE SALAD
500g leftover roast lamb, shredded or roughly chopped
2 garlic cloves, crushed
2 tsp paprika
2 tbsp tomato purée
2 tsp ground cumin
1 tsp ground coriander
2 tbsp olive oil
75g pea shoots
½ cucumber, peeled into ribbons
2–3 cooked beetroots, cut into wedges
100g feta, crumbled
Few mint sprigs, leaves picked

FOR THE COUSCOUS
200g dried couscous
275ml hot chicken stock

FOR THE DRESSING
4 preserved lemons
1 tsp ground cumin
1 tbsp paprika
Juice ½ lemon
150ml olive oil

1. For the salad, mix the lamb, garlic, paprika, tomato purée, cumin, coriander, olive oil, 100ml water and plenty of seasoning in a medium pan. Heat gently, stirring occasionally, until piping hot and the sauce clings to the lamb. Set aside.

2. Meanwhile, put the couscous and some seasoning into a heatproof bowl. Pour over the hot chicken stock, cover with a plate or cling film and set aside for 5min, before fluffing up with a fork.

3. To make the dressing, scrape out the insides of the preserved lemons and discard. Add the rinds to the small bowl of a food processor, with the cumin, paprika, lemon juice, olive oil and a large pinch of salt. Whizz until as fine as you can get it, then set aside.

4. Spoon the couscous on to a large serving plate. Top with the pea shoots and cucumber ribbons, followed by the cooked beetroot and lamb. Sprinkle over the feta and mint leaves. Drizzle over some of the dressing and serve with the remaining dressing on the side.

Hands-on time: 10min
Cooking time: about 5min
Serves 4

PER SERVING 866cals, 53g protein, 52g fat
(13g saturates), 45g carbs (8g total sugars), 5g fibre

Banh Mi Salad

This veggie dish is inspired by the flavours and textures of the popular Vietnamese street food baguette.

FOR THE PICKLES
75ml rice wine vinegar
3 tbsp caster sugar
4 medium carrots, peeled and cut into matchsticks
20cm daikon/mooli radish, peeled and cut into matchsticks
1 fresh jalapeño or 1 large green chilli, deseeded and finely sliced

FOR THE DRESSING
3 tbsp mayonnaise, vegan, if you like
1 tbsp sriracha
Finely grated zest ½ lime, plus 2 tbsp juice
1 garlic clove, crushed

FOR THE SALAD
150g dried rice noodles
280g extra firm tofu, cut into 1cm-wide batons
2 tbsp cornflour
2 tbsp vegetable oil
1 cucumber
25g bunch coriander, leaves picked and roughly chopped
25g bunch mint, leaves picked and roughly chopped
5 tbsp store-bought crispy fried onions

1. For the pickles, mix the vinegar, sugar and 1 tsp salt in a large bowl to dissolve the sugar. Add the carrots, daikon/mooli and jalapeño/chilli, then stir to coat and set aside.

2. Whisk together the dressing ingredients in a large serving bowl and set aside.

3. For the salad, bring a large pan of water to the boil and cook the noodles according to the pack instructions. Drain, run under cold water to cool completely, then drain again and empty into a serving bowl. Toss to coat.

4. Next, pat dry the tofu batons with kitchen paper. Put the cornflour into a shallow bowl and season well. Gently toss the tofu in the cornflour to coat. Heat the oil in a large non-stick frying pan over a medium heat. Fry the tofu, turning occasionally, until golden and crisp. Set aside.

5. Shave the cucumber into ribbons into the serving bowl using a Y-shaped peeler (discard the seedy core). Drain the pickles and add to the bowl with the tofu and most of the herbs. Toss gently to coat. Garnish with the remaining herbs and the crispy onions and serve.

Hands-on time: 35min
Cooking time: about 10min
Serves 4

PER SERVING 554cals, 15g protein, 25g fat (6g saturates), 65g carbs (23g total sugars), 6g fibre

Rainbow Beetroot and Orange Salad

Whichever colour you choose, sweet, earthy beetroots pair beautifully with nutty sesame, sweet orange and tangy goat's cheese.

3 oranges
4 medium mixed beetroot (about 500g), peeled
    (see GH Tips)
1 tbsp white sesame seeds
¾ tsp caster sugar
3 tbsp extra virgin olive oil
1 tbsp cider vinegar
4 spring onions, finely sliced
125g rindless soft goat's cheese, crumbled

FOR THE TAHINI CREAM
100g tahini (see GH Tips)
1 small garlic clove, crushed
2 tbsp lemon juice
1 tbsp maple syrup
100g Greek-style yogurt

◆ GH TIPS
We used red, candied and golden beetroot for our salad. If you're using multi-coloured beetroot, marinate them in separate bowls to avoid the different colours bleeding into each other.

Always stir tahini well before measuring it out as the oil separates during storage.

1. Squeeze the juice from 1 of the oranges into a large bowl. Slice the top and bottom off the remaining 2 oranges and sit them on a board. Cut away all the peel and white pith. Working one at a time, hold an orange over the juice bowl and carefully cut between the membranes to separate the segments. Squeeze any remaining juice from the membranes into the bowl and set aside the segments on a plate. Whisk ½ tsp fine salt into the juice bowl.

2. Slice the beetroot as thinly as possible – a mandoline is best for this. Add to the juice bowl (see GH Tips), toss to coat and set aside for 1hr.

3. Meanwhile, toast the sesame seeds in a small frying pan over a low heat for 2–3min. Sprinkle in the sugar and a large pinch of salt and fry, stirring, for 7–8min until caramelised and deep golden. Tip on to a plate to cool.

4. For the tahini cream, whisk the tahini, garlic, lemon juice and maple syrup in a medium bowl. Whisk in the yogurt and check the seasoning.

5. To serve, strain the beetroot, reserving the juices. Measure 4 tbsp of the juice back into the large bowl and whisk in the olive oil, cider vinegar and some seasoning. Add the beetroot, orange segments and spring onions and toss gently to coat.

6. Spread the tahini cream on to a large platter. Arrange the beetroot mixture on top and dot over the goat's cheese. Drizzle over any remaining dressing, sprinkle with the caramelised sesame seeds and serve.

V **GF**

Hands-on time: 30min, plus marinating
Cooking time: about 10min
Serves 8

PER SERVING 251cals, 9g protein, 18g fat
(6g saturates), 12g carbs (11g total sugars), 4g fibre

Spicy Thai Beef Salad

Thai basil has an aromatic, slight aniseed flavour that pairs well with mint and mango, but you could swap it for coriander if you prefer. Toasted ground rice is a traditional choice to add crunch and flavour to Thai salads.

FOR THE DRESSING
5 tbsp lime juice (about 3 limes)
2 tbsp fish sauce
2 tsp sugar
2–3 bird's eye chillies, deseeded and sliced
4 fresh kaffir lime leaves, de-veined and finely shredded (see GH Tip)
1 echalion shallot, thinly sliced into rings

FOR THE SALAD
1½ tbsp Thai sticky rice or other short grain rice
2 tsp vegetable oil
2 x 200g beef fillet steaks, trimmed
½ cucumber, sliced into half moons
1 mango, peeled, de-stoned and shredded/julienned
100g mizuna or wild rocket
25g bunch mint, leaves picked
25g bunch Thai basil, leaves picked
40g salted peanuts, roughly chopped

◆ GH TIP
If you can't find fresh kaffir lime leaves, you can finely crumble in dried leaves, or use the grated zest of 1 lime. It won't have quite the same aroma, but will be close.

1. For the dressing, mix together the lime juice, fish sauce and sugar in a small bowl until the sugar dissolves. Stir in the chillies, shredded lime leaves and shallot rings and set aside.

2. For the salad, toast the rice in a frying pan over a medium-high heat, shaking frequently, until it is a deep golden-brown, about 5–10min. Tip on to a plate, leave to cool completely, then grind to a coarse powder with a pinch of salt using a pestle and mortar.

3. Return the pan to a high heat and add the oil. Pat dry the steaks using kitchen paper and fry for 4–6min, turning halfway, until well browned on the outside but still rare in the middle. Remove to a plate and leave to rest for 5min while you assemble the rest of the salad.

4. In a large bowl, toss half the dressing with the cucumber, mango, salad leaves, herbs and most of the peanuts. Tip on to a large platter (or divide among 4 plates). Thinly slice the steaks and arrange on top. Spoon over the remaining dressing and scatter over the remaining peanuts and the ground toasted rice. Serve.

Hands-on time: 30min, plus cooling
Cooking time: about 15min
Serves 4

PER SERVING 297cals, 27g protein, 13g fat (4g saturates), 15g carbs (9g total sugars), 3g fibre

Warm Piri-piri Chicken, Chorizo and Chickpeas

A zingy dressing, inspired by the Portuguese favourite, takes everyday chicken to the next level.

400g skinless chicken breasts, sliced into chunky strips
190g pack cooking chorizo sausages, sliced
400g baby plum tomatoes, halved
2 x 400g tins chickpeas, drained
90g pack wild rocket leaves

FOR THE PIRI-PIRI DRESSING
2 tbsp sherry vinegar
Zest and juice 1 lemon
½ tsp runny honey
3 tbsp olive oil
1 red chilli, deseeded and finely chopped
¼ tsp sweet smoked paprika
1 tbsp chopped fresh oregano
½ small garlic clove, crushed

1. For the dressing, whisk together the vinegar, lemon zest and juice, honey and oil in a bowl until combined. Stir in the chilli, paprika, oregano and garlic and season. Pour half the dressing into a jug and set aside.

2. Add the chicken to the dressing left in the bowl and set aside to marinate briefly.

3. Meanwhile, heat a frying pan over a medium high heat, add the chorizo and fry for 2–3min, stirring occasionally, until it is beginning to crisp and much of the fat has rendered out. Remove to a plate with a slotted spoon, then discard all but 1 tbsp of the fat and return the pan to the heat.

4. Add the chicken and marinade to the pan and fry for 8–10min, turning halfway and basting the chicken in the marinade until it is golden and cooked through.

5. Put the tomatoes and chickpeas into a large bowl. Add the chorizo and most of the rocket, then season with black pepper. Pour over a little of the reserved dressing and toss together. Divide among 4 plates, then top with the chicken and reserved rocket leaves. Serve with the remaining dressing, if you like.

Hands-on time: 10min, plus marinating
Cooking time: about 15min
Serves 4

PER SERVING 496cals, 44g protein, 22g fat (6g saturates), 25g carbs (5g total sugars), 9g fibre

Smoked Mackerel and Giant Couscous Salad

Use cooked smoked chicken in place of the mackerel, if you like.

500ml chicken stock
200g giant couscous
100g bag baby spinach
200g Tenderstem broccoli, stalks trimmed
2 tbsp extra virgin olive oil
1 tsp ground cumin
1 lemon, zest finely grated and juice
300g smoked, peppered mackerel fillets, skinned
   and flaked
150g dried apricots, roughly chopped
Small bunch coriander, roughly chopped
3 spring onions, finely sliced
25g pine nuts

1. Bring the chicken stock to the boil in a medium
   pan, add the couscous and boil for 6–8min until
   tender. Add the spinach to the pan and stir to
   wilt. Drain and transfer to a large serving bowl.

2. Bring a medium pan of water to the boil and
   cook the broccoli for 3min until tender, then
   drain and rinse under cold water.

3. In a small bowl, mix together the oil, cumin,
   lemon zest and juice. Stir into the couscous
   along with half the flaked mackerel fillets.

4. Stir through the broccoli, apricots, coriander,
   spring onions and pine nuts, and top with the
   remaining mackerel fillets to serve.

Hands-on time: 15min
Cooking time: 10min
Serves 4

PER SERVING 589cals, 27g protein, 35g fat
(6g saturates), 40g carbs (15g total sugars), 6g fibre

Zesty Pork Salad Cups

This Thai-inspired salad is traditionally served in lettuce leaves. Take the components to the table and let guests assemble their own cups.

1 tbsp sunflower oil
500g lean pork mince
1 tbsp fish sauce
Zest and juice 1 lime, plus wedges to garnish
1–2 red chillies, deseeded and finely chopped
½ tbsp soft brown sugar
½ red onion, finely chopped
Large handful each coriander and mint leaves,
    roughly chopped
2 little gem lettuces, leaves separated
40g roasted peanuts, finely chopped

1. Heat the oil in a wok or frying pan. Add the pork and cook over a high heat for 5–8min until browned and cooked through. Set aside.

2. In a large serving bowl, mix together the fish sauce, lime zest and juice, chillies, brown sugar and red onion. Stir in the pork and most of the coriander and mint. Check the seasoning.

3. Take the pork mixture, lettuce leaves, peanuts, reserved herbs and lime wedges to the table and let people dig in.

◆ GH TIP
For a more substantial meal, you could serve this salad with boiled rice.

Hands-on time: 15min
Cooking time: about 10min
Serves 4

PER SERVING 266cals, 30g protein, 14g fat (3g saturates), 4g carbs (3.5g total sugars), 2g fibre

Chicken and Roasted Chickpea Salad

This salad uses minimal ingredients to create maximum flavour, thanks in part to the delicious tahini dressing. Use leftover cooked chicken if you have some.

2 x 400g tins chickpeas, drained and rinsed
2 tbsp harissa paste
4 medium skinless chicken breasts
1½ tbsp olive oil
250g kale, roughly chopped, woody stems discarded
3 tbsp tahini
Juice ½ lemon
½ tbsp tamari

1. Preheat the oven to 220°C (200°C fan) mark 7. In a small roasting tin, mix together the chickpeas, harissa and plenty of seasoning. Roast for 15min, until lightly crisp. Set aside to cool. Reduce the oven to 200°C (180°C fan) mark 6.

2. Put the chicken on a baking tray, drizzle with 1 tbsp of the oil and season. Cook in the oven for 20–25min, until cooked through.

3. Cook the kale in a large pan of boiling water for 5min, until tender. Drain and rinse briefly under cold water to stop the cooking. Meanwhile, whisk together the tahini, lemon juice, tamari, remaining ½ tbsp oil, some seasoning and 4 tbsp water in a small bowl.

4. Divide the kale and chickpeas among 4 bowls. Top with sliced cooked chicken and drizzle over the dressing. Serve.

Hands-on time: 20min
Cooking time: about 40min
Serves 4

PER SERVING 439cals, 41g protein, 19g fat (3g saturates), 21g carbs (2g total sugars), 11g fibre

Curried Paneer Salad

Serve this delicious salad hot or at room temperature. If you like things a little spicier, swap the mild curry paste for a medium or hot version.

250g brown basmati and wild rice mix (see GH Tip)
400g paneer, cut into 2cm chunks
3 tbsp mild curry paste
1 tbsp vegetable oil
3 tbsp mango chutney
Juice 1 lime
200g baby spinach
200g baby plum tomatoes, halved

1. Put the rice in a bowl, cover with cold water and leave to soak for 30min. Drain and rinse well in a sieve under cold running water.

2. Empty the drained rice into a medium pan (that has a lid) and add 500ml water. Bring to the boil over a high heat, cover and simmer gently for 20–25min, until the rice is tender and all the water has been absorbed. Empty into a serving bowl and season.

3. Meanwhile, in a separate bowl, mix together the paneer, curry paste, oil and plenty of seasoning. Heat a large non-stick frying pan over a medium heat and fry the paneer for 5min, turning frequently, until browned all over.

4. Mix the mango chutney and lime juice into the rice, followed by the spinach and tomatoes. Top with the paneer and serve.

◆ GH TIP
A white basmati and wild rice mix would work well too, but may require a shorter cooking time, so check the pack instructions.

Hands-on time: 20min, plus soaking
Cooking time: about 30min
Serves 4

PER SERVING 653cals, 34g protein, 32g fat (16g saturates), 55g carbs (9g total sugars), 4g fibre

Warm Lentil Bistro Salad

We've grilled the cheese on top for ease, but you can serve this warm salad with goat's cheese croutes on the side, if you prefer.

75g smoked diced pancetta
2 x 250g pouches cooked Puy lentils
40g sundried tomatoes, chopped
40g roast peppers from a jar, drained and chopped
75g pitted green olives, roughly chopped
125g cherry tomatoes, halved or quartered
Large handful parsley, roughly chopped
2 x 100g goat's cheese rounds
40g walnuts, roughly chopped

FOR THE DRESSING
2 tbsp extra virgin olive oil (or use the oil from the sundried tomato jar)
2 tbsp red wine vinegar
1 tbsp runny honey
1 tbsp Dijon mustard

1. Preheat the grill to high. For the salad, heat a large, shallow casserole dish or ovenproof frying pan (see GH Tip) over a medium heat. Fry the pancetta for 5min, or until golden. Add the lentils and turn to coat in the oil and heat through.

2. Meanwhile, in a small bowl, mix the dressing ingredients with some seasoning. Add the sundried tomatoes, peppers, olives, cherry tomatoes and dressing to the dish/pan and bubble for a few seconds. Remove the pan from the heat and mix through most of the parsley.

3. Slice the goat's cheese rounds in half horizontally through their depth and place on top of the lentils. Grill for 5min, or until bubbling and golden. Scatter over the walnuts and remaining parsley. Serve.

◆ GH TIP
If you don't have an ovenproof frying pan, transfer the salad to an ovenproof serving dish at the end of step 2.

Hands-on time: 15min
Cooking time: about 15min
Serves 4

PER SERVING 598cals, 29g protein, 38g fat (13g saturates), 29g carbs (7g total sugars), 10g fibre

Halloumi Couscous Salad

This grain-based salad is incredibly versatile, and you can easily change up the flavours by adding your favourite nuts and seeds.

100g couscous
125g halloumi
1 tsp olive oil
Large handful parsley, roughly chopped
25g sultanas or raisins
15g pumpkin seeds
15g pitted black olives, halved
125g cooked beetroot, roughly chopped

FOR THE DRESSING
½ tbsp wholegrain or Dijon mustard
1½ tbsp olive oil
1 tbsp white wine vinegar
¼–½ tsp caster sugar

1. Whisk together the dressing ingredients in a small bowl with some seasoning and set aside. Next, empty the couscous into a medium heatproof bowl and just cover with freshly boiled water from the kettle. Cover the bowl with a plate or cling film and set aside for 5min.

2. Meanwhile, cut the halloumi into 3–5mm thick slices and brush with the oil. Heat a medium frying pan over a medium heat and fry the halloumi for 3–4min per side, until deep golden and crisp. Remove from the heat.

3. Stir the couscous with a fork, breaking up any clumps. Mix in the dressing, parsley, sultanas/raisins, seeds, olives, beetroot and halloumi. Check the seasoning and serve.

◆ GH TIP
Try using bulgur wheat or chickpeas instead of couscous. Chopped sundried tomatoes or capers are a good alternative to olives.

Hands-on time: 15min
Cooking time: about 10min
Serves 2

PER SERVING 607cals, 26g protein, 31g fat (13g saturates), 55g carbs (17g total sugars), 5g fibre

Grilled and Chilled Watermelon Salad

Grilling watermelon makes it even juicier and gives it an almost meaty texture. Don't be tempted to brown the watermelon too far in advance, however, as the grill marks will dissolve back into the fruit.

1kg watermelon
Vegetable oil, to grease
100g rocket
3 spring onions, finely sliced
Handful mint leaves, torn
125g feta, crumbled

FOR THE DRESSING
½ tbsp Dijon mustard
3 tbsp balsamic vinegar
4 tbsp extra virgin olive oil

1. Slice the skin and white pith off the watermelon and cut into 2cm-thick slices. If the seeds are hard (from a larger melon), poke them out with a skewer as best you can. Cut the slices into triangles (the exact size doesn't really matter).

2. Lightly oil the bars of your barbecue or griddle pan. Barbecue or griddle the watermelon pieces over a high heat for 8–10min on one side only (do this in batches if necessary), or until dark char marks form on the melon. Remove to a large baking tray in a single layer, charred-side-up, and chill for 1-2hr.

3. To make the dressing, whisk together all the ingredients with some seasoning.

4. To serve, arrange the rocket on a large platter. Scatter over half the spring onions, mint and feta, then drizzle over half the dressing. Arrange the chilled watermelon on top and scatter over the remaining spring onions, mint and feta. Finish with the remaining dressing and serve.

◆ GET AHEAD
Prepare the recipe to the end of step 3 up to 2hr ahead. Cover and chill the dressing.

Hands-on time: 20min, plus chilling
Cooking time: about 20min
Serves 8

PER SERVING 126cals, 3g protein, 9g fat (3g saturates), 8g carbs (8g total sugars), 1g fibre

Spicy Prawn and Peanut Noodle Salad

This no-cook salad is super-quick to assemble. Double the quantities for a delicious next-day lunch.

1 small cucumber, finely sliced into half moons
½ tbsp caster sugar
1½ tbsp white wine vinegar
450g cooked rice noodles (we used flat ribbon noodles)
3 tbsp vegetable oil
1 tbsp soy sauce
1 tbsp runny honey
1 red chilli, deseeded and finely chopped
350g cooked and peeled king prawns
2 spring onions, finely sliced
50g roasted and salted peanuts, roughly chopped
Small handful coriander, roughly chopped

1. In a bowl, mix together the cucumber, caster sugar and ½ tbsp of the white wine vinegar. Set aside.

2. Put the noodles in a heatproof bowl and cover with just-boiled water. Leave to warm through for 5min, then drain well and tip into a large serving bowl.

3. In a small jug, mix the oil, soy sauce, honey, chilli and remaining 1 tbsp white wine vinegar. Pour over the noodles and toss together with the prawns, spring onions and marinated cucumber. Sprinkle over the peanuts and coriander and serve.

Hands-on time: 15min
Serves 4

PER SERVING 348cals, 21g protein, 16g fat (2g saturates), 30g carbs (6g total sugars), 3g fibre

5

Pasta & Grains

Chorizo and Kale Risotto

All that's needed are a few key ingredients to make this unusual and tasty risotto.

2 tbsp sunflower oil
125g chorizo sausage, chopped into small chunks
1 onion, finely chopped
125g kale, shredded (tough stalks removed)
300g risotto rice
1.1–1.2 litres hot chicken or vegetable stock
100g Parmesan cheese, grated, plus extra
   to serve (optional)

1. Heat 1 tbsp of the oil in a large pan over medium heat and fry the chorizo until golden and the oil is red. Empty into a small bowl and set aside. Add the remaining oil to the pan and gently fry the onion for 10min until softened.

2. In a large pan of boiling water, cook the kale for 5min until tender. Drain well and set aside.

3. Add the rice to the onion pan and fry, stirring, for 1min. Add a ladleful of stock and stir frequently until the liquid has been absorbed. Keep adding stock, a ladleful at a time, continuing to stir frequently while the rice absorbs the liquid. Continue cooking in this way until the rice is tender but retains a tiny bite – about 15–17min.

4. Lift the chorizo out of the bowl and add to the pan (leaving the red oil behind), with the kale and Parmesan. Mix together and check the seasoning. Take the pan off the heat, cover and leave for 2min. Divide among 4 warmed bowls, drizzle with the chorizo oil and serve with extra Parmesan, if you like.

Hands-on time: 25min
Cooking time: about 40min
Serves 4

PER SERVING 589cals, 30g protein, 22g fat (9g saturates), 67g carbs (4g total sugars), 3g fibre

Cheeseburger Macaroni Cheese

We've grilled our mac 'n' cheese for speed, but you could cook it in the oven, if you like.

1 tbsp olive oil
1 onion, finely sliced
400g beef mince
300g macaroni
40g butter
1½ tbsp American-style yellow mustard
40g plain flour
500ml milk
75g Cheddar, coarsely grated
75g Red Leicester, coarsely grated
75g gherkins (drained weight), sliced
Green salad, to serve (optional)

◆ GH TIP
The American-style yellow mustard delivers that classic tang, but you can use Dijon or wholegrain mustard instead.

1. Heat the oil in a large, deep, oven-safe frying pan or skillet over medium-high heat and cook the onion and beef for 5min, stirring to break up any clumps, or until the meat is browned and the onion softened.

2. Meanwhile, cook the pasta in a large pan of boiling salted water according to the pack instructions. Preheat grill to high.

3. Tip the mince mixture into a bowl. Melt the butter and mustard in the empty pan over a medium heat. Add the flour and cook, stirring, for 1min. Remove the pan from the heat and gradually stir in the milk to make a smooth sauce. Return the pan to the heat and cook, stirring, until thickened and bubbling. Stir through most of the cheeses and plenty of seasoning. Drain the pasta and stir into the sauce along with the gherkins and mince mixture. Check the seasoning.

4. Sprinkle over the remaining cheese and grill for 5min, or until golden and bubbling. Serve with a crisp green salad, if you like.

Hands-on time: 5min
Cooking time: about 20min
Serves 4

PER SERVING 869cals, 45g protein, 44g fat (22g saturates), 71g carbs (10g total sugars), 5g fibre

Spinach and Ricotta Cannelloni

Prepare this classic Italian vegetarian main dish when you have some extra time and freeze it. Then on a busy day, you have a homemade meal you can cook from frozen.

FOR THE TOMATO SAUCE
1 tbsp extra virgin olive oil
2 garlic cloves, crushed
1 tbsp mixed dried herbs
3 x 400g tins plum tomatoes
1 tbsp balsamic vinegar
Small handful basil, leaves picked and roughly chopped
Green salad, to serve (optional)

FOR THE FILLING
500g spinach
350g ricotta
50g vegetarian Italian-style hard cheese (or Parmesan,
    if vegetarian not required)
¼ tsp freshly grated nutmeg
250g dried cannelloni

FOR THE TOPPING
250g mozzarella

◆ GET AHEAD
Prepare to end of step 3 (no need to preheat the oven) in a freezer-safe dish. Wrap and freeze for up to 1 month. To serve, either defrost in the fridge and complete the recipe or, to cook from frozen, preheat the oven to 160°C (140°C fan) mark 3, cover the dish with foil and cook for 1hr. Remove the foil, turn up the oven to 200°C (180°C fan) mark 6 and cook for 20min more, until golden and bubbling.

Hands-on time: 35min
Cooking time: about 1hr
Serves 6

PER SERVING 462cals, 27g protein, 21g fat
(12g saturates), 40g carbs (11g total sugars), 6g fibre

1. For the tomato sauce, heat the oil in a large pan over a medium heat. Add the garlic and cook for 1min. Add the remaining sauce ingredients and some seasoning. Simmer for 30min, stirring occasionally and breaking up the tomatoes with the back of a wooden spoon, until thick.

2. Meanwhile, for the filling, put the spinach into a colander in the sink and pour over a full kettle of just-boiled water to wilt (you may need to do this in batches). When cool enough to handle, lift up handfuls of the spinach and firmly squeeze out the excess moisture. Roughly chop, then put into a large bowl. Mix in the ricotta, cheese, nutmeg and plenty of seasoning. Transfer the mixture to a large piping bag fitted with a large plain nozzle (or snip a hole in the bottom).

3. Preheat the oven to 200°C (180°C fan) mark 6. To assemble, spread half the tomato sauce in the base of a 2.5 litre ovenproof serving dish (about 35 x 40cm). Pipe filling into each cannelloni tube and arrange in a single layer on top of the sauce, then top with the remaining sauce. Tear the mozzarella into strips and arrange on top of the sauce.

4. Cook in the oven for 30min, or until golden and bubbling. Serve with a green salad, if you like.

Easy Courgette and Leek Lasagne

Quark is low in fat but high in protein, so it makes the perfect creamy base for this light, veg-filled lasagne.

---

2 tsp olive oil
2 garlic cloves, crushed
1 tbsp fresh thyme leaves, finely chopped
400g tin plum tomatoes
2 medium leeks, about 350g, finely sliced
3 medium courgettes, about 500g, coarsely grated
250g tub quark
¼ tsp freshly grated nutmeg
150g fresh lasagne sheets
50g feta, crumbled
15g Italian-style vegetarian hard cheese, finely grated

1. Preheat the oven to 200°C (180°C fan) mark 6.
   Heat 1 tsp of the oil in a medium pan over a low
   heat, add the garlic and thyme and cook for 2–3min,
   until starting to sizzle. Add the tomatoes and some
   seasoning, increase the heat to medium-high and
   bubble for 12–15min, stirring regularly, until the
   tomatoes have broken down and reduced.

2. Meanwhile, heat the remaining oil in a large
   frying pan over a medium-high heat. Add the leeks
   and courgettes and cook for 10–15min, stirring
   occasionally, until softened and any moisture has
   evaporated from the pan. Remove from the heat,
   then stir in the quark, nutmeg and some seasoning.

3. Spread half the leek mixture over the base of a
   1.8–2 litre ovenproof serving dish (a rough 21cm
   square one works well) and arrange half the pasta
   sheets on top. Spoon over half the tomato sauce.
   Repeat the layers once more. Sprinkle over the feta,
   hard cheese and freshly ground black pepper.

4. Cook in the oven for 25–30min, until browned
   and bubbling. Serve.

Hands-on time: 20min
Cooking time: about 50min
Serves 4

PER SERVING 277cals, 21g protein, 7g fat
(3g saturates), 30g carbs (11g total sugars), 6g fibre

Nduja and Aubergine Pasta

A soft, spicy salami from Calabria in Italy, nduja is all the rage. Raw cooking chorizo would make a good alternative here.

1 tbsp olive oil
2 small aubergines, cut into finger-sized strips
100g nduja, skin removed if needed
2 x 400g tins cherry tomatoes
2 tsp dried oregano
1 tbsp red wine vinegar
2 tsp sugar
350g rigatoni or other pasta
15g basil, leaves picked

1. Heat 1 tbsp oil in a large, deep frying pan over a high heat and fry the aubergines, stirring occasionally, for 6–8min, until browned. Tip on to a plate.

2. Add the nduja to the pan, breaking it up with a wooden spoon, and fry for 2min. Stir in the tomatoes, oregano, vinegar, sugar and some seasoning. Bring to the boil, then tip in the aubergines and bubble vigorously for 15min, stirring occasionally, until the sauce is slightly reduced and the tomatoes are bursting.

3. Meanwhile, cook the pasta in a large pan of boiling salted water according to the pack instructions.

4. Drain the pasta and add to the aubergine pan along with most of the basil, then stir gently to coat and check the seasoning. Divide among 4 bowls and garnish with the remaining basil leaves. Serve.

Hands-on time: 5min
Cooking time: about 25min
Serves 4

PER SERVING 546cals, 16g protein, 17g fat (6g saturates), 77g carbs (14g total sugars), 9g fibre

Truffle Carbonara

For a meaty addition, cook a little diced pancetta along with the mushrooms. If you can't get hold of truffle paste, use a little truffle oil instead.

25g butter
50g dried breadcrumbs
Small handful parsley, finely chopped
Finely grated zest 1 lemon
200g chestnut mushrooms, finely sliced
500g fresh tagliatelle
3 medium eggs
2 tbsp minced truffle/truffle paste
100g Parmesan, finely grated

1. Melt half the butter in a large frying pan over a medium-high heat and fry the breadcrumbs for 2min, or until golden. Tip into a bowl and stir through the parsley and lemon zest. Set aside.

2. Add the remaining butter and mushrooms to the pan and fry for 5min, or until the mushrooms are golden and any liquid in the pan has evaporated. Meanwhile, cook the pasta in a large pan of boiling salted water according to the pack instructions.

3. In a small bowl, whisk the eggs, truffle mince/paste, most of the cheese and plenty of freshly ground black pepper. Drain the pasta, reserving a small cupful of the cooking water.

4. Remove the mushroom pan from the heat and add the pasta, egg mixture and about 75ml of the reserved pasta water. Toss together for 1min, adding a little more pasta water to make it glossy, if needed. Warm over very low heat, if needed.

5. Divide among 4 bowls and sprinkle over the herby crumb and remaining cheese. Serve.

Hands-on time: 5min
Cooking time: about 10min
Serves 4

PER SERVING 648cals, 31g protein, 22g fat (10g saturates), 78g carbs (3g total sugars), 6g fibre

Speedy Gnocchi with Sage Butter

Using ready-made mashed potato makes home-made gnocchi more achievable as a midweek meal. Swap the spinach for any greens you like.

750g shop-bought or leftover mashed potato, chilled
200g '00' flour or plain flour, plus extra to dust
1 medium egg
150g butter, chopped
8 whole sage leaves
100g baby spinach
50g Italian-style vegetarian hard cheese, finely grated, plus extra, to serve (optional)

1. Scoop the mash into a bowl and sift over the flour. Make a well in the centre and add the egg. Bring together with your hands, then tip on to a lightly floured work surface and knead gently for 1min to make a soft dough. Wrap in foil or cling film and chill for 5min to firm up slightly.

2. Bring a large pan of salted water to the boil. Lightly flour a work surface and divide the dough into quarters. Roll each piece into a 2cm-thick sausage, then slice each sausage into 2cm pieces.

3. Melt the butter in a large non-stick frying pan over a low heat. Add the sage leaves and spinach and fry, stirring occasionally, for 1min. Meanwhile, cook the gnocchi in the boiling water for 1min, or until they bob to the surface. Increase the heat under the frying pan to high and shake the pan to create an emulsion.

4. Lift the cooked gnocchi out of the water with a slotted spoon and transfer to the frying pan with the cheese, shaking the pan gently and adding some of the gnocchi cooking water to create a creamy sauce. Serve the gnocchi, sprinkled with more cheese, if using.

◆ GET AHEAD
Prepare to the end of step 2, then put the cut gnocchi on a lightly floured baking sheet. Chill for up to 5hr, or freeze. If freezing, bag up once solid and freeze for up to 1 month. Complete the recipe to serve, adding an extra 1min cooking time if frozen.

Hands-on time: 20min, plus chilling
Cooking time: about 5min
Serves 4

PER SERVING (without extra cheese) 765cals, 17g protein, 49g fat (31g saturates), 61g carbs (1g total sugars), 4g fibre

Crispy Cod with Pearl Barley Risotto

Pearl barley retains a slight chew but is a tasty alternative to rice in this recipe.

---

1 tbsp olive oil
1 onion, finely chopped
200g pearl barley
1.2 litres fish stock
15g plain flour
4 skinless cod loins (roughly 125g each)
25g butter
150g each frozen peas and frozen leaf spinach
Small handful mint, leaves picked and sliced (see GH Tip)
Large handful watercress (see GH Tip)

1. Heat ½ tbsp of the oil in a large pan over a medium heat and fry the onion for 5min, until softened. Stir in the pearl barley and cook, stirring, for 1min. Add the stock and some seasoning, then bring to the boil. Simmer, stirring frequently, for 40–45min, until the barley is tender (it will retain a slight chew).

2. When the risotto is nearly ready, mix the flour and some seasoning on a plate. Pat dry the cod loins with kitchen paper and coat in the flour mixture (shake off the excess).

3. Heat the butter and remaining ½ tbsp oil in a large non-stick frying pan over a high heat. When foaming, add the fish and cook for 3min, then turn and cook for 1min, before removing the pan from the heat to finish cooking.

4. Meanwhile, stir the peas and spinach into the risotto and cook to defrost and heat through. Stir through the mint and check the seasoning.

5. Divide the risotto among 4 shallow bowls and top with the crispy cod and watercress. Serve.

◆ GH TIP
If you don't have any fresh mint, then 1 tsp of dried will do the trick. You can also replace the watercress with rocket.

Hands-on time: 15min
Cooking time: about 55min
Serves 4

PER SERVING 444cals, 32g protein, 12g fat (4g saturates), 51g carbs (4g total sugars), 4g fibre

Beef and Guinness Ragù

Easy to double up and freeze, this hearty recipe is ideal on a chilly evening.

2 tsp olive oil
1 small onion, finely chopped
200g beef braising steak, cut into 2.5cm pieces
1 tbsp plain flour
1 carrot, peeled and roughly chopped
1 tsp wholegrain mustard
1 tsp dried thyme
200ml Guinness
400g tin chopped tomatoes
1 tbsp tomato purée
150g pappardelle pasta

TO SERVE
Parmesan, grated (optional)

1. Heat 1 tsp of the oil in a medium pan (that has a lid) over a medium heat and fry the onion for 5min, until softened. Meanwhile, pat dry the beef with kitchen paper, then toss in a bowl with the flour and some seasoning.

2. Empty the onion into a separate bowl. Return the pan to medium-high heat with the remaining 1 tsp oil, then fry the beef until browned all over, about 10min. Add the carrot, then return the onion to the pan. Stir in the mustard, thyme and Guinness, then bring to the boil, scraping up any stuck-on goodness from the base of the pan. Simmer for 5min, then stir in the chopped and puréed tomatoes and some seasoning.

3. Cover the pan and simmer for 1hr, stirring occasionally, until the beef is almost tender. Remove the lid and simmer for 20min, stirring frequently, to thicken.

4. Bring a medium pan of salted water to the boil, then cook the pasta according to the pack instructions. Drain and serve topped with the beef ragù and Parmesan, if you like.

Hands-on time: 20min
Cooking time: about 1hr 40min
Serves 2

PER SERVING (without Parmesan) 572cals, 36g protein, 11g fat (3g saturates), 76g carbs (17g total sugars), 9g fibre

Meatball Gnocchi Bake

The tomato sauce is cooked in the pan with the meatballs, which makes this comfort-food supper even easier. You could use pork mince, if you prefer.

FOR THE MEATBALLS
½ small onion, finely chopped
1 garlic clove, crushed
1 tsp dried mixed herbs
300g beef mince (5% fat)
40g dried breadcrumbs
1 medium egg
½ tbsp olive oil

FOR THE TOMATO SAUCE
½ small onion, finely chopped
1 garlic clove, crushed
2 celery sticks, finely chopped
2 tsp dried basil or dried mixed herbs
2 x 400g tins chopped tomatoes
2 tbsp tomato purée

TO FINISH
400g fresh gnocchi
100g frozen peas
125g mozzarella, torn into small pieces
Green salad, to serve (optional)

1. To make the meatballs, mix together all the ingredients in a medium bowl with plenty of seasoning.

2. Heat a large, shallow casserole dish or non-stick frying pan (that has a lid) over a medium heat. Using your hands, shape the meatball mixture into walnut-sized balls and add to the pan. Brown all over.

3. Lower the heat and make the tomato sauce in the same casserole/pan with the balls: push all the meatballs to one side of the pan, and to the empty side add the onion, garlic and celery and cook for 5min. Add the dried herb(s), tomatoes, tomato purée and some seasoning and gently mix everything together. Bring up to a bubble.

4. Preheat the grill to high. Carefully stir the gnocchi into the pan, then cover and simmer gently for 5min more. Uncover and cook for a few min to reduce the sauce slightly. Sprinkle over the peas and gently mix them in. Scatter over the mozzarella.

5. Grill for 5min, or until golden and bubbling. Serve with a green salad, if you like.

Hands-on time: 30min
Cooking time: about 30min
Serves 4

PER SERVING 501cals, 25g protein, 19g fat (11g saturates), 52g carbs (14g total sugars), 7g fibre

Koftas with Broccoli Couscous and Zesty Yogurt

Supercharge your midweek meal with tasty greens – we've grated broccoli into the couscous to add extra goodness.

FOR THE KOFTAS
500g beef mince
2 shallots, finely chopped
2 garlic cloves, crushed
2 tsp paprika
2 tsp ground coriander
2 tsp ground cumin
1 tsp oil

FOR THE COUSCOUS
1 medium head broccoli
350ml vegetable stock
100g couscous
Juice 1 lemon

FOR THE YOGURT
250g Greek yogurt
2 tbsp roughly chopped dill
1 preserved lemon, deseeded and finely chopped

YOU'LL ALSO NEED
12 wooden skewers, soaked in water for 30min

1. Make the koftas. Put all the ingredients, except the oil, into a large bowl with ¼ tsp fine salt and mix well (using your hands is easiest). Divide the mixture into 12 and squeeze each portion into a sausage shape around the end of a skewer. Arrange on a non-stick baking tray and chill for 10min.

2. Meanwhile, preheat the grill to medium. For the couscous, hold the broccoli stalks and coarsely grate just the florets to couscous-sized pieces (or cut them off and pulse in a food processor). Bring the stock to the boil in a medium pan, add the grated broccoli and simmer for 2min, then remove from the heat and stir in the couscous, lemon juice and plenty of seasoning. Cover and leave to absorb for 10min. Uncover and fluff up with a fork.

3. For the yogurt, mix together all the ingredients in a small bowl with some seasoning.

4. Brush the koftas with the oil and grill for 8–10min, turning halfway, or until golden and cooked through. Serve with the couscous and yogurt alongside.

Hands-on time: 30min, plus soaking and chilling
Cooking time: about 12min
Serves 4

PER SERVING 520cals, 36g protein, 29g fat (13g saturates), 26g carbs (7g total sugars), 6g fibre

Paella Rice Cakes

You can, of course, eat this paella as soon as it's ready, but here we've shaped ours into cakes and cooked them in the oven to crisp up the outside.

Large pinch saffron
800ml hot vegetable or chicken stock
2 tbsp olive oil, plus extra to brush
1 onion, finely chopped
1 red or green pepper, deseeded and finely chopped
2 garlic cloves, crushed
1 tsp smoked paprika
250g paella rice
100g fine green beans, finely chopped
100g frozen peas
Small handful parsley, finely chopped, plus extra
    to garnish
50g pitted black olives, chopped
60g Manchego cheese, grated
125g chorizo ring, de-skinned and chopped
Lemon wedges, to serve

◆ GET AHEAD
Prepare to end of step 4 up to 1 day ahead.
Cover and chill. Complete the recipe to serve.

1. Stir the saffron into the stock and set aside until needed. Heat the oil in a large, deep frying or paella pan and gently cook the onion and pepper for 10min, until softened. Stir in garlic and paprika and cook for 1min.

2. Add the rice and some seasoning and stir to coat in the oil, cooking for 1min. Add the green beans and saffron stock. Turn up the heat, bring to the boil, then turn down the heat to low and cook for 20min, with minimal stirring.

3. Remove the pan from the heat, sprinkle the peas on top and set aside to cool completely. Once cool, stir through the parsley, olives and grated Manchego. Check the seasoning.

4. Line a baking tray with parchment. Shape the paella mixture into 8 patties, squeezing together firmly, and space apart on the lined tray. If you have time, chill them for 30min to firm up.

5. Preheat the oven to 200°C (180°C fan) mark 6. Brush the tops of the paella cakes with oil and cook in the oven for 30min, or until piping hot and crisp. Just before they are due to be ready, fry the chorizo in a dry pan over a medium heat until it is crisp and it has released some of its oil.

6. Serve the paella cakes with the chorizo (and its oil) spooned over. Garnish with parsley and serve with lemon wedges for squeezing over.

Hands-on time: 30min, plus cooling and (optional)
    chilling
Cooking time: about 1hr 5min
Serves 4

PER SERVING 590cals, 19g protein, 28g fat
(10g saturates), 62g carbs (9g total sugars), 6g fibre

Quinoa 'Paella'

High in protein and fibre, quinoa makes this vegan paella-style dish filling and healthy. If you like, swap the butter beans for chickpeas.

500ml hot vegetable stock
Pinch saffron (optional)
1 tbsp olive oil
1 onion, finely chopped
1 red pepper, deseeded and cut into 1cm pieces
4 garlic cloves, crushed
2 tsp hot smoked paprika
200g quinoa, rinsed under cold water
200g passata
200g green beans, trimmed
175g chargrilled artichokes, drained
400g tin butter beans, drained and rinsed
150g frozen peas
100g pitted dry black olives, roughly chopped
Juice ½ lemon, plus wedges to serve
Large handful parsley, roughly chopped

1. Infuse the vegetable stock with the saffron, if using. Heat the oil in a large, deep frying or paella pan (that has a lid) over a medium heat and fry the onion and red pepper, uncovered, for 5min, until softened. Add the garlic and paprika and fry for 2min.

2. Stir the quinoa into the pan with the vegetable stock, passata and plenty of seasoning. Cover and simmer for 15min, adding the green beans for the final 5min.

3. Stir in the artichokes, butter beans, peas, olives, lemon juice and half the parsley. Recover with the lid and simmer for 5min, until the quinoa is tender and all the liquid has been absorbed. Check the seasoning, garnish with the remaining parsley and serve with lemon wedges.

Hands-on time: 15min
Cooking time: about 35min
Serves 4

PER SERVING 405cals, 17g protein, 12g fat (2g saturates), 49g carbs (14g total sugars), 17g fibre

Speedy Chicken 'Risotto'

Orzo pasta makes for a quick alternative to risotto rice in this recipe, which can be on the table in less than 15 minutes. If you have a little more time, add in a grated onion with the garlic and cook for an extra couple of minutes.

1 tbsp olive oil
2 garlic cloves, crushed
300g orzo pasta
Pinch saffron
700ml hot chicken stock
150g fresh or frozen peas
300g cooked skinless chicken, shredded
75g Parmesan, finely grated

1. Heat the oil in a large, deep frying pan over a medium heat and cook the garlic for 1min, until fragrant. Stir through the orzo and saffron, then pour in the chicken stock. Bring to the boil and simmer for 4min, adding the peas for the final 1min, or until the orzo is tender and all the stock has been absorbed.

2. Stir through the chicken and most of the Parmesan, then season. Divide between 4 bowls and sprinkle over the remaining Parmesan. Serve.

◆ GH TIP
Stir through some fresh basil pesto for an added herby hit.

Hands-on time: 5min
Cooking time: about 10min
Serves 4

PER SERVING 535cals, 44g protein, 13g fat (5g saturates), 58g carbs (4g total sugars), 6g fibre

Spaghetti Puttanesca Grill

Our twist on the classic puttanesca is grilled and on the table in less than half an hour.

300g spaghetti
300g Tenderstem broccoli, chopped
3 tbsp olive oil
3 garlic cloves, finely sliced
6 anchovy fillets, roughly chopped
2 tbsp capers, drained and rinsed
Large pinch chilli flakes
100g pitted green olives, chopped
2 x 400g tins cherry tomatoes
25g breadcrumbs
25g Parmesan cheese, grated

1. Bring a large pan of salted water to the boil and cook the spaghetti until al dente, according to pack instructions, adding the broccoli for the final 3min of cooking time. Drain both and toss in 1 tbsp of the oil.

2. Meanwhile, heat the remaining oil in a large frying pan, add the garlic and cook over a low heat until just beginning to colour. Add the anchovies and stir to dissolve. Add the capers, chilli and olives, and increase the heat. Add the tomatoes and bubble for about 8min until the sauce is thickened.

3. Preheat the grill to high. Toss the drained pasta and broccoli in the sauce, then season and transfer to an ovenproof dish (about 20.5 x 30.5cm). Scatter over the breadcrumbs and Parmesan, then grill until golden and bubbling.

Hands-on time: 15min
Cooking time: about 20min
Serves 4

PER SERVING 508cals, 19g protein, 15g fat (3g saturates), 69g carbs (11g total sugars), 10g fibre

Spanish Baked Risotto

Inspired by classic paella flavours, this baked risotto has all the taste without the endless standing and stirring in front of the hob.

1 tbsp olive oil
120g pack diced chorizo
400g risotto rice
300g cherry tomatoes
1 litre hot chicken stock
2 roasted red peppers from a jar, deseeded and sliced
Large bunch parsley, chopped
Lemon wedges, to serve

1. Preheat the oven to 200°C (180°C fan) mark 6. Heat the oil in a large casserole or ovenproof pan (that has a lid) over a high heat and fry the chorizo for 2min until golden.

2. Add the rice and cook for 1min, stirring. Add the cherry tomatoes, stock and some seasoning, then bring to the boil. Cover and cook in the oven for 25min until the stock is absorbed and the rice is tender.

3. Stir through the red peppers and parsley, then check the seasoning. Serve with lemon wedges.

Hands-on time: 5min
Cooking time: about 30min
Serves 4

PER SERVING 555cals, 21g protein, 13g fat (4g saturates), 88g carbs (4g total sugars), 3g fibre

Smoked Haddock Carbonara

Cooking the haddock in the pasta water gives a deliciously smokey flavour.

400g dried spaghetti
2 undyed smoked haddock fillets (about 300g)
75g diced pancetta
25g butter
3 garlic cloves, crushed
3 medium eggs
100g Parmesan, finely grated
Small handful parsley, finely chopped

1. Cook the pasta in a large pan of boiling salted water, according to the pack instructions, until al dente. Add the haddock to the pan for the final 5min (turning the heat down to a simmer).

2. Meanwhile, fry the pancetta in a large frying pan over a high heat for 5min, until golden and crisp. Add the butter and garlic; fry for 1min. Set aside.

3. Whisk together the eggs, most of the cheese and plenty of ground black pepper. Remove the fish with a slotted spoon and drain the pasta, reserving a small cupful of cooking water. Flake the fish.

4. Add the pasta to the pan with the egg mixture and about 3 tbsp reserved pasta water. Toss over a gentle heat for 1min to coat, adding a little more pasta water, if needed. Fold through the flaked fish and check the seasoning. Serve topped with ground pepper, the remaining Parmesan and the parsley.

Hands-on time: 15min
Cooking time: about 15min
Serves 4

PER SERVING 719cals, 44g protein, 27g fat (13g saturates), 73g carbs (2g total sugars), 5g fibre

Chicken Linguine

This creamy linguine showcases plenty of lovely Italian ingredients.

---

1 tsp olive oil
225g chestnut mushrooms, quartered
300g chicken thigh fillets, cut into finger-sized strips
75g pancetta cubes
300g linguine
¾ tsp wholegrain mustard
1 tbsp thyme leaves
250g ricotta
40g Grana Padano, grated, plus extra to serve (optional)

1. Bring a large pan of salted water to the boil. Meanwhile, heat the oil in a large frying pan over a medium-high heat and fry the mushrooms, chicken and pancetta until all the liquid has evaporated and they are taking on some colour.

2. Cook the linguine in the boiling water according to the pack instructions. Drain, reserving a large mugful of the starchy cooking water.

3. Stir the mustard, large pinches of salt and pepper and most of the thyme into the chicken. Add the pasta, all the cheese and most of the reserved cooking water.

4. Stir well over a medium heat, until it forms a smooth sauce. Check the seasoning. Serve sprinkled with the remaining thyme and extra Grana Padano, if using.

Hands-on time: 20min
Cooking time: about 20min
Serves 4

PER SERVING (without extra cheese) 610cals, 37g protein, 26g fat (12g saturates), 56g carbs (3g total sugars), 4g fibre

Orecchiette with Sicilian Pesto

Sicilian pesto is similar to its Genoese cousin but is primarily flavoured with tomatoes and almonds.

325g orecchiette
50g blanched almonds
250g cherry tomatoes
2 garlic cloves, crushed
Small bunch basil
40g Pecorino, finely grated, plus extra to serve
4 tbsp extra virgin olive oil
8 pancetta slices, roughly chopped

1. Cook the pasta in a large pan of boiling salted water according to the pack instructions.

2. Meanwhile, pulse the almonds in a food processor until roughly chopped. Add the tomatoes, garlic, basil (including stalks), Pecorino and plenty of seasoning, then pulse until fairly smooth. With the motor running, slowly pour in the oil until incorporated. Check the seasoning.

3. Fry the pancetta in a large, non-stick frying pan over a medium heat, until golden. Reduce the heat to low and stir through the pesto. Drain the orecchiette, reserving a little of the cooking water, and add the pasta to the pancetta pan. Stir in a little cooking water to loosen, and cook until warmed through.

4. Divide among 4 bowls, sprinkle over the extra Pecorino and serve.

Hands-on time: 15min
Cooking time: about 15min
Serves 4

PER SERVING 595cals, 19g protein, 29g fat (7g saturates), 61g carbs (4g total sugars), 6g fibre

Green Spaghetti

This is a garlicky sauce, but you can reduce the number of cloves for a milder flavour.

200g cavolo nero or kale, thickly shredded, woody stems discarded
350g spaghetti
200g frozen peas
3 garlic cloves, peeled
50g vegetarian Italian-style hard cheese (or Parmesan, if you do not need it to be vegetarian), finely grated
150g ricotta

1. Bring a large pan of water to the boil and cook the cavolo nero for 5min, or until just tender. Lift out with a slotted spoon into a blender (keep the water boiling).

2. Add the spaghetti to the pan and cook according to the pack instructions. Drain, reserving 200ml of the cooking water, and return the spaghetti to the empty pan (off the heat).

3. Add the peas, garlic, hard cheese, reserved water and plenty of seasoning to the blender with the cavolo nero and whizz until smooth. Pour into the spaghetti pan; toss gently to combine, then return the pan to a low heat to warm through.

4. Divide among 4 bowls and spoon a dollop of ricotta on to each. Serve.

Hands-on time: 15min
Cooking time: about 20min
Serves 4

PER SERVING 482cals, 23g protein, 10g fat (5g saturates), 70g carbs (6g total sugars), 9g fibre

Tapenade Lamb Chops with Bulgur Wheat

If you don't want to use feta, sprinkle lemon zest and juice over this dish instead.

2 large courgettes, thickly sliced
2 tsp olive oil
8 lamb loin chops
5 tbsp green olive tapenade
200g bulgur wheat
75g feta, crumbled

1. Preheat the grill to high. Toss the courgettes with the oil and some seasoning and arrange on a large non-stick baking tray. Brush the lamb with 2 tbsp of the tapenade, then put on top of the courgettes and season with plenty of ground black pepper.

2. Grill for 10–12min, turning the chops and courgettes halfway through, or until the meat is golden-brown and the courgettes are tender.

3. Meanwhile, cook the bulgur wheat in a medium pan of salted boiling water for 8–10min, until just tender. Carefully remove a small cupful of the starchy cooking water, then drain thoroughly.

4. In a small bowl, whisk the remaining 3 tbsp tapenade with just enough of the cooking water to give a drizzling consistency. Divide the bulgur wheat, courgettes and lamb chops among 4 plates, sprinkle over the feta and drizzle with the tapenade. Serve.

Hands-on time: 15min
Cooking time: about 12min
Serves 4

PER SERVING 816cals, 42g protein, 53g fat (23g saturates), 40g carbs (3g total sugars), 5g fibre

Sweet Chilli Salmon and Freekeh

Freekeh is wheat that has been harvested while still green, then roasted to create a distinct smokey flavour.

200g freekeh
300g Tenderstem broccoli, cut into 2.5cm pieces
150g frozen broad beans
5 tbsp sweet chilli sauce
Juice 2 limes
4 salmon fillets (around 500g)
2 ripe avocados, de-stoned and roughly chopped
2 spring onions, thinly sliced

1. Put the freekeh into a large pan of salted water over a medium-high heat. Bring to the boil, then reduce the heat and simmer for 35min until tender (freekeh retains a chew). Add the broccoli for the final 5min of cooking and the broad beans for the final 1min. Drain, skinning the broad beans, if you like (see GH Tip).

2. Meanwhile, preheat the oven to 200°C (180°C fan) mark 6 and line a baking tray with foil. Mix 3 tbsp sweet chilli sauce and the juice of 1 lime in a large bowl with plenty of seasoning. Add the salmon and turn to coat. Arrange the fillets on the prepared tray, skin-side down (if present), and brush over any sauce left in the bowl. Cook for 15min, until the fish flakes when lightly pressed.

3. Empty the drained freekeh on to a large serving plate. Flake over the cooked salmon (discard any skin) and gently toss through the avocado, spring onions, remaining sweet chilli sauce and lime juice, plus lots of seasoning. Serve.

◆ GH TIP
Skinning the broad beans isn't necessary, but reveals them in all their bright green beauty.

Hands-on time: 20min
Cooking time: about 40min
Serves 4

PER SERVING 672cals, 44g protein, 30g fat
(6g saturates), 49g carbs (12g total sugars), 15g fibre

Sausage and Fennel Lasagne

Instead of sausage meat, you could use about eight of your favourite sausages. Simply peel off and discard the skins.

1 large fennel bulb
1 tbsp olive oil
450g pork sausage meat
1 tsp fennel seeds
1 garlic clove, crushed
1 courgette, coarsely grated
1 tbsp plain flour
200ml white wine
9 lasagne sheets
175g grated mozzarella

FOR THE WHITE SAUCE
750ml milk
50g butter
50g plain flour
75g Parmesan, grated

1. Preheat the oven to 200°C (180°C fan) mark 6. Slice the fronds off the fennel bulb and reserve. Finely chop the remaining fennel (core and all). In a large frying pan, heat the oil and gently fry the fennel for 5min until just beginning to soften. Add the pork and cook over a medium heat for about 10min, breaking up with a spoon.

2. Add the fennel seeds, garlic and courgette to the pan and fry for 2min. Stir in the flour, then pour in the wine. Simmer for 5min.

3. Soak the lasagne sheets in a single layer in freshly boiled water – a large oven tray is ideal – while you make the white sauce. In a medium pan, gradually bring the milk, butter and flour to the boil, whisking constantly, until thickened. Simmer over a low heat for 5min, then stir in the Parmesan and season well. Drain the lasagne.

4. Spoon a third of the pork mixture into the base of a 2 litre baking dish. Top with a quarter each of the white sauce and mozzarella, then add a layer of lasagne sheets (not overlapping). Repeat the layers twice more, finishing with a layer of white sauce and mozzarella.

5. Cook in the oven for 30-35min until golden and bubbling. Sprinkle over the reserved fennel fronds and serve.

Hands-on time: 15min
Cooking time: about 1hr
Serves 6

PER SERVING 767cals, 33g protein, 37g fat (19g saturates), 67g carbs (11g total sugars), 6g fibre

Pies, Galettes & Tarts

Red Onion Tarte Tatin

Make onions the star of the show with this plant-based centrepiece. Swap the thyme for rosemary, if you like.

320g ready-rolled puff pastry
25g butter
3 juniper berries, crushed
1 tbsp thyme leaves, plus extra, to garnish (optional)
4–5 small red onions, each cut into 3 slices
2 tbsp redcurrant jelly
50ml red wine

1. Preheat the oven to 200°C (180°C fan) mark 6. Unroll the pastry and, using an ovenproof frying pan that's 23cm across the top, cut a rough circle the same size as the top of the pan (roll out the pastry a little more first, if needed). Slide the pastry on to a baking sheet, prick all over with a fork and chill until needed.

2. Melt the butter in the pan over a medium heat. Stir through the juniper berries and thyme, and cook for 1min, until fragrant. Lower the heat, then arrange the onion slices (using tongs, if needed) to cover the base of the pan. Cook gently for 20min, until the onions have softened.

3. In a bowl, mix the redcurrant jelly, wine and some seasoning. Pour into the onion pan, turn up the heat and bubble for 5min, until slightly reduced.

4. Working quickly, lay the pastry over the onions and tuck the edges down slightly into the pan. Cook for 25–30min, or until puffed and golden.

5. Carefully remove the pan from the oven and wrap the handle with an oven glove or tea towel (to remind you it's hot!). Leave to cool for 5min before inverting on to a serving plate. Garnish with thyme sprigs, if you like, and serve in slices.

◆ GET AHEAD
Prepare to end of step 3 up to 3hr ahead.
Cool, cover and set aside at room temperature.
Complete the recipe to serve.

Hands-on time: 20min, plus cooling
Cooking time: about 55min
Serves 6

PER SERVING 181cals, 2g protein, 10g fat (5g saturates), 18g carbs (8g total sugars), 2g fibre

Spring Vegetable Tart

This zesty vegetarian centrepiece makes use of in-season produce and ready-rolled pastry, and is quick and easy to prepare.

320g ready-rolled shortcrust pastry
1 egg, beaten
250g ricotta
Finely grated zest and juice 1 lemon
75g mature Cheddar, finely grated
1 tbsp mint leaves, finely chopped, plus extra
   small leaves to garnish
40g spring greens, finely shredded (woody
   cores discarded)
2 tbsp olive oil
4 spring onions
75g radishes, sliced
40g walnuts, roughly chopped

◆ GET AHEAD
Prepare to end of step 2 up to a day ahead.
Cool completely and store the pastry in an
airtight container at room temperature.
Complete the recipe to serve.

1. Line a baking sheet with baking parchment, then unroll the pastry on to the baking sheet. Fold in all the sides to create a 2cm-wide border, then crimp the border with your fingers. Chill for 30min.

2. Preheat the oven to 200°C (180°C fan) mark 6. Prick the pastry inside the border well with a fork, then brush all over with beaten egg. Cook for 15–20min, until the pastry is golden and sandy to the touch.

3. In a bowl, mix together the ricotta, lemon zest and juice, Cheddar, mint and some seasoning. In a separate bowl, toss the spring greens with 1 tbsp of the olive oil. Trim the spring onions to remove the root and some of the tougher green leaves at the top, then slice lengthways into quarters.

4. Spread the ricotta mixture inside the tart border and scatter over the spring greens. In the empty bowl, toss the spring onions, radishes and remaining oil. Arrange on top of the greens. Return to the oven for 15–18min, until the vegetables are tender.

5. Allow the tart to cool slightly, then scatter over walnuts and mint leaves to garnish. Serve warm or at room temperature.

Hands-on time: 20min, plus chilling and cooling
Cooking time: about 40min
Serves 4 as a main or 6 as a side

PER SERVING (for 6) 457cals, 13g protein, 35g fat
(13g saturates), 22g carbs (2g total sugars), 3g fibre

Festive Salmon Parcel

Despite its appearance, filo is one of the easiest pastries to handle and makes this recipe instantly impressive.

Large handful fresh parsley
2 sprigs fresh tarragon
Finely grated zest 1 lemon
3 tbsp olive oil, plus extra to brush
2 tbsp flaked almonds
270g filo pastry sheets
750g side of fresh salmon, skinless, with small bones removed (see GH Tip)
Lemon wedges, to serve

1. Preheat the oven to 200°C (180°C fan) mark 6. Put the parsley, tarragon, lemon zest, oil and some seasoning into a food processor and whizz until well combined but still with some texture. Add the almonds and pulse briefly to break up.

2. On a large baking tray, arrange a single layer of filo sheets into a rough 40.5cm square (overlapping the sheets in the middle) – it doesn't matter if the pastry hangs over the sides of the tray. Top with a second layer of filo in the same way. Next, put the skinned salmon along the centre of the pastry and top with the herb mixture. Brush the top layer of visible pastry with some oil, then pull that layer up and over the salmon, lightly scrunching the pastry into frills. Repeat with the bottom layer of pastry. Use the remaining filo to add more frills to the top of the parcel, then brush these with a little more oil.

3. Cook for 20min until golden. Transfer to a serving board or platter and garnish with the lemon wedges. Serve immediately in slices.

◆ GET AHEAD
Prepare to the end of step 1 up to 1hr ahead. Transfer to a bowl, cover and keep at room temperature. Complete the recipe to serve.

◆ GH TIP
Buy salmon as even in width as possible, so everyone gets an equal slice.

Hands-on time: 15min
Cooking time: about 20min
Cuts into 6 slices

PER SLICE 500cals, 30g protein, 32g fat (5g saturates), 23g carbs (1g total sugars), 0g fibre

Courgette and Ricotta Tarts

Impress guests with these elegant tarts – almost too pretty to cut into!

2 tsp olive oil, plus extra to grease
4 filo pastry sheets
100g ricotta
3 tbsp finely grated vegetarian Italian-style hard cheese
50ml whole milk
1 large egg
Finely grated zest 1 lemon
2 large courgettes

1. Preheat the oven to 180°C (160°C fan) mark 4. Grease 2 x 10cm fluted tart tins. Trim the filo sheets into 8 rectangles, each 23 x 12.5cm. Cover with a damp tea towel so they don't dry out.

2. Lightly brush one filo rectangle with oil and gently press into a tin (there will be overhang). Repeat with the remaining filo, using 4 rectangles per tin and laying the sheets at 45° angles to each other (so they don't fully overlap).

3. Beat together the cheeses, milk, egg, lemon zest, and some seasoning. Spoon into the pastry cases.

4. Using a mandoline, slice the courgettes into thin strips. Roll one strip into a tight spiral. Wrap another strip around the outside of the spiral, then keep going until your courgette spiral is large enough to mostly fill the tin. Gently place in the ricotta. Repeat with the remaining courgettes. Brush the visible courgettes with a little oil.

5. Cook the tarts for 30min, or until golden and the filling is set (dab off any moisture from the courgettes with kitchen paper). Cool in the tins for 5min. Serve warm or at room temperature.

◆ GET AHEAD
Make up to 6hr ahead. Cool completely in the tin, cover and store at room temperature. Serve at room temperature or warm (in tins) in an oven preheated to 180°C (160°C fan) mark 4 for 5min.

Hands-on time: 25min, plus cooling
Cooking time: 30min
Serves 2

PER SERVING 398cals, 17g protein, 14g fat (6g saturates), 49g carbs (6g total sugars), 4g fibre

Buckwheat and Greens Galette

Buckwheat gives this vegetarian pastry a nutty taste. Swap the asparagus for Tenderstem broccoli, if you like.

FOR THE PASTRY
100g buckwheat flour
100g plain flour, plus extra to dust
110g unsalted butter, chilled and chopped
1 medium egg, beaten

FOR THE FILLING
200g baby spinach
150g full-fat cream cheese
50g Cheddar, grated
Finely grated zest 1 and juice ½ lemon
200g asparagus, trimmed and roughly chopped
1 tsp olive oil
1 medium egg, beaten

◆ GET AHEAD
Make the pastry up to a day ahead. Chill. To serve, allow the pastry to soften at room temperature for 15min before continuing the recipe.

Hands-on time: 25min, plus chilling
Cooking time: about 40min
Serves 4

PER SERVING 594cals, 17g protein, 41g fat (24g saturates), 38g carbs (3g total sugars), 4g fibre

1. First, make the pastry. In a food processor, pulse the flours with ¼ tsp fine salt until combined. Add the butter and pulse until the mixture resembles fine breadcrumbs. Alternatively, mix the dry ingredients in a large bowl and rub in the butter with your fingers. Add the egg and pulse/mix until the pastry comes together. Tip on to a work surface, shape into a disc, then wrap and chill for 30min.

2. Meanwhile, make the filling. Put the spinach into a colander in the sink and pour over a full kettle of just-boiled water to wilt. When cool enough to handle, lift up handfuls of the spinach and firmly squeeze out the excess moisture.

3. In a medium bowl, mix together the squeezed spinach, cream cheese, Cheddar, lemon zest and juice and some seasoning. In another bowl, toss the asparagus with the oil.

4. Lightly flour a large sheet of baking parchment and roll out the pastry on it to a rough 35cm circle. Slide the pastry on its parchment on to a large baking sheet. Spread over the spinach mixture, leaving a 5cm border around the edges. Arrange the asparagus on the filling, then fold in the pastry so it just begins to cover the filling (don't worry if it looks a little rustic). Chill for 30min.

5. Preheat the oven to 190°C (170°C fan) mark 5. Brush the folded pastry with beaten egg. Cook the galette for 30–40min, or until the pastry is golden brown. Serve.

Roasted Squash and Red Chicory Tart with Salsa Verde

Keep things informal with one shareable tart or, for a more sophisticated effect, divide the pastry into six and bake individual tarts.

½ large butternut squash (about 500g), peeled, deseeded and sliced into 1cm thick wedges
2 tbsp olive oil
3 red chicory, trimmed and quartered
3 red onions, finely sliced
½ tsp fennel seeds
320g ready-rolled vegan puff pastry
200g tub oat crème fraîche

FOR THE SALSA VERDE
Large bunch flat-leaf parsley
Small handful basil leaves
1 heaped tsp capers in brine, drained
½ garlic clove, finely grated
4 tbsp extra virgin olive oil
2 tsp vegan red wine vinegar

1. Preheat the oven to 220°C (200°C fan) mark 7 and line a large baking tray with baking parchment. Toss the butternut squash with ½ tbsp oil, season and spread out on the prepared tray. Roast for 10min. Toss the chicory with another ½ tbsp oil and add to the tray, roasting for a further 10min. Set aside.

Hands-on time: 20min, plus resting
Cooking time: about 45min
Serves 6

PER SERVING 440cals, 6g protein, 30g fat (11g saturates), 33g carbs (10g total sugars), 6g fibre

2. Meanwhile, heat the remaining 1 tbsp olive oil in a frying pan over a medium heat. Add the onions, cover and cook for 10min, stirring occasionally, until softened. Uncover, stir in the fennel seeds and cook for 10min more until golden, then set aside.

3. Lower the oven temperature to 200°C (180°C fan) mark 6. Unroll the pastry sheet and put on a large sheet of baking parchment. Score a border 1cm in from the edge, taking care not to cut all the way through the pastry. Prick the middle all over with a fork. Slide the pastry (still on the parchment) on to a large baking sheet and cook in the oven for 15min, until puffed up.

4. Remove the pastry from the oven and, with the back of a spoon, gently press down the pastry inside the border. Spread the oat fraîche evenly over the pastry inside the border. Scatter over the onions, then arrange the squash and chicory on top. Return to the oven for 10min.

5. Meanwhile, make the salsa verde. Put all the ingredients in the small bowl of a food processor or a small high-speed blender with 2 tbsp water and pulse to a rough or smooth sauce, as you prefer.

6. Set the tart aside for 10min to allow the oat fraîche to thicken before slicing and serving dolloped with the salsa verde.

◆ GH TIP
You can make the salsa verde by hand – finely chop the herbs and capers, then toss with the garlic, oil and vinegar. This gives a chunkier finish but will taste just as good.

Spinach and Feta Pie (Spanakopita)

We've baked this classic Greek pie in a round tin for extra crispiness. The ricotta adds a creamy texture, but you can swap it for extra feta, if you prefer.

800g spinach
4 spring onions, finely chopped
150g feta, crumbled
150g ricotta
Small handful dill, roughly chopped
Small handful mint, leaves picked and roughly chopped
2 medium eggs, beaten
Finely grated zest 1 lemon
¼ tsp freshly grated nutmeg
50g butter, melted
6 filo pastry sheets
1 tsp sesame seeds
Green salad, to serve (optional)

Hands-on time: 25min, plus cooling
Cooking time: about 55min
Serves 6

PER SERVING 302cals, 14g protein, 19g fat
(10g saturates), 17g carbs (4g total sugars), 5g fibre

1. Preheat the oven to 200°C (180°C fan) mark 6. Put the spinach into a colander in the sink, then pour over a full kettle of just-boiled water to wilt (you may need to do this in batches). When cool enough to handle, lift up handfuls of the spinach and firmly squeeze out the excess moisture. Roughly chop.

2. In a large bowl, mix the spring onions, feta, ricotta, herbs, eggs, lemon zest, nutmeg, cooled spinach and plenty of seasoning until combined.

3. Lightly brush a 20.5cm round cake tin (either springform or loose-bottomed) with some of the melted butter. Brush the top of a filo sheet with butter and press (butter-side up) into the tin. Repeat with a further 3 sheets, rotating them so the base and sides of the tin are covered, leaving the excess hanging over the top of the tin. Spoon in the filling and smooth to level.

4. Cut the remaining 2 filo sheets into rough circles just larger than 20.5cm – use your cake tin as a template. Brush the top of each with butter, then set on top of the filling (butter-side up). Scrunch in the overhanging filo, brush with the remaining butter and sprinkle over the sesame seeds.

5. Put the tin on a baking tray (to catch any leaking butter) and cook in the oven for about 45min, covering with foil after 15min. Remove the tray from the oven, then carefully remove the outside of the cake tin. Re-cover the top with foil and return to the oven for 5–10min to crisp up the sides of the pastry. Leave to cool for 10min before transferring to a board or plate. Serve with a green salad, if you like.

Salmon, Asparagus and Pea Quiche

Any leftovers make for a lovely lunch straight from the fridge. For a quicker dinner, use ready-made shortcrust pastry.

FOR THE PASTRY
175g plain flour, plus extra to dust
100g unsalted butter, chilled and chopped
1 tsp dried thyme
1 tsp dried rosemary

FOR THE FILLING
3 medium eggs
125ml double cream
125g crème fraîche
2 tsp Dijon mustard
25g Parmesan, finely grated
150g asparagus spears, woody ends trimmed
75g frozen garden peas
150g hot smoked salmon, skinned and flaked

1. First, make the pastry. Using a food processor, pulse the flour and butter until the mixture resembles fine breadcrumbs. Alternatively, rub the butter into the flour using your fingers. Pulse/mix in the dried herbs and a large pinch of fine salt, followed by 2 tbsp ice-cold water. Pulse/mix until the pastry just comes together. Tip on to a work surface, shape into a disc, then wrap and chill for 30min.

2. Lightly flour a work surface and roll out the pastry, then use to line a 20.5cm round, 3.5cm deep fluted tart tin. Trim the excess pastry and prick the base all over with a fork. Chill for 10min.

3. Preheat the oven to 190°C (170°C fan) mark 5. Line the pastry in the tin with a large sheet of baking parchment and fill with baking beans. Cook for 20min, until the pastry sides are set. Carefully remove the parchment and baking beans. Return the tin to the oven for 12–15min, until the pastry is lightly golden and feels sandy to the touch. Remove from the oven and turn down the oven temperature to 170°C (150°C fan) mark 3.

4. Meanwhile, make the filling. In a large jug, whisk the eggs, cream, crème fraîche, mustard, Parmesan and plenty of seasoning. Roughly chop all but 3 of the asparagus spears and scatter into the pastry case (still in the tin), along with the peas and flaked salmon. Pour in the cream mixture and arrange the whole spears on top (they may sink a little).

5. Cook for 50–55min, or until the filling is golden and just set. Allow to rest for 5min before transferring to a serving plate or board. Serve warm or at room temperature.

Hands-on time: 25min, plus chilling and resting
Cooking time: about 1hr 30min
Serves 6

PER SERVING 530cals, 16g protein, 40g fat (23g saturates), 26g carbs (3g total sugars), 2g fibre

Veggie Lentil Filo Pie

With a spicy filling topped with crisp pastry, this pie is bound to become a new favourite. For a meaty addition, add chopped chicken thighs with the lentils, or stir in cooked prawns before finishing in the oven.

3 tbsp vegetable oil
1 onion, finely chopped
175g red split lentils
1 large sweet potato (about 300g), cut into 1.5cm pieces
1 tbsp Thai red curry paste
2 garlic cloves, crushed
5cm piece fresh root ginger, peeled and grated
400g tin coconut milk
400ml vegetable stock
175g baby spinach
4 large filo pastry sheets (about 145g)

1. Heat 1 tbsp of the oil in a large pan over low heat and fry the onion for 5min. Meanwhile, wash the lentils well in a sieve under cold running water and drain.

2. Stir the lentils, sweet potato, Thai curry paste, garlic, ginger and some seasoning into the pan and fry for 1min. Pour in the coconut milk and stock. Bring to the boil over high heat, then turn down the heat and simmer for 15min, until the lentils are cooked through and beginning to break down and the potatoes are tender. Stir in the spinach and check the seasoning.

3. Preheat the oven to 190°C (170°C fan) mark 5. Empty the lentil mixture into a 1.5–2 litre ovenproof serving dish.

4. Brush the top of each filo sheet with oil, scrunch up lightly and use to top the lentil mixture. Cook in the oven for 15–20min, until the filo is golden and the filling is piping hot. Serve.

Hands-on time: 20min
Cooking time: about 45min
Serves 4

PER SERVING 597cals, 17g protein, 28g fat (16g saturates), 66g carbs (11g total sugars), 8g fibre

Chicken and Mushroom Pot Pie

With the sauce coming from ready-made soup, this might be the easiest chicken pie you'll ever make.

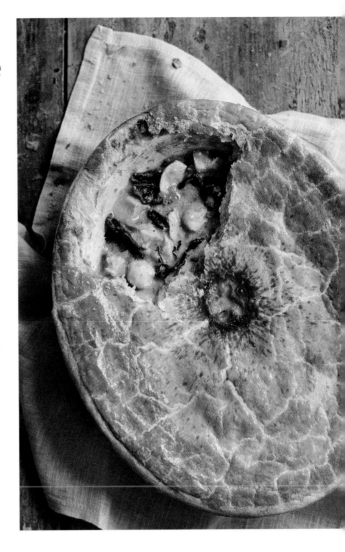

25g dried wild mushrooms
1 leek, halved lengthways and finely sliced
2 x 295g tins low-fat condensed mushroom soup
50ml milk
200g ready-cooked chestnuts, chopped
4 skinless chicken breasts, cut into 2cm chunks
320g ready-rolled puff pastry
1 medium egg, beaten

1. Put the mushrooms and sliced leek into a 1.8 litre pie or baking dish. Cover with freshly boiled water and set aside for 20min to soften. Drain and return the mixture to the dish. Preheat the oven to 190°C (170°C fan) mark 5.

2. Mix the soup and milk into the leek mixture, then stir in chestnuts, chicken and some salt and freshly ground black pepper.

3. Unroll the pastry and make sure it will cover the top of the dish, with 3cm excess around all the sides. If needed, roll out the pastry a bit more. Brush the rim and outer top 3cm of the dish sides with some egg. Lay the pastry on top and, if needed, snip the overhang to 3cm using kitchen scissors. Press the pastry on to the sides of the dish to seal, then brush with more egg. Snip a cross in the centre of the pastry.

4. Bake in the middle of the oven for 1hr. Carefully remove from the oven and set aside to rest for 10min. Serve.

Hands-on time: 30min, plus softening and resting
Cooking time: about 1hr
Serves 4

PER SERVING 555cals, 39g protein, 28g fat (12g saturates), 34g carbs (3g total sugars), 2g fibre

Individual Beetroot Wellington

Enjoy a 'roast' even on meat-free days with this eye-catching Wellington, made with a heavenly combination of earthy beetroot and creamy goat's cheese.

1 medium raw beetroot (about 100g unpeeled weight)
75g baby leaf spinach
½ tbsp Dijon mustard
Freshly grated nutmeg, to taste
Plain flour, to dust
250g ready-made puff pastry (from a block)
25-40g goat's cheese, crumbled
1 medium egg, beaten

◆ GET AHEAD
Prepare to end of step 5 up to 6hr ahead.
Complete the recipe to serve.

Hands-on time: 25min, plus cooling and chilling
Cooking time: 1hr 35min
Serves 1

PER SERVING 761cals, 21g protein, 46g fat (30g saturates), 64g carbs (9g total sugars), 5g fibre

1. Preheat the oven to 200°C (180°C) mark 6. Wash the beetroot and wrap in foil. Roast on a baking tray for 1hr, or until you can easily push a knife into the centre. Cool.

2. Meanwhile, put the spinach into a sieve in the sink and pour over boiled water from the kettle to wilt. Run the spinach under cold water until cool, then firmly squeeze out all the excess moisture. Put into a bowl and mix in the mustard, nutmeg and some seasoning. Set aside.

3. Wearing gloves to protect your hands, peel off the beetroot skin, then remove a thin slice from the root end so it stands up.

4. Lightly flour a work surface and roll out a third of the pastry to make a rough 16cm square. Transfer to a baking sheet lined with baking parchment. Sit the beetroot in the middle, then make a tight nest of the spinach mixture around it. Top the spinach with a halo of cheese, then brush the visible pastry with beaten egg.

5. Roll out the remaining pastry until it's large enough to cover the filling. Lay over the filling, working out any air pockets and pressing the edges together to seal. Trim the excess and crimp around the edge. Brush all over with egg. Chill for 20min.

6. Reheat the oven to 200°C (180°C) mark 6. Re-glaze the pastry with egg and cook for 35min, until golden. Serve.

Bombay Vegetable Turnovers with Radish Raita

A cross between a samosa and a pasty, these vegetable parcels are flavoured with the spices of Bombay potatoes and served with a cooling yogurt sauce.

1 tbsp vegetable oil
1 small onion, finely sliced
2 garlic cloves, crushed
1 green finger chilli, finely chopped
2 tsp brown mustard seeds
2 tsp garam masala
1 tsp turmeric
75g frozen peas
250g mixed roasted vegetables, such as potatoes,
    parsnips and carrots, cut into 1cm pieces
Plain flour, to dust
500g block ready-made puff pastry
1 medium egg, beaten
1 tsp nigella seeds, to sprinkle

FOR THE RAITA
½ cucumber, peeled, halved lengthways and deseeded
200g Greek-style yogurt
4 fat radishes, cut into matchsticks
Small handful mint leaves, finely chopped
1 tbsp lemon juice

◆ GET AHEAD
Prepare to the end of step 2 up to a day ahead, then arrange on a lined baking tray, cover and chill. Make the raita up to 1hr ahead. Complete the recipe to serve.

Hands-on time: 40min, plus cooling
Cooking time: about 30min
Serves 4

PER SERVING 518cals, 12g protein, 31g fat
(17g saturates), 45g carbs (8g total sugars), 4g fibre

1. Heat the oil in a large frying pan over a medium heat, add the onion with a pinch of salt and fry for 7–8min, until softened. Add the garlic and chilli, fry for 2min, then add the spices and stir for 1min. Add the peas, cook for 2min, until tender, then remove from the heat. Stir in the roasted vegetables and season. Cool.

2. Preheat the oven to 220°C (200°C fan) mark 7 and line a large baking tray with baking parchment. Lightly flour a work surface and roll out the pastry to a 33cm square, about 3mm thick. Trim any wonky edges, then cut into 4 even squares. Put a quarter of the vegetable mixture on one diagonal half of each rectangle (leaving a border), then brush around the edges with egg. Fold the empty half of the pastry over the vegetables and press the edges to seal.

3. Transfer the turnovers to the prepared tray and brush all over with egg. Cut a few slashes into the top of each parcel and scatter over the nigella seeds. Cook for 12–15min until dark golden and crisp.

4. Meanwhile, make the raita. Coarsely grate the cucumber, then squeeze the flesh in your hands over a sink to remove the excess juice. Mix in a bowl with the remaining ingredients and some seasoning. Serve with the turnovers.

Portobello Pithiviers

An elegant main that can easily be made vegan by using a vegan pastry and a melted dairy-free spread rather than egg to glaze.

2 medium portobello mushrooms, each about 8.5cm across
1 tsp olive oil
320g ready-rolled puff pastry
1 egg, beaten

FOR THE STUFFING
1 tsp olive oil
1 echalion shallot, finely chopped
1 tsp freshly chopped rosemary
60g spinach
15g walnuts, finely chopped

◆ GET AHEAD
Prepare to the end of step 4 up to a day ahead. Complete the recipe to serve.

Hands-on time: 30min, plus cooling and chilling
Cooking time: about 55min
Makes 2 pithiviers

PER PITHIVIER 481cals, 12g protein, 32g fat (17g saturates), 34g carbs (2g total sugars), 3g fibre

1. Preheat the oven to 200°C (180°C fan) mark 6. Put the mushrooms in a small roasting tin, gill-side up. Drizzle over the oil and season. Roast for 20min, until almost tender, then flip over and roast for 5min more (this helps with evaporating some of the liquid). Set aside to cool completely.

2. Meanwhile, make the stuffing. Heat the oil in a medium frying pan over a low heat and fry the shallot for 5min, until softened. Add the rosemary and fry for 1min. Add the spinach and fry, stirring, until wilted and any moisture in the pan has evaporated. Remove from the heat, add the walnuts and leave to cool. Check the seasoning.

3. To assemble, allow the pastry to sit at room temperature for 5min. Line a baking tray with baking parchment. Unroll the pastry and stamp out 4 circles, each about 12.5cm – they need to be at least 4cm larger than your mushrooms. Lay 2 circles on the lined tray and top with the mushrooms, gill-side up. Spoon the stuffing on to the mushrooms, mounding it neatly.

4. Brush the pastry border with some beaten egg, then lay the remaining 2 circles on top, to cover, and press firmly on the edges to seal (remove any air bubbles). Trim the excess pastry, leaving a 1cm border. Crimp the edges and brush all over with more egg. With a small, sharp knife, score curved lines from the centre of the top of each pastry to the edges. Chill for 30min.

5. Preheat the oven to 200°C (180°C fan) mark 6. Cut a steam hole in the centre of each pithivier. Cook for 25–30min, or until golden and puffed. Serve.

Mixed Pepper and Goat's Cheese Puff Pastry Plait

This plaited pastry looks elaborate but is straightforward to assemble.

350g ready-roasted mixed peppers (drained weight)
375g ready-rolled puff pastry
50g soft goat's cheese
2 thyme sprigs, leaves removed
1 medium egg, beaten
½ tsp poppy seeds

1. Preheat the oven to 190°C (170°C fan) mark 5. Put the drained peppers on kitchen paper and dry thoroughly with more kitchen paper.

2. Unwrap the pastry and put on a baking tray so the short end is in front of you. Spread the goat's cheese in a line towards you down the middle third of the pastry, then top the cheese with the peppers. Sprinkle over the thyme leaves and season well with freshly ground black pepper.

3. With a sharp knife, cut 2cm wide slits, running 1cm away from the peppers to the edges of the pastry, slanting the slits towards you. Brush the pastry with beaten egg.

4. Fold the pastry ends over the filling, then, starting at the end furthest away from you, fold in the pastry strips, alternating sides, over the pepper mixture to give a plait effect. Brush the top with egg and sprinkle with poppy seeds.

5. Cook the plait for 30–40min until the pastry is deep golden. Serve warm or at room temperature in slices.

◆ GET AHEAD
Prepare to the end of step 4 up to 4hr ahead. Cover and chill. Unwrap and complete the recipe to serve.

Hands-on time: 15min
Cooking time: about 40min
Serves 8

PER SERVING 224cals, 5g protein, 14g fat
(7g saturates), 17g carbs (2g total sugars), 1g fibre

Lamb and Lentil Filo Parcels

These parcels are perfect for freezing ahead and can be cooked from frozen.

4 tbsp olive oil
1 red onion, finely chopped
1 large carrot, finely chopped
250g lamb mince
2 tbsp harissa paste
1 tsp ground cinnamon
1 tsp ground cumin
150g dried brown lentils, rinsed
1 red pepper, finely diced
6 filo pastry sheets
Salad, to serve

1. Heat 1 tbsp of the oil in a large deep frying pan over a medium heat and fry the onion and carrot for 10min, until softened and lightly golden. Stir in the lamb, then cook for 8–10min until browned all over. Add the harissa, cinnamon and cumin and cook for 2min, then add the lentils, red pepper, 800ml water and some seasoning.

2. Bring to the boil, cover and simmer for 20–25min, until the lentils have absorbed the liquid and are tender. Check seasoning and allow to cool.

3. Preheat the oven to 200°C (180°C fan) mark 6. Working 1 sheet at a time, cut the filo in half to make 2 smaller rectangles, brush the tops with oil and stack. Spoon a sixth of the lamb mixture into the centre of the filo, then bring up the pastry edges and press them together above the meat to seal into a parcel. Place on a baking tray lined with baking parchment. Repeat with the remaining pastry, oil and lamb filling. Brush the tops of parcels with a little more oil.

4. Cook for 12–15min, until golden brown and piping hot. Serve with salad.

◆ GET AHEAD
Prepare to end of step 3 (do not preheat the oven). Wrap in cling film and freeze for up to 1 month. Unwrap and cook from frozen in an oven preheated to 200°C (180°C fan) mark 6, allowing 8min extra, or until golden and piping hot.

Hands-on time: 25min, plus cooling
Cooking time: about 1hr
Serves 6

PER SERVING 373cals, 18g protein, 15g fat (4g saturates), 39g carbs (5g total sugars), 6g fibre

Beef Wellington with Port Gravy

Nothing says special occasion quite like a beef Wellington, and the combination of Parma ham, porcini paste and garlic spinach in ours makes for a taste sensation that's well worth the effort.

FOR THE WELLINGTON
750–800g centre-cut beef fillet
1 tbsp olive oil, plus extra to grease
25g butter
2 garlic cloves, crushed
450g baby leaf spinach, any woody stalks removed
Freshly grated nutmeg, to taste
8 Parma ham slices
2 tbsp porcini and truffle paste (see GH Tip)
Plain flour, to dust
500g block ready-made puff pastry
1 medium egg, beaten
Poppy seeds, to garnish (optional)

FOR THE PORT GRAVY
1 tsp olive oil
75g pancetta lardons
1 echalion shallot, finely chopped
3 tbsp plain flour
200ml ruby port
500ml beef stock
1 tbsp redcurrant jelly

◆ GET AHEAD
Prepare to the end of step 4 up to 1 day ahead, loosely cover with foil and chill. Make the gravy up to 1 day ahead, then cool, cover and chill. Complete the recipe to serve, reheating the gravy in a pan.

Hands-on time: 1hr, plus cooling, chilling and resting
Cooking time: about 1hr
Serves 6

PER SERVING 797cals, 49g protein, 43g fat (23g saturates), 43g carbs (7g total sugars), 2g fibre

1. For the Wellington, pat dry the beef fillet with kitchen paper. Heat the oil in a large frying pan over a high heat and fry the beef for 8–10min, turning regularly, until browned all over (including the ends). Cool on a wire rack set over a baking tray.

2. Melt the butter in the same pan, add the garlic and cook for 30sec. Add half the spinach, season with salt, pepper and nutmeg, then cook until slightly wilted. Add the remaining spinach and cook, stirring, until completely wilted. Drain in a colander in the sink. When the spinach is cool enough to handle, squeeze out all the excess moisture with your hands, then dry thoroughly on kitchen paper.

3. Lay 2 large overlapping sheets of cling film on a work surface. Arrange slices of Parma ham, slightly overlapping, in the centre, in a rectangle large enough to completely cover the beef (including the ends). Top with spinach, leaving a 2.5cm border. Brush the fillet with porcini paste and set in the centre of the spinach. Using the cling film to help, wrap the ham and spinach around the fillet, then roll up into a cling film-wrapped log, twisting the ends tightly to secure. Chill for at least 30min (or up to 6hr).

4. Line a baking tray with baking parchment. Lightly flour a work surface and roll out the pastry to a rectangle large enough to completely enclose the beef. Cut a 2.5cm strip from one edge and set aside. Re-roll the pastry sheet to

its original size and brush all over with egg. Unwrap the beef and set in the centre of the pastry. Fold in the short edges of the pastry, then wrap up. Put seam-side down on the prepared tray and brush all over with egg. Stamp or cut out small stars from the reserved pastry, stick on top and brush with egg. Chill for at least 30min (or up to 24hr).

5. Preheat the oven to 220°C (200°C fan) mark 7. Heat a sturdy baking tray in the oven for 10min. Brush the Wellington all over with more egg and sprinkle over the poppy seeds, if using. Lift on to preheated baking tray (still on the parchment) and cook for 10min. Reduce the oven temperature to 200°C (180°C fan) mark 6 and cook for 35–40min (for medium), until the pastry is a deep golden brown (if you have a meat thermometer, it should read 60°C when inserted into centre of the fillet).

6. Meanwhile, make the gravy. Heat the oil, pancetta and shallot in a pan over a medium heat and cook, stirring occasionally, until the pancetta is golden and the shallots are tender. Stir in the flour and cook for 1min. Gradually add the port, whisking to avoid lumps, then whisk in the stock. Increase the heat to high and bubble vigorously for 5min, until thickened. Whisk in the redcurrant jelly and check the seasoning. Set aside.

7. Remove the Wellington from the oven and rest for 10min. Transfer to a serving plate or board and serve with the gravy, reheated if needed.

◆ GH TIP
If you can't find porcini paste, you can use Dijon mustard instead.

Feed a Crowd

Prawn and Crayfish Cocktail Salad

A sophisticated take on the classic prawn cocktail. Use cooked lobster instead of our mix of prawns and crayfish tails for an even more lavish option.

2 ripe avocados
Juice 1 lemon, plus wedges to serve
4 Little Gem lettuces, quartered lengthways
16 mixed radishes, thinly sliced
350g cooked and peeled tiger or king prawns
150g cooked and peeled crayfish tails

FOR THE SAUCE
100g mayonnaise
2 tbsp salad cream
2 tbsp tomato ketchup
1 tbsp brandy
Tabasco, to taste

1. Halve, stone and peel the avocados. Slice them lengthways into slim wedges, then put in a bowl with half the lemon juice and toss gently with your hands to coat. Set aside.

2. To make the sauce, whisk all the ingredients in a small bowl and season with salt, pepper and lemon juice to taste.

3. Divide the lettuce, avocado wedges, radishes, prawns and crayfish among 8 plates. Drizzle over the sauce and serve with lemon wedges.

◆ GET AHEAD
Make the sauce a day ahead, then cover and chill. Complete the recipe to serve.

Hands-on time: 15min
Serves 8

PER SERVING 231cals, 12g protein, 18g fat (2g saturates), 3g carbs (3g total sugars), 2g fibre

Truffled Mushroom Pâté with Parmesan Crisps

Earthy mushrooms and truffle oil pair beautifully, while tofu adds a silky lightness to the pâté.

75g butter
3 echalion shallots, finely chopped
30g dried porcini mushrooms
800g chestnut mushrooms, finely sliced
175g silken tofu, drained
175g cream cheese
2 tbsp Pedro Ximénez sherry or Marsala
1 tbsp soy sauce
½–1 tbsp truffle oil

FOR THE CRISPS
150g Parmesan or vegetarian Italian-style hard cheese, finely grated
2 tbsp plain flour

TO SERVE
100g chopped walnuts
Handful parsley, finely chopped
Crispbreads (optional)

◆ GET AHEAD
Prepare up to end of step 4 up to 2 days ahead. Chill the pâté and store the cooled crisps in an airtight container at room temperature. Complete the recipe to serve.

Hands-on time: 30min, plus chilling
Cooking time: about 30min
Serves 8

PER SERVING 361cals, 16g protein, 29g fat (13g saturates), 7g carbs (3g total sugars), 3g fibre

1. Heat a third of the butter in a large, deep frying pan over a medium heat and cook the shallots for 10min, stirring occasionally, until softened. Scrape on to a plate. Meanwhile, cover the dried porcini with just-boiled water from the kettle and leave to soak until needed.

2. Heat a little more butter in the empty shallot pan and fry the chestnut mushrooms until tender and any moisture has evaporated – do this in 2–3 batches, adding extra butter as needed.

3. Whizz the shallots and mushrooms with the tofu in a food processor until smooth. Drain the porcini and add to the processor with the remaining pâté ingredients. Pulse briefly and check the seasoning. Divide among 8 small bowls or ramekins, cover with cling film and chill for 2hr, until the pâté is firmer.

4. Meanwhile, make the Parmesan crisps. Preheat the oven to 200°C (180°C fan) mark 6 and line 2 baking trays with baking parchment. Mix the Parmesan, flour and some freshly ground black pepper in a bowl. Spoon tablespoons of the mixture, spaced well apart, on to the lined trays and gently pat into 4 x 7cm rectangles – you should have 16. Cook in the oven for 8–10min until melted and golden. Cool completely on the trays, then lift off with a palette knife.

5. To serve, mix the walnuts and parsley and sprinkle over the pâté. Serve with the Parmesan crisps and some crispbreads, if you like.

Potato, Pea and Paneer Samosas with Mango Yogurt Dip

These are great, fresh from the fryer, as a party nibble or starter. You could, of course, cook fresh potatoes for this, but you need such a small quantity that tinned ones are a great choice.

FOR THE SAMOSAS
2 tsp vegetable oil, plus extra to deep-fry
1 onion, finely chopped
2 garlic cloves, crushed
2 tsp cumin seeds
1 tsp garam masala
½ tsp ground turmeric
1–2 green finger chillies, deseeded and finely chopped (optional)
100g frozen petits pois
300g tin cooked new potatoes, drained and cut into 5mm pieces
100g paneer, coarsely grated
6 filo pastry sheets (220–230g), defrosted if frozen (see GH Tip)

FOR THE YOGURT DIP
Small handful mint leaves, finely chopped
200g natural yogurt
2 tbsp smooth mango chutney

YOU'LL ALSO NEED
Cooking thermometer

Hands-on time: 1hr
Cooking time: about 40min
Makes 24 samosas

PER SAMOSA (with 1 tsp dip) 119cals, 3g protein, 8g fat (1g saturates), 9g carbs (2g total sugars), 1g fibre

1. For the samosas, heat the oil in a medium-large frying pan over a low-medium heat and cook the onion for 10min, until softened and lightly golden. Stir in the garlic, spices and chilli (if using) and cook for 2min, until fragrant. Stir in the petits pois and cook for 2–3min to defrost.

2. Remove the pan from the heat and stir in the potatoes. Using a fork or potato masher, crush half the mixture roughly in the pan, then add the grated paneer and plenty of seasoning and mix together.

3. Lay one sheet of filo lengthways in front of you (keep the remaining sheets covered with a damp tea towel). Cut the sheet into 4 even strips, roughly 11 x 23cm (see GH Tip). Working with 1 strip at a time, brush the edges lightly with water, then put a scant 2 tbsp of the samosa filling at the bottom of the strip. Fold the pastry diagonally from the bottom left corner, wrapping it tightly over the filling to form a triangle and pinching the pastry edges together to seal. Continue to tightly fold the triangle diagonally up the pastry strip, maintaining the triangle shape. Tuck the end of the strip into the parcel and press gently to seal (use a little extra water to stick if needed). Repeat with the remaining pastry and filling to make 24 samosas, covering the finished samosas with cling film or a tea towel as you go.

4. Fill a large, wide, heavy-based pan with oil so it's 3cm deep. Heat the oil to 180°C, then fry the samosas in batches of 6–8 (depending on the size of your pan), for 5–7min each, turning occasionally with a slotted spoon, until deep golden brown. Lift out on to kitchen paper using the slotted spoon, then repeat to cook the remaining samosas, monitoring the oil temperature as you go.

5. Meanwhile, make the yogurt dip. Mix the mint, yogurt and a pinch of salt in a serving bowl. Lightly swirl through the mango chutney, thinning the chutney first with a little water if it's very thick. Serve the samosas with the mango yogurt for dipping.

◆ GET AHEAD
The samosas are best eaten freshly fried, but will keep covered and chilled for 2–3 days (the pastry will soften but they will still be delicious). Alternatively, prepare to the end of step 3 up to 2hr ahead. Transfer to a baking tray lined with baking parchment, wrap tray tightly with cling film and chill. Complete the recipe to serve.

◆ GH TIP
The size of filo pastry sheets varies with the brand, so you may need to use more sheets to get the same number of correctly sized pastry strips – however, the overall pack weight should be about the same.

Rainbow Summer Rolls

Summer rolls are traditionally served in Vietnam with a rich peanut sauce, but the fresh, fruity flavours of these rainbow rolls pair beautifully with the spicy, tangy, fish sauce-based dip called nuoc cham.

50g dried rice vermicelli noodles
½ mango, peeled
1 carrot, peeled
½ cucumber
½ red pepper, deseeded
75g purple cabbage, core removed
12 ready-made rice paper spring roll wrappers
12 large cooked, peeled king prawns, halved lengthways
   (see GH Tips)
24 large mint leaves
6 soft lettuce leaves, halved
2 tbsp roasted salted peanuts, chopped

FOR THE DIPPING SAUCE
1½ tbsp caster sugar
1 tbsp rice vinegar
1 tbsp fish sauce
1 tbsp lime juice
1 small garlic clove, crushed
1 red bird's eye chilli, finely sliced

◆ GET AHEAD
The rolls are best eaten fresh, but will keep for up to 12hr in an airtight container, separated by baking parchment.

◆ GH TIPS
A julienne peeler will make quick work of preparing the carrot and cucumber.

You could replace the prawns with cooked, shredded chicken, or leave them out altogether, if you like.

Hands-on time: 35min
Makes 12 rolls

PER ROLL (with 1 tsp dipping sauce) 80cals, 4g protein, <1g fat (<1g saturates), 15g carbs (4g total sugars), 1g fibre

1. Put the noodles into a heatproof bowl and cover with just-boiled water from the kettle. Leave to soften for 8–10min (or according to the packet instructions), then drain and rinse under cold water to cool. Drain again and set aside.

2. Meanwhile, cut the mango, carrot, cucumber (discarding the seedy core) and red pepper into fine matchsticks (see GH Tips). Finely shred the cabbage.

3. Fill a large baking tray with just-warm water. Dip a spring roll wrapper into the water for 10–15sec, until slightly softened (it will continue to soften as you work). Shake off the excess water and lay flat on a board. In a horizontal line across the centre of the wrapper, lay 2 prawn halves and 2 mint leaves, then put half a lettuce leaf on top. Arrange some noodles, mango, vegetables and peanuts in the centre of the wrapper, leaving a 3–4cm border at the top and bottom, and 5cm at the sides. Fold in the wrapper sides, then fold the base up over the filling. Continue to roll up tightly to seal, being careful not to tear the wrapper. Repeat to make 12 rolls.

4. To make the dipping sauce, mix the sugar with 2 tbsp just-boiled water in a small bowl until dissolved. Stir in the remaining ingredients and serve with the rolls.

Cheesy Hedgehog Bread

An utterly irresistible tear-and-share delight that can be cooked either on the barbecue or in the oven.

125g butter, softened
2 garlic cloves, crushed
3 rosemary sprigs, leaves picked and finely chopped
2 tsp runny honey
1 large loaf crusty white bread (about 500g)
200g Camembert, cut into 1cm pieces

1. If not barbecuing, preheat the oven to 190°C (170°C fan) mark 5. Mix the butter, garlic, rosemary, honey and some seasoning in a small bowl until combined. Set aside.

2. Cut the top of the loaf into a crosshatch pattern, spacing the cuts 2.5cm apart and cutting almost down to the base of the loaf. Sit the loaf on a large sheet of foil.

3. Using your fingers, spread the butter mixture into the cuts and all over the top of the bread. Now push the Camembert pieces into the cuts. Wrap the loaf loosely in foil.

4. If cooking in the oven, put on a baking tray and cook in the oven for 25–30min, until the cheese is melted, and the bread is golden and crisp. If barbecuing, cook over low heat for 15min, covering with a lid if your barbecue has one, until the cheese is melted, and the bread is golden and crisp. Serve immediately.

◆ GET AHEAD
Prepare to end of step 3 up to 1 day ahead and chill. Complete the recipe to serve.

Hands-on time: 10min
Cooking time: about 30min
Serves 8

PER SERVING 354cals, 12g protein, 20g fat
(12g saturates), 32g carbs (3g total sugars), 2g fibre

Boston Baked Beans

These are typically made with salt pork, though we've used lardons for ease, and cooked slowly to form a thick stew, rich in colour with a caramelised crust. The aim is to just keep the beans covered with liquid, so they form a thick and shiny, glaze-like sauce.

500g dried haricot beans, soaked overnight in cold water
2 onions
1 carrot, roughly chopped
2 bay leaves
2 garlic cloves, peeled
1 tbsp vegetable oil
200g smoked bacon lardons
125g black treacle
1½ tbsp Dijon mustard
1 tsp cider vinegar, if needed

1. Drain the soaked beans and put into a large pan. Cut 1 onion into quarters and add to the pan with the carrot, bay leaves and garlic cloves. Cover well with cold water. Bring to the boil over a high heat, then simmer for 45min (topping up with water as needed), until the beans are tender but not falling apart. Using a slotted spoon, lift out and discard the onion, carrot and garlic. Drain the beans, reserving the cooking liquid.

2. Meanwhile, finely chop the remaining onion. Heat the oil in a large casserole dish over a medium heat and fry the lardons for 5min, until golden and crisp. Add the onion and cook, stirring occasionally, for 5min until softening.

3. Preheat the oven to 180°C (160°C fan) mark 4. Add the drained beans and bay leaves to the casserole dish. Measure the treacle into a large jug and mix in the mustard and enough of the reserved cooking water to make it up to 700ml (reserve the remaining cooking water). Grind in plenty of black pepper and add a few large pinches of salt.

4. Stir the treacle mixture into the casserole dish and smooth the beans into an even layer. Add more reserved cooking water, if needed, to just cover the top of the beans. Bring to a simmer on the hob, then cook in the oven, uncovered, for 4hr. You'll need to stir every hour or so and top up with reserved cooking water if the top beans aren't submerged. The beans should be completely tender and a few of them bursting. There should also be a dark brown crust on the surface (avoid stirring in final 1hr of cooking to let this form). The beans take a long time as the treacle slows down the rate of cooking. If your cooking water runs out, top up with just-boiled water.

5. Remove from the oven and stir the beans well to allow a thick starchy sauce to form. Check the seasoning, adding a splash of cider vinegar for acidity, if needed. Serve.

◆ GET AHEAD
Make the recipe up to 3 days ahead. Cool, cover and chill. To serve, reheat gently on the hob, adding just-boiled water, if needed, to loosen. Check the seasoning.

Hands-on time: 15min, plus overnight soaking
Cooking time: about 5hr
Serves 8

PER SERVING 350cals, 18g protein, 8g fat (3g saturates), 43g carbs (15g total sugars), 15g fibre

Giant Sausage Roll Wreath

A fun way to serve a perennial favourite – we guarantee this festive wreath will be popular any time of year!

½ tbsp olive oil
2 red onions, finely sliced
2 tbsp balsamic vinegar
1 tbsp caster sugar
600g sausage meat
Handful fresh sage leaves, finely chopped
2 garlic cloves, crushed
2 x 320g packs ready-rolled puff pastry
2 tbsp English mustard
1 medium egg, beaten
¾ tsp poppy seeds

YOU'LL ALSO NEED
Star cutters in different sizes

1. Heat the oil in a medium pan over a medium heat. Add the onions and cook for 15min, stirring occasionally, until softened. Add the vinegar and sugar and stir until the sugar dissolves. Cook for 4min, or until the onions become sticky and caramelised. Empty into a large bowl and allow to cool.

2. Stir the sausage meat, sage, garlic and plenty of seasoning into the onion bowl.

3. Lay a long sheet (about 70cm) of baking parchment in front of you, with one of the long edges closest to you. Unroll a sheet of pastry on to the parchment, again with a long edge closest to you. Trim off a rough 25 x 8cm pastry rectangle from a short side, put on a plate, cover and chill.

4. Lay the second unrolled sheet of pastry next to the first, with a short edge overlapping by 2cm (press to stick together), to create one large rectangle about 25 x 62cm. Brush with the mustard.

5. Arrange the filling in a sausage shape along the length of the rectangle, just below the centre. Fold the top of the pastry down over the filling and press the long edges to seal, working out any air bubbles. Trim any excess pastry and press it along the seal with a fork. Carefully bend the sausage roll into a ring, pressing and sealing the 2 ends together. Transfer to a large baking sheet, still on the baking parchment, then trim the parchment to fit. Chill for 30min.

6. Preheat the oven to 200°C (180°C fan) mark 6. Using the cutters, stamp out star shapes from the reserved pastry rectangle. Brush the sausage ring with a little egg to glaze, then stick the stars on top and brush with more egg. Sprinkle over the poppy seeds and cook for 40–45min, until the pastry is a deep golden brown. Transfer to a large serving plate or board. Serve hot, or at room temperature, in slices.

Hands-on time: 30min, plus cooling and chilling
Cooking time: about 1hr 5min
Serves 8

PER SERVING 461cals, 17g protein, 30g fat (13g saturates), 29g carbs (6g total sugars), 3g fibre

◆ GET AHEAD
Prepare to the end of step 5 up to a day ahead.
Wrap tightly and chill. Complete the recipe
to serve.

Chicken, Pistachio and Ham Pie

This layered pie can be served hot or finished with a flavourful jelly and served cold, so is a great choice both for entertaining at home and a picnic.

FOR THE PASTRY
Vegetable oil, to grease
700g plain flour
115g lard, cut into cubes
115g butter, cut into cubes
1 egg, beaten

FOR THE FILLING
1 tbsp vegetable oil
1 onion, finely chopped
650g skinless chicken thigh fillets
60g pistachio kernels, roughly chopped
2 tbsp thyme leaves, roughly chopped
175g pulled ham
1 tbsp wholegrain mustard

FOR THE JELLY (OPTIONAL)
200ml chicken stock
1½ sheets platinum grade leaf gelatine

◆ GET AHEAD
Prepare to end of step 9 and freeze the cooked pie whole, or in slices, well-wrapped, for up to 1 month. To serve, defrost in the fridge, then serve chilled or allow to come to room temperature.

Hands-on time: 45min, plus cooling and (overnight) chilling
Cooking time: about 1hr 30min
Serves 12

PER SERVING 454cals, 22g protein, 22g fat (9g saturates), 41g carbs (1g total sugars), 2g fibre

1. Grease a 20.5cm round springform tin and set on a large baking tray. To make the pastry, put the flour and 1 tsp fine salt into a food processor. Next, melt the lard, butter and 250ml water in a small pan over low heat. Turn up the heat and bring to the boil.

2. With the motor running on the food processor, add the hot lard mixture to the dry ingredients and whizz until the pastry nearly comes together. Tip on to a work surface and knead until smooth.

3. Break off two-thirds of the pastry (wrap the remaining third). Roll out and use to line the greased tin, pressing well into the edges and leaving some pastry hanging over the sides. (Don't worry if it breaks – just work it back into place, as this won't make the pastry tough.) Chill for 10min.

4. Preheat the oven to 180°C (160°C fan) mark 4. To make the filling, heat the oil in a small frying pan over a low heat and cook the onion for 5min, until softened. Tip into a large bowl and leave to cool for a few minutes.

5. Meanwhile, pulse the chicken in a food processor until it resembles mince. Empty into the onion bowl along with the pistachios, thyme, 1 tsp fine salt and ½ tsp freshly ground black pepper. In a separate bowl, mix together the ham and mustard.

6. Press half the chicken mixture into the pastry-lined tin. Top with the ham in an even layer, then press on the remaining chicken mixture.

7. Roll out the remaining pastry until large enough to cover the filling. Lift on to the tin and press the edges to seal. Trim the excess pastry, then crimp the edges, making sure the crimping sits inside the tin or the cooked pie will be hard to remove. Brush the top of the pastry with beaten egg (set the rest of the egg aside). Poke a hole in the centre of the lid with the handle of a wooden spoon.

8. Cook for 40min, then carefully unclip and remove the outside ring of the tin (leaving the pie on its base on the baking tray). Brush all over with the rest of the egg and return to the oven for 35–40min to set the sides and cook through. Take out of oven, set aside to cool slightly for 10min, then serve (if serving hot).

9. To serve the pie cold with jelly, pour the stock for the jelly into a pan and add the gelatine. Leave to soak (off the heat) for 5min, then heat gently, until the gelatine dissolves. Empty into a jug. Using a funnel or with a steady hand, pour a little stock into the hole. Keep adding stock until the pie will take no more (you may not need it all). Leave to cool for 30min, then chill overnight.

10. Allow to come up to room temperature before serving in slices (or serve chilled, if you prefer).

Spiced Spatchcock Chicken with New Potatoes and Tomatoes

Roasting the chicken over vegetables gives them extra flavour as they mingle with the roasting juices. The recipe makes more spice rub than you'll need – store the extra in a sealed jar at room temperature for up to a month and use on barbecued meats and veg.

600g miniature new potatoes, halved if large
1½ tbsp olive oil
1 large whole chicken (about 1.8kg)
40g butter, melted
300g cherry tomatoes on the vine
1 large lemon, cut into 6 wedges

FOR THE SPICE RUB
2 tbsp hot or sweet smoked paprika
1½ tbsp light brown soft sugar
1 tsp English mustard powder
1 tsp ground cumin
2 tsp dried thyme
1 tsp garlic granules

◆ GET AHEAD
Prepare to the end of step 3 up to a day ahead. Sit the chicken on top of the potatoes, cover the roasting tin with foil and chill. To serve, allow to come to room temperature for 30min. Position the chicken on top of the rack and complete the recipe to serve.

Hands-on time 15min, plus resting. Cooking time about 50min
Serves 6

PER SERVING 567cals, 40g protein, 36g fat (12g saturates), 21g carbs (7g total sugars), 3g fibre

1. Preheat the oven to 200°C (180°C fan) mark 6. In a small bowl, mix all the ingredients for the spice rub with 1½ tsp fine salt. Put the potatoes in a medium-large roasting tin and toss through 1 tbsp of the oil and 2 tsp of the spice rub. Spread into a single layer.

2. Put the chicken breast-side down on a board. Using sturdy kitchen scissors, cut along each side of the backbone and discard. Turn the chicken over and press down hard on the breast to flatten it (you should hear it crack). Pat dry with kitchen paper.

3. Stir half the remaining spice rub into the melted butter and brush it all over the chicken. Arrange breast-side up on a sturdy metal cooling rack (that fits above the potato roasting tin) and position it on top of the tin.

4. Roast for 35min. Remove the chicken and potatoes from the oven, add the tomatoes and lemon wedges to the tin and drizzle over the remaining ½ tbsp oil. Position the chicken above the tin again and return to the oven for 10–15min, or until the chicken is cooked through and the potatoes are tender.

5. Remove from the oven and rest in a warm place for 10min. Transfer the chicken to a board and the potatoes, tomatoes and lemon wedges to a serving dish. Serve with chilli and lime squash and apple 'slaw (see right), if you like.

Chilli and Lime Buttered Squash Wedges

If you wash butternut squash, there's no need to peel it before roasting – the skin softens and caramelises during cooking.

1 medium butternut squash (about 1kg), trimmed, halved and deseeded
60g butter, softened
1 red chilli, deseeded and finely chopped
Small handful coriander leaves, finely chopped
Finely grated zest 1 lime
50g feta, crumbled (optional)

1. Preheat the oven to 200°C (180°C fan) mark 6. Cut each butternut half into 3 equal pieces lengthways and put into a roasting tin. In a small bowl, mash together the butter, chilli, coriander, lime zest and plenty of seasoning. Rub 1 tbsp of the butter mixture over the wedges (using your fingers is easiest) and set the rest of the butter aside at room temperature. Roast the squash for 30–40min, until tender.

2. Transfer to a serving dish, dot over the remaining butter and turn the wedges gently in it so it melts. Sprinkle over the feta (if using) and serve.

◆ GET AHEAD
Prepare to end of step 1 up to an hour ahead, then cool, cover and keep at room temperature. Dot over the remaining butter and return to a hot oven to melt, then complete the recipe.

Hands-on time: 10min
Cooking time: about 40min
Serves 6

PER SERVING 151cals, 3g protein, 10g fat (6g saturates), 11g carbs (6g total sugars), 3g fibre

Apple 'Slaw with Buttermilk Dressing

A fresh, fruity and crunchy side dish, this 'slaw is great as an accompaniment to any summer meal.

1 each green and red apple (unpeeled)
Juice 1 lemon
1 pointed sweetheart/hispi green cabbage (about 600g), cored and finely shredded
½ red onion, finely sliced
150ml buttermilk
3 tbsp mayonnaise
2 tsp Dijon mustard
1 tbsp cider vinegar
1 garlic clove, crushed

1. Cut the apples into matchsticks, discarding the cores. Working quickly to stop them discolouring, put the pieces into a large serving bowl with the lemon juice and toss to coat. Add the cabbage and onion.

2. In a small bowl or jug, whisk the remaining ingredients with plenty of seasoning. Add the dressing to the serving bowl and toss gently to mix and coat (using your hands is easiest). Serve.

◆ GET AHEAD
Make up to 4hr ahead, then cover and chill. To serve, allow to come to room temperature for 30min.

Hands-on time: 20min
Serves 6

PER SERVING 121cals, 4g protein, 6g fat (1g saturates), 10g carbs (10g total sugars), 5g fibre

Fennel and Almond Crusted Salmon with Beetroot and Horseradish Dip

A herby crumb transforms a simple salmon into a dinner party-worthy main course. The punchy beetroot dip balances the rich, succulent fish.

1kg side of fresh salmon, skin on, trimmed and with small
  bones removed
1 tbsp Dijon mustard
75g panko breadcrumbs
50g blanched almonds, whizzed in a food processor
  until coarse
25g Parmesan, finely grated
1 tbsp fennel seeds, lightly crushed
Finely grated zest 1 lemon
2 tbsp each fresh tarragon and parsley, finely chopped
4 tbsp olive oil, plus extra to grease

FOR THE BEETROOT AND HORSERADISH DIP
300g cooked beetroot, drained
50g blanched almonds, toasted
1 tbsp hot horseradish sauce
3 tbsp soured cream
1 tbsp fresh tarragon, chopped
Juice ½ lemon

◆ GET AHEAD
Make the crumb topping up to a few hours ahead.
Cover and set aside. Complete the recipe to serve.
Make the beetroot dip up to 1 day ahead, then
cover and chill. Remove from the fridge 30min
before serving.

1. Preheat the oven to 190°C (170°C fan) mark 5. Put the salmon, skin-side down, in a large roasting tin lined with baking parchment and lightly oiled. Brush with the mustard to coat.

2. In a bowl, mix together the breadcrumbs, almonds, Parmesan, fennel seeds, lemon zest, chopped herbs, olive oil and some seasoning. Spread evenly over the salmon, pressing gently so that it sticks.

3. Roast in the oven for 20–30min until just cooked through – the time will vary depending on the thickness of your fillet, so check regularly from 20min.

4. Meanwhile, make the dip: in a food processor, whizz the beetroot with the almonds and horseradish. Add the soured cream, tarragon and lemon juice, whizz again briefly, then season to taste. Serve the salmon with the dip, soured cream potato salad and dill pickled cucumber (see right), if you like.

Hands-on time: 15min
Cooking time: 30min
Serves 8

PER SERVING (with dip) 439cals, 35g protein, 28g fat (5g saturates), 12g carbs (5g total sugars), 3g fibre

Soured Cream Potato Salad

A dressing of vinegar and soured cream rather than mayonnaise makes for a lighter, fresher potato salad. Use Jersey Royals, if you can find them.

1.2kg baby new potatoes, halved if large
2 tbsp white wine vinegar
1 tbsp Dijon mustard
150ml soured cream
Small bunch dill, chopped

1. Cook the potatoes in a large pan of boiling salted water for 15–20min until completely tender. Drain well, then tip on to a baking tray and toss with the vinegar. Spread out in a single layer and leave to cool to room temperature.

2. In a large bowl, mix the mustard with the soured cream, most of the dill and some seasoning. Toss in the potatoes, then transfer to a serving bowl. Sprinkle with the remaining dill and serve straight away.

◆ GET AHEAD
Make up to 1 day ahead, reserving the dill to garnish. Cover and chill. Take out of the fridge 30min before serving, transfer to a serving bowl and scatter with the reserved dill.

Hands-on time: 10min
Cooking time: about 20min
Serves 6

PER SERVING 202cals, 5g protein, 5g fat (3g saturates), 32g carbs (4g total sugars), 4g fibre

Dill Pickled Cucumber with Apple and Avocado

Cucumber pickles lightly in just half an hour. Combined with sweet apple and creamy avocado, it makes for a fresh, light accompaniment to rich salmon.

---

3 tbsp white wine vinegar
1 tbsp caster sugar
Small bunch dill, finely chopped
2 cucumbers
3 tbsp olive oil
3 avocados, halved, de-stoned and sliced
1 Pink Lady apple, sliced into matchsticks

1. In a large bowl, mix together the vinegar, sugar, most of the dill and a large pinch of salt. Peel the cucumbers into ribbons using a Y-shaped peeler (discard the seedy core) and add to the bowl. Mix gently and set aside for 30min to pickle lightly. Drain the liquid into another bowl, then add 3 tbsp back in with the olive oil. Season.

2. Add the avocados and most of the apple to the large bowl and toss together. Check the seasoning. Spoon on to a serving plate, scatter over the remaining dill and apple, and serve immediately to keep the colour and crunch.

Hands-on time: 15min, plus pickling
Serves 6

PER SERVING 235cals, 2g protein, 21g fat (4g saturates), 8g carbs (7g total sugars), 4g fibre

Vanilla Panna Cotta and Champagne Jelly

A creamy panna cotta base combines with pear, pomegranate seeds and satsuma segments in a sweetened cranberry Champagne jelly for a dessert that is as stunning as it is delicious.

14 sheets platinum-grade leaf gelatine
150ml elderflower cordial
100ml cranberry juice
2 Comice pears, peeled
2 tbsp lemon juice
2 satsumas
100g pomegranate seeds, plus extra to decorate
350ml Champagne (see GH Tip)
475ml double cream
75ml semi-skimmed milk
3 tbsp icing sugar, plus extra to dust
1½ tsp vanilla extract

TO DECORATE (OPTIONAL)
Few cranberries
Few rosemary sprigs
Orange zest, pared

1. Put 9 of the gelatine leaves in a bowl, cover with cold water and leave to soak for 5min, until softened.

2. In a medium pan, heat the elderflower cordial and cranberry juice until just steaming. Lift the gelatine out of the water (squeeze out the excess) and stir into the hot liquid to dissolve. Pour into a large jug and set aside to cool slightly.

Hands-on time: 25min, plus soaking and 8hr chilling
Cooking time: about 5min
Serves 10

PER SERVING 343cals, 4g protein, 26g fat (16g saturates), 17g carbs (17g total sugars), 1g fibre

3. Meanwhile, using a melon baller or a metal teaspoon measure, scoop as many balls as you can from each pear (avoiding the core). Working quickly, put the balls into a bowl and coat in the lemon juice.

4. Separate the satsuma segments, removing the pith from each, then arrange the segments in the base of a 1.75 litre jelly mould or cake tin. Add the pomegranate seeds, then drain the pear balls and add to the mould/tin. Slowly stir the Champagne into the elderflower mixture, then gently pour over the fruit. Chill for 4hr, or until set.

5. Soak the remaining 5 gelatine leaves as before. In a medium pan, heat the cream, milk, icing sugar and vanilla extract until just steaming. Remove from the heat. Lift the gelatine out of the water (squeeze out the excess) and stir into the hot liquid to dissolve.

6. Leave to cool completely, then pour over the set Champagne jelly and chill for 4hr, or until set.

7. To serve, dip the outside of jelly mould/tin in just-boiled water for a few seconds, dry, then invert the jelly on to a serving plate or stand. Give the mould/tin a single firm shake. If the jelly doesn't come out first time, dip, dry and try again. Decorate with pomegranate seeds, cranberries, rosemary and orange zest and dust with a little icing sugar (it will cling to the rosemary), if you like. Serve.

◆ GET AHEAD
Prepare to end of step 6 up to 3 days ahead.
Cover and chill. Complete the recipe to serve.

◆ GH TIP
You can use Prosecco or Cava here, if you prefer.

Tiramisu

It's perhaps the most iconic Italian dessert, yet Tiramisu actually only dates back to the 1960s, when it was said to have been first served in a restaurant in Treviso, northern Italy. It's simple to make but needs at least 4hr to sit, so is an ideal get-ahead option.

3 medium eggs, separated
200ml double cream
80g caster sugar
250g mascarpone
200ml espresso or strong black coffee, cooled
3 tbsp sweet marsala
3 tbsp dark rum
24 (or a 200g pack) savoiardi biscuits
Cocoa powder, to dust

◆ GET AHEAD
Complete the recipe up to 2 days ahead.

◆ GH TIP
Sweet marsala is a must in tiramisu, but you can swap the dark rum for brandy, or leave it out altogether for a less alcoholic version.

1. Put the egg whites in one bowl, the yolks in another, and the double cream in a third. Add the sugar to the yolks and, using a handheld electric whisk, beat until pale and thick, about 3–4min.

2. Add half the mascarpone to the egg yolk mixture and beat until combined, then beat in the remaining mascarpone. Next, whisk the double cream until it just holds its shape (no need to clean the beaters first).

3. Scrape the cream into the mascarpone bowl and beat to combine. Clean the beaters, then whisk the egg whites until they hold stiff peaks. Fold the whites into the mascarpone mixture, trying to keep in as much air as possible

4. Mix the espresso/coffee, marsala and rum in a shallow bowl. Working 2 biscuits at a time, dip half the biscuits into the espresso mixture for 1–2sec per side – you want them to soak up liquid but not get too soft. Once soaked, arrange the biscuits in the base of a 1.5 litre serving dish.

5. Spoon half the mascarpone mixture into the dish and spread in an even layer. Repeat the layering once more with the remaining biscuits, boozy coffee and mascarpone mixture. Dust generously with cocoa powder and chill for at least 4hr before serving.

Hands-on time: 30min, plus chilling
Serves 6

PER SERVING 577cals, 9g protein, 39g fat (25g saturates), 42g carbs (30g total sugars), 0g fibre

Orange and Chai-spiced Trifle

Chai tea bags have a lovely blend of black tea and spices ready to infuse, but you could use whole spices like cinnamon, ginger and cardamom and strain the infused milk through a fine sieve. For an alcohol-free version, use orange juice instead of Cointreau.

1 lemon swiss roll (about 230g)
50ml Cointreau
50g marmalade

FOR THE CUSTARD
1 vanilla pod
600ml whole milk
1 chai tea bag
5 medium egg yolks
75g caster sugar
2 tbsp cornflour

FOR THE CANDIED ORANGE PEEL
150g caster sugar
Pared zest 1 large orange, cut into thin strips

TO SERVE
400ml double cream
1 tbsp icing sugar
2 tbsp Cointreau
Finely grated zest 1 orange

1. Cut the swiss roll into 1½cm-thick slices and arrange in the base and slightly up the sides of a 1.5–2 litre trifle dish. Mix the Cointreau and marmalade and spoon it over the sponge base. Chill while you make the custard.

Hands-on time: 40min, plus infusing, cooling and chilling
Cooking time: about 45min
Serves 8

PER SERVING 617cals, 6g protein, 35g fat (21g saturates), 63g carbs (54g total sugars), 1g fibre

2. Halve the vanilla pod lengthways and scrape out the seeds. Add the seeds and pod to a medium pan with the milk and tea bag and heat until steaming. Set aside to infuse for 10min. Discard the vanilla pod. Lift out the teabag, squeeze over the pan to extract the flavour and discard.

3. In a heatproof bowl, mix the egg yolks, caster sugar and cornflour until combined. Gradually stir in the warm milk mixture. Return the mixture to the pan and cook over medium heat, stirring constantly, until thickened. Pour back into the empty bowl, lay baking parchment or cling film directly on the surface of the custard and leave to cool completely.

4. Meanwhile, make the candied orange peel. Heat the sugar with 250ml water in a wide pan over a low heat, stirring until sugar dissolves. Turn up the heat to medium-high, bring to the boil, then add the peel. Bubble for 10min. Turn down the heat and simmer gently for 15–20min until the peel is tender and translucent (being careful that the sugar doesn't colour and caramelise). Using a slotted spoon, lift the peel on to a baking sheet lined with baking parchment. Cool.

5. Spoon the cooled custard into the trifle dish and smooth to level. Chill for 30min–1hr, until the custard has set a bit more.

6. When ready to serve, whisk the cream, icing sugar and Cointreau to soft peaks. Fold through the grated orange zest. Spoon on to the custard layer, then sprinkle with candied orange zest. Serve.

Al Fresco

Picnic Pizza Bread

A medley of Mediterranean flavours will make this speedy filled ciabatta loaf a hit with the whole family. Just add sunshine!

1 large ciabatta loaf
4 tbsp olive tapenade
150g pot mild creamy goat's cheese
150g Peppadew peppers
285g jar artichoke antipasto
2 tbsp olive oil
Large handful salad leaves, such as rocket, spinach or watercress, plus extra to serve

1. Split open the bread horizontally and scoop out a little of the dough from both sides and discard.

2. Spread both the cut sides of the ciabatta with the tapenade. Spread the goat's cheese on just one side, then top with a layer of Peppadew peppers and a layer of artichokes, and drizzle with the olive oil.

3. Add the salad leaves and cover with the other side of bread. Press down well, wrap tightly in clingfilm and leave for 10min. Serve thickly sliced with extra salad leaves on the side.

Hands-on time: 10min, plus standing
Serves 4

PER SERVING 480cals, 17g protein, 27g fat (9g saturates), 37g carbs (4g total sugars), 6g fibre

Tomato Sausage Rolls

Sausage rolls are always a favourite. We've given ours a sophisticated twist with basil and sweet chutney.

___

320g ready-rolled puff pastry
4 tbsp tomato chutney
450g sausage meat
Small handful fresh basil, chopped
1 medium egg, beaten
Sesame seeds, to sprinkle

1. Unroll the puff pastry sheet and cut into 2 long strips. Spread 2 tbsp tomato chutney on to each (leaving a 2.5cm border), then divide the sausage meat and some basil between both. Brush the long borders with the beaten egg, then roll, seal and cut each long roll into 6 pieces.

2. Preheat the oven to 200°C (180°C fan) mark 6. Brush the rolls with egg and sprinkle with sesame seeds, then arrange on a lined baking sheet. Cook for 20–25min until golden.

Hands-on time: 10min
Cooking time: about 25min
Makes 12 rolls

PER ROLL 244cals, 8g protein, 15g fat (6g saturates), 14g carbs (2g total sugars), 1g fibre

Roasted Pepper and Chorizo Picnic Frittatas

Making a frittata in a muffin tin is a clever way to create individual, portable portions – perfect for a picnic or light lunch.

___

100g sliced roasted peppers
300g cooked, sliced potatoes
100g diced and fried chorizo
6 large eggs
150ml crème fraîche
50g Manchego, grated
1 heaped tbsp chopped parsley

1. Preheat the oven to 180°C (160°C fan) mark 4. Line a 12-hole muffin tin with squares of baking parchment. Divide the roasted peppers, cooked potatoes and chorizo among the cases.

2. Whisk the eggs with the crème fraîche and some seasoning. Stir in the cheese and parsley, then divide among the cases.

3. Bake for 20min, until golden. Allow to cool, then serve, or place in an airtight container for easy transportation.

◆ GET AHEAD
Make up to a day ahead, leave to cool, then cover and chill. Serve chilled or at room temperature.

Hands-on time: 10min, plus chilling
Cooking time: 20min
Makes 12 mini frittatas

PER MINI FRITTATA 165cals, 8g protein, 12g fat (6g saturates), 5g carbs (1g total sugars), 1g fibre

Stuffed Picnic Loaf

Versatile and easy to pack while still looking impressive, this loaf will be the centrepiece of the picnic blanket.

Round crusty loaf
1 tbsp extra virgin olive oil
Antipasti of your choice – we used salami and jarred roasted peppers
Sliced or soft cheese – we used drained mozzarella
Salad leaves

1. Slice off the top third of the crusty loaf and hollow out the inside to leave a 3cm shell.

2. Brush the inside of the loaf with the oil, then fill with layers of antipasti, cheese and salad. Put the 'lid' back on, wrap well in cling film and chill overnight. Unwrap and slice to serve.

Hands-on time: 10min, plus overnight chilling
Serves 6

PER SERVING 344cals, 15g protein, 16g fat (6g saturates), 33g carbs (3g total sugars), 3g fibre

Creamy Garlic Prawn Toasts

These lusciously rich and cheesy treats make a fantastic canapé, snack or lunch. You could also use cooked crayfish or even lobster.

100g soured cream
50g mayonnaise
2 garlic cloves, crushed
50g Cheddar cheese, coarsely grated
2 tbsp chopped chives
200g cooked and peeled king prawns, roughly chopped
12 baguette slices
½ tsp paprika or cayenne pepper

1. Preheat the oven to 200°C (180°C fan) mark 6. In a bowl, mix the soured cream, mayonnaise, garlic, half the Cheddar and most of the chives. Season well, then stir in the prawns to coat.

2. Arrange the baguette slices on a baking tray. Spoon the prawn mixture on top of each, then sprinkle over the remaining cheese and the paprika or cayenne pepper.

3. Cook in the oven for 8–10min, or until the toasts turn golden and the cheese is bubbling. Scatter over the remaining chives and serve.

Hands-on time: 10min
Cooking time: about 10min
Makes 12 toasts

PER SERVING 144cals, 7g protein, 7g fat (2g saturates), 14g carbs (1g total sugars), 1g fibre

Chilli and Coriander Grissini with Spiced Lentil Houmous

Adjust the amount of chilli to suit your spice preference. You could swap the coriander for parsley or basil, if you like.

FOR THE GRISSINI
200g strong white bread flour, plus extra to dust
7g sachet fast-action dried yeast
1 tbsp olive oil
1 tbsp runny honey
1 tsp dried chilli flakes
Small handful coriander, roughly chopped

FOR THE HOUMOUS
150g split red lentils, rinsed
400ml vegetable stock
400g tin chickpeas, drained and rinsed
1 garlic clove, crushed
3 tbsp tahini
Juice 1 lemon
½ tsp ground cinnamon
1 tsp garam masala
2 tsp mild chilli powder, plus extra to sprinkle
2 tbsp olive oil, plus extra to drizzle

◆ GET AHEAD
Make the grissini up to 1 day ahead. Cool, then store in an airtight container. Make houmous up to 3 days ahead, then cover and chill. To serve, allow the houmous to come up to room temperature and garnish.

Hands-on time: 30min, plus rising and cooling
Cooking time: about 30min
Serves 8

PER SERVING 248cals, 10g protein, 6g fat (1g saturates), 36g carbs (3g total sugars), 4g fibre

1. First make the grissini. In the bowl of a freestanding mixer fitted with a dough hook, or in a large bowl, combine the flour, yeast, oil, honey, chilli flakes, coriander, ½ tsp fine salt and 125ml tepid water. Mix to make a soft but not sticky dough – add a little extra water if the mixture looks dry.

2. If making by hand, tip the dough on to a lightly floured work surface and knead for 8–10min, until smooth and elastic. If using a freestanding mixer, knead for 5min. Cover the bowl and set aside in a warm place to rise for 1hr, or until doubled in size.

3. Preheat the oven to 190°C (170°C fan) mark 5 and line 2 large baking sheets with baking parchment. Scrape the dough on to a lightly floured work surface and divide into 16 even pieces. Using your hands, roll each piece into a thin sausage, about 25cm long. Place on the prepared baking sheets, spacing apart, and bake for 15–20min, or until golden. Leave to cool on the sheets.

4. Meanwhile, make the houmous. Put the lentils and stock in a pan over medium-high heat, bring to the boil, then simmer for 20min, until the lentils are mushy and the liquid has been absorbed. Set aside to cool.

5. Pulse the lentils, chickpeas, garlic, tahini, lemon juice and spices in a food processor until fairly smooth. With the motor running, gradually pour in the oil, whizzing until smooth. Thin with a little just-boiled water, if you like. Check the seasoning (it can take a fair amount), then spoon into a serving bowl.

6. To serve, sprinkle the houmous with a little chilli powder and drizzle with oil. Serve with the grissini for dipping.

◆ GH TIP
For a vegan version, swap the honey for caster sugar and check your stock.

Pissaladière Pinwheels

Inspired by a French classic, these savoury bites shaped like windmills are an eye-catching nibble and fun for picnics.

1 tbsp olive oil
1 onion, finely sliced
100g cherry tomatoes, halved
¼ tsp dried thyme
320g ready-rolled puff pastry
Plain flour, to dust
8 anchovy fillets in oil, drained
1 medium egg, beaten
15g Gruyère cheese, finely grated
4 pitted black olives, halved

◆ GET AHEAD
Bake up to 3 days ahead, then cool and chill in an airtight container. To serve, reheat the windmills on a baking sheet in an oven preheated to 200°C (180°C fan) mark 6 for 10min, or allow to come to room temperature.

◆ GH TIP
For a fun way to serve these appetisers, push a paper straw into the cooked pastries to resemble a toy windmill.

Hands-on time: 30min, plus cooling and chilling
Cooking time: about 45min
Makes 8 pinwheels

PER PINWHEEL 202cals, 5g protein, 13g fat (8g saturates), 17g carbs (2g total sugars), 1g fibre

1. Heat the oil in a medium pan (that has a lid) over a low heat. Add the onion and a splash of water, then cover and cook for 15min, until softened and golden. Stir in the cherry tomatoes and thyme. Turn up the heat to medium and cook, uncovered, for 6–8min, until the tomatoes have broken down. Set aside to cool completely.

2. Unroll the pastry sheet on to a lightly floured work surface. Use a rolling pin to roll the pastry longer, so the long edge measures 41cm. Using a sharp knife, trim the pastry into a 20.5 x 41cm rectangle, then cut into 8 equal squares. Arrange the squares on a baking tray, spacing them apart, and chill for 15min.

3. Preheat the oven to 200°C (180°C fan) mark 6. On each square, make a 5cm-long diagonal cut from each corner toward the centre. Spoon an eighth of the cooled onion mixture into the centre of each square. Working one square at a time, bring a left-hand side of a sliced corner into the centre, lightly press the point down, then repeat with the left-hand side of the other sliced corners to create a 'windmill' effect. Repeat with the remaining squares.

4. Halve each anchovy fillet lengthways, then cut each strip in half to make shorter lengths. Lay an anchovy strip along every straight edge of the pastry windmills. Brush all the visible bare pastry with the beaten egg, then sprinkle over the grated cheese and press half an olive into the centre of each windmill.

5. Cook in the oven for 15–20min, until golden and risen. Serve warm or at room temperature.

Bruschetta Bar

This DIY starter is just the ticket when friends come round. There's enough to serve 6 and guests can help themselves, allowing you to join the party.

Toasted Ciabatta Slices

Cut a loaf of ciabatta into 18 x 2.5cm slices. Brush both sides of each slice with olive oil and toast on a hot griddle pan for 2min per side, until charred and crisp.

Hands-on time: 45min
Cooking time: 35–40min
Makes 18 toasts to serve 6

◆ GET AHEAD
Griddle the toasts up to 2hr ahead.

Crab, Fennel and Chilli Toasts

200g white crabmeat
Finely grated zest 1 lemon
1 tbsp olive oil
1 small fennel bulb, finely diced (keep the fronds to garnish)
½–1 red chilli, deseeded and finely chopped
Toasted ciabatta slices

1. Mix together the crabmeat, lemon zest, olive oil, fennel bulb, chopped chilli and some seasoning. Cover and chill until needed. Serve with the toasted ciabatta slices.

PER TOAST 109cals, 9g protein, 4g fat (1g saturates), 8g carbs (1g total sugars), 1g fibre

Goat's Cheese, Parma Ham and Basil Drizzle Toasts

6 Parma ham slices
Large handful basil leaves
4 tbsp olive oil
Squeeze lemon juice
75g soft goat's cheese
Toasted ciabatta slices

1. Fry the Parma ham in a hot frying pan for 1–2min per side until crispy and golden. Set aside on kitchen paper.

2. Whizz the basil in a food processor with the olive oil and lemon juice until it's as smooth as you can get it.

3. Serve the goat's cheese, crispy Parma ham and basil oil with the toasted ciabatta slices.

◆ GET AHEAD
Cook the Parma ham up to 2hr ahead.
Whizz the basil oil up to 1hr ahead.
Complete the recipe to serve.

PER TOAST 172cals, 7g protein, 12g fat (4g saturates), 8g carbs (1g total sugars), 1g fibre

Roasted Carrot Houmous Toasts

300g carrots
1 tbsp olive oil
400g tin chickpeas (drained and rinsed)
3 tbsp tahini
3 tbsp lemon juice
3 tbsp olive oil, plus extra to serve
2 garlic cloves, crushed
1½ tsp ground cumin
Handful pumpkin seeds
Toasted ciabatta slices

1. Preheat the oven to 200°C (180°C fan) mark 6. Thinly slice the carrots and toss on a baking tray with the olive oil and some seasoning. Roast for 35-40min, turning halfway through, until golden.

2. Empty the roast carrots into a food processor and add the chickpeas, tahini, lemon juice, olive oil, crushed garlic, cumin and a splash of water. Whizz until smooth. Check the seasoning, adding water to thin or lemon juice to sharpen. Transfer to a bowl, drizzle with extra olive oil and sprinkle over some pumpkin seeds. Serve with the toasted ciabatta slices.

◆ GET AHEAD
Make the houmous up to 3 days ahead. Cover and chill. Remove from the fridge 1hr before serving – you may want to stir through some more oil to loosen. Complete the recipe.

PER TOAST 232cals, 7g protein, 14g fat (2g saturates), 18g carbs (4g total sugars), 6g fibre

Asparagus with Maple-balsamic Dressing

A scattering of finely sliced red onion with a maple syrup and balsamic dressing really makes this side dish sing.

1kg asparagus spears, woody ends trimmed
125ml extra virgin olive oil, plus 1 tbsp to drizzle
1 tsp sesame seeds
4 tbsp balsamic vinegar
2½ tbsp maple syrup
2 tsp Dijon mustard
¼ red onion, thinly sliced

1. Preheat the oven to 220°C (200°C fan) mark 7. Put the asparagus in a baking tray, drizzle over 1 tbsp olive oil, season and toss to coat. Roast for 10–12min, until tender, adding the sesame seeds for the final 2 min.

2. Meanwhile, make the dressing. Whisk the vinegar, maple syrup, mustard and some seasoning in a bowl. Gradually whisk in the olive oil, until combined.

3. Tip the asparagus into a serving dish and scatter over the onion. Drizzle over a little of the dressing and serve with the rest of the dressing in a small bowl on the side.

◆ GET AHEAD
Make the dressing up to 2 days ahead; cover and chill. To serve, allow to come to room temperature, whisk to recombine, then complete the recipe.

Hands-on time: 15min
Cooking time: about 12min
Serves 8

PER SERVING 186cals, 4g protein, 14g fat (2g saturates), 9g carbs (9g total sugars), 3g fibre

Crunchy Green Salad with Mint Dressing

This fabulous salad is a great mixture of textures and flavours with a refreshing minty dressing.

300g mange tout
300g sugar snap peas
200g radishes, trimmed and finely sliced
100g pea shoots or watercress

FOR THE DRESSING
Juice 1½ lemons
25g bunch mint, leaves picked and finely sliced
2 tbsp runny honey
1 tbsp wholegrain mustard
2 garlic cloves, crushed
2 tbsp olive oil

1. For the dressing, whisk all the ingredients in a small bowl with some seasoning. Set aside.

2. Bring a large pan of water to the boil and blanch the mange tout and sugar snap peas, in batches if needed, for 1–2min. Drain, then rinse under cold running water until completely cool. Drain again and thoroughly pat dry with kitchen paper

3. In a large serving bowl, toss the mange tout and sugar snaps with the radishes and pea shoots or watercress. Just before serving, drizzle over the dressing and toss gently to combine.

Hands-on time: 15min, plus cooling
Cooking time: about 5min
Serves 8

PER SERVING 75cals, 4g protein, 3g fat (<1g saturates), 7g carbs (6g total sugars), 3g fibre

Potato and Sweetcorn Sunshine Salad

Potato salad gets a modern makeover with a zingy dressing and crunchy chicory.

1.2kg new potatoes
2 tbsp sunflower seeds
250g chicory, thickly sliced widthways
198g tin sweetcorn, drained
3 spring onions, finely sliced

FOR THE DRESSING
Juice 1 lime
6 tbsp mayonnaise
2 tbsp crème fraîche
1 tbsp Dijon mustard
¼ tsp dried mixed herbs

1. Put the potatoes into a pan of salted water. Bring to the boil, then reduce the heat and simmer for 13–15min, until just tender. Drain and leave to cool.

2. Meanwhile, toast the sunflower seeds in a dry frying pan over a medium heat for 1–2min, shaking the pan frequently. Allow to cool.

3. For the dressing, whisk all the ingredients in a large bowl with some seasoning.

4. Roughly chop the cooled potatoes and add to the dressing bowl with the chicory and sweetcorn. Toss gently to coat. Tip into a serving bowl or dish, scatter over the spring onions and sunflower seeds and serve.

Hands-on time: 20min, plus cooling
Cooking time: about 15min
Serves 8

PER SERVING 250cals, 5g protein, 13g fat (2g saturates), 28g carbs (4g total sugars), 4g fibre

Courgette and Feta Filo Tart

Using filo pastry makes this quiche lovely and light. We used dill but if you don't like it, you can use parsley instead.

2 courgettes (about 450g)
1 tbsp olive oil, plus extra to brush
1 shallot, finely chopped
4 medium eggs
250ml double cream
2 tsp freshly chopped dill
3-4 sheets filo pastry
150g feta

◆ GET AHEAD
Make up to a day ahead. Cool completely in the tin, then cover and chill. To serve, preheat the oven to 180°C (160°C fan) mark 4 and cook in the tin for 10min.

1. Trim and peel the courgettes into long ribbons using a Y-shaped peeler, stopping when you get to the core (do not discard). Put the ribbons on a board in a single layer, then sprinkle with salt to draw out moisture. Set aside.

2. Coarsely grate or finely chop the courgette cores. Heat the oil in a medium frying pan over a low heat and fry the shallot for 5min, until softened. Turn up the heat to medium, add the grated/chopped courgette cores and fry for 5min more until softened, then tip into a bowl. Leave to cool for 5min.

3. Whisk the eggs, cream and dill into the cooled courgette mixture. Season lightly.

4. Preheat the oven to 150°C (130°C fan) mark 2. Lightly brush a 23cm round, deeply fluted tart tin at least 3.5cm deep with some oil. Brush the top of a filo sheet with oil. Press the filo sheet into the tin (oiled-side up). Repeat with more filo sheets, rotating them as you layer so that the base and sides of the tin are completely covered, and pressing the sheets together well so that there are no gaps. Lightly scrunch the excess pastry hanging over the sides to make a rim.

5. Pat the courgette ribbons dry with kitchen paper. Loosely curl half the ribbons and arrange in the pastry case, then crumble in most of the feta. Pour in the egg and courgette mixture, making sure it runs into all the gaps, then swirl on the remaining courgette ribbons. Crumble over the remaining feta.

6. Put the tin on a baking sheet and cook in the oven for about 50min–1hr, or until the pastry is golden and the filling is set. Leave to cool for 10min in the tin, then transfer to a board or cake stand and serve in slices.

Hands-on time: 20min, plus cooling
Cooking time: about 1hr 10min
Makes 8 slices

PER SLICE 308cals, 9g protein, 26g fat (14g saturates), 9g carbs (2g total sugars), 1g fibre

Shaved Fennel and Samphire Salad

This pretty salad makes a great side for grilled fish or meat for a special meal.

FOR THE SALAD
2 medium oranges
½ small red onion, finely sliced
1 large fennel bulb, cored and finely sliced, fronds reserved
100g samphire

FOR THE DRESSING
1 tsp Dijon mustard
1 tsp cider vinegar
2 tbsp extra virgin olive oil

1. Finely grate the zest of half an orange into a small bowl and set aside for the dressing. Using a sharp serrated knife, slice off the peel and any white pith from both oranges, then slice horizontally across the segments into rounds. Cut each slice in half to make semi-circles, picking out and discarding any pips.

2. Put the orange slices in a large bowl with the red onion and sliced fennel and gently toss together to combine (the acid from the oranges will help the onion and fennel to soften and mellow the onion slightly).

3. Bring a medium pan of water to the boil and cook the samphire for 3min, until just tender. Drain and cool under cold running water. Drain well again and add to the bowl with the orange, onion and fennel.

4. To make the dressing, whisk the mustard, vinegar and some seasoning into the reserved orange zest. Whisk in the olive oil to make a thick dressing.

5. Tip the salad on to a large platter in an even layer, then drizzle over the dressing. Scatter over the reserved fennel fronds and serve.

Hands-on time: 15min
Cooking time: about 5min
Serves 4 as a side

PER SERVING 101cals, 2g protein, 6g fat (1g saturates), 8g carbs (8g total sugars), 4g fibre

Roast Stuffed Salmon

A generous, tasty stuffing transforms sides of salmon into a surprisingly simple showstopper that can be made ahead.

25g butter
125g pancetta, diced
1 large onion, finely chopped
200g fresh brown or seeded breadcrumbs
2 eating apples, cored and coarsely grated
25g pine nuts, toasted
3 tbsp thyme leaves, chopped
Juice 1 lemon
2 sides of salmon (about 850g each), with small bones removed
Vegetable oil, to grease

◆ GET AHEAD
Prepare to the end of step 3 up to 3hr ahead. Chill. Complete recipe to serve.

1. Preheat the oven to 220°C (200°C fan) mark 7. In a medium frying pan, melt the butter and fry the pancetta and onion for 4–5min, until just cooked. Empty into a large bowl and allow to cool completely.

2. Stir the breadcrumbs, apples, pine nuts, thyme, lemon juice and plenty of seasoning into the pancetta bowl.

3. Check the salmon for bones (pull any out with tweezers and discard). Pat the fish dry with kitchen paper and lay one piece, skin-side down, on a large chopping board. Spoon and press the stuffing evenly on top of the fish. Lay the second side of salmon on top, skin-side up, and secure in place along the length with pieces of knotted string. Carefully transfer to a large greased roasting tin.

4. Roast for 30–35min, or until the salmon is just cooked through and golden at the edges. Transfer to a platter and serve.

Hands-on time: 20min, plus cooling
Cooking time: about 40min
Serves 8

PER SERVING 561cals, 53g protein, 32g fat (8g saturates), 14g carbs (5g total sugars), 3g fibre

Chicken Coxinhas

Shredded chicken and spiced cream cheese are wrapped in dough that softly steams inside its crispy crumb coating when fried.

1 large skinless chicken breast (about 160g)
500ml hot chicken stock
25g butter
450g plain flour, plus extra to dust
4 spring onions, trimmed
1 tsp vegetable oil, plus extra to deep-fry
1 garlic clove, crushed
100g full-fat cream cheese
1½ tsp hot paprika, plus extra to sprinkle
Finely grated zest 1 lime, plus 1–2 tsp juice

FOR THE COATING
50g plain flour
2 medium eggs, beaten
125g fine dried breadcrumbs

YOU'LL ALSO NEED
Cooking thermometer

1. Put the chicken and stock into a medium pan. Bring to a simmer over medium heat, then reduce the heat and cook gently for 12min, or until the chicken is cooked through. Lift the chicken on to a plate to cool, then finely shred.

2. While the chicken is cooling, remove the stock pan from the heat and stir in the butter to melt. Mix in the flour and a pinch of salt to make a thick, fairly lumpy dough. Scrape on to a plate, cover loosely with cling film and set aside to cool for 10min.

Hands-on time: about 1hr, plus cooling
Cooking time: about 35min
Makes 16 balls

PER BALL 197cals, 7g protein, 7g fat (2g saturates), 26g carbs (1g total sugars), 1g fibre

3. Meanwhile, slice the white ends of the spring onions and finely chop the green (keep separate). Heat the 1 tsp oil in a small frying pan over low heat and cook the sliced white spring onions and garlic for 3min, until softened. Empty into a bowl and mix in the shredded chicken, green spring onions, cream cheese, paprika, lime zest and juice (to taste) and plenty of seasoning. Set aside.

4. Generously flour a work surface and knead the dough for 10min, until smooth and shiny. Divide into 16 golf-ball sized pieces. Put one piece in the palm of your hand and flatten to a rough 9cm circle. Put a scant 1 tbsp chicken filling in the centre and carefully bring up the edges of the dough to encase it, pinching to seal and create a pear/teardrop shape. Place on a baking tray lined with baking parchment. Repeat with the remaining dough and filling.

5. For the coating, put the flour, beaten eggs and breadcrumbs into 3 separate bowls. Coat each coxinha in flour (tap off excess), then egg, then breadcrumbs. Return to the lined tray.

6. Fill a large, deep, heavy-based pan with oil so it's 7cm deep. Heat the oil to 180°C. Using a slotted spoon, lower 6 coxinha into the oil and cook for 4–5min, until deep golden (over-cooking will cause them to split). Lift out on to kitchen paper. Repeat with remaining coxinhas, monitoring the oil temperature as you go.

7. Sprinkle the coxinhas with a little salt and paprika and serve.

◆ GET AHEAD

Prepare to end of step 5 up to 2 days ahead. Cover and chill. To serve, allow to come to room temperature before frying. The cooked coxinhas will also keep covered and chilled for a couple of days. Serve at room temperature. These are great hot from the fryer, but once cooled, they also make a delightful portable snack for picnics or lunch boxes.

Herby Vegetable and Ricotta Tart

A colourful tart with a delicious herby pastry, which can be made ahead for stress-free entertaining.

FOR THE PASTRY
125g butter, chilled and cubed
275g plain flour, plus extra to dust
25g mixed herbs, finely chopped (we used basil, chives and thyme leaves)

FOR THE FILLING
100g baby corn, halved lengthways
2 large mixed colour peppers, deseeded and thickly sliced
1 large courgette, trimmed, halved and thickly sliced
1 red onion, thickly sliced
1½ tbsp olive oil
125g baby spinach
200g ricotta
100ml double cream
4 large eggs
15g dill, roughly chopped
60g pitted black olives
30g pine nuts, lightly toasted

1. First make the pastry. Using a food processor, pulse the butter and flour until the mixture resembles fine breadcrumbs. Alternatively, rub the butter into the flour using your fingers. Pulse/mix in the chopped herbs, followed by 4 tbsp cold water, until the pastry just comes together. Tip on to a work surface, shape into a disc, then wrap and chill while you prepare the filling.

Hands-on time: 40min, plus chilling and cooling
Cooking time: about 1hr 40min
Cuts into 8 slices

PER SLICE 438cals, 12g protein, 29g fat (16g saturates), 31g carbs (4g total sugars), 4g fibre

2. Preheat the oven to 220°C (200°C fan) mark 7. For the filling, put the baby corn, peppers, courgette and red onion on a baking tray and toss through 1 tbsp olive oil and some seasoning. Roast for 20–25min, turning halfway, until charred at the edges. Cool slightly.

3. Meanwhile, heat the remaining ½ tbsp oil in a large frying pan or wok, add the spinach and cook, stirring, until wilted. Remove to a board, leave to cool slightly, then roughly chop.

4. Lightly flour a work surface and roll out the pastry. Use it to line a 25cm round, 3cm deep tart tin. Trim the edges to neaten, prick the base all over with a fork and freeze for 5–10min, until solid.

5. Line the pastry in the tin with a large sheet of baking parchment and fill with baking beans. Cook for 15–20min, until the pastry sides are set. Carefully remove the parchment and beans and return to the oven for 10min, until the pastry is lightly golden and feels sandy to the touch.

6. In a jug, whisk the ricotta, cream, eggs, dill and plenty of seasoning, until combined. Scatter half the spinach, roasted vegetables, olives and pine nuts into the pastry case (still in its tin). Pour in the ricotta mixture, then scatter over the remaining spinach, vegetables, olives and pine nuts, making sure they are partially submerged.

7. Cook for 45min, or until the pastry is golden and the filling is set, covering loosely with foil after 20min if the tart is getting too brown. Cool in the tin for 5min, then transfer to a cake stand or plate and serve warm or at room temperature.

◆ GET AHEAD
Make the tart a day ahead. Cool (still in the tin), then cover and chill. To serve, cover with foil and reheat in the tin in an oven preheated to 220°C (200°C fan) mark 7 for 20–25min, until heated through.

9

Slowly Does It

Prawn and Chorizo Jambalaya

This is the ideal dinner for when you're in need of something simple and comforting.

250g cooking chorizo, sliced into 3mm rounds
1 each green and red pepper, deseeded and chopped
1 onion, finely chopped
2 celery sticks, finely chopped
2 garlic cloves, crushed
1 tsp dried thyme
1 tbsp Cajun seasoning
400g tin chopped tomatoes
500ml chicken stock
Few drops Tabasco, to taste
300g easy-cook long-grain rice
200g cooked peeled king prawns
Large handful flat-leaf parsley, roughly chopped
Lemon wedges, to serve

1. Put all the ingredients except the rice, prawns, parsley and lemon wedges into a slow cooker. Season well. Cover with the lid and cook on low for 4hr.

2. Increase the slow cooker setting to high, stir in the rice, then re-cover with the lid and cook for a further 30min or until the rice is cooked. Add the prawns, cover and cook for a further 5min, or until they are hot. Stir in most of the parsley and check the seasoning. Sprinkle over the remaining parsley and serve with lemon wedges.

Hands-on time: 15min
Cooking time: about 4hr 35min
Serves 4

PER SERVING 634cals, 35g protein, 22g fat (8g saturates), 71g carbs (10g total sugars), 6g fibre

Greek Lamb Stew

This hearty and warming stew, flavoured with cinnamon, is packed with slow-cooked vegetables and just the thing for a cold day.

1 tbsp olive oil
250g diced lamb leg
1 onion, finely chopped
1 aubergine, cut into 2cm pieces
2 red peppers, deseeded and sliced
3 garlic cloves, crushed
400g tin chopped tomatoes
1 tbsp tomato purée
300ml chicken stock
50g pitted black olives
2 tsp dried oregano
1 cinnamon stick
2 bay leaves
2 courgettes, halved lengthways and cut into 5mm-thick slices
200g bulgur wheat
50g feta, crumbled
Small handful dill, chopped

1. Heat the oil in a large pan or casserole (that has a lid) over a medium-high heat and brown the lamb pieces all over. Transfer to a bowl. Add the onion to the pan/casserole, then lower the heat and cook gently for 5–10min until softened. Add the aubergine and peppers and cook for a further 5min until starting to brown.

2. Stir in the garlic, fry for 1min, then return the lamb to the pan with the tinned tomatoes, tomato purée, stock, olives, oregano, cinnamon stick, bay leaves and some seasoning. Bring to the boil, then turn down the heat, cover and simmer for 45min.

3. Uncover and stir in the courgettes, then re-cover and simmer for a further 30min. Remove the lid and simmer for 15min more, until the lamb is tender and the sauce has thickened.

4. During the final 15min of cooking, bring the bulgur wheat and 400ml water to the boil in a medium pan. Cook over a low heat for 10–12min, until the water has been absorbed and the bulgur wheat is tender.

5. Check the seasoning of the stew, scatter over the feta and dill and serve with bulgur wheat.

Hands-on time: 30min
Cooking time: about 1hr 45min
Serves 4

PER SERVING 427cals, 26g protein, 16g fat (6g saturates), 50g carbs (13g total sugars), 11g fibre

Slow Cooker Ham and Red Lentil Stew

This hearty stew is deliciously easy, as the slow cooker does all the work! We used carrots, parsnips and potatoes, but you can use any leftover roast veg you like.

2 tsp olive oil
2 red onions, finely sliced
3 rosemary sprigs
2 x 400g tins chopped tomatoes
150g red lentils, rinsed under cold water
200g cooked ham, in a chunk if possible
300g mixed roasted vegetables, in large pieces
700ml hot gluten-free vegetable stock
300g savoy cabbage, spring greens or kale, shredded

1. Heat the oil in a large frying pan over a medium heat, add the onions and fry for 10min, stirring occasionally, until softened. Add the rosemary and cook for a further 2min. Scrape the mixture into a slow cooker.

2. Stir in the tomatoes, lentils, ham, vegetables and stock. Cover with the lid and cook on high for 4hr, or until the lentils are very tender.

3. Remove the ham from the stew and shred with 2 forks. Return to the slow cooker with the cabbage, greens or kale. Re-cover and cook for 45min more, until the cabbage is cooked. Remove the rosemary and season generously with freshly ground black pepper and salt, if needed.

◆ GH TIP
No slow cooker? Cook the stew in a large covered pan for 45–55min, or until the lentils are very tender. Shred the ham and add the cabbage for the final 10min.

Hands-on time: 20min
Cooking time: about 5hr
Serves 4

PER SERVING 379cals, 25g protein, 8g fat (1g saturates), 46g carbs (22g total sugars), 12g fibre

Slow Cooker Thai Red Curry

This dish couldn't be easier, and can also be made on the hob (see GH Tips).

1 tbsp vegetable oil
8 bone-in, skin-on chicken thighs
4 tbsp Thai red curry paste
2 tbsp fish sauce
1 sweet potato, cut into 3cm pieces
1 aubergine, cut into 3cm pieces
150g mixed exotic/wild mushrooms, sliced if large
1 red chilli, deseeded and sliced
400ml tin coconut milk

TO SERVE
Small handful Thai basil, roughly torn
Lime wedges
Cooked basmati rice

1. Heat the oil in a large frying pan over a medium-high heat and brown the chicken, skin-side down, for 10min, until golden.

2. Transfer the chicken to a slow cooker and stir in the remaining ingredients and a generous pinch of salt. Cover and cook on low for 3hr, until the chicken and sweet potato are cooked and tender.

3. Check the seasoning, garnish with Thai basil and serve with lime wedges and rice.

◆ GH TIPS
If you don't have a slow cooker, make the curry on the hob: at step 2, cook over a low heat (covered) for 45min–1hr.

For a thicker curry, strain the finished liquid into a pan, setting aside the chicken and veg. Mix 1½ tbsp cornflour with 2 tbsp of the liquid to a smooth paste, then add to the pan and bring to a boil, stirring. Bubble for a few minutes, stirring occasionally, until thickened. Return the chicken and veg to the sauce and serve.

Hands-on time: 15min
Cooking time: about 3hr 15min
Serves 4

PER SERVING 843cals, 50g protein, 62g fat (26g saturates), 18g carbs (7g total sugars), 6g fibre

Duck and Sausage Cassoulet

This hearty dish is deliciously versatile. Serve it as a stew once you've stirred the duck back in or, as is more traditional, baked with a crispy breadcrumb topping.

4 duck legs
2 tsp olive oil
6 chunky pork sausages
100g smoked bacon lardons
1 onion, finely chopped
1 carrot, finely chopped
1 celery stick, finely chopped
4 garlic cloves, crushed
4 ripe plum tomatoes (about 400g), roughly chopped
Handful thyme sprigs, leaves picked
2 bay leaves
500ml chicken stock
2 x 400g tins haricot beans, drained and rinsed
Cooked greens, to serve (optional)

FOR THE CRUMB
50g fresh or dried breadcrumbs
1 garlic clove, crushed
Handful parsley, finely chopped

◆ GET AHEAD
Prepare to the end of step 5. Cool, then freeze the cassoulet mixture and breadcrumbs separately for up to 3 months. To serve, defrost in the fridge, then return the cassoulet to a casserole dish. Reheat on the hob for 10min, adding a splash of water if needed. Complete the recipe to serve.

Hands-on time: 30min, plus cooling
Cooking time: about 2hr 15min
Serves 6

PER SERVING 716cals, 54g protein, 42g fat (14g saturates), 26g carbs (6g total sugars), 9g fibre

1. Preheat the oven to 180°C (160°C fan) mark 4. Pat dry the duck legs with kitchen paper, season all over and arrange on a wire rack set over a roasting tin. Roast for 1hr 30min, or until the meat is pulling away from the bones. Cool (reserving the fat in the roasting tin).

2. Meanwhile, heat the oil in a large casserole dish (that has a lid) over a medium heat. Brown the sausages all over. Remove to a plate. Add the lardons, onion, carrot and celery to the casserole and cook for 8–10min, until softened and starting to brown. Stir in the garlic and cook for 2min, until fragrant.

3. Stir in the tomatoes, thyme, bay leaves, stock and some seasoning. Bring to the boil, then return the sausages to the casserole. Reduce the heat to low, cover and cook for 1hr, removing the lid for the final 15min.

4. Chunkily shred the duck meat and skin from the bones, discarding any fatty bits. Stir the shredded duck into the casserole with the beans. Check the seasoning.

5. In a small bowl mix the breadcrumbs with the garlic, parsley, 2 tbsp of the reserved duck fat, and some seasoning.

6. Sprinkle the crumb mixture over the casserole in an even layer and cook in the oven, uncovered, for 45min, or until bubbling and golden brown. Serve with some cooked greens.

Pork and Cheddar Cobbler

The perfect winter warmer. Swap the thyme for rosemary or sage, if you like.

1.5kg boneless pork shoulder
2 tbsp plain flour
1 tbsp English mustard powder
2 tbsp olive oil
2 onions, finely sliced
2 carrots, finely chopped
1 celery stick, finely sliced
2 garlic cloves, crushed
1 tbsp fresh thyme leaves, roughly chopped
400ml good-quality cider
400ml chicken stock

FOR THE COBBLER
175g self-raising flour
½ tbsp baking powder
75g mature Cheddar, grated
1 tbsp fresh thyme leaves, roughly chopped
100ml cider
2 medium eggs

◆ GET AHEAD
Prepare to the end of step 4 (no need to preheat the oven) and leave the pork to cool completely before topping with the cobbler. Wrap and freeze for up to 1 month. To serve, defrost in the fridge. Complete the recipe, cooking for 30–35min, or until piping hot (cover with foil if the cobbler is browning too quickly).

1. Remove and discard the skin and excess fat from the pork, then cut into rough 2cm chunks. Toss the pork chunks in the flour, mustard powder and plenty of seasoning. Heat 1 tbsp of the oil in a large, shallow casserole dish (that has a lid) over a medium-high heat. Fry the pork, in batches if needed, until browned all over. Using a slotted spoon, put on a plate.

2. Add the remaining oil to the casserole and lower the heat to medium. Cook the onions, carrots and celery for 10min, stirring occasionally, until softened. Stir through the garlic and thyme and cook for 2min, until fragrant.

3. Return the pork (and any juices) to the casserole with the cider, stock and plenty of seasoning. Bring to the boil, then cover and simmer over low heat for 1hr, until the pork is tender. Remove from the heat.

4. Preheat the oven to 200°C (180°C fan) mark 6. For the cobbler, in a large bowl, mix the flour, baking powder, Cheddar, thyme and plenty of seasoning. Add the cider and one egg and stir until combined. Spoon on to the casserole in 12 equal dollops.

5. Beat the remaining egg and brush a little over the cobbler to glaze. Cook in the oven for 25min, or until piping hot and golden. Serve.

Hands-on time: 30min
Cooking time: about 1hr 50min
Serves 6

PER SERVING 628cals, 64g protein, 22g fat (8g saturates), 35g carbs (8g total sugars), 4g fibre

Beef and Ale Casserole

You can't go wrong with this mix of hearty tender beef, and cheesy dumplings.

50g plain flour
1.2kg chuck, stewing or casserole beef steak, trimmed and
   cut into 5cm chunks
3 tbsp olive oil
250ml beef stock
2 large onions, finely sliced
2 large carrots, peeled and cut into 2.5cm chunks
200g button mushrooms, halved if large
1 bay leaf
4 thyme sprigs
500ml ale

FOR THE DUMPLINGS
100g plain flour
1 tsp baking powder
50g butter, chilled, coarsely grated
1 tbsp finely chopped flat-leaf parsley, plus extra
   to garnish
1 tsp thyme leaves
50g extra-mature Cheddar, grated

◆ GET AHEAD

Make to the end of step 2 up to 3 days ahead, then cool, cover and chill. To serve, reheat thoroughly in a slow cooker, then complete the recipe.

To freeze ahead, make to end of step 2, then cool. Transfer to a suitable container and freeze for up to 1 month. To serve, defrost overnight in the fridge. Reheat in a slow cooker on high until piping hot and complete the recipe.

1. Put the flour in a large bowl and season. Add a third of the beef and toss to coat. Heat 1 tbsp of the oil in a large frying pan over a medium heat. Shake the excess flour from the beef, then add to the pan and brown. Remove to a slow cooker with a slotted spoon. Repeat until all the beef is browned, adding fresh oil to the pan between batches.

2. Add the stock to the pan, stirring to scrape up any sticky bits, then pour into the slow cooker. Stir in the onions, carrots, mushrooms, bay leaf and thyme. Pour in the ale and season. Cover with the lid and cook on high for 4hr.

3. After 4hr, make the dumplings. Mix together all the ingredients, apart from the cheese, in a bowl with plenty of seasoning, or pulse in a small food processor until the mixture resembles breadcrumbs. Add the cheese and mix/pulse, then sprinkle over 2–3 tbsp cold water and stir/pulse until the dough comes together. Roll into 8 balls. Uncover the stew, and arrange the dumplings on top, spacing them apart. Re-cover with the lid and cook on high for 1–1hr 30min. Check the seasoning, garnish and serve.

Hands-on time: 45min
Cooking time: about 5hr 45min
Serves 6

PER SERVING 562cals, 55g protein, 23g fat (10g saturates), 27g carbs (7g total sugars), 4g fibre

Venison Bourguignon with Cheese Cobbler

Farmed venison makes for a wonderfully luxurious special-occasion stew, and the mild game flavour works so well in a rich bourguignon, but you could use beef braising steak instead.

500g small shallots, peeled
2 tbsp olive oil
200g smoked bacon lardons
1.5kg diced venison
3 garlic cloves, crushed
2 tbsp tomato purée
2 tbsp plain flour
500ml French Pinot Noir or other red wine
1 beef stock cube, crumbled
6 thyme sprigs, leaves picked
2 bay leaves
3 tbsp Cumberland sauce (or use redcurrant jelly)
250g baby chestnut mushrooms

FOR THE COBBLER
200g self-raising flour, plus extra to dust
25g butter, chopped
½ tbsp English mustard powder
100g mature or vintage Red Leicester or Cheddar, grated
150ml buttermilk, plus 2 tbsp to glaze

◆ GET AHEAD
Make up to the end of step 2 a couple of days ahead, then cool, cover and chill. Reheat thoroughly before completing the recipe to serve.

Hands-on time: 55min
Cooking time: about 3hr 20min
Serves 6

PER SERVING 713cals, 72g protein, 26g fat (11g saturates), 39g carbs (9g total sugars), 4g fibre

1. Finely slice half the shallots, reserving the smallest ones for later. Heat 1 tbsp of the oil in a large ovenproof pan or casserole (that has a lid) over a medium-high heat, and cook the lardons for 4–5min, until golden. Remove to a plate with a slotted spoon. Add the sliced shallots to the pan or casserole and cook for 4–5min, until softened. Meanwhile, pat dry the venison with kitchen paper.

2. Add the venison, garlic, tomato purée and flour to the pan or casserole and cook, stirring occasionally, for 5min. Stir in the wine, increase the heat to high, bring to the boil and bubble for 2–3min, scraping the base of the pan or casserole to dissolve any sticky bits. Return the lardons to the pan or casserole with the stock cube, thyme, bay leaves, Cumberland sauce, 100ml water and some seasoning. Cover and cook over low heat for 2hr, or until the venison is tender.

3. Meanwhile, make the cobbler. In a medium bowl, rub together the flour and butter using your fingertips. Add the mustard powder, 75g cheese and some seasoning, mix to combine, then stir in the buttermilk to create a slightly sticky dough. Tip on to a lightly floured surface, roll out to 1.5cm thick and stamp out 12 stars using a 7cm cutter, re-rolling the trimmings. Place on a lightly floured plate, cover and chill until needed.

4. Preheat the oven to 200°C (180°C fan) mark 6. Heat the remaining 1 tbsp oil in a large frying pan over a medium-high heat. Add the mushrooms and reserved (whole) shallots and cook, stirring occasionally, for 4–5min, until golden. Stir into the pan or casserole and check

the seasoning. Re-cover with the lid and cook in the oven for a further 20min.

5. Carefully remove the pan or casserole from the oven. Arrange the cobbler stars on top of the bourguignon in a circle. Brush with buttermilk and sprinkle over the remaining 25g cheese. Return to the oven, uncovered, for 20–25min until the cobbler is golden on top. Serve with Horseradish Crème Fraîche (see right).

◆ HORSERADISH CRÈME FRAÎCHE

Mix 125g crème fraîche, 3 tbsp horseradish sauce and 1 tsp finely chopped thyme leaves with a pinch of salt and 1–2 tsp runny honey, to taste. Chill until needed.

PER TBSP 47cals, <1g protein, 5g fat (3g saturates), 1g carbs (1g total sugars), <1g fibre

Smokey Shredded Beef Brisket

Enjoy barbecue flavours without the hassle of firing up the grill.

1 tbsp vegetable oil
2kg boneless rolled beef brisket, string/elastic removed
2 onions, thickly sliced
1 litre beef stock
4 garlic cloves, peeled
4 bay leaves
Soft buns, to serve (optional)
Coleslaw, to serve (optional)

FOR THE BOURBON SAUCE
300ml bourbon or whisky
100g light brown soft sugar
100g tomato ketchup
100ml cider vinegar
½ tbsp smoked paprika (sweet or hot)
1 tsp cayenne pepper
2 tsp ground cumin
1 tbsp onion granules
1 tbsp garlic granules

◆ GET AHEAD
Prepare to end of step 4 up to 3 days ahead.
Cool the meat in the liquid, then cover and
chill. Cool the sauce, cover and chill. To serve,
lift the meat out of the liquid and shred. Reheat
in a pan with the sauce until piping hot, adding
a splash of the cooking liquid if it looks dry.

1. Heat the oil in a large frying pan over a
   medium-high heat and brown the brisket
   all over. Transfer to a slow cooker (cut the
   brisket in half if you can't fit it in whole).

2. Add the onions to the pan and cook over
   a low-medium heat, stirring occasionally,
   until deep golden. Gradually stir in the stock,
   scraping up any sticky brown bits from the
   base of the pan, then bring to the boil.

3. Pour the onion mixture over the beef, add
   the garlic cloves and bay leaves, and season.
   Cover and cook on low for 8hr, until the meat
   is tender and falling apart.

4. Make the sauce 30min before serving. Set
   aside 1 tbsp of the bourbon/whisky in a small
   bowl, then stir together the remaining sauce
   ingredients with some seasoning in a large pan.
   Simmer for 15–20min, stirring occasionally, until
   thickened. Stir in the reserved bourbon/whisky
   and set aside.

5. Lift the brisket out of the cooking liquid on
   to a board and roughly shred with 2 forks.
   Add to the sauce and stir to coat. Serve in soft
   buns with coleslaw, alongside your favourite
   vegetables, if you like.

Hands-on time: 35min
Cooking time: about 8hr 15min
Serves 8

PER SERVING (without buns and coleslaw) 702cals,
46g protein, 41g fat (17g saturates), 16g carbs
(15g total sugars), 0g fibre

◆ GH TIP
Cool and chill or freeze the excess cooking liquid
to use as the base for another soup or stew.

Guinness and Pearl Barley Irish Stew

This lamb stew is packed with bacon, pearl barley and veggies. Serve it with seasonal greens – and more Guinness, of course!

1 tbsp vegetable oil
150g smoked streaky bacon, roughly chopped
500g diced boneless lamb shoulder
500ml lamb stock
2 tbsp plain flour
440ml can Guinness or other stout
2 onions, sliced
2 celery sticks, finely chopped
400g potatoes, peeled, cut into large chunks
2 parsnips, peeled, cut into thick discs
2 bay leaves
2 thyme sprigs
100g pearl barley, rinsed and drained
Buttered wilted cabbage, to serve (optional)

◆ GET AHEAD
Complete the recipe up to 3 days ahead, then cool, cover and chill. To serve, reheat until piping hot in a pan, thinning with a little stock or water if needed.

1. Heat the oil in a large frying pan over a medium-high heat. Add the bacon and fry, stirring occasionally, until crisp. Remove to a slow cooker with a slotted spoon. Add the lamb to the pan and brown all over (in batches if needed). Remove with a slotted spoon and add to the slow cooker.

2. Add the stock to the pan and bubble for a couple of minutes, stirring to scrape up any sticky brown bits from the base of the pan.

3. Add the flour to the slow cooker and stir to coat the meat. Pour in the stock, then the Guinness. Add the remaining ingredients, season lightly and stir, ensuring the potatoes and parsnips are covered in liquid. Cover with a lid and cook on low for 6hr, until the meat and vegetables are tender. Serve with buttered wilted cabbage, if you like.

Hands-on time: 45min
Cooking time: about 6hr 30min
Serves 4

PER SERVING 810cals, 47g protein, 37g fat (14g saturates), 63g carbs (13g total sugars), 8g fibre

Cheat's Macaroni Cheese

There's no white sauce to make with this simple recipe – throw it all in the slow cooker for easy-peasy comfort food.

800ml whole milk, plus extra if needed
250g mature Cheddar, grated, plus extra to serve
50g Italian-style vegetarian hard cheese, finely grated, plus extra to serve
100g full-fat cream cheese
1 tsp English mustard powder
400g macaroni pasta
200g frozen peas

1. Put the milk, cheeses, mustard powder and plenty of seasoning into the slow cooker. Stir well, then add the macaroni and mix again. Cover with the lid and cook on low for 1hr until the pasta is just cooked and the sauce is creamy.

2. Put the peas in a sieve in the sink and pour over a kettle of boiling water. Drain, then stir into the macaroni. Re-cover and cook for a further 20–30min.

3. Stir in a splash of milk to loosen, if you like, then serve the pasta sprinkled with extra cheese and ground black pepper.

Hands-on time: 10min
Cooking time: about 1hr 30min
Serves 4

PER SERVING 901cals, 43g protein, 41g fat (25g saturates), 87g carbs (14g total sugars), 8g fibre

Chicken Cacciatore

Meaning 'hunter's chicken', this Italian classic is made with chicken thighs cooked in a rustic tomato sauce.

2 tbsp olive oil
500g bone-in, skin-on chicken thighs
40g plain flour
1 onion, finely chopped
150ml red wine
3 garlic cloves, crushed
2 bay leaves
2 rosemary sprigs, leaves picked and finely chopped
5 anchovy fillets in oil, drained and roughly chopped
400g tin plum tomatoes, chopped
200ml chicken stock
2 mixed peppers, deseeded and sliced
100g pitted olives
Cooked rice or polenta, to serve (optional)

◆ GH TIP
Chicken thighs remain juicy and tender with long, slow cooking, but you can use skin-on breasts, if you prefer.

1. Heat half the oil in a large, deep frying pan over a medium heat. Toss the chicken in the flour and add to the pan, skin-side down. Fry until a dark golden brown, then turn and brown the other side. Remove to a plate, skin-side up.

2. Add the remaining oil to the pan and fry the onion until beginning to soften, about 5min. Increase the heat to high, add the wine and bubble until reduced by half. Stir in the garlic, herbs and anchovies. Cook for 2min, stirring. Pour in the tomatoes and chicken stock and bring to the boil.

3. Pour the mixture into the slow cooker, stir in the peppers and set the thighs on top. Cover and cook on high for 3hr.

4. Remove the chicken to a plate and keep warm. Pour the sauce into a wide, shallow pan. Stir in the olives and bubble over a high heat for 10min to reduce and thicken slightly. Return the chicken to the sauce and check the seasoning. Serve with rice or polenta.

Hands-on time: 25min
Cooking time: about 3hr 30min
Serves 4

PER SERVING 483cals, 28g protein, 31g fat (7g saturates), 17g carbs (9g total sugars), 5g fibre

Deliciously Simple Braised Lamb

Cooking a joint of lamb in the slow cooker makes it wonderfully tender and provides an almost instant gravy.

Half leg of lamb (about 1kg)
2 garlic cloves, sliced
Small handful rosemary sprigs
150ml red wine
200ml lamb or chicken stock
2 tbsp cornflour
1 tsp redcurrant jelly
Dash of gravy browning (optional)

◆ GET AHEAD
Cook the lamb 1 day ahead. Cool in its liquid, then cover and chill. To serve, empty into a large pan, cover with a lid and reheat gently until piping hot (about 30–40min). Make the gravy in the slow cooker or the pan, cooking for less time.

1. Use a small sharp knife to make small incisions all over the lamb, then push a slice of garlic and a small sprig of rosemary into each cut. Season the lamb all over and put into the slow cooker. Pour in the wine and stock. Cover and cook on low for 4hr.

2. Working quickly, uncover and turn over the lamb joint, then re-cover with the lid (don't leave the lid up for long as the heat will rapidly escape). Cook for a further 4–5hr, until tender.

3. Transfer the lamb to a warm plate, cover tightly with foil and leave to rest in a warm place while you make the gravy. Turn the slow cooker setting to high. In a small bowl, mix the cornflour with a splash of the cooking liquid to a smooth paste, then whisk into the slow cooker, followed by the redcurrant jelly and gravy browning, if using. Leave to simmer, uncovered, for 30min while the lamb rests. Check the seasoning.

4. Slice the lamb and serve with the gravy and your favourite vegetables.

Hands-on time: 20min, plus resting
Cooking time: about 9hr 30min
Serves 6

PER SERVING 354cals, 33g protein, 21g fat (9g saturates), 5g carbs (1g total sugars), 0g fibre

Sticky Pork Belly Buns

Melt-in-the-mouth juicy pork, sweet sticky sauce and pillowy buns – does street food get any better than this?

FOR THE FILLING
600g boneless pork belly (see GH Tips)
4 tbsp hoisin sauce
1 tbsp soy sauce
3 tbsp Shaoxing rice wine or dry sherry
2 garlic cloves, crushed
3cm piece fresh root ginger, peeled and grated
1 tbsp runny honey

FOR THE BUNS
75ml milk
½ tbsp vegetable oil, plus extra to grease
250g plain flour
20g caster sugar
½ tsp fast-action dried yeast

FOR THE TOPPINGS
2 spring onions, finely shredded
½ cucumber, sliced into batons
Small handful coriander leaves
1 red chilli, finely sliced (optional)

YOU WILL ALSO NEED
1–2 large steamer baskets

◆ GH TIPS
If you don't fancy making your own buns you can buy them ready-made, or try using lettuce leaves as wraps instead.

Look for pork belly with even layers of meat and fat. If there's a big layer of fat under the skin, you may prefer to cut it off before serving.

Hands-on time: 40min, plus (overnight) marinating, rising and resting
Cooking time: about 2hr 40min
Makes 8 buns

PER BUN 359cals, 18g protein, 17g fat (6g saturates), 33g carbs (9g total sugars), 2g fibre

1. For the filling, use a sharp knife to deeply score the skin of the pork belly in a tight criss-cross pattern, going right into the fat layer beneath (this will make it easier to eat later). Mix the hoisin, soy sauce, Shaoxing or sherry, garlic and ginger in a roasting tin or ovenproof dish in which the pork will fit fairly snugly. Add the pork and turn to coat. Place skin-side up, cover and chill for at least 2hr, ideally overnight.

2. Preheat the oven to 180°C (160°C fan) mark 4. Pour 200ml water into the tin/dish and cover with foil (making sure the foil doesn't touch the pork skin). Roast for 2hr 30min, basting occasionally, or until very tender.

3. Meanwhile, for the buns, heat the milk in a small pan until warm. Remove from the heat and mix in the oil and 75ml cold water. Mix the flour, sugar, yeast and ½ tsp fine salt in a large bowl, then make a well in the centre. Pour in the milk mixture and mix by hand until the dough comes together, then knead briefly in the bowl for 1–2min. Cover and leave to rise in a warm place for 1hr, or until doubled in size.

4. Tip the dough on to a clean surface and knead for 10min, until smooth and bouncy. If the dough is sticking, grease the surface lightly. Divide and shape into 8 neat balls, then roll each ball into a 3mm thick oval. Brush the ovals lightly on both sides with oil and fold in half widthways, gently pressing together the sides. Put on individual squares of baking parchment, then cover loosely with greased cling film (oil-side down) and leave to rise for 45min-1hr, or until slightly puffed.

◆ GET AHEAD
Steam the buns up to 3hr ahead. Once cool, cover loosely with a tea towel. To serve, reheat following the method in step 5 for 4–5min, or until puffed and warm. Complete the recipe.

5. Put the buns in a steamer basket, spacing apart (you will need to do this in batches if you only have one basket). Cover with the steamer lid and sit the basket over a large pan half-filled with boiling water. Steam over a medium heat for 15min, until light and puffy. Remove the lid immediately to avoid condensation dripping on to the buns.

6. Once cooked, leave the pork to rest somewhere warm for 20min (or until the buns are ready).

Meanwhile, strain the cooking juices into a small pan, and skim off and discard any excess fat. Stir in the honey and bubble over a medium heat until reduced and syrupy.

7. Cut the pork into 16 slices. Pile into the steamed buns and drizzle over the sauce. Finish with the toppings and serve.

Slow-braised Chicken with Leek, Rosemary and Cheddar Dumplings

Slowly cooking your chicken ensures it stays succulent, and your dumplings will soak up the maximum flavour by steaming alongside the meat in the braising liquid.

1 tbsp olive oil
1 medium free-range chicken (about 1.5kg)
200g smoked bacon lardons
400g leeks, thickly sliced
2 sticks celery, sliced
2 large garlic cloves, finely chopped
2 bay leaves
250ml dry white wine
300g Chantenay carrots, or normal carrots cut into large chunks
300g baby parsnips, peeled and quartered lengthways
350ml hot chicken stock

FOR THE DUMPLINGS
125g self-raising flour
1 tsp English mustard powder
25g cold butter, cubed
1 tsp very finely chopped rosemary leaves
1 tbsp finely chopped parsley, plus extra to serve
25g mature Cheddar cheese, grated
2 tbsp natural yogurt
Buttered seasonal green veg, to serve

Hands-on time: 30min
Cooking time: 2hr 30min
Serves 4

PER SERVING 956cals, 63g protein, 52g fat (16g saturates), 41g carbs (12g total sugars), 10g fibre

1. Preheat the oven to 140°C (120°C fan) mark 1. Heat the oil to high in a frying pan large enough to fit your chicken. When hot, add the chicken, breast-side down, and sear, turning a couple of times, until it is golden all over. Remove and set aside on a plate. Discard any fat in the pan.

2. Add the lardons, and fry until crisp and golden. Remove to a plate with a slotted spoon, discarding most of the fat. Reduce the heat to medium, add the leeks and fry for 10min until tender and just golden, then remove about a quarter of them and set aside on a plate (roughly chop and reserve these for the dumplings). Increase the heat to high, return the lardons to the pan with the celery, garlic, bay leaves and wine, then bring to a boil and simmer for a couple of minutes. Transfer to a large roasting tin.

3. Sit the chicken in the roasting tin, breast-side up, and nestle the carrots and parsnips around it. Season. Set the roasting tin over the heat on the hob, pour over the hot stock and bring to the boil, then cover tightly with foil and cook in the oven for 1hr 15min.

4. Meanwhile, make the dumplings: mix the flour, mustard powder and ½ tsp fine salt in a bowl. Rub in the butter with your fingertips, then stir in the reserved cooked leek, rosemary, parsley and cheese. Add the yogurt and 2 tbsp cold

water, mixing well to combine. Divide into 8 dumplings, about 40g each.

5. After 1hr 15min, remove the casserole from the oven. Dot the dumplings around the chicken, ensuring they are partly submerged. Re-cover with foil and return to the oven for a further 45min, uncovering the casserole for the final 15min until cooked through – the juices should

run clear when a skewer is inserted into the thickest part of the leg.

6. Lift out the chicken on to a board and carve – it should be very tender. Serve the casserole in bowls, topped with the sliced chicken, buttered greens and extra parsley.

On the BBQ

Harissa Aubergine

This vegan-friendly main is super simple but looks oh-so-impressive served up on a platter.

2 medium aubergines
2½ tbsp harissa paste
2 tbsp maple syrup
1 tbsp lemon juice
½ tbsp olive oil, plus extra to drizzle
4 tbsp pomegranate seeds
Small handful mint or coriander leaves, roughly chopped

1. Halve the aubergines lengthways and score the flesh in a criss-cross pattern with a small sharp knife, being careful not to cut through the skin. In a small bowl, mix the harissa, maple syrup and lemon juice with some seasoning.

2. Brush the skin side of the aubergines with the olive oil, then brush the flesh with half the harissa mixture. Barbecue or griddle, skin-side down, over medium heat for 10min, until the skin is charred and the flesh is tender.

3. Brush the flesh side with the remaining harissa, then turn and barbecue/griddle flesh-side down for 5min, until browned. Transfer to a serving board or plate, using a palette knife or thin-edged spatula if the aubergine is sticking to the bars. Sprinkle over the pomegranate seeds and herbs, drizzle with extra oil and serve.

Hands-on time: 15min
Cooking time: about 15min
Serves 4

PER SERVING 88cals, 2g protein, 3g fat (0g saturates), 12g carbs (10g total sugars), 5g fibre

American-style Smokey BBQ Brisket

Slow-cooking brisket gives meltingly tender and juicy results. Pop this in the oven in the morning, then simply finish on the barbecue – or even a griddle – for an impressive centrepiece.

1.5kg beef brisket joint (flat, not rolled)
2 tbsp light muscovado sugar
3 tbsp sweet smoked paprika
1 tbsp English mustard powder
2 tsp ground coriander
1 tsp garlic granules
200ml hot beef stock

FOR THE BBQ SAUCE
2 tsp vegetable oil, plus extra to grease
1 onion, finely chopped
50g light muscovado sugar
75g tomato ketchup
75ml bourbon whiskey
1 tbsp cider vinegar

◆ GET AHEAD
Prepare to end of step 1 up to a day ahead. Cover and chill the brisket, and store the remaining spice mixture at room temperature. To serve, remove the brisket from fridge 30min before adding the stock to the tin and completing the recipe.

1. Preheat the oven to 150°C (130°C fan) mark 2. Pat the brisket dry with kitchen paper and put into a roasting tin that will hold it snugly. Mix the sugar and spices with 2 tsp salt and some freshly ground black pepper. Rub half the spice mixture all over the beef.

2. Pour the hot stock around the beef, cover the tin tightly with foil and cook for 4–5hr (this will vary considerably according to how thick your brisket is), until very tender.

3. Meanwhile, make the sauce. Heat the oil in a medium pan over low heat and fry the onion for 15min, stirring occasionally, until softened and golden. Add the remaining spice mixture and cook, stirring, for 2min. Stir in the remaining sauce ingredients, bring to a simmer and bubble for 15min. Whizz until smooth, then check the seasoning. Set aside.

4. Preheat a barbecue or griddle to low and lightly grease the bars. Whisk 100ml of the liquid from the beef roasting tin into the barbecue sauce. Using tongs, lift the beef on to the barbecue or griddle. Brush with a little of the sauce, cover with a lid if your barbecue has one and cook for 15–20min, turning carefully a few times, until lightly charred all over. Remove to a board and cut into slices or shred with 2 forks and serve with the remaining sauce.

Hands-on time: 25min
Cooking time: about 5hr 20min
Serves 8

PER SERVING 493cals, 37g protein, 31g fat (13g saturates), 14g carbs (13g total sugars), 1g fibre

Korean Chicken Burgers

Sweet, spicy and smokey, this versatile sauce will be your new go-to barbecue accompaniment. We've used chicken for this recipe, but next time try it with salmon fillets.

1 small carrot
100g mooli
50g radishes, sliced
Small handful mint, roughly chopped
1 tsp each black and white sesame seeds (or 2 tsp of either)
Vegetable oil, to brush
2 tbsp plain flour
2 tbsp cornflour
8 boneless, skinless chicken thighs (about 800g)

TO SERVE
4 brioche buns, halved
8 tbsp kimchi
4 tsp mayonnaise

FOR THE BARBECUE SAUCE
2 tsp cornflour
2 tbsp soy sauce
3 tbsp dark brown sugar
3 tbsp sriracha
1 tbsp rice wine vinegar
1 tbsp runny honey
½ tsp sesame oil
2 garlic cloves, crushed
2cm piece fresh root ginger, grated

◆ GET AHEAD
Make the barbecue sauce up to 3 days ahead.
Cool and keep in a sealed jar in the fridge.

1. Make the barbecue sauce: in a small bowl, mix the cornflour with 1 tbsp water. Put the remaining ingredients and 75ml water into a pan. Heat gently to dissolve the sugar. Add the cornflour mix, bring to the boil and simmer, whisking, until thickened, about 3min. Set aside.

2. Peel the carrot and mooli into ribbons or julienne. Mix in a bowl with the radishes, mint and sesame seeds, then set aside.

3. Heat a large griddle pan/pan/barbecue over medium-high heat and brush with oil. In a large bowl, mix the flour and cornflour with some seasoning. Toss the chicken in the mixture, tapping off the excess. Cook for about 10min, turning halfway, or until cooked through and charred. Toast the buns.

4. Serve the chicken in the buns with the barbecue sauce, vegetable mix, kimchi and mayonnaise.

Hands-on time: 25min
Cooking time: about 20min
Serves 4

PER SERVING 669cals, 41g protein, 31g fat (8g saturates), 56g carbs (26g total sugars), 3g fibre

Nectarine and Feta Salad

Sweet and salty, this simple salad will complement barbecued main dishes well. You can swap the nectarines for peaches – just make sure they're not too soft.

3 tbsp olive oil, plus extra to grease
1 tbsp balsamic vinegar
½ tbsp runny honey
4 ripe nectarines, de-stoned and quartered
140g rocket
200g feta, roughly crumbled
Large handful roughly chopped soft herb(s), we used parsley
50g walnuts, toasted and roughly chopped

1. Make the dressing by whisking together the olive oil, balsamic vinegar, honey and plenty of seasoning. Set aside.

2. Lightly grease the bars of a barbecue or griddle pan. Barbecue/griddle the nectarine slices over high heat for 5–6min, turning carefully halfway with tongs and a thin spatula or palette knife if the fruit is sticking. Arrange the rocket on a large serving plate and top with the nectarines, feta, herbs and walnuts. Drizzle over the dressing and serve.

Hands-on time: 15min
Cooking time: about 6min
Serves 6

PER SERVING 250cals, 9g protein, 18g fat (6g saturates), 11g carbs (11g total sugars), 3g fibre

New Potato Skewers with Satay Sauce

If you fancy it a little spicier, add some finely chopped red chilli.

32 baby new potatoes (about 750g)
½ tbsp vegetable oil

FOR THE SATAY SAUCE
Juice ½ lime
6 tbsp smooth peanut butter
2 tbsp tamari
2 tbsp sweet chilli sauce
150ml coconut milk

YOU'LL ALSO NEED
8 wooden skewers, soaked in water for 30min

1. Parboil the potatoes in a large pan of boiling water for 10min, or until fairly tender. Drain well.

2. Meanwhile, heat the sauce ingredients in a small pan, stirring occasionally, until combined and slightly thickened. Transfer to a bowl and set aside.

3. In a bowl, toss the potatoes with the oil and some seasoning, then thread on to skewers. Barbecue over high heat for 10–15min, turning halfway, or on a baking sheet under a medium grill for 10–15min, turning halfway. Serve on or off the skewers with the satay sauce.

Hands-on time: 15min, plus soaking
Cooking time: about 25min
Makes 8 skewers

PER SERVING 116cals, 2g protein, 4g fat (3g saturates), 17g carbs (4g total sugars), 2g fibre

Lamb and Red Pepper Kofte

The addition of red pepper purée to the lamb mince helps keep these mini kebabs light and juicy.

FOR THE KOFTE
2 red peppers, halved and deseeded
400g lamb mince (20% fat)
1 medium egg
50g fresh white breadcrumbs
1 tsp ground cumin
1 tsp ground coriander
2 tbsp finely chopped mint
1 tbsp vegetable oil
Flatbreads, to serve

FOR THE YOGURT DRIZZLE
150g Greek-style yogurt
2 tbsp lemon juice
2 garlic cloves, crushed

YOU'LL ALSO NEED
6 wooden skewers, soaked in water for 30min

◆ GET AHEAD
Prepare to end of step 1 up to a day ahead. Cover and chill. Complete the recipe to serve.

1. For the kofte, whizz half a pepper in the small bowl of a food processor to a purée. Scrape into a large bowl. Cut the remaining peppers into 24 chunks and set aside. Add the lamb mince, egg, breadcrumbs, spices, mint and 1 tsp fine salt to the pepper purée and mix (with your hands is easiest) until well combined.

2. Divide the lamb mixture into 24 portions and roll into rough rugby ball shapes, about 4.5cm long and 2.5cm wide. Thread 4 on to each skewer, squeezing gently to help them stick, alternating with chunks of red pepper.

3. Brush the kofte all over with the oil and barbecue/grill the skewers over/under medium-high heat for 10–12min, turning regularly, until golden and cooked through.

4. Meanwhile, make the yogurt drizzle. Whisk all the ingredients with some seasoning. Serve the cooked kofte in flatbreads with the yogurt on the side.

Hands-on time: 30min, plus soaking
Cooking time: about 12min
Serves 6

PER SERVING (without flatbread) 226cals, 16g protein, 14g fat (6g saturates), 7g carbs (3g total sugars), 1g fibre

Pomegranate and Dukkah Lamb Cutlets

This Egyptian spice mix works wonderfully with lamb. If you don't need the dish to be dairy free, serve with minty yogurt, if you like, to dip.

FOR THE DUKKAH
1½ tbsp coriander seeds
1½ tbsp cumin seeds
60g chopped roasted hazelnuts
40g sesame seeds

FOR THE LAMB
16 lamb cutlets
3 tbsp pomegranate molasses
Extra virgin olive oil, to drizzle
75g pomegranate seeds
Small handful mint, leaves picked and finely shredded

1. To make the dukkah, finely grind the coriander and cumin seeds with a pestle and mortar. Empty into a shallow bowl and mix in the hazelnuts, sesame seeds and ½ tsp each fine salt and freshly ground black pepper. Set aside.

2. Preheat a barbecue or grill to medium heat. Brush the cutlets on both sides with pomegranate molasses, then press firmly into the dukkah to coat.

3. If cooking under the grill, arrange on a baking sheet. Barbecue/grill for 5–10min for pink meat (depending on the thickness), turning midway through. Cook for longer if you prefer. Leave to rest on a board for 3min.

4. Arrange on a serving board or platter, drizzle with a little oil and scatter over the pomegranate seeds and mint. Serve.

Hands-on time: 25min, plus resting
Cooking time: about 10min
Makes 16 cutlets

PER CUTLET 371cals, 18g protein, 32g fat (14g saturates), 3g carbs (2g total sugars), 1g fibre

Shawarma-spiced Cauliflower Steaks

Cauliflower takes big flavours really well, and this recipe marries punchy ingredients from the Middle East and North Africa for a dish that will have everyone wanting a portion.

2 large cauliflowers
3 tbsp shop-bought or home-made shawarma spice mix (see GH Tip)
100g butter, melted
1 garlic clove, crushed
3 tbsp tahini
2 tbsp lemon juice
100g natural yogurt
Oil, to grease
2 tbsp pomegranate molasses
3 tbsp pomegranate seeds
Handful fresh coriander, leaves picked
2 tbsp pine nuts

◆ GH TIP
To make shawarma spice, mix 2 tsp each ground cinnamon, sumac and cumin; ½ tsp each ground allspice and ground black pepper; and ¼ tsp each ground nutmeg and cardamom.

Hands-on time: 25min
Cooking time: about 40min
Serves 4

PER SERVING 457cals, 11g protein, 36g fat
(15g saturates), 19g carbs (13g total sugars), 7g fibre

1. Remove any damaged or dirty outer leaves from the cauliflowers, but leave on firm, undamaged green leaves. Cut 2 x 1½cm thick slices from the centre of each cauliflower, cutting through the root. Set aside the rest of the cauliflower for another recipe.

2. Whisk together the shawarma spice mix, melted butter, garlic and plenty of salt. In a separate bowl, whisk the tahini, lemon juice and yogurt; set aside.

3. Lightly oil the barbecue bars and brush the cauliflower steaks all over with a little of the spiced butter. Barbecue in a single layer over low heat for 35–40min, carefully turning and brushing with more butter a few times during cooking, until the cauliflower is tender. Alternatively, preheat the oven to 220°C (200°C fan) mark 7. Arrange the cauliflower steaks on a baking tray lined with baking parchment; brush with flavoured butter. Cook for 20–25min, turning and brushing with more butter halfway through.

4. Spread half the tahini yogurt on a platter, put the cooked cauliflower steaks on top and brush with any remaining spiced butter. Drizzle over the pomegranate molasses and the remaining tahini yogurt, and scatter over pomegranate seeds, fresh coriander leaves and pine nuts.

Sticky Sausages

Sticky, sweet and incredibly moreish, these sausages won't hang around for long!

2 tbsp olive oil
2 garlic cloves, crushed
3 tbsp runny honey
3 tbsp hoisin sauce
2 tbsp wholegrain mustard
16 raw cocktail sausages or 12 chipolatas

YOU'LL ALSO NEED
8–12 wooden skewers, soaked in water for 30min

1. In a large bowl, mix the oil, garlic, honey, hoisin, mustard and plenty of seasoning. Put half the sauce into a small pan and set aside.

2. Add the sausages to the sauce in the bowl and stir to coat. To barbecue, thread 4 cocktail sausages or 3 chipolatas on to double skewers. (This stops the sausages spinning on the skewer, making them easier to turn.) Cook over medium heat for about 15min, turning halfway and basting with any leftover marinade as you go, until cooked through. Alternatively, put the sausages (without skewers) into an ovenproof serving dish and cook in an oven preheated to 190°C (170°C fan) mark 5 for 25min, stirring halfway.

3. Meanwhile, bubble the sauce in pan over medium-high heat for 5min, until reduced. Remove from the heat and pour into a small bowl. Serve with the sausages.

Hands-on time: 15min, plus soaking
Cooking time: about 15min
Serves 6

PER SERVING 221cals, 7g protein, 15g fat (4g saturates), 14g carbs (11g total sugars), 1g fibre

Chicken Tikka Skewers

Classic chicken tikka is cooked in an ultra-hot oven called a tandoor. Using a barbecue at home gives a similar charred and smokey result to this classic dish.

125g Greek-style yogurt
4 garlic cloves, crushed
5cm piece fresh root ginger, peeled and finely grated
Juice 1 lemon, plus wedges to serve
1 tbsp tomato purée
2 tbsp runny honey
1 tbsp ground cumin
1 tbsp ground coriander
1 tsp turmeric
1 tsp paprika
2 tsp chilli powder (mild or hot)
6 large skinless boneless chicken breasts (about 900g), cut into 3–4cm pieces
350g mango chunks or cherry tomatoes, or a mixture
Handful coriander, roughly chopped

YOU'LL ALSO NEED
8 wooden skewers, soaked in water for 30min

1. In a large, non-metallic bowl, mix the yogurt, garlic, ginger, lemon juice, tomato purée, honey, spices and 1 tsp fine salt. Add the chicken and stir to coat. Cover and leave to marinate in the fridge for at least 4hr, or ideally overnight.

2. Thread the chicken on to skewers, alternating with chunks of mango and/or tomatoes. Barbecue or grill over/under medium heat for 8–10min, turning occasionally, or until cooked through. Scatter over the coriander and serve with lemon wedges for squeezing over, if you like.

Hands-on time: 20min, plus (overnight) marinating and soaking
Cooking time: about 10min
Makes 8 skewers

PER SERVING 184cals, 26g protein, 4g fat (2g saturates), 10g carbs (10g total sugars), 2g fibre

Smokey Pulled Pork with Cola Barbecue Sauce

Cooked low and slow, pork shoulder becomes meltingly tender. For best results, you'll need a coal barbecue to finish this recipe, or you can use a hot oven.

1 onion, thickly sliced
2.2kg boneless pork shoulder
1½ tbsp smoked sweet paprika
1 tbsp English mustard powder
2 tsp light brown soft sugar

FOR THE BARBECUE SAUCE
1 small apple, peeled and grated, core discarded
½ onion, coarsely grated
1 red chilli, deseeded and finely chopped
40g light brown soft sugar
250g tomato ketchup
150ml cola
4 tbsp cider vinegar
2 tbsp soy sauce

TO SERVE (OPTIONAL)
White buns, halved
Coleslaw, dairy free, if needs be

Hands-on time: 35min
Cooking time: about 6hr
Serves 12

PER SERVING (meat and sauce only) 257cals, 35g protein, 7g fat (2g saturates), 13g carbs (13g total sugars), 0g fibre

1. Preheat the oven to 150°C (130°C fan) mark 2. For the pork, arrange the onion slices in the base of a deep casserole dish (that has a lid) and put the pork on top, skin-side up. In a small bowl, mix the paprika, mustard powder, sugar and 2 tsp sea salt, then rub it all over the pork. Add 250ml water to the casserole (taking care not to pour it over the pork), then cover with the lid and cook for 4hr 30min–5hr, until pork is very tender (it should pull apart easily with 2 forks).

2. Meanwhile, make the barbecue sauce. Mix all the ingredients in a small pan and bring to the boil over a medium heat. Bubble for 15–20min, stirring occasionally, until thickened and reduced. Purée with a stick blender and set aside until needed.

3. Carefully transfer the pork to a board. Brush all over with a thin layer of barbecue sauce. Barbecue over low indirect heat (push coals to one side and set the pork over the coal-free side), with a disposable roasting tray underneath to catch any drips. Cover the barbecue with a lid (if possible) and cook for 45min, turning carefully and brushing with more sauce a couple of times. Alternatively, finish the pork in the oven: increase the heat to 220°C (200°C fan) mark 7. Set the pork on a baking tray and brush liberally with barbecue sauce, then cook for 20–25min, until the outside is lightly charred.

4. Remove and discard the skin and most of the visible fat from the pork. Shred the meat with 2 forks. Add the remaining barbecue sauce and toss to coat. Serve in buns with coleslaw, if you like.

◆ GET AHEAD
Prepare to the end of step 1 a day ahead.
Cool, cover and chill. Bring to room
temperature for 1hr, then complete the
recipe. The barbecue sauce keeps for 1 week
chilled in an airtight jar.

◆ GH TIP
If you can't cover your barbecue, don't worry:
the pork will still taste delicious. You can
add smoking chips to the coals, if you like.

Sweet Chilli Prawn and Chicken Burgers

Our favourite Chinese takeaway dish, sesame prawn toast, reimagined in burger form – irresistible!

FOR THE BURGER
300g chicken thigh fillets
400g raw peeled king prawns
4 spring onions, roughly chopped
2 tbsp cornflour
3 tbsp sweet chilli sauce, plus extra to serve
100g sesame seeds, white or a mixture of black and white
Oil, to grease and rub
6 brioche or sesame burger buns, split

FOR THE SALAD
½ small firm white cabbage (about 250g), finely shredded
Juice 1 lemon
2 tsp caster sugar
3 tbsp mayonnaise

◆ GET AHEAD
Prepare to the end of step 3 up to 12hr ahead.
Complete the recipe to serve.

1. To make the burgers, trim and discard any sinews from the chicken. Roughly chop, then pulse in a food processor with half the prawns, the spring onions and 1½ tsp fine salt, until the mixture resembles mince. Empty into a large bowl. Roughly chop the remaining prawns and add to the bowl with the cornflour and sweet chilli sauce. Mix thoroughly (with your hands is easiest). Cover and chill for 30min.

2. Put the sesame seeds on a small plate. Divide the burger mixture equally into 6 balls. Roll the balls gently in the sesame seeds, then shape into flattened patties about 1½ cm thick. Arrange on a lightly greased plate, cover and chill for 1hr to firm up.

3. Meanwhile, make the salad. Mix all the ingredients in a large bowl with some seasoning. Chill until needed.

4. Rub the burger patties with a little oil, then barbecue over low heat for 12–15min, or until cooked through, turning midway through. Towards the end of cooking, barbecue the burger buns (cut-side down), until toasted. Serve the cooked burgers in buns with the salad, drizzled with extra sweet chilli sauce.

Hands-on time: 30min, plus chilling
Cooking time: about 15min
Makes 6 burgers

PER BURGER 542cals, 31g protein, 26g fat (5g saturates), 44g carbs (15g total sugars), 5g fibre

Sauces and Dips

These full-of-flavour options will enhance all your barbecued main dishes.

Smokey Tomato Sauce

A great all-rounder to dip your chips in or spread on top of burgers. Use hot smoked paprika if you like your sauce a little spicy.

Heat **1 tbsp oil** in a medium pan and fry **1 finely chopped onion** until softened. Stir in **1 crushed garlic clove**, **3 tbsp sweet smoked paprika** and **1½ tbsp tomato purée** and cook for 2min, until fragrant. Stir in a **400g tin chopped tomatoes**, **1 tbsp light brown soft sugar**, **½ tbsp cider vinegar** and **1 tsp salt**. Bring to the boil, then reduce the heat to low and simmer for 20min, until slightly reduced. Stir in a **dash of Worcestershire sauce** and check the **seasoning**. For a smooth sauce, whizz with a stick blender. Cool, cover and chill until needed (up to 5 days).

Serves 8

PER SERVING 40cals, 1g protein, 1g fat (<1g saturates), 5g carbs (5g total sugars), 1g fibre

Roasted Garlic and Chipotle Mayo

Use a low-fat mayonnaise, if you prefer, for this warming and gently spiced dip.

Preheat the oven to 200°C (180°C fan) mark 6. Slice the top off **1 small garlic bulb**, then wrap the bulb loosely in foil and roast for 40min. Remove from the oven and cool. Squeeze the garlic cloves out of their skins into a bowl. Mash thoroughly, then mix in **125g mayonnaise**, **100g half-fat crème fraîche**, **1 tbsp chipotle paste** and some **seasoning**. Chill in the fridge, covered, until needed (up to 3 days).

 Serves 8

Per 1tbsp 130cals, 1g protein, 14g fat (2g saturates), 1g carbs (1g total sugars), <1g fibre

Green Goddess Dip

This vibrant green dip is fresh, herby and creamy – ideal for dipping raw vegetables, crisp salad leaves or salty crisps.

In a food processor, whizz **2 peeled and destoned ripe avocados**, **2 crushed garlic cloves**, the leaves from **25g mint** and **25g basil**, **75g soured cream**, the juice of **2 limes**, **2 tsp fish sauce** or **2 finely chopped anchovy fillets**, and a **pinch of salt** until smooth. Chill in the fridge, covered, until needed (up to 2 days).

Serves 8

PER SERVING 98cals, 1g protein, 9g fat (3g saturates), 2g carbs (1g total sugars), 2g fibre

Sticky Peanut Baby Back Ribs

Cooking ribs in foil parcels steams them so they're deliciously tender, and you can then caramelise them on the barbecue still in the foil without the risk of them sticking to the bars.

3 tbsp smooth peanut butter
2 tbsp tomato ketchup
1 tbsp fish sauce
4 tbsp soy sauce
3 tbsp runny honey
2 x 450g pork loin rib racks
Juice 1 lime, plus extra wedges to serve
75g roasted salted peanuts, roughly chopped
3 spring onions, chopped

1. Preheat the oven to 150°C (130°C fan) mark 2. In a small bowl, whisk together the peanut butter, ketchup, fish sauce, 2 tbsp soy sauce and 1 tbsp honey.

2. Lay 2 large sheets of heavy-duty kitchen foil on a work surface and put a rack of ribs in the centre of each. Brush the peanut sauce all over the ribs. Fold up the foil and scrunch the edges together to make sealed parcels around the ribs. Arrange side-by-side on a large baking tray and cook in the oven for 1hr–1hr 15min, or until very tender and the meat is pulling away from the bones.

3. Once the ribs are cooked, open up the foil parcels so the ribs are fully exposed and pour the juices into a small pan. Add the remaining soy sauce and honey to the pan and whisk to combine. Bring to the boil and bubble vigorously until reduced and sticky. Remove from the heat and whisk in the lime juice.

4. Brush some of the glaze all over the ribs, then put the open foil parcels over medium barbecue heat and cook for 15–20min, turning the ribs a couple of times and basting with more glaze, until sticky and charred. Brush with any remaining glaze, sprinkle over the chopped peanuts and spring onions and serve with lime wedges for squeezing over.

Hands-on time: 20min
Cooking time: about 1hr 40min
Serves 8

PER SERVING 306cals, 26g protein, 18g fat (6g saturates), 9g carbs (7g total sugars), 1g fibre

Mango Chutney-glazed Paneer and Vegetable Kebabs

If you've not tried paneer, a firm Indian cheese, you're in for a treat. Instead of melting, it goes crisp and chewy in the high heat, making it a great option for vegetarians and meat-lovers alike.

FOR THE CORIANDER DIP
2 green chillies, deseeded and chopped
1 small garlic clove, crushed
30g coriander, roughly chopped
200g Greek-style yogurt

FOR THE KEBABS
2 tbsp vegetable oil
1½ tsp garam masala
2 x 226g blocks paneer, each cut into 12 pieces
Mixed colour peppers, deseeded and cut into 2.5cm chunks
1 courgette, halved lengthways and cut into 2.5cm chunks
4 spring onions, cut into 2.5cm pieces
3 tbsp smooth mango chutney
1 tsp nigella seeds (optional)

YOU'LL ALSO NEED
6 metal skewers or wooden skewers, soaked in water for 30min

◆ GET AHEAD
Make the dip up to a day ahead – cover and store in the fridge until needed.

1. First make the dip. In the small bowl of a food processor, whizz the chillies, garlic and coriander with 50g of the yogurt until smooth. Scrape into a serving bowl and mix in the remaining yogurt and some salt. Cover and chill until needed.

2. For the kebabs, mix the oil and garam masala with a generous pinch of salt in a large bowl. Mix through the paneer, peppers, courgette and spring onions until they are well coated. Thread on to skewers, alternating the paneer and vegetables.

3. Barbecue/grill the skewers over/under medium-high heat for 10–12min, turning often, until lightly charred. Mix the mango chutney with the nigella seeds, if using, and stir in a drop of hot water to loosen. Brush all over the skewers and cook for a further 2–3min, until caramelised. Serve with the dip alongside.

Hands-on time: 30min, plus soaking
Cooking time: about 15min
Serves 6

PER SERVING 358cals, 22g protein, 26g fat (14g saturates), 8g carbs (8g total sugars), 2g fibre

Rubs and Butters

Parmesan, Tomato and Basil Butter

Add slices to hot grilled fish or chicken, or toss through steamed greens or pasta.

In the small bowl of a food processor, whizz 4 sun-dried tomatoes from a jar (drained) with ½ tsp freshly ground black pepper until fairly smooth. Add 125g softened unsalted butter and whizz again, until combined. Pulse in 50g finely grated Parmesan and 1 basil sprig until well combined. Scrape on to a sheet of baking parchment or cling film, wrap into a sausage shape and chill until needed (up to 1 week).

Makes 150g/serves 10

PER 15g SERVING 117cals, 2g protein, 12g fat (8g saturates), 1g carbs (<1g total sugars), <1g fibre

Whipped Miso Butter

Salty, sweet and delicately garlicky, you'll want to slather this on everything, from steak to toast.

Put 125g softened butter, 2 tbsp brown miso paste and 1 crushed garlic clove in a medium bowl and beat with a handheld electric whisk for 2min, until well-combined and pale. Add 1 tbsp soy sauce and 1 tbsp runny honey and beat to combine. Scrape on to a sheet of baking parchment or cling film, wrap into a sausage shape and chill until needed (up to 1 week).

 Makes 150g/serves 10

PER 15g SERVING 105cals, 1g protein, 11g fat (7g saturates), 2g carbs (1g total sugars), 0g fibre

Piri Piri Rub

Use this on meat, fish and vegetables before grilling, or as a seasoning afterwards. Mix in a little lemon zest just before using, if you like, for a zingy hit.

Mix ½ tbsp hot chilli powder, 40g light brown soft sugar, ½ tsp garlic granules, ½ tsp onion powder, 3 tbsp sweet smoked paprika, ½ tsp chilli flakes and 2 tsp each ground cumin, dried oregano, dried thyme and salt. Store in an airtight container at room temperature for up to 3 months.

Makes 8 tbsp/serves 24

PER 1 TSP SERVING 15cals, 0g protein, 0g fat (0g saturates), 2g carbs (2g total sugars), 0g fibre

Griddled Doughnut Sandwiches

Doughnuts make a wonderfully luxurious bun for ice-cream sandwiches. Pick your preferred sauce – or why not make all three and mix and match!

FOR THE STRAWBERRY SAUCE
250g strawberries (hulled weight)
40g caster sugar
Finely grated zest and juice ½ lemon (keep separate)
1 tbsp cornflour

FOR THE CARAMEL SAUCE
150g granulated sugar
50g butter, chopped
75ml whipping or double cream
Sea salt flakes (optional)

FOR THE CHOCOLATE SAUCE
150g dark chocolate, roughly chopped
150ml whipping or double cream
2 tbsp golden syrup
15g butter

TO SERVE
8 ring doughnuts or yum yums
Ice cream

1. First, make the strawberry sauce. Roughly chop the strawberries and put into a medium pan with the sugar, lemon zest and 50ml water. Bubble, stirring occasionally, until the strawberries are mushy and the liquid is syrupy, about 12min. Whizz in a blender until smooth.

Hands-on time: 40min, plus cooling
Cooking time: about 40min
Makes 8 sandwiches

PER SERVING (with 1 scoop of ice cream and 1 tsp of each sauce) 537cals, 6g protein, 35g fat (20g saturates), 48g carbs (33g total sugars), 2g fibre

2. Whisk the lemon juice and cornflour together in a medium pan. Pass the strawberry mixture through a fine sieve into the pan. Cook over a medium heat, whisking, until thickened (the mixture will need to boil). Cool.

3. For the caramel sauce, heat the sugar and 60ml water in a medium pan over low heat, stirring occasionally, until the sugar dissolves. Turn up the heat and bubble, swirling the pan (not stirring), until the mixture is a golden caramel colour. Remove the pan from the heat and carefully mix in the butter (it will foam up), followed by the cream. Allow to cool. Mix in some sea salt, if you like, to make salted caramel.

4. For the chocolate sauce, melt the ingredients in a heatproof bowl set over a pan of barely simmering water to make a glossy sauce. Set aside.

5. To serve, split the doughnuts/yum yums through their middles. Barbecue or griddle over a medium-high heat for 2–3min per side, until both sides have charred stripes (cook in batches if needed). Transfer to a board to cool slightly.

6. Serve the doughnuts filled with a scoop of your favourite ice cream and your chosen sauce, or all 3, to drizzle over.

◆ GET AHEAD
Make the strawberry and caramel sauces up to 1 week ahead. Cover and chill. Allow the strawberry sauce to come up to room temperature before serving. Microwave the caramel sauce for 10sec, or gently heat in a small pan, to loosen. Make the chocolate sauce up to 3 days ahead. Cover and chill. To serve, warm through gently in a heatproof bowl over a pan of simmering water, thinning with a little milk, if needed.

Poultry

Roast Chicken with Orzo

Make sure to buy a free-range bird for this recipe – you'll be rewarded with better flavour in the meat as well as the pasta, which absorbs the juices.

2 tbsp olive oil
1 medium whole chicken (about 1.7kg)
2 carrots, cut into 1.5cm pieces
1 leek, finely sliced
2 celery sticks, sliced
100g pancetta lardons
1 lemon, cut into 6 wedges
1 tarragon sprig, plus extra leaves, chopped, to garnish
500–700ml hot chicken stock
300g orzo pasta

1. Preheat the oven to 190°C (170°C fan) mark 5. Heat the oil over a medium-high heat in a casserole dish (that has a lid) that will hold the chicken with some space around it. Untruss the chicken and brown in the casserole, breast-side down, until the breast is golden. Remove the chicken to a board.

2. Add the carrots, leek, celery and pancetta to the dish and cook for 5min, until beginning to brown. Stir in the lemon wedges, tarragon sprig and plenty of seasoning. Return the chicken to the casserole dish, breast-side up. Pour in enough stock to come halfway up the sides of the chicken, then bring to the boil.

3. Put on the lid and cook in the oven for 50min. Remove the lid, scatter the orzo around the chicken, making sure it's submerged in the stock, then re-cover and return to the oven for 20min. Check the chicken is cooked – a meat thermometer inserted into the thickest part of the breast should read 72°C or higher.

4. Carefully transfer the casserole to a board and leave to rest for 10min. Scatter over the chopped tarragon and serve.

Hands-on time: 30min, plus resting
Cooking time: about 1hr 30min
Serves 6

PER SERVING 677cals, 47g protein, 36g fat (11g saturates), 39g carbs (4g total sugars), 5g fibre

Lime and Caper Chicken with Green Rice

Cooking rice in a mixture of puréed vegetables and stock is a great way to add extra nutrition and bags of flavour to a simple meal.

8 chicken thighs or mix of thighs and drumsticks
75g butter, softened
3 garlic cloves, crushed
Finely grated zest and juice 2 limes, kept separate
Large bunch coriander, leaves and stalks separated
4 tbsp capers, drained
225g long grain rice
1 green pepper, deseeded and chopped
1 large green chilli, deseeded
350ml hot vegetable stock
2 tsp vegetable oil
3 spring onions, roughly chopped

1. Preheat the oven to 200°C (180°C fan) mark 6. Make 3 or 4 deep cuts in each chicken piece and put into a shallow roasting tin.

2. In a small bowl, mash the butter, garlic, lime zest and plenty of seasoning. Finely chop half the coriander leaves and mix into the butter. Rub all over the chicken and into the cuts. Scatter over the capers and roast for 40–45min, basting halfway through, until the chicken is cooked through and crisp.

3. Meanwhile, thoroughly rinse the rice in a sieve under cold water, then drain. In a blender or food processor, whizz the pepper, green chilli and coriander stalks with half the stock, until fairly smooth. Add the remaining stock and whizz again.

4. Heat the oil in a medium pan over a low-medium heat, then fry the spring onions for 2min. Add the drained rice and stir to coat. Add the vegetable purée and a pinch of salt. Bring to a gentle simmer, stir once and cover with a lid. Reduce the heat to very low and cook for 12min (without boiling or stirring). Remove the lid, stir once with a fork, then cover with a clean tea towel and leave to rest (off the heat) for 10min.

5. Drizzle the lime juice over the rice and fork through gently. Serve the chicken with the rice, scattered with the remaining coriander leaves and with the buttery juices from the roasting tin spooned over.

Hands-on time: 25min, plus resting
Cooking time: about 45min
Serves 4

PER SERVING 697cals, 36g protein, 39g fat (15g saturates), 50g carbs (3g total sugars), 3g fibre

Miso-glazed Griddled Chicken with Sticky Rice Salad

The various elements of this taste fairly simple by themselves, but on the plate they come together to create something quite special.

150g sushi or sticky rice
2 tbsp mirin
2 tbsp white miso paste
3cm piece fresh root ginger, peeled and grated
1 tbsp maple syrup
1 tbsp soy sauce
1 large red chilli, deseeded and finely chopped
4 medium skinless chicken breasts
4 baby pak choi, halved lengthways
1 tsp sesame oil
100g pea shoots
125g radishes, thinly sliced
3 spring onions, finely sliced

◆ GH TIP
For a more intense flavour, marinate the chicken in the miso mixture overnight in the fridge.

1. Wash the rice well in a bowl of cold water, rubbing the grains together with the palms of your hands as if polishing them. Drain away any cloudy water and repeat (several times if necessary) until the water remains clear. Drain the rice and put into a medium pan. Add enough water to just cover the rice and a generous pinch salt.

Hands-on time: 25min
Cooking time: about 25min
Serves 4

PER SERVING 335cals, 33g protein, 5g fat (1g saturates), 40g carbs (7g total sugars), 2g fibre

2. Bring to the boil over a medium-high heat, stirring occasionally, then reduce to a simmer. Cover with a lid and cook for 8min, until the rice is tender. Remove from the heat and leave to steam, covered, for 5min. Uncover, drizzle over the mirin and mix gently to coat. Set aside to cool slightly.

3. Meanwhile, in a large bowl, mix together the miso, ginger, maple syrup, soy and most of the chilli. With a sharp knife, slash the top of each chicken breast a few times to allow the flavours to penetrate. Add the chicken to the bowl and rub the miso mixture all over and into the slashes. Cook in a hot non-stick griddle pan over a medium heat for 12–15min, turning halfway, until the chicken is cooked through. Remove to a plate and keep warm.

4. Rub the halved pak choi with the sesame oil, then place cut-side down on the griddle pan and cook for 4min, until slightly softened. Meanwhile, in a large bowl, mix the pea shoots, radishes and spring onions. Add the cooled (but still warm) rice and toss gently (with your hands is easiest, though it will be sticky). Divide the rice mixture, chicken and pak choi between 4 plates. Sprinkle over the remaining chopped red chilli and serve.

Turkey Sichuan Noodles

This Asian-inspired noodle dish is a wonderful way to use up leftover turkey, but you could also use shredded roast beef or chicken.

2 tbsp sesame oil
400g leftover turkey, shredded
300g fresh sprouts, shredded (see GH Tip)
4cm piece fresh root ginger, peeled and finely grated
2 garlic cloves, crushed
2 tsp Sichuan peppercorns, crushed using a pestle
    and mortar
1 red chilli, deseeded and finely chopped
250ml chicken stock
5 tbsp soy sauce
1 tbsp rice wine vinegar
1 tbsp chilli oil
600g wok-ready thick udon noodles
2 spring onions, finely sliced, to garnish

1. Heat the sesame oil in a large wok or deep frying pan over a high heat. Add the turkey and stir-fry until piping hot and slightly crispy, about 5min. Add the sprouts, ginger, garlic, crushed Sichuan peppercorns and red chilli and stir-fry for 1min.

2. Next add the stock, soy sauce, vinegar and chilli oil and fry for 2min, stirring occasionally, until slightly reduced.

3. Add the noodles and gently toss to soften and heat through. Garnish with the spring onions and serve.

◆ GH TIP
If you have leftover sprouts from another meal, use these and fry them alongside the meat.

Hands-on time: 25min
Cooking time: 15min
Serves 6

PER SERVING 310cals, 31g protein, 7g fat (1g saturates), 29g carbs (4g total sugars), 5g fibre

Sticky Chicken and Pak Choi

One of those recipes that, once tried, you'll turn to time and time again. The sauce is wonderful spooned over rice, too.

8 skin-on chicken pieces, we used thighs and drumsticks
6 baby pak choi
2 tsp sesame seeds
3 spring onions, finely sliced

FOR THE SAUCE
1 tbsp vegetable oil
4 tbsp soy sauce
2 tbsp hoisin sauce
3 tbsp sweet chilli sauce
3 garlic cloves, crushed
5cm piece fresh root ginger, peeled and finely grated
Finely grated zest and juice 1 lime
Cooked basmati rice, to serve (optional)

1. Preheat the oven to 190°C (170°C fan) mark 5. Mix the sauce ingredients in a large roasting tin or ovenproof serving dish. Add the chicken and turn to coat in the sauce. Roast for 15min.

2. Meanwhile, slice the leafy tops off the pak choi and set aside. Slice the cores in half lengthways.

3. Carefully remove the tin/dish from the oven and add the pak choi cores, turning to coat in the sauce. Spoon the sauce over the chicken, then return to the oven for 15min.

4. Nestle the pak choi leaves into the tin/dish, spooning over the sauce, then return to the oven for 5min, until wilted and the chicken is cooked through and the sauce is glossy. Sprinkle over the sesame seeds and spring onions and serve with rice, if you like.

◆ GH TIP
If your sauce is still thin after roasting, strain into a pan and bubble over hob heat for a few min to thicken.

Hands-on time: 15min
Cooking time: about 35min
Serves 4

PER SERVING (without rice) 453cals, 60g protein, 20g fat (4g saturates), 8g carbs (6g total sugars), 3g fibre

Chicken Schnitzel Bagel Burgers

Crunchy, chewy, mustardy... This bagel burger has it all! We've used traditional bagels but try seeded bagels, if you like.

FOR THE RÉMOULADE
300g celeriac, peeled
50g mayonnaise
50g crème fraîche
Finely grated zest and juice ½ lemon
2 tsp wholegrain mustard

FOR THE CHICKEN SCHNITZEL
4 small skinless chicken breasts
25g plain flour
2 medium eggs, beaten
100g fresh white breadcrumbs
Vegetable oil, to fry

TO SERVE
4 bagels, halved
Handful rocket
2 tomatoes, sliced

Hands-on time: 30min
Cooking time: about 12min
Makes 4 burgers

PER BURGER 756cals, 48g protein, 27g fat
(6g saturates), 77g carbs (8g total sugars), 7g fibre

1. To make the rémoulade, cut the celeriac into thin slices, then cut the slices into matchstick-sized pieces. Alternatively, coarsely grate the celeriac. Put into a bowl, then mix in the remaining ingredients and some seasoning. Cover and chill until needed.

2. For the schnitzel, working one chicken breast at a time, slice in half through its depth, but leave one side attached. Open out and put between 2 sheets of baking parchment, then bash with a rolling pin to an even thickness. Repeat with the remaining breasts.

3. Next, put the flour, eggs and breadcrumbs into 3 separate shallow bowls. Mix some seasoning into the flour. Dip the flattened chicken pieces first into the flour to coat and gently tap off the excess. Next, coat them in egg and then finally dip the chicken into the breadcrumbs, pressing them on to cover, if needed.

4. To fry, pour enough oil into a large frying pan so it's 5mm deep. Heat the oil over a medium heat for a few minutes. Add the breaded chicken pieces (in batches if needed) and fry for 3min per side, or until golden and cooked through. Using tongs, transfer to a board lined with kitchen paper. Fry the remaining chicken, monitoring the oil temperature.

5. Meanwhile, toast the bagels and place the bottoms on to 4 plates. Top each with rocket and some tomato slices. Lay on the chicken schnitzels, spoon on some rémoulade and top with the bagel lids. Serve with any remaining rémoulade alongside.

Kadhai Chicken Chargha Spiced Curry

Traditionally a north Indian dish, kadhai chargha is made with marinated pieces of chicken that are fried in whole spices to form a light sauce that coats all the succulent meat. Serve with roti or naan bread and mint chutney.

FOR THE MARINADE
6–8 garlic cloves
1 tsp Kashmiri chilli powder (see GH Tip)
1 tsp ground coriander
½ tsp ground turmeric
½ tsp garam masala
2 tbsp Greek yogurt
900g bone-in, skinless chicken thighs and drumsticks

TO SERVE
3 tbsp vegetable oil
½ tsp cumin seeds
2–3 dried Kashmiri red chillies
4cm piece fresh root ginger, peeled and coarsely grated
1 red chilli, thinly sliced
Handful coriander, finely chopped
Mint raita (optional)

◆ GH TIP
Kashmiri chilli powder has an intense red colour and is less fiery than regular chilli powder. If you can't find it, use paprika.

1. For the marinade, use a pestle and mortar to grind the garlic into a smooth paste. Scrape into a non-metallic bowl and mix in the remaining spices and yogurt. Add the chicken and stir to coat. Cover and chill for 2–3hr, ideally overnight.

2. To serve, heat the oil in a large, heavy-based pan (that has a lid) over medium heat. Add the cumin seeds and dried chillies. Sizzle for 10sec. Tip in the marinated chicken pieces (and any marinade from the bowl) and fry for 5–7min, turning frequently.

3. Turn down the heat to low, season with salt and freshly ground black pepper, then cover and cook for 15min. Stir in the ginger, sliced red chilli and coriander. Re-cover and cook for 5–7min, until the chicken is cooked through.

4. Lift out the chicken on to a board. Turn up the heat under the sauce and bubble hard for 5min to reduce. Check the seasoning. Return the chicken to the pan and turn to coat. Serve with mint raita, if you like.

Hands-on time: 20min, plus (overnight) marinating
Cooking time: about 35min
Serves 4

PER SERVING 444cals, 42g protein, 30g fat (7g saturates), 2g carbs (1g total sugars), <1g fibre

Chermoula Griddled Chicken with Couscous Salad

Chermoula is used here as a marinade for the chicken, but it's also wonderful dolloped on top of veggies or fish.

4 medium skinless chicken breasts
100g couscous
Finely grated zest ½ and juice 1 lemon, keep separate
2 tbsp extra virgin olive oil
2 medium carrots, peeled and coarsely grated
50g pitted green olives
100g rocket

FOR THE CHERMOULA
20g bunch flat-leaf parsley
20g bunch coriander
1 garlic clove, crushed
½ tsp ground cumin
½ tsp paprika
1 tsp Aleppo pepper
½ preserved lemon, deseeded and finely chopped
100ml olive oil
1 tbsp red wine vinegar

FOR THE YOGURT SAUCE
250g Greek-style yogurt
1–2 preserved lemons, to taste, deseeded and finely chopped
2 tsp dried mint

1. For the chermoula, whizz all the ingredients with some seasoning in a food processor until finely chopped. Scrape into a large bowl.

2. Using a sharp knife, slash the top of each chicken breast a few times (to allow the flavours to penetrate). Add to the bowl and rub the chermoula all over the meat and into the slashes. Cook on a hot non-stick griddle pan over a medium heat for 15–20min, turning halfway, until cooked through. Remove to a plate and keep warm.

3. Meanwhile, put the couscous into a large heatproof bowl with the lemon zest, half the lemon juice and 150ml just-boiled water. Cover the bowl and leave to soak for 10min.

4. In a separate bowl, mix all the yogurt sauce ingredients with some seasoning. Fluff up the couscous with a fork, then fork through the olive oil, remaining lemon juice and some seasoning. Add the carrot, olives and rocket, then mix.

5. Spoon the couscous on to a large platter or divide between 4 plates. Serve with the chicken and the yogurt sauce.

Hands-on time: 30min
Cooking time: about 20min
Serves 4

PER SERVING 576cals, 36g protein, 35g fat (9g saturates), 26g carbs (7g total sugars), 5g fibre

Crunchy Peanut Butter Chicken

Firm tofu would work well for a meat-free version of this satay dish. You can also use crunchy peanut butter for extra texture.

1 tbsp sesame oil
4 boneless, skinless chicken thighs (about 300g), cut into strips
2 mixed colour peppers, we used yellow and red, deseeded and finely sliced
2 garlic cloves, crushed
2 tbsp tamarind paste
2 tbsp peanut butter
400ml tin full-fat coconut milk
2 red apples, cored and cut into matchsticks
½ tsp sugar, to taste
1 red chilli, deseeded and finely sliced
2 spring onions, finely sliced
2 tbsp salted peanuts, roughly chopped
Cooked basmati rice, to serve

1. Heat the sesame oil in a large, deep frying pan or wok over a medium-high heat. Cook the chicken and peppers, stirring occasionally, until the chicken is browned all over.

2. Add the garlic, tamarind paste and peanut butter and cook for 2min, until fragrant. Stir through the coconut milk and plenty of seasoning. Bring to the boil, then turn down the heat and simmer for 10min, until slightly reduced and the chicken is cooked through. Stir in the apples and check the seasoning, adding a little sugar, if needed.

3. Garnish with the chilli, spring onions and peanuts, and serve with cooked basmati rice.

Hands-on time: 15min
Cooking time: about 20min
Serves 4

PER SERVING (without rice) 455cals, 22g protein, 31g fat (18g saturates), 20g carbs (16g total sugars), 5g fibre

Chicken, Chorizo and Bean Stew

Chorizo adds great flavour to this hearty stew, but if you're not a fan, use 100g smoked bacon lardons instead.

1 tbsp olive oil
1 fennel bulb (about 275g)
1 large onion, finely sliced
2 skinless chicken breasts (about 250g)
100g chorizo ring, skinned and cut into 5mm-thick slices
400g tin chopped tomatoes
400ml chicken stock
400g haricot beans, drained and rinsed
Finely grated zest and juice ½ lemon
Large handful parsley, roughly chopped

1. Heat the oil in a large, deep frying pan over a low heat. Halve, core and finely slice the fennel (reserve any feathery fronds to garnish). Add the fennel, onion and a large pinch of salt to the pan and cook for 5min, until softened. Add the whole chicken breasts and chorizo slices, then turn up the heat to medium and cook until the chicken is lightly golden (it doesn't need to be cooked through yet).

2. Stir in the tomatoes, stock, and some salt and freshly ground black pepper. Bring to the boil, then simmer over medium heat for 15min, or until the chicken is cooked through.

3. Lift the chicken on to a board and shred using 2 forks. Return to the pan with the haricot beans, lemon zest and juice and most of the parsley. Heat through and check the seasoning. Garnish with the remaining parsley and any reserved fennel fronds. Serve.

◆ GH TIP
For some extra richness, garnish the stew with grated Manchego cheese and serve with crusty bread

Hands-on time: 15min
Cooking time: about 30min
Serves 4

PER SERVING 323cals, 30g protein, 12g fat (4g saturates), 19g carbs (9g total sugars), 9g fibre

Chicken and Pineapple Satay Skewers with Rainbow Salad

Nutty, sweet and oh-so good, we've paired these moreish skewers with a refreshing, crunchy salad.

435g tin pineapple chunks in juice, drained and
  juice reserved
4 tbsp smooth peanut butter
4 skinless chicken breasts, cut into 2.5cm pieces
2 tbsp roasted peanuts, roughly chopped
2 spring onions, finely sliced

FOR THE SALAD
¼ red cabbage, cored
1 carrot
2 small peppers, we used red and yellow
75g sugar snap peas

FOR THE DRESSING
5cm piece fresh root ginger, finely grated
2 garlic cloves, crushed
Juice 1 lime
2 tbsp kicap manis
1 tbsp soy sauce
2 tbsp sweet chilli sauce
2 tsp vegetable oil

YOU'LL ALSO NEED
8 wooden skewers, soaked in water for 30min

1. To make the dressing, whisk all the ingredients together in a large bowl with 2 tbsp reserved pineapple juice. In a separate bowl, mix the peanut butter with 5 tbsp of the dressing, then add the chicken and toss to coat. Whisk 2 tbsp pineapple juice into the remaining dressing and set aside. Preheat the grill to high.

2. Push the chicken and pineapple on to the skewers, alternating them, and put on to a foil-lined baking tray. Brush with any remaining marinade and set aside.

3. To make the salad, finely shred the cabbage and cut the rest of the vegetables into matchsticks.

4. Grill the skewers for 10min, turning halfway, until the chicken is cooked through. Just before serving, add the salad veg to the dressing and toss to coat. Check the seasoning. Serve the skewers sprinkled with peanuts and spring onions and the salad on the side.

Hands-on time: 30min, plus soaking
Cooking time: about 10min
Serves 4

PER SERVING 419cals, 36g protein, 16g fat (4g saturates), 30g carbs (27g total sugars), 5g fibre

Chicken Fajita Bowl with Cauliflower Rice

Serving the spicy chicken with cauliflower rice makes this a low-carb meal, but you could substitute cooked brown basmati rice, if you prefer.

4 medium skinless chicken breasts, cut into
    finger-sized strips
2 mixed colour peppers, deseeded and cut into 1cm strips
1 red onion, cut into 8 wedges through the root
2 tsp hot smoked paprika
1 tsp ground cumin
Juice 2 limes
1 tbsp olive oil
400g cauliflower florets (about 1 medium cauliflower)
Large handful coriander, roughly chopped
4 tbsp guacamole, to serve
4 tbsp reduced-fat soured cream, to serve

1. Mix the chicken, peppers, onion, spices, lime juice and 1 tsp fine salt in a large non-metallic bowl. Cover and chill for at least 30min (or up to 6hr).

2. Brush a large griddle or frying pan with oil and heat over a medium-high heat. Cook the chicken and veg mixture for 8–10min, turning regularly, until the chicken is cooked.

3. Meanwhile, make the cauliflower rice. Whizz the florets in a food processor until they resemble rice. Heat a large frying pan over medium heat. Add the cauliflower and cook for 5min, stirring, until tender and piping hot. Stir through the coriander and plenty of seasoning.

4. Divide the cauliflower rice between 4 bowls, top with the chicken mixture and serve with the guacamole and soured cream.

Hands-on time: 20min, plus marinating
Cooking time: about 15min
Serves 4

PER SERVING 297cals, 32g protein, 12g fat
(3g saturates), 12g carbs (9g total sugars), 5g fibre

Apricot and Sage Stuffed Turkey Breasts

Flavoursome stuffed turkey breast fillets make a nice change from a whole roast bird.

2 tsp vegetable oil
½ onion, finely chopped
40g dried apricots, finely chopped
Small handful sage, leaves picked and roughly chopped
75g fresh breadcrumbs
40g blue cheese, crumbled
1 medium egg, lightly beaten
6 turkey breast fillets (about 750g total)
6 rashers streaky bacon

1. Heat the oil in a medium frying pan over a medium heat and fry the onion for 10min, until softened. Tip into a large bowl and leave to cool.

2. Preheat the oven to 200°C (180°C fan) mark 6. Line a baking tray with baking parchment and set aside. Stir the apricots, sage, breadcrumbs, blue cheese, egg and some seasoning into the cooled onion.

3. Make a deep horizontal slit in the side of each turkey breast fillet, being careful not to go all the way through. Stuff the slits with the apricot and sage mixture.

4. Using the back of a large knife, run along the length of a bacon rasher on a board, stretching it out as long as it will go. Repeat with the remaining rashers. Wrap a rasher around each stuffed turkey breast, then arrange on the lined baking tray.

5. Cook for 20–25min, or until breasts are cooked through. Serve.

◆ GET AHEAD
Prepare to end of step 4 up to 1 day ahead (no need to preheat the oven), then cover and chill. Uncover and complete the recipe to serve.

◆ GH TIP
Use 1 tsp dried sage instead of fresh, if you prefer.

Hands-on time: 20min, plus cooling
Cooking time: about 35min
Serves 6

PER SERVING 311cals, 39g protein, 11g fat (4g saturates), 13g carbs (4g total sugars), 1g fibre

Romesco-style Chicken Traybake

We've used all the flavours of Spanish Romesco, a roasted red pepper and almond sauce, to create this delicious traybake.

2 tbsp olive oil
600g baby new potatoes, halved
4 medium skin-on chicken breasts
1 tbsp plain flour
1 tbsp smoked sweet paprika
2½ tbsp sherry vinegar
2 garlic cloves, crushed
1 tbsp runny honey
150g roasted peppers from a jar (about 3),
    roughly chopped
25g flaked almonds
Large handful parsley, roughly chopped
Bread, to serve (optional)

1. Preheat the oven to 200°C (180°C) mark 6. In a large bowl, mix 1 tbsp of the oil, the potatoes and some seasoning to coat. Empty into a large ovenproof serving dish and roast for 15min.

2. Meanwhile, cut a few slits into the top of each chicken breast, then put into the empty bowl with the remaining 1 tbsp oil, the flour, ½ tbsp paprika and some seasoning. Mix to coat. Add the chicken to the potatoes, skin-side up, and roast for 30min.

3. In a small bowl, mix together the remaining ½ tbsp paprika, the vinegar, garlic, honey and some seasoning. Add the peppers to the roasting tin, drizzle over the vinegar sauce and scatter over the almonds. Return to the oven for 10–15min, until the chicken is cooked through and the potatoes are golden and tender. Sprinkle over the parsley and serve with bread to mop up the juices, if you like.

Hands-on time: 20min
Cooking time: about 1hr
Serves 4

PER SERVING 459cals, 50g protein, 14g fat
(2g saturates), 33g carbs (6g total sugars), 4g fibre

Teriyaki Turkey Balls with Soba Noodles

These Asian-inspired meatballs may become your new favourite way to enjoy turkey mince. Soba is the Japanese name for buckwheat, which gives these noodles their distinctive, nutty flavour.

400g turkey thigh mince
4 tbsp fresh breadcrumbs, white or brown
2 garlic cloves, crushed
1 tbsp vegetable oil
3 tbsp teriyaki sauce
1 tbsp runny honey
2 tsp white sesame seeds
150g soba noodles
150g sugar snap peas, julienned
1 medium carrot, peeled and julienned
Juice ½ lime, plus extra wedges, to serve
Handful coriander leaves

1. Mix the turkey, breadcrumbs, half the garlic and plenty of seasoning in a large bowl. Divide and roll into 20 meatballs (about 20g each).

2. Heat the oil in a large frying pan over a medium-high heat. Add the meatballs and fry, turning regularly, until golden and just cooked through, about 15min. Add the remaining garlic, teriyaki sauce, honey and sesame seeds and bubble until the sauce has reduced and the meatballs are coated.

3. Meanwhile, cook the soba noodles in boiling salted water according to the pack instructions, adding the sugar snaps and carrots for the final 1min of cooking. Drain, then rinse briefly under cold water and drain again. Add the noodle mixture to the meatball pan and toss to coat. Stir in the lime juice, sprinkle with coriander and serve with extra lime wedges for squeezing over.

◆ GH TIP
Although made from buckwheat, many soba noodles do contain some wheat flour – check the brand you choose is gluten-free, if you need it to be.

Hands-on time: 30min
Cooking time: about 20min
Serves 4

PER SERVING 436cals, 38g protein, 12g fat (3g saturates), 42g carbs (12g total sugars), 4g fibre

Zesty Green Chicken Stew

If you can't find fresh tarragon, use 1 tsp dried instead.

1 tbsp olive oil
3 medium skinless chicken breasts, cut into
    finger-sized strips
750ml chicken stock
200g small broccoli florets
2 x 400g tins butter beans, drained and rinsed
200g frozen peas
Finely grated zest 1 lemon
100g half-fat crème fraîche
Small handful tarragon, finely chopped
Crusty bread, to serve (optional)

1. Heat the oil in a large deep frying pan over
   a medium heat and fry the chicken for 3min
   (it doesn't need to be cooked through yet).
   Add the stock and bring to the boil. Add the
   broccoli and simmer for 5min, until the chicken
   is cooked through and the broccoli is tender.

2. Stir through the butter beans and peas and
   bring back to the boil. Add the lemon zest and
   mix through the crème fraîche and tarragon.
   Check the seasoning. Ladle into 4 bowls and
   serve with crusty bread, if you like.

Hands-on time: 15min
Cooking time: about 15min
Serves 4

PER SERVING 363cals, 38g protein, 10g fat (4g saturates),
24g carbs (6g total sugars), 13g fibre

Chicken Molé

A lovely Mexican dish, similar in flavour to a chilli con carne. The small hit of chocolate adds great depth.

1 tbsp sunflower oil
4 chicken thigh fillets
1 onion, finely chopped
¾–1 tbsp ancho or chipotle chilli paste, to taste
1 tsp ground cumin
½ tsp ground cinnamon
400g tin chopped tomatoes
2 x 400g tins kidney beans, drained and rinsed
250g basmati rice
25g dark chocolate (at least 70% cocoa solids), chopped
Green salad, to serve (optional)

1. In a large pan, heat the oil over a high heat and brown the chicken on both sides. Turn down the heat, add the onion and cook for 5min.

2. Stir in the chilli paste and spices, cook for 1min, then add the tomatoes and kidney beans. Bring to a boil, then simmer, covered, for 20min.

3. Meanwhile, cook the rice according to the pack instructions.

4. Lift out the chicken on to a board. Continue cooking the sauce, uncovered, for 5min to reduce. Shred the chicken and stir back into the sauce with the chocolate. Check the seasoning and serve with rice and salad, if you like.

Hands-on time: 20min
Cooking time: about 40min
Serves 4

PER SERVING 612cals, 34g protein, 16g fat (4g saturates), 78g carbs (13g total sugars), 12g fibre

12

Meat

Cannellini Bean and Meatball Stew

This hearty stew is perfect for chilly evenings, and freezes well. You can use all beef mince for the meatballs, if you prefer.

FOR THE MEATBALLS
300g beef mince
100g pork mince
50g fresh breadcrumbs
1 medium egg
2 tsp olive oil

FOR THE STEW
2 tsp olive oil
1 onion, finely chopped
2 celery sticks, finely chopped
1 small carrot, finely chopped
2 garlic cloves, crushed
1 tbsp tomato purée
2 rosemary sprigs, leaves picked and finely chopped
   (or use 2 tsp dried)
400g tin cannellini beans, drained and rinsed
400g tin plum tomatoes
125ml red wine
200ml vegetable stock
Crusty bread to serve (optional)

1. For the meatballs, mix the beef, pork, breadcrumbs and egg in a bowl with some seasoning. Shape into 16 balls. Heat the oil in a large, deep non-stick frying pan or casserole dish over a medium-high heat. Add the meatballs and cook for 5min, until browned all over. Remove to a plate.

2. For the stew, reduce the heat under the pan/casserole to low and add the oil. Stir in the onion, celery and carrot and cook for 5min, until slightly softened. Add the garlic, tomato purée and rosemary, and fry for a couple of minutes. Stir in the beans, tomatoes, wine, stock and plenty of seasoning.

3. Bring to the boil, breaking down the tomatoes with a wooden spoon. Reduce the heat, add the meatballs and bubble gently for 10min, stirring occasionally, until they are cooked through and the sauce has thickened slightly. Check the seasoning and serve with crusty bread, if you like.

Hands-on time: 20min
Cooking time: about 25min
Serves 4

PER SERVING 412cals, 29g protein, 20g fat (7g saturates), 23g carbs (9g total sugars), 7g fibre

Summer Spiced Ham with Pineapple Salsa

A glorious glazed ham makes a super centrepiece, and this tropical take is perfect for sunny days. You can use smoked or unsmoked gammon, but smoked adds an almost barbecued flavour.

3kg boneless smoked/unsmoked gammon
1 onion, sliced
2 bay leaves
1 tsp black peppercorns
2 whole star anise
1 litre fresh pineapple juice (not from concentrate)
3 tbsp dark brown soft sugar
Pinch dried chilli flakes (optional)

FOR THE SALSA
1 medium-sized ripe pineapple
1 red pepper, deseeded and finely chopped
2 spring onions, halved and sliced
1 large red chilli, deseeded and finely chopped
Finely grated zest and juice 1 lime
Handful coriander, roughly chopped

1. Weigh the gammon and calculate the cooking time, allowing 20min per 450g, plus 20min.

2. Put the gammon in a pan (with a lid) just big enough to hold it, and add the onion, bay leaves, peppercorns and star anise. Add 750ml pineapple juice and top up with cold water to cover. Cover with the lid and bring to the boil over a medium-high heat. Reduce the heat and simmer very gently for the calculated cooking time.

3. Remove the ham from the cooking liquid (reserve the liquid) and put on a board. Leave to cool slightly. Preheat the oven to 220°C (200°C fan) mark 7. Meanwhile, put the reserved pineapple juice in a small pan, bring to the boil and bubble until reduced, about 15min.

4. Remove any string from the ham. Using a sharp knife, slice off the skin, leaving a good layer of fat. Score a close diamond pattern into the fat.

5. Line a roasting tin that will just fit the ham with a double layer of foil. Add the ham (fat-side up). Brush the reduced pineapple juice over the meat and into the fat, then sprinkle the fat with the sugar and dried chilli flakes (if using). Add a large mugful of the reserved cooking liquid to the roasting tin. Roast for 25–35min, until an even golden brown.

6. Meanwhile, make the salsa. Slice the skin off the pineapple and use the tip of a knife or vegetable peeler to remove the brown 'eyes'. Cut into quarters vertically and slice out the woody core. Finely dice the flesh. Add to a serving bowl and mix in the remaining salsa ingredients and a generous pinch of salt.

7. Slice the ham and serve with the salsa.

Hands-on time: 25min, plus cooling
Cooking time: about 3hr
Serves 8, with leftovers

PER SERVING (if serving 8) 579cals, 66g protein, 28g fat (9g saturates), 14g carbs (14g total sugars), 1g fibre

◆ GET AHEAD
Poach the gammon 1–2 days ahead, cool
completely in the cooking liquid, then cover
and chill (still in liquid). Bring to room
temperature before completing the recipe
to serve. The finished ham and salsa will keep
well in the fridge for up to 4 days. Bring up to
room temperature before serving.

Crusted Venison with Red Wine and Juniper Gravy

This showstopper looks impressive but is deceptively easy. Ask your butcher to French trim your venison.

---

2 venison racks, about 1.5kg total (French trimmed and fat removed from meat)
150g fresh white breadcrumbs
1 garlic clove, crushed
Large handful parsley, finely chopped
2 tbsp thyme leaves
4 tbsp olive oil, plus 1 tbsp to brush
1 tbsp Dijon mustard

FOR THE GRAVY
1 tbsp olive oil
2 shallots, finely sliced
½ tbsp plain flour
1 garlic clove, bashed
3 thyme sprigs
300ml red wine
10 juniper berries, crushed
300ml beef stock
3 tbsp redcurrant jelly

◆ GET AHEAD
Prepare to the end of step 3 up to 1 day ahead. Cover and chill. To serve, uncover and allow to come to room temperature for 20min, then complete the recipe.

Hands-on time: 45min, plus coming up to room temperature, cooling and resting
Cooking time: about 45min
Serves 6

PER SERVING (with 2 cutlets) 426cals, 40g protein, 14g fat (3g saturates), 25g carbs (7g total sugars), 0g fibre

1. Remove the venison from the fridge and allow it to sit at room temperature for 20min. In a large bowl, mix together the breadcrumbs, garlic, parsley, thyme, oil and some seasoning until combined.

2. Preheat the oven to 200°C (180°C fan) mark 6. Weigh the venison racks separately, then calculate the average weight and work out the cooking time, allowing 20min per 450g for pink meat.

3. Brush the 1 tbsp oil over the meat and season well. Heat a large, non-stick frying pan over a high heat and brown the racks (in batches, if needed) for 3min. Lift into a roasting tin (reserving the pan) and set aside to cool slightly. Brush the venison with the mustard, then press on the breadcrumb mixture to cover the top of the meat.

4. Roast the racks for the calculated cooking time (an average 750g rack should take about 33min). To check whether it's cooked to pink, insert a metal skewer into the centre of the meat and hold it for 5sec – it should come out warm. If not, return the tin to the oven for a further 2min and check again.

5. When cooked, transfer the racks to a board, cover with foil and leave to rest for 20min.

6. Meanwhile, make the gravy. Heat the oil in the reserved frying pan and gently fry the shallots

for 4min, until softened. Stir in the flour, garlic and thyme sprigs and cook for 1min. Mix in the wine and juniper berries, increase the heat to high and simmer for 2min, until reduced by half. Add the stock and redcurrant jelly and simmer until slightly reduced, about 4min. Check the seasoning. Strain into a warmed jug.

7. Transfer the racks to a serving platter and serve with the gravy.

◆ GH TIP
Venison racks are typically sold with 8 bones, so we've kept them whole (rather than trimming to 2 x 6 bone racks). This means some lucky guests will get 3 cutlets each!

Pork Schnitzel on Stroganoff Noodles

You could swap the pork for high-welfare British veal, or butterflied skinless chicken breasts, if you like.

2 pork loin steaks (about 300g), excess fat trimmed
25g plain flour
1 medium egg, beaten
60g dried breadcrumbs
2 tsp sweet smoked paprika
4 tbsp vegetable oil
1 small onion, finely sliced
125g baby chestnut mushrooms, halved
4 tbsp brandy
½ tsp freshly grated nutmeg
100g soured cream
2 tbsp chopped chives, plus extra to garnish
125g tagliatelle
½ lemon, cut into 4 wedges

1. Put the pork steaks on a board and cover with baking parchment. With a rolling pin, carefully flatten them to an even 5mm thickness, then peel off the parchment and pat dry with kitchen paper.

2. Put the flour, egg and breadcrumbs into 3 separate shallow bowls. Season the flour and mix 1 tsp paprika into the breadcrumbs.

3. Coat each pork steak in flour (tap off the excess), then dip into the beaten egg, followed by the breadcrumbs to coat. Transfer to a plate and chill while you make the stroganoff.

4. Heat ½ tbsp of the oil in a large frying pan over a low-medium heat and cook the onion for 8min, until softened. Increase the heat to medium, add another ½ tbsp oil and the mushrooms and cook for 5min, until lightly browned. Add the brandy and remaining 1 tsp paprika and bubble for 30sec, then stir in the nutmeg, soured cream and chives. Check the seasoning, then cover and keep warm.

5. Cook the tagliatelle in a large pan of boiling water for 10min, or according to the pack instructions, until al dente. Meanwhile, heat the remaining 3 tbsp oil in a separate large, non-stick frying pan over a medium heat and fry the coated pork for 5–8min, turning once, or until golden and cooked through.

6. Drain the tagliatelle, reserving a cupful of the cooking water. Add the pasta to the stroganoff sauce with enough of the reserved cooking water to make a silky sauce, tossing to coat. Add a little lemon juice to taste, if needed.

7. Divide the stroganoff between 2 shallow bowls or plates, top each with a schnitzel and garnish with chives. Serve with the remaining lemon wedges for squeezing over.

Hands-on time: 30min
Cooking time: about 25min
Serves 2

PER SERVING 927cals, 45g protein, 41g fat (10g saturates), 75g carbs (7g total sugars), 5g fibre

Côte de Boeuf with Rosemary Salt Fries and Truffle Mayo

Côte de boeuf is the French name for a single bone-in ribeye steak, which makes a superb special occasion meal for two, especially when paired with crispy chips and a rich dip.

4 tbsp vegetable oil
500g large Maris Piper potatoes, unpeeled
1 côte de boeuf (about 700–800g)
25g butter
2 rosemary sprigs, plus 2 tsp finely chopped leaves
1–2 tsp coarse sea salt, to taste
1–2 tbsp truffle oil
3 tbsp thick mayonnaise

1. Preheat the oven to 220°C (200°C fan) mark 7. Bring a medium pan of salted water to the boil. Line the base of a large roasting tin with baking parchment (to stop the chips sticking) and add 3½ tbsp of the oil. Heat in the oven for 10min.

2. Slice the potatoes into 1cm-wide chips. Parboil for 4min, then drain well and leave to steam dry for a couple of minutes. Carefully add the chips to the hot oil, turning to coat. Cook in the oven on the top shelf for 45–50min, turning halfway through, or until golden and crisp.

3. Meanwhile, pat dry the beef with kitchen paper and season lightly with salt. Heat the remaining ½ tbsp oil in an ovenproof frying pan over a high heat and brown the beef all over. Add the butter, rosemary sprigs and some freshly ground black pepper.

4. Spoon the melting butter over the steak, then transfer to the bottom shelf of the oven and cook for 15–20min, basting occasionally, for medium-rare – a digital thermometer should read 55°C when inserted into the thickest part of the steak. Remove from the oven, cover loosely with foil and leave to rest in a warm place for 10min.

5. Using a pestle and mortar, bash the sea salt and chopped rosemary until fairly finely ground. Set aside. In a small bowl, whisk the truffle oil into the mayonnaise.

6. Toss the rosemary salt into the cooked chips. Serve with the steak and truffle mayo.

Hands-on time: 25min, plus cooling and resting
Cooking time: about 55min
Serves 2

**PER SERVING 1,060cals, 74g protein, 63g fat
(13g saturates), 47g carbs (3g total sugars), 5g fibre**

Pork Tacos

A speedy supper that's on the table in less than 30 minutes. Swap the pork mince for beef and use a ready-made spice mix in place of the individual herbs and spices, if you like – look for ones labelled taco or fajita seasoning.

1 tbsp olive oil
500g pork mince
2 garlic cloves, crushed
1 tbsp dried oregano
1 tbsp ground cumin
½ tbsp sweet smoked paprika
1 tsp dried chilli flakes

FOR THE SALSA
1 red onion, finely chopped
1 red chilli, deseeded and finely chopped
4 large ripe tomatoes, chopped
Juice 1 lime

TO SERVE
8 hard taco shells
125g Cheddar, coarsely grated
4tbsp soured cream
Large handful coriander, roughly chopped

1. Mix all the salsa ingredients with some seasoning in a bowl. Set aside. Warm the taco shells according to the pack instructions.

2. Heat the oil in a large frying pan over high heat and cook the mince, stirring to break up any clumps, until browned all over. Turn down the heat to medium and stir through the garlic, oregano, spices and plenty of seasoning. Cook for 2min. Add the salsa and cook for 2min, until the tomatoes have broken down a little and the pork is cooked through.

3. Spoon the pork mixture into the taco shells and top with the Cheddar, soured cream and chopped coriander. Serve.

Hands-on time: 10min
Cooking time: about 10min
Serves 4

PER SERVING 554cals, 35g protein, 36g fat (14g saturates), 22g carbs (6g total sugars), 3g fibre

Lemongrass Pork Meatball Banh Mi

Originating in the streets of Saigon, this French-Vietnamese street-food favourite elevates the humble sandwich to new heights.

FOR THE PICKLES
1½ tbsp rice wine vinegar
1 tsp caster sugar
1 small carrot, peeled and cut into matchsticks
5cm daikon or mooli, peeled and cut into matchsticks

FOR THE PORK MEATBALLS
Small handful coriander, stalks and leaves separated
½ lemongrass stick, finely chopped
1 garlic clove
½ tbsp fish sauce
1 tsp runny honey
½ tbsp soy sauce
150g pork mince (5% fat)
½ tbsp vegetable oil

TO SERVE
1 medium baguette
2 tbsp Brussels pâté (optional)
1 tbsp mayonnaise
Sriracha hot sauce (optional)

1. Start by making the lightly pickled vegetables. Mix the vinegar, sugar and a large pinch of salt in a medium bowl to dissolve the sugar. Add the carrot and daikon, stir to coat, then set aside.

2. For the pork meatballs, finely chop the coriander stalks and bash to a paste with the lemongrass and garlic using a pestle and mortar. Scrape into a bowl and mix in the remaining meatball ingredients, apart from the oil, until well combined. Shape into 8 meatballs.

3. Heat the oil in a medium non-stick frying pan over a low-medium heat. Add the meatballs and fry, turning frequently, until deeply golden and cooked through, about 12–15min.

4. To serve, cut the baguette in half lengthways and spread over the pâté, if using, followed by the mayonnaise. Drain the vegetables, then load on to the bread and top with the meatballs. Scatter over the coriander leaves and drizzle with sriracha, if you like. Halve and serve.

Hands-on time: 30min
Cooking time: about 15min
Serves 2

PER SERVING 426cals, 25g protein, 18g fat (3g saturates), 40g carbs (8g total sugars), 3g fibre

Beef Massaman Curry

This mild curry is a delicious balance of sweet, savoury and spice flavours.

400ml tin coconut milk
4 tbsp Massaman curry paste
600g beef chuck steak or boneless shin, trimmed and cut into large chunks (see GH Tip)
500g new potatoes, quartered
2 small onions, roughly chopped
1 bay leaf
1 cinnamon stick
1 tbsp palm sugar or demerara sugar
1 tbsp tamarind paste
1 tbsp fish sauce
50g roasted salted peanuts
200g sticky rice
Large handful Thai basil, torn if large, to serve
Lime wedges, to serve

◆ GET AHEAD

Prepare the curry to the end of step 2 up to a day ahead, then cool, cover and chill. To serve, reheat gently until piping hot, adding a splash of water if needed. Complete the recipe to serve.

◆ GH TIP

Beef chuck from the shoulder, or shin are both well-marbled cuts of meat, resulting in a tastier curry. Avoid pre-diced lean casserole meat for this recipe, which can be dry.

1. Heat a large pan over a medium heat. Add 2 tbsp coconut milk and the curry paste and fry for 1min. Add the beef and fry until browned all over, about 5min.

2. Stir in the remaining coconut milk, and the potatoes, onions, bay leaf, cinnamon stick, sugar, tamarind paste, fish sauce, peanuts and 300ml just-boiled water from a kettle. Bring to the boil, then reduce the heat slightly and bubble gently for 45min, until the beef is almost tender and the sauce has reduced by at least half. Cover with a lid and cook on a low heat for 20–30min, or until the beef is just tender, stirring regularly to prevent the sauce from sticking to the bottom of the pan.

3. When the curry has about 20min left to cook, wash the rice well in a bowl of cold water, rubbing the grains together with the palms of your hands as if polishing them. Drain away any cloudy water and repeat until water remains clear. Put the rice in a medium pan with 300ml water and bring to the boil over a medium-high heat. Cover, reduce the heat and simmer gently for 10–15min, until the water is absorbed and the rice is tender.

4. Check the curry seasoning, and remove the cinnamon stick and bay leaf. Garnish with Thai basil and serve with the rice and lime wedges.

Hands-on time: 20min
Cooking time: about 1hr 25min
Serves 4

PER SERVING 840cals, 41g protein, 41g fat (22g saturates), 74g carbs (12g total sugars), 5g fibre

Beef Burritos

A tasty alternative to fajitas that the whole family will enjoy.

FOR THE REFRIED BEANS
25g butter
1 small onion, finely chopped
2 x 400g tins kidney beans, drained and rinsed
1 tsp ground cumin
1-2 red chillies, deseeded and finely chopped
3 tbsp soured cream
Finely grated zest and juice ½ lemon

FOR THE FILLING
1 tbsp vegetable oil
1 onion, finely chopped
2 garlic cloves, crushed
400g lean beef steak mince
1 red pepper, deseeded and sliced
2 tsp smoked paprika, sweet or hot
2 tsp ground coriander
2 tbsp tomato purée
250g microwave pack basmati rice
195g tin sweetcorn, drained

TO SERVE
4 large flour tortillas
Guacamole
Soured cream
Cheddar cheese, grated

1. Heat the butter in a medium pan over a low heat and gently fry the onion for 15min, until completely softened. Meanwhile, whizz the kidney beans and 200ml water in a food processor until smooth.

2. Add the cumin and chillies to the onion and fry for 1min, then scrape in the bean mixture. Simmer for 15min, stirring occasionally, until thickened. Stir in the soured cream, lemon zest and juice, and check the seasoning.

3. Meanwhile, make the filling: heat the oil in a large pan over a medium heat, then fry onion for 10min, until softened. Add the garlic and fry for 1min. Add the beef mince and fry, stirring to break up the mince, until well browned.

4. Add the pepper, paprika, coriander, tomato purée and plenty of seasoning to the mince. Fry for a few minutes until the pepper is just tender, then stir in the rice, sweetcorn and a splash of water. Heat through, breaking up the rice. Check the seasoning.

5. To serve, warm the tortillas according to the pack instructions. Spread a large spoonful of the beans on to a tortilla, then top with a quarter of the mince mixture and some guacamole, soured cream and grated cheese. Roll up and enjoy!

Hands-on time: 25min
Cooking time: about 35min
Serves 4

PER SERVING (without guacamole, soured cream or cheese) 635cals, 38g protein, 19g fat (9g saturates), 69g carbs (10g total sugars), 16g fibre

Green Bean and Pork Sichuan Stir-fry

Frying the beans first gives an authentic texture to this dish. Sichuan pepper has a fascinating hot and numbing aromatic flavour that is positively addictive.

300g green beans, trimmed
2 tbsp vegetable oil
4 spring onions, chopped
2 garlic cloves, crushed
½–1 tsp dried chilli flakes
1½–2 tsp Sichuan peppercorns, lightly crushed
400g pork mince
100g pak choi or tat soi, stalks shredded, leaves
   roughly chopped
1 tbsp sugar
2 tbsp soy sauce
Rice or noodles, to serve

1. Slice the beans in half to make shorter lengths. Heat 1½ tbsp of the oil in a large wok or deep frying pan over a high heat. Add the beans and fry, stirring occasionally, for 4–5min, until slightly browned and blistered. Remove to a plate with a slotted spoon.

2. Add the remaining ½ tbsp oil to the wok/pan. Fry the spring onions, garlic, chilli flakes and crushed peppercorns for 30sec, stirring. Add the pork and stir fry until opaque.

3. Return the beans to the wok/pan with the pak choi/tat soi, sugar and soy sauce. Stir-fry for 2–3min, until the vegetables are just tender. Serve with rice or noodles.

Hands-on time: 15min
Cooking time: about 15min
Serves 4

PER SERVING 264cals, 21g protein, 16g fat (4g saturates), 8g carbs (7g total sugars), 3g fibre

Crispy Pistou-stuffed Rack of Pork

Pistou is a herby Provençal sauce often served on top of a bean soup, but we've stuffed ours inside a crispy pork rack.

100g seeded bread, roughly chopped
3 garlic cloves
125g basil, leaves and stalks
125ml extra virgin olive oil
1 tsp flaked sea salt, plus extra to sprinkle
2kg pork rack (ask your butcher to score the rind)

1. Preheat the oven to 220°C (200°C fan) mark 7. In the small bowl of a food processor, whizz the bread to crumbs, then tip into a bowl. Next, whizz the garlic, basil, oil and salt to a chunky consistency. Scrape into the breadcrumb bowl with some freshly ground black pepper and mix.

2. Make a 'flap' along the length of the pork joint by partially cutting the skin and fat away from the meat, leaving it attached at the bottom. Press the pistou mixture beneath the flap, then tie the flap back in place along the length of the joint with kitchen string. Weigh the joint and calculate the cooking time, allowing 25min per 450g. Sit the pork in a roasting tin that will just hold it.

3. Season the skin with flaked sea salt and roast for the calculated time, turning down the oven to 180°C (160°C fan) mark 4 after the first 40min. If the stuffing is getting too dark, cover it with a strip of foil. A meat thermometer inserted into the centre of the meat should read at least 70°C.

4. Transfer the pork to a board, cover loosely with foil and leave to rest in a warm place for 30–45min. Serve in slices.

◆ GET AHEAD
Prepare to end of step 2 up to 1 day ahead (don't preheat the oven). Cover and chill. To serve, dry the skin with kitchen paper and complete recipe.

◆ GH TIP
Seeded bread gives the stuffing a little crunch, but swap it for wholemeal or sourdough, if you prefer.

Hands-on time: 25min, plus resting
Cooking time: about 1hr 55min
Serves 8

PER SERVING 547cals, 49g protein, 35g fat (11g saturates), 8g carbs (1g total sugars), 1g fibre

Stuffed and Rolled Pork with Gravy

Pork fillet is still economical and, when paired with flavour-boosting ingredients, definitely impresses.

2 x 450g pork loin fillets
12 rashers streaky bacon
1 tbsp vegetable oil

FOR THE STUFFING
1 tbsp vegetable oil
1 onion, finely chopped
1 small eating apple, peeled, cored and finely chopped
2 tsp dried sage
40g fresh white breadcrumbs
1 medium egg

FOR THE GRAVY
500ml chicken stock
2 tbsp plain flour
75ml white wine

◆ GET AHEAD
Prepare to the end of step 4 up to 3hr ahead. Cover and chill. Complete the recipe to serve.

◆ GH TIP
Swap the white wine for a fruity cider to echo the apple flavour of the stuffing, if you prefer.

1. Start by making the stuffing: heat the oil in a medium frying pan and gently cook the onion for 8min, stirring occasionally, until softened. Stir in the apple, sage and some seasoning and cook for a few min. Set aside to cool.

2. Preheat the oven to 220°C (200°C fan) mark 7. To butterfly the pork, position one fillet in front of you on a chopping board. Holding a knife parallel to the board, make a horizontal cut along the length of the fillet about 1cm up from board; stop cutting just before you reach the opposite edge of the pork, so the pork remains in one piece. Open out the fillet and make further slices to flatten it out and create as large a rectangle as possible with an even thickness. Repeat with the second fillet.

3. Lay 6 rashers of bacon side by side on the board, with about 1cm space between the slices. Lay a pork fillet cut-side up on top of the bacon with the long side running across the strips (adjust the bacon rashers, if needed).

4. Mix the breadcrumbs and egg into the cooled onion mixture. Top the pork on the bacon with half the stuffing, spreading to level. Starting from one of the long edges, roll up the fillet (leave the bacon where it is), then move the rolled fillet to the base of the bacon strips and wrap them around the loin, stretching them a little as you go. Secure in place with pieces of kitchen string. Repeat with the remaining bacon, pork loin and stuffing.

5. Heat the oil in a large frying pan over a medium-high heat. Brown the fillets on all sides, then lift out on to a baking tray, setting the pan aside to make gravy later. Continue cooking the fillets in the oven for 25–30min or until cooked through.

Hands-on time: 50min, plus cooling
Cooking time: about 55min
Serves 6

PER SERVING 439cals, 51g protein, 20g fat (6g saturates), 11g carbs (4g total sugars), 1g fibre

6. When cooked, lift the fillets on to a board and cover loosely with foil. Discard the excess fat from the baking tray, then add a splash of water and, using a wooden spatula, scrape up all the flavoursome cooked brown bits from the base. Empty into a jug and add the stock.

7. To make the gravy, return the frying pan to a medium heat and add the flour. Cook, stirring, for 1min. Gradually add the wine, followed by the stock, then return to medium hob heat, stirring constantly, until thickened. Check the seasoning and strain through a fine sieve into a jug.

8. Remove the string from the pork and cut into thick slices. Serve with the gravy.

Lamb Korma

Using shop-bought paste means this curry comes together quickly. Lamb neck fillet is tender, so doesn't need long to cook, but you can swap it for chicken breast, if you like.

1 tbsp vegetable oil
1 large onion, finely sliced
350g lamb neck fillet, cut into 2cm chunks
4 tbsp korma spice paste
6 tomatoes, roughly chopped
50g ground almonds
250g natural yogurt, plus extra to drizzle
Large handful coriander, roughly chopped
Small handful toasted flaked almonds (optional)
Rice or naan bread, to serve

1. Heat the oil in a large pan over a medium-high heat, then cook the onion for 10min, until softened. Add the lamb and cook for 10min, stirring occasionally, until cooked through.

2. Stir in the spice paste, tomatoes and plenty of seasoning and cook, stirring occasionally, until the tomatoes have broken down.

3. Add the ground almonds and yogurt and cook for 2min, thinning with a little water if needed. Check the seasoning and garnish with a drizzle of yogurt, the coriander and a sprinkle of toasted flaked almonds, if you like. Serve with rice or naan bread.

◆ GET AHEAD
Prepare to end of step 2 up to a day ahead, then cool, cover and chill. To serve, reheat until piping hot and complete the recipe.

Hands-on time: 20min
Cooking time: about 30min
Serves 4

PER SERVING (including almonds) 401cals, 26g protein, 28g fat (8g saturates), 11g carbs 9g total sugars), 3g fibre

Sausage, Bean and Kale One-pot

Using one pan for this dish saves on washing-up, and the delicious meaty flavours from frying the sausages enrich the broth of this light but hearty stew.

1 tbsp olive oil
8 pork sausages
1 large red onion, chopped
2 garlic cloves, crushed
3 rosemary sprigs, leaves picked and finely chopped
800ml chicken stock
4 ripe tomatoes (about 400g), roughly chopped
400g tin cannellini beans, drained and rinsed
200g shredded kale, woody stalks discarded
40g Parmesan, finely grated

1. Heat the oil in a large pan over a medium heat and fry the sausages for 6–8min, until browned. Add the onion and a pinch of salt, then turn down the heat a little and fry for 5–7min, until the onion has softened. Add the garlic and rosemary and fry for 1min.

2. Pour in the stock and bring to the boil. Add the tomatoes, then turn up the heat to medium and simmer for 10min, or until the sausages are cooked through, adding the beans and kale for the final 3min.

3. Stir through half the Parmesan and season (it can take plenty of freshly ground black pepper). Serve sprinkled with the remaining Parmesan.

◆ GH TIP
Swap the rosemary for any woody herb that you prefer – thyme or sage would both work well.

Hands-on time: 15min
Cooking time: about 30min
Serves 4

PER SERVING 561cals, 29g protein, 36g fat (13g saturates), 25g carbs (9g total sugars), 12g fibre

Miso Pork Meatballs with Kale Crisps and Butter Bean Mash

Miso paste adds umami and depth to these meatballs, which are served with a smooth mash and crispy kale.

FOR THE MEATBALLS
4 spring onions, finely chopped
2 garlic cloves, crushed
3cm piece fresh root ginger, peeled and grated
2 tbsp white miso paste
400g lean pork mince
2 tsp vegetable oil
2 tbsp soy sauce
1 tbsp runny honey

FOR THE MASH
3 x 400g tins butter beans, drained and rinsed
Juice ½ lemon

FOR THE KALE
150g bag sliced kale, woody stems removed
2 tsp oil

Hands-on time: 25min
Cooking time: about 25min
Serves 4

PER SERVING 410cals, 33g protein, 15g fat (4g saturates), 30g carbs (7g total sugars), 13g fibre

1. Preheat the oven to 180°C (160°C fan) mark 4. For the meatballs, mix most of the spring onions (reserving some for garnish), the garlic, ginger, miso paste and pork in a bowl with some seasoning. Shape into 16 balls and put on a baking tray lined with baking parchment.

2. Next, mix the kale in a bowl with the 2 tsp oil, then spread on to a baking tray and cook in the oven for 10min, until crisp and lightly golden.

3. Meanwhile, heat the oil for the meatballs in a large frying pan over a medium-high heat. Fry the meatballs for 10–15min, turning frequently, until golden and just cooked through. Add the soy sauce, honey and 2 tbsp water and bubble for 2min, until the meatballs are coated in the sticky glaze.

4. Meanwhile, make the mash. Bring 300ml water to the boil in a large pan and add the beans. Simmer for 5min, then mash with a potato masher. Mix in the lemon juice and plenty of seasoning, and loosen with some just-boiled water, if needed.

5. To serve, divide the mash between 4 bowls and top with the kale. Add the meatballs, drizzle over any remaining pan sauce and scatter over the remaining spring onions.

Beef Bulgogi Bibimbap

There is so much flavour in this bowl that it's worth the time it takes to make and assemble. Use pork fillet in place of the beef, if you like.

250–300g sirloin steak, fat discarded, thinly sliced (see GH Tip)
2 tbsp gochujang chilli paste
2½ tbsp soy sauce
5 tsp sesame oil
400g mixed stir-fry vegetables
4cm piece fresh root ginger, peeled and grated
2 x 250g microwave packs brown basmati rice
4 medium eggs
3 spring onions, thinly sliced
1 tsp black or white sesame seeds, or a mix
Kimchi, to serve

◆ GH TIP
Freeze the steaks (in their packaging) for 10min to make them easier to slice thinly.

1. Mix the beef, gochujang and 2 tbsp of the soy sauce in a non-metallic bowl. Cover and chill for at least 10min (or up to 12hr). Preheat the oven to 200°C (180°C fan) mark 6.

2. Heat 1 tsp sesame oil in a large non-stick frying pan (one that has a lid) over high heat. Add the vegetables and stir-fry for 1min, then add a splash of water, cover with the lid and cook for 3–4 min, until just tender. Remove to a plate, dress with ½ tbsp soy sauce, then cover and keep warm.

3. Add 2 tsp of the oil to the empty pan and stir-fry the ginger for 1 min until aromatic. Add the rice, stirring to break up any clumps, and fry for 3–4min until piping hot. Transfer to a baking tray and put in the oven to keep warm and crisp up while you cook the beef.

4. Add 1 tsp more sesame oil to the frying pan and stir-fry the beef for 2–3min. Transfer to a clean bowl, cover and keep warm.

5. Wipe the pan clean with kitchen paper. Add the remaining 1 tsp oil and fry the eggs until crisp on the bottom and just set on top, about 4 min. Divide the rice between 4 bowls and top with the vegetables, beef and fried eggs. Garnish with spring onions and sesame seeds. Serve each bowl with a spoonful of kimchi.

Hands-on time: 30min, plus chilling
Cooking time: about 30min
Serves 4

PER SERVING 467cals, 29g protein, 17g fat (4g saturates), 48g carbs (6g total sugars), 3g fibre

Red Pepper and Lamb Lahmacun

A little lamb mince goes a long way in these crisp and easy flatbreads, inspired by Turkey's answer to the pizza.

FOR THE DOUGH
2 tsp runny honey
2 tbsp olive oil
325g plain flour, plus extra to dust
7g sachet fast-action dried yeast

FOR THE TOPPING
250g lamb mince (10% fat)
150g roasted red peppers from a jar (drained weight), finely chopped
2 garlic cloves, crushed
2 tsp ground cumin
Handful coriander or parsley, roughly chopped

FOR THE SALAD
½ cucumber, deseeded and finely chopped
4 tbsp pomegranate seeds
1 tbsp cider or white wine vinegar
1 medium raw beetroot (about 125g), peeled and cut into matchsticks

Hands-on time: 40min, plus rising
Cooking time: about 15min
Serves 4

PER SERVING 496cals, 21g protein, 13g fat (4g saturates), 71g carbs (7g total sugars), 5g fibre

1. First, prepare the dough. In a jug, mix the honey with 200ml tepid water to dissolve, then add the oil. In a large bowl, mix the flour, yeast and 1 tsp fine salt. Add the honey-water and mix to bring the dough together. Empty on to a lightly floured work surface and knead for 5–10min, until smooth and elastic. Return to the bowl, cover with cling film and leave to rise in a warm place for 1hr, or until well risen.

2. Meanwhile, make the topping. Mix the lamb mince, peppers, garlic, cumin and coriander/parsley in a bowl with plenty of seasoning. Cover and chill until needed.

3. Preheat the oven to 240°C (220°C fan) mark 9 and put in 2 large baking sheets to heat up. Turn out the dough and knead briefly to knock out the air. Divide into 4. Roll out each piece on a lightly floured surface to a rough 30 x 15cm oval. Lay out 2 large sheets of baking parchment and put 2 bases on each. Spread the lamb mixture on to the dough in a thin layer, going all the way to the edges.

4. Carefully remove a baking sheet from the oven and slide 2 lahmacun on to it (still on the parchment). Repeat with the other baking sheet. Cook in the oven for 15min, or until crisp.

5. Meanwhile, toss the cucumber and pomegranate seeds in a bowl with the vinegar and a pinch of salt. Pat dry the shredded beetroot on kitchen paper, then mix gently into the cucumber mixture. Remove the lahmacun from the oven and transfer to plates or boards. Serve with the salad.

Tandoori Roast Lamb with Couscous Pilaf

This Indian-inspired twist on roast lamb comes with a side dish of couscous, roasted under the meat to soak up all the juices.

FOR THE LAMB
2 onions
40g fresh root ginger, peeled
4 garlic clove
Finely grated zest and juice 1 lemon (keep separate)
4 tbsp tandoori spice mix
250g Greek-style yogurt
1 tbsp sugar
2kg whole lamb leg on the bone
200g couscous
300–400ml hot vegetable stock

FOR THE YOGURT DRIZZLE
Large handful coriander leaves
200g Greek-style yogurt
Juice 1 lemon

1. For the lamb, roughly chop one of the onions, then whizz to a paste in the small bowl of a food processor with the ginger and garlic. Scrape into a bowl and mix in the lemon zest, tandoori spice mix, yogurt, sugar and a generous pinch of salt. Thinly slice the remaining onion and scatter in the base of a roasting tin that just fits the lamb.

2. Pat dry the lamb with kitchen paper and make 20 or so deep cuts all over the meat with the point of a sharp knife. Put the lamb in the roasting tin. Use a teaspoon (or your finger) to push the yogurt mixture into the cuts, then smear the rest all over the leg. If you have time, cover the lamb and marinate in the fridge for at least 8hr (up to 24hr).

3. Preheat the oven to 200°C (180°C fan) mark 6. Drizzle the lemon juice over the lamb. Cover the tin with foil and roast for 1hr 30min for medium-rare (cook for longer/shorter as you prefer). After 45min, carefully remove the tin from the oven and remove the foil. Spoon any marinade from the tin back over the lamb. Sprinkle the couscous around the lamb and stir it gently into the juices. Add enough stock so the couscous is just covered, then return to the oven (uncovered) for the remaining cooking time.

4. Lift the lamb on to a board, loosely cover with foil and leave to rest in a warm place for 30–45min. Mix the couscous gently with a fork to coat in all the juices in the tin. Cover the tin with foil and set aside.

5. For the yogurt drizzle, finely chop half the coriander leaves and mix with the yogurt, lemon juice and some seasoning. Thin with a little water if needed. Spoon the couscous on to a large serving platter, set the rested lamb on top and scatter over the remaining coriander. Serve in slices with the drizzle.

Hands-on time: 25min, plus (optional) marinating and resting
Cooking time: about 1hr 30min
Serves 8

PER SERVING 609cals, 45g protein, 35g fat (13g saturates), 29g carbs (8g total sugars), 3g fibre

Fish & Seafood

Piri Piri Salmon with Herby Rice

Swap the salmon for another type of fish, if you like – cod loins or tuna steaks work particularly well.

225g white basmati and wild rice mix
350ml vegetable stock
1 garlic clove, crushed
1 tbsp sweet smoked paprika
1 tsp mild chilli powder
½ tsp ground cumin
½ tsp dried chilli flakes
½ tsp each dried oregano and dried thyme
2 tbsp olive oil
4 skinless salmon fillets (about 120g each)
Finely grated zest and juice 1 lime
Large handful coriander, roughly chopped

FOR THE SLAW
½ red cabbage, cored and finely shredded
½ red onion, finely sliced
2 tbsp Dijon mustard
250g natural yogurt
Juice 2 limes

1. Preheat the oven to 200°C (180°C fan) mark 6. Rinse the rice under cold water, then drain. Add to a medium pan with the stock and simmer over a medium heat. Stir, then cover with a lid. Reduce the heat to low and cook for 17min. Remove from heat and set aside, with the lid on.

2. Meanwhile, mix the garlic, spices, dried herbs, oil and seasoning in a bowl. Put the salmon on a baking tray lined with baking parchment. Brush with the spice mix. Oven roast for 15min, or until the salmon flakes when pressed.

3. Meanwhile, mix together all the slaw ingredients and season well.

4. Uncover the rice, sprinkle over the lime zest, juice and coriander and fork through to mix. Divide among 4 plates and serve with the salmon and slaw.

Hands-on time: 10min
Cooking time: about 20min
Serves 4

PER SERVING 553cals, 36g protein, 20g fat (4g saturates), 56g carbs (10g total sugars), 4g fibre

Fragrant Fish Tagine

Harissa is a great flavour booster to keep in the fridge and gives extra punch to this spicy one-pan baked fish dish.

1 large onion, finely sliced
2 yellow peppers, deseeded and roughly chopped
2 tbsp olive oil
500ml fish stock
Pinch saffron (optional)
1½ tsp ground cinnamon
2 tsp ground cumin
1 tbsp harissa paste
Finely grated zest and juice 1 orange
400g tin chopped tomatoes
175g couscous
100g pitted green olives
300g chunky white fish fillets or loins, skin
    removed (see GH Tip)
Large handful parsley, roughly chopped
25g flaked almonds, toasted, to serve

1. Preheat the oven to 180°C (160°C fan) mark 4. Mix the onion, peppers and oil in a large roasting tin or ovenproof serving dish with a large pinch of salt. Cook in the oven for 20min, stirring midway, until softened and beginning to brown.

2. Meanwhile, in a large jug, mix the stock, saffron (if using), spices, harissa, orange zest and juice with some seasoning.

3. Remove the tin/dish from the oven and stir in the stock and tomatoes. Return to the oven for 20min.

4. Mix in the couscous and olives, nestle in the fish, cover with foil and return to the oven for 15min.

5. Roughly flake the fish and check the seasoning, then garnish with parsley and almonds and serve.

◆ GH TIP
Frozen fish fillets would work well here (cook from frozen), but choose chunky ones to avoid overcooking.

Hands-on time: 20min
Cooking time: about 55min
Serves 4

PER SERVING 417cals, 24g protein, 14g fat
(2g saturates), 45g carbs (12g total sugars), 7g fibre

Shallot, Cider and Tarragon Mussels with Garlic Bread

Sustainable, seasonal (when there's an 'R' in the month) and great value, mussels make a delicious midweek meal. Try this with clams for an elegant dinner-party starter, too.

2kg prepared mussels
25g garlic butter, plus extra to serve
1 tbsp olive oil
3 large shallots, finely sliced
500ml dry cider
200ml vegetable or fish stock
Handful tarragon leaves, chopped
Crusty bread, toasted, to serve

1. Sort through the mussels to remove any open ones, clean under running water and remove any barnacles and beards with a cutlery knife. Firmly tap any open mussels – if they close, they are fine to use, but discard any that remain open.

2. Melt the garlic butter and oil in a very large pan with a tight-fitting lid over a medium heat. Add the shallots and cook for 10min, until soft.

3. Increase the heat, pour in the cider and stock, then cover and bring to the boil. Tip in the mussels and cover again. Simmer for 5min, shaking occasionally, until the mussels have fully opened (discard any that remain closed).

4. Stir through most of the tarragon and divide the mussels among 4 bowls, then sprinkle over the remaining tarragon. Serve with toasted bread spread with garlic butter.

Hands-on time: 5min
Cooking time: 15min
Serves 4

PER SERVING 501cals, 61g protein, 22g fat (9g saturates), 5g carbs (5g total sugars), 1g fibre

Cod and Lentils

If you can't find tinned beluga lentils, use Puy lentils instead. Similarly, you can use regular cauliflower florets if the sweet-stemmed version is elusive.

2 x 400g tins beluga lentils, drained and rinsed
200g cherry tomatoes, halved
3 spring onions, thinly sliced
160g pack sweet-stemmed cauliflower, trimmed
75g pitted green olives
1 tbsp wholegrain mustard
100ml fish stock
½ lemon, thinly sliced (seeds discarded)
1 tbsp olive oil
1 tsp butter
4 skin-on cod fillets (about 125g each)
Small handful parsley, roughly chopped

1. Preheat the oven to 200°C (180°C fan) mark 6. Empty the lentils into a large ovenproof serving dish or roasting tin and mix through tomatoes, spring onions, cauliflower, olives, mustard, fish stock and seasoning. Lay on the lemon slices and cook in oven for 20min.

2. Meanwhile, heat the oil and butter in a large non-stick frying pan until foaming. Pat dry the fish skin with kitchen paper, then fry skin-side down for 5min until crisp. Carefully set the fish on top of the lentils, skin-side up, and cook for 5min more, until the fish is cooked and flakes when pressed. Scatter over the parsley and serve.

◆ GH TIP
If you prefer skinless cod fillets, cook the fish in the oven for just 10min.

Hands-on time: 15min
Cooking time: about 25min
Serves 4

PER SERVING 304cals, 32g protein, 8g fat (2g saturates), 21g carbs (3g total sugars), 12g fibre

Prawn and Courgette Curry with Roasted Cauliflower

This dairy-free, soupy curry cooks while the cauliflower roasts. Use broccoli instead of cauliflower, if you prefer.

FOR THE ROASTED CAULIFLOWER
2 tbsp vegetable oil
2 tsp korma curry paste
½ tsp ground turmeric
1 tsp black onion seeds
Finely grated zest and juice 1 lime, keep separate
600g small-medium cauliflower florets

FOR THE CURRY
1 tbsp vegetable oil
1 large onion, finely sliced
5cm piece fresh root ginger, peeled and finely grated
3 tbsp korma curry paste
1 tsp cumin seeds
300g baby new potatoes, halved
400g tin full-fat coconut milk
500g courgettes, trimmed and roughly chopped
300g frozen raw peeled king prawns
Large handful coriander, roughly chopped

1. Preheat the oven to 200°C (180°C fan) mark 6. For the cauliflower, mix the oil, curry paste, turmeric, onion seeds, lime zest and some seasoning in a bowl. Add the cauliflower and mix to coat.

2. Tip the cauliflower mixture into a roasting tin, cover with foil and roast for 30min. Uncover, squeeze over the lime juice and return to the oven for 10min, or until tender and beginning to char slightly around the edges.

3. Meanwhile, make the curry. Heat the oil in a large, shallow casserole dish or deep frying pan. Cook the onion and a pinch of salt for 10min, until softened. Stir in the ginger, curry paste and cumin seeds and cook for 1min, until aromatic.

4. Add the potatoes, turn up the heat and cook for 2min. Stir in the coconut milk and 200ml water. Bring to the boil and bubble for 5–10min, or until the potatoes are almost tender.

5. Stir in the courgettes and bubble for 3min, until the veg are tender. Add the prawns and cook until bright pink and piping hot. Stir in the coriander, check the seasoning and serve with the roasted cauliflower.

Hands-on time: 25min
Cooking time: about 40min
Serves 4

PER SERVING 493cals, 23g protein, 30g fat (16g saturates), 28g carbs (13g total sugars), 8g fibre

Smoked Cheesy Fish Pie

If you don't want to use prawns in this comforting dish, just use 250g more haddock.

75g butter
50g plain flour
500ml semi-skimmed milk
1 tbsp Dijon mustard
125g smoked Cheddar, grated
250g skinless smoked haddock, in large pieces
150g raw peeled king prawns
198g tin mixed sweetcorn and peppers, drained
2 soft-boiled eggs, peeled
125g ciabatta or other crusty bread, cut into 2cm pieces
Green peas or green salad, to serve

1. Preheat the oven to 180°C (160°C fan) mark 4. Melt 50g butter in a large pan over a medium heat. Mix in the flour to make a thick paste. Cook, stirring, for 3min. Remove from the heat; gradually mix in the milk to form a smooth sauce.

2. Return the pan to the heat and bring to the boil, stirring. Simmer for 5min, until thickened. Stir in the mustard, 75g cheese and some seasoning.

3. Stir in the haddock, prawns and sweetcorn mix, then spoon into a roughly 1.5 litre ovenproof serving dish. Slice the boiled eggs into quarters and nestle into the sauce, spacing them apart.

4. Melt the remaining 25g butter in a separate pan, add the bread cubes and some salt and toss to coat. Scatter the bread, then the remaining 50g cheese, over the pie filling. Cook in the oven for 30min, or until the sauce is bubbling and golden. Serve with green peas or a green salad.

◆ GET AHEAD
Assemble the pie 1 day ahead, leaving the white sauce to cool completely before assembling. Cover and chill. Cook, for an extra 5–10min, if needed, ensuring the filling is piping hot in the centre.

Hands-on time: 20min
Cooking time: about 45min
Serves 4

PER SERVING 601cals, 41g protein, 37g fat (19g saturates), 33g carbs (8g total sugars), 2g fibre

Mediterranean Cod en Papillote with Crushed Potatoes

Crushing the potatoes part-way through cooking helps to get them extra crispy, but you could skip this step, if you like.

750g baby new potatoes, halved if large
3 tbsp olive oil
2 tsp dried oregano
200g cherry tomatoes, halved
1 small courgette, thinly sliced
4 skinless cod loins or fillets (about 120g each)
1 lemon, thinly sliced and deseeded
75g pitted Kalamata olives, halved
2 tbsp capers, drained
Small handful dill, roughly chopped

1. Preheat the oven to 200°C (180°C fan) mark 6. Mix the potatoes, 2 tbsp of the oil, the oregano and plenty of seasoning in a roasting tin. Cook for 15–20min, then lightly crush with a potato masher. Return to the oven for 10min, or until golden and crisp.

2. Meanwhile, prepare 4 squares of baking parchment, each measuring 30 x 30cm. Fold each square in half, then open out again. Pile the tomatoes and courgette slices on to one side of each parchment square and top each with a piece of fish. Lay the lemon slices on top and scatter over the olives, capers and dill. Drizzle over the remaining oil and add plenty of seasoning.

3. Working one square at a time, fold the empty half of the baking parchment over the fish, then tightly fold/roll in the edges to make a sealed parcel. Repeat to make 3 more parcels, then transfer them on to a baking tray.

4. Cook for 15min, or until the fish is cooked through. (Press a fillet through the parcel – it should flake slightly under your finger. Serve the parcels with the potatoes.

Hands-on time: 15min
Cooking time: about 30min
Serves 4

PER SERVING 324cals, 26g protein, 10g fat (2g saturates), 31g carbs (5g total sugars), 5g fibre

Katsu Cod Fishcakes

The curry sauce for these fishcakes can be made and chilled a day ahead. Reheat to serve.

FOR THE FISHCAKES
500g floury potatoes, peeled and cut into 4cm pieces
1 tbsp vegetable oil, plus extra to fry
1 onion, finely sliced
2 tsp medium curry powder
1 red chilli, deseeded and thinly sliced
500g skinless cod fillets, cut into 2cm pieces
3 tbsp plain flour
2 medium eggs, beaten
100g panko breadcrumbs

FOR THE CURRY SAUCE
1 tsp vegetable oil
1 onion, finely chopped
3cm piece fresh root ginger, peeled and finely grated
2 garlic cloves, crushed
1 tbsp medium curry powder
3 tbsp plain flour
500ml chicken or vegetable stock
1 tbsp runny honey
Pak choi, wilted, to serve

1. For the fishcakes, in a medium pan, cover the potatoes with cold water and bring to the boil. Reduce the heat and simmer for 10–13min, until tender. Drain well, then leave to steam dry for 5min. Return the potatoes to the pan and mash with plenty of seasoning, until smooth. Set aside to cool.

2. Heat 1 tbsp oil in a small pan over a medium heat and cook the onion for 10min, until softened. Stir in the curry powder and chilli and cook for 2min, until fragrant. Set aside to cool.

3. Add the onion mixture to the potato pan, together with the cod and plenty of seasoning. Mix and shape into 8 patties. Arrange on a baking tray lined with baking parchment. Chill for 30min to firm up.

4. Meanwhile, make the curry sauce. Heat the oil in a medium pan over a medium heat and cook the onion for 10min, until softened. Stir in the ginger, garlic, curry powder and flour and cook for 1min. Remove from the heat and gradually mix in the stock. Return to the heat and cook, stirring, until thickened. Stir through the honey and some seasoning. Whizz with a stick blender for a smooth sauce, if you like.

5. For the fishcakes, put the flour, eggs and breadcrumbs into 3 separate shallow bowls. Coat a fishcake first in flour, gently shaking off the excess. Next coat in egg, then in breadcrumbs to cover. Repeat with remaining fishcakes.

6. Preheat the oven to 200°C (180°C fan) mark 6. To fry, heat a shallow layer of oil in a large non-stick frying pan over high heat. Fry 4 fishcakes for 2min per side, or until golden. Return to the lined tray. Repeat with the remaining fishcakes, then transfer the fishcakes to the oven and cook for 20min, until piping hot.

7. Reheat the sauce, if needed, and serve with the fishcakes and wilted pak choi.

Hands-on time: 45min, plus cooling and chilling
Cooking time: about 1hr
Serves 4

PER SERVING 573cals, 38g protein, 15g fat (2g saturates), 69g carbs (10g total sugars), 7g fibre

Side of Salmon with Anchovy and Caper Butter

This butter works well with other fish and seafood, too, so make extra and keep it in the fridge or freezer.

100g unsalted butter, softened
3 tbsp capers, drained
3 anchovy fillets in oil, drained and roughly chopped
Small handful soft green herbs, such as parsley and coriander, finely chopped
3 lemons
850g side of salmon, skin on
150g samphire

1. Preheat the oven to 200°C (180°C fan) mark 6. Mix the butter, capers, anchovies, herbs and the finely grated zest from 1 of the lemons in a bowl and season well.

2. Line a large roasting tin with baking parchment and lay the salmon on top, skin-side down. Check for and tweezer out any bones, then rub the flavoured butter over the flesh. Cut one of the unzested lemons into thin slices and lay on top of the salmon. Cut the remaining 2 lemons into wedges and scatter around the fish.

3. Roast for 10min, then remove from the oven and scatter the samphire around the fish and gently toss in the buttery juices. Return to the oven for 10–15min, until the salmon is cooked through and the samphire is just tender.

4. Transfer to a platter and spoon over any buttery juices from the roasting tin. Serve.

◆ GET AHEAD
Make the flavoured butter up to 1 day ahead. Cover and chill. Alternatively, keep the butter wrapped in the freezer for up to 3 months. To serve, defrost if necessary, then allow to soften at room temperature before completing the recipe.

Hands-on time: 15min
Cooking time: about 25min
Serves 6

PER SERVING 391cals, 32g protein, 28g fat
(12g saturates), 1g carbs (<1g total sugars), 2g fibre

Seabass Coconut Curry with Paratha

This south Indian-style curry is wonderfully fragrant and light. The rolling technique used for the paratha forms their recognisable layers, and they make the perfect accompaniment.

FOR THE PARATHA
200g stoneground wholewheat (atta) flour, plus
  extra to dust (see GH Tip)
2 tbsp natural yogurt
Ghee, melted, to brush (or use vegetable oil)

FOR THE CURRY
1 tsp coconut oil
1 tsp black mustard seeds
½ tsp fennel seeds
10 dried curry leaves
1 onion, finely sliced
4 garlic cloves, crushed
5cm piece fresh root ginger, peeled and grated
1-2 green chillies, deseeded and finely chopped
1 tsp ground turmeric
¼ tsp ground cinnamon
5 tomatoes, roughly chopped
300ml light coconut milk
4 sea bass fillets (roughly 125g each), skinned and
  roughly chopped
Juice ½ lemon
Large bunch coriander, roughly chopped

1. Start by making the paratha. Put the flour and
   a pinch of salt into a medium bowl, make a well
   in the centre and add the yogurt and 80ml tepid
   water. Stir to combine, then bring together with
   your hands to form a soft dough. Tip on to a
   work surface and knead for 5–8min, until smooth.
   Shape into a ball, return to the empty bowl and

Hands-on time: 30min, plus resting and chilling
Cooking time: about 35min
Serves 4

PER SERVING 498cals, 33g protein, 22g fat
(9g saturates), 40g carbs (9g total sugars), 7g fibre

cover with a damp, clean tea towel. Leave to rest
for at least 10min (or up to 2hr).

2. Once the dough has rested, divide it into 4 and
   roll out each piece on a lightly floured surface to
   a rough 10 x 30cm rectangle. Brush the top of the
   rectangles with ghee/oil and dust with some flour
   (this helps to define the flaky layers). Working
   one rectangle at a time, fold the dough in half
   lengthways, twist it tightly from one end as if
   making a cheese straw. Lifting up one end, coil
   the twist back on to itself, so it's about 5cm tall,
   tucking the end you are holding under the coil.
   Flatten slightly and transfer to a plate. Repeat with
   the remaining paratha dough and chill for 10min.

3. Meanwhile, make the curry. Heat the oil in a large,
   deep frying pan over a medium heat. Add the
   mustard and fennel seeds and curry leaves, and
   fry until the seeds start to pop. Stir in the onion,
   garlic, ginger, chilli and 2 tbsp water and cook for
   5min, until the onion is softened.

4. Add the turmeric, cinnamon and tomatoes, and fry
   for 2min before adding the coconut milk, 300ml
   water and seasoning. Bring to the boil, then simmer
   for 20min, adding the fish for the final 5min.

5. Meanwhile, roll each paratha coil into a 15cm
   circle. Heat a large frying pan over a medium-high
   heat. Dry fry the parathas 1 at a time until flaky
   and golden brown, about 2min per side.

6. Once the curry has reduced, season it with lemon
   juice and sprinkle over the coriander. Serve with
   the paratha.

◆ GH TIP
If you can't find wholewheat
atta flour, plain white flour
will also work.

Prawn Saganaki with Courgette Noodles

Tinned cherry tomatoes make a fruity and delicious sauce, but you could use tinned plum tomatoes instead.

---

2 tbsp olive oil, plus extra to drizzle
4 garlic cloves, crushed
¼–½ tsp crushed chilli flakes, to taste
2 x 400g tins cherry tomatoes
150ml white wine, we used Chardonnay
1 tsp sugar
4–5 courgettes (about 1.1kg), spiralized or peeled into ribbons using a Y-shaped peeler, then cut in half lengthways
Large handful dill, roughly chopped
300g raw peeled jumbo king prawns
75g feta, crumbled
1 small baguette, sliced (optional)

1. Heat 1 tbsp oil in a large, deep frying pan over a medium heat. Add the garlic and chilli flakes and cook, stirring, for 1–2min, until fragrant. Add the tomatoes, wine, sugar and some seasoning. Bring to the boil, then reduce the heat slightly and bubble gently for 20–25min, until reduced.

2. Meanwhile, heat the remaining 1 tbsp oil in a large frying pan or wok over a medium heat. Add the courgettes and fry for 6–7min, until tender, turning gently to avoid breaking them up. Stir in most of the dill and season generously.

3. Stir the prawns into the tomato sauce and cook for 3–4min, until opaque. Check the seasoning.

4. Arrange the courgettes on a platter, or in 4 bowls, and spoon on the prawn sauce. Sprinkle over the feta, remaining dill and some black pepper. Drizzle with oil; serve with the bread, if you like.

Hands-on time: 15min
Cooking time: about 35min
Serves 4

PER SERVING 374cals, 27g protein, 12g fat (4g saturates), 33g carbs (14g total sugars), 6g fibre

Haddock Florentine Bake

Baked with spinach and ready-made cheese sauce, this haddock recipe is an easy and tasty alternative to the classic fish pie.

1½ tbsp olive oil
2 leeks, finely sliced
175g baby spinach
500g fresh cheese sauce
500g skinless haddock fillets, cut into 2cm chunks
75g dried breadcrumbs

1. Preheat the oven to 200°C (180°C fan) mark 6. Heat 1 tbsp of the oil in a medium hob-proof casserole dish over a medium heat. Cook the leeks for 10min, stirring occasionally, until softened. Stir through the spinach and cook for a couple of minutes more, until wilted.

2. Remove from the heat and stir through the cheese sauce, haddock and plenty of seasoning.

3. Mix the breadcrumbs with the remaining oil and plenty of seasoning. Scatter over the haddock mixture and cook in the oven for 25min, until golden and bubbling. Serve.

◆ GH TIP
If you don't have a suitable casserole dish, simply cook the filling in a medium pan to the end of step 2, then transfer to an ovenproof serving dish to continue cooking.

Hands-on time: 15min
Cooking time: about 40min
Serves 4

PER SERVING 371cals, 34g protein, 16g fat (7g saturates), 23g carbs (4g total sugars), 3g fibre

Caponata Cod Traybake

A twist on the traditional Sicilian stew. Swap the parsley for mint or basil, if you like.

---

2 large aubergines, finely chopped
1 celery stick, finely sliced
500g tomatoes, roughly chopped
3 tbsp olive oil, plus extra to brush
1 tbsp capers, drained
100g pitted black olives
40g sultanas
1 tbsp red wine vinegar
4 skinless cod loin fillets (about 125g each)
4 lemon slices
2 tbsp pine nuts
Large handful parsley, roughly chopped
Crusty bread, to serve (optional)

1. Preheat the oven to 200°C (180°C fan) mark 6. Mix the aubergines, celery, tomatoes, oil and plenty of seasoning in a large roasting tin. Roast for 20min, stirring halfway through, until the tomatoes have started to break down and the aubergines have softened.

2. Remove from the oven and mix through the capers, olives, sultanas and vinegar. Set the cod fillets on top, brush each with a little oil, then season and top with the lemon slices. Scatter the pine nuts into the tin. Cover the tin with foil and return to the oven for 10min, or until the fish is cooked.

3. Garnish with parsley and serve with crusty bread, if you like.

◆ GH TIP
Swap the cod for any other chunky skinless fish you prefer, such as salmon.

Hands-on time: 15min
Cooking time: about 30min
Serves 4

PER SERVING (without bread) 337cals, 26g protein, 18g fat (3g saturates), 14g carbs (14g total sugars), 7g fibre

Lime and Coriander Fishcakes

These salmon and prawn fishcakes are zesty and fragrant in equal measure. You could swap the salmon for another meaty fish, such as cod.

500g floury potatoes, peeled and cut into 4cm chunks
250g salmon fillets
200g cooked and peeled king prawns, roughly chopped
2 spring onions, finely sliced
Small handful coriander, roughly chopped
2tbsp sweet chilli sauce
Finely grated zest 2 limes and juice of 1, plus wedges
   to serve
75g dried breadcrumbs
40g desiccated coconut
25g plain flour
2 medium eggs, beaten
Vegetable oil, to fry
Green salad and tartare sauce, to serve (optional)

◆ GET AHEAD
Prepare the fishcakes to the end of step 4. Layer in a freezer-safe container between sheets of baking parchment and freeze for up to 1 month. To serve, defrost overnight in the fridge and complete the recipe.

1. Put the potatoes into a large pan, cover with cold water and bring to the boil. Bubble for 10–13min, until tender. Drain thoroughly and leave to steam dry in a colander for 5min. Return the potatoes to the pan and mash with plenty of seasoning until smooth. Set aside to cool slightly.

2. Meanwhile, put the salmon in a medium pan with 400ml water. Bring to the boil over a medium heat, then reduce to a gentle simmer and cook for 4–5min, until the fish is opaque and just cooked. Carefully remove with a slotted spoon to a plate lined with kitchen paper. When cool enough to handle, flake the fish into large chunks, discarding the skin (if present).

3. Add the flaked salmon, prawns, spring onions, coriander, sweet chilli sauce, lime zest and juice and plenty of seasoning to the mashed potato. Stir very gently until just combined, avoiding breaking up the salmon too much. Shape into 8 even patties.

4. Mix the breadcrumbs and dessicated coconut in a shallow bowl, then put the flour and eggs into 2 separate shallow bowls. Coat each fishcake in flour (tap off the excess), then the egg and finally the breadcrumb mixture. Put on a baking tray lined with baking parchment and chill for at least 30min.

5. Heat a thin layer of oil in a large frying pan over a medium-high heat and fry the fishcakes for 3–4min per side (in batches if necessary), or until nicely golden. Drain on a plate lined with kitchen paper and keep warm while you fry the second batch.

6. Serve with lime wedges, and a green salad and tartare sauce, if you like.

Hands-on time: 30min, plus chilling
Cooking time: about 35min
Serves 4

PER SERVING 562cals, 31g protein, 27g fat
(8g saturates), 47g carbs (7g total sugars), 5g fibre

Crunchy Nutty Prawn and Noodle Satay Salad

Yes, you read that right, these prawns have a crispy crumb made from breakfast cereal! Needless to say, these satay noodles are incredibly moreish.

1½ tbsp cornflour
1 medium egg, beaten
50g Kellogg's Crunchy Nut, roughly crushed
100g raw peeled king prawns
Coconut or vegetable oil, to fry
150g fresh or cooked fine rice noodles
½ cucumber, cut into matchsticks, seedy core discarded
1 large carrot, peeled and cut into matchsticks
Small handful mint leaves, shredded

FOR THE SATAY SAUCE
1 tsp coconut or vegetable oil
2 garlic cloves, crushed
1–2 red birds eye chillies, to taste, deseeded and finely chopped
½ tbsp light brown soft sugar
1 tbsp soy sauce
2 tbsp peanut butter
100ml coconut milk
Juice ½ lime, plus wedges to serve

◆ GH TIP
If you like, put the coated prawns on a baking tray lined with baking parchment and cook in an oven preheated to 220°C (200°C fan) mark 7, for 5–6min, until firm.

1. To make the satay sauce, heat the oil in small pan, then fry the garlic and chilli(es) until aromatic. Add the sugar, soy, peanut butter and coconut milk. Bubble until slightly thickened, then stir in the lime juice. Check the seasoning, then set aside.

2. Put the cornflour into a shallow bowl and mix in some seasoning. Put the beaten egg and crushed Kellogg's Crunchy Nut into 2 separate shallow bowls. Toss the prawns in cornflour, then coat in egg, before coating in cereal.

3. Heat enough oil in a medium frying pan to come 5mm up the sides of the pan. Fry the prawns for 2min per side, turning gently, until golden and firm (see GH Tip). Set aside.

4. Suitably discard the oil. Return the pan to a medium heat, add the noodles, cucumber and carrot, then cook for 1–2min. Mix through the sauce to coat and heat through. Divide between 2 shallow bowls, top with the prawns and scatter over the mint. Serve with the lime wedges.

Hands-on time: 25min
Cooking time: about 15min
Serves 2

PER SERVING 640cals, 21g protein, 30g fat (16g saturates), 69g carbs (21g total sugars), 6g fibre

Crispy Salmon Teriyaki Stir-Fry

Brushing the salmon with cornflour helps to crisp it up and helps to give great texture to this Asian-inspired recipe.

4 skin-on salmon fillets
1 tbsp cornflour
½ tbsp vegetable oil
½ tbsp sesame oil
300g pack stir-fry vegetables
300g fresh egg noodles

FOR THE SAUCE
6 tbsp teriyaki sauce
Juice ½ lime
2 garlic cloves, crushed
3cm piece fresh root ginger, peeled and finely grated
½ red chilli, deseeded and finely chopped

1. In a small bowl, mix together the sauce ingredients. Next, use a pastry brush to lightly brush the salmon on all sides with the cornflour. Heat the vegetable oil in a large non-stick frying pan over medium heat.

2. Fry the salmon fillets, skin-side down, for 5min, then flip and fry for 2min more. Add half the sauce and cook until sticky, spooning the sauce over the salmon to coat.

3. Meanwhile, in a separate medium frying pan or wok, heat the sesame oil over a high heat. Add the stir-fry vegetables and stir-fry for 3min, until just tender. Add the remaining sauce and the noodles, then cook until piping hot and coated in the sauce.

4. Divide the noodle mixture between 4 bowls and top with the salmon.

◆ GH TIP
If you can't find fresh egg noodles, buy dried noodles and cook following the pack instructions. Drain and add in step 3.

Hands-on time: 15min
Cooking time: about 10min
Serves 4

PER SERVING 548cals, 35g protein, 28g fat
(5g saturates), 36g carbs (13g total sugars), 3g fibre

Cod with Gremolata on Soft Polenta

Use any chunky, sustainably sourced white fish you like for this speedy supper.

15g dried wild/mixed mushrooms, broken into
   small pieces
900ml hot chicken or vegetable stock
1 tbsp olive oil
4 skinless chunky cod or other white fish
   fillets (approx 500g)
75g butter
Lemon juice, to taste
150g quick-cook/1-minute polenta

FOR THE GREMOLATA
2 garlic cloves
40g walnuts
25g flat-leaf parsley
Finely grated zest 1 lemon

1. In a medium pan, soak the dried mushrooms in the stock for 10min, until softened.

2. Meanwhile, make the gremolata. Roughly chop the garlic, then add the walnuts and parsley to the board and chop them all together until fine. Scrape into a bowl, mix in the lemon zest and a pinch of salt, then set aside.

3. Heat the oil in a large non-stick frying pan over a high heat. Pat dry the fish fillets with kitchen paper and season all over with salt and freshly ground black pepper. Fry for 6-7min (depending on the thickness), turning halfway, until golden and just cooked through. Add 25g butter to the pan with a squeeze of lemon juice and, as the butter melts, spoon it over the fish.

4. While the fish is cooking, bring the stock and mushrooms to the boil over a medium heat. Pour in the polenta, whisking with a large balloon whisk. Cook, whisking, for 1-2min, until thickened. Remove from the heat and stir in the remaining butter and plenty of seasoning. Divide the polenta among 4 plates, top with the fish, then scatter over the gremolata and serve.

Hands-on time: 20min
Cooking time: about 10min
Serves 4

PER SERVING 503cals, 34g protein, 28g fat
(11g saturates), 28g carbs (1g total sugars), 4g fibre

Ligurian Fish Stew

There are countless variations of this stew, so adapt it to include your favourite fish.

1 tsp extra virgin olive oil, plus extra to drizzle (optional)
1 large fennel bulb, sliced
2 garlic cloves, crushed
1½ tsp each fennel and cumin seeds
Large pinch dried chilli flakes, or more to taste
1 red pepper, deseeded and roughly chopped
400ml fish stock
2 x 400g tins chopped tomatoes
500g skinless white fish, we used haddock, cut
　　into big dice
Large handful parsley, roughly chopped
Toasted bread, to serve (optional)

1. Heat the oil in a large pan. Add the fresh fennel and garlic, then cook gently, covered, for 10min until softened. Meanwhile, bash the fennel and cumin seeds roughly in a pestle and mortar.

2. Add the seed mixture and dried chilli to the pan along with the red pepper and some seasoning. Fry for 5min, then stir in the stock and tomatoes. Bring up to boil and bubble for 10min, stirring occasionally.

3. Add the fish to the pan, then continue to cook for 5min, or until the fish is just cooked through. Fold through most of the parsley and check the seasoning. Garnish with the remaining parsley and some oil (if you like). Serve as it is or with slices of toasted bread.

Hands-on time: 15min
Cooking time: about 30min
Serves 4

PER SERVING 180cals, 25g protein, 4g fat (1g saturates), 9g carbs (9g total sugars), 4g fibre

Smoked Salmon Poké Bowl

We've swapped traditional raw fish for smoked salmon in this midweek marvel. Other smoked fish, such as mackerel, would also work well.

FOR THE PICKLED CUCUMBER
1 large cucumber
2 tsp rice vinegar
2 tsp caster sugar

FOR THE RICE
175g sushi or short-grain rice
2 tbsp rice vinegar
½ tbsp caster sugar

TO SERVE
2 hot smoked salmon fillets (around 200g), flaked
150g radishes, thinly sliced
1 carrot, cut into matchsticks
2 nori sheets, finely sliced
2 tbsp sliced pickled ginger
2 tsp toasted sesame seeds

1. Make the pickled cucumber. Peel the cucumber into ribbons, discarding the seedy core. Add to a bowl and mix in the vinegar and sugar. Set aside.

2. Prepare the rice. Wash well in a bowl of cold water, rubbing the grains together with the palms of your hands as if polishing them. Drain away any cloudy water and repeat (several times if necessary) until the water remains clear. Put the rice into a medium pan and pour in water until it comes 1cm above the rice. Bring to the boil, stirring occasionally, then lower the heat to a simmer. Cover and cook for 8min, until the rice is tender. Take the pan off the heat and leave covered for 5min.

3. Meanwhile, heat the vinegar, sugar and 1 tsp salt in a small pan to dissolve the sugar. Take off the heat. Transfer the rice to a bowl and gently mix in the vinegar seasoning.

4. Divide the rice between 4 bowls, top with pickled cucumber, salmon, veg, nori, ginger and sesame seeds and serve.

Hands-on time: 20min
Cooking time: about 15min
Serves 4

PER SERVING 304cals, 18g protein, 7g fat (1g saturates), 42g carbs (6g total sugars), 3g fibre

Meatless
Marvels

Smokey Halloumi Mushrooms

These cheese-topped mushrooms use the same spice rub as our spatchcock chicken recipe on p156 and make for a great main course or accompanying side.

60g butter, melted
1 garlic clove, crushed
Finely grated zest 1 lemon
6 Portobello mushrooms
250g halloumi, cubed
100g rocket, to serve

FOR THE SPICE RUB
2 tbsp hot or sweet smoked paprika
1½ tbsp light brown soft sugar
1 tsp English mustard powder
1 tsp ground cumin
2 tsp dried thyme
1 tsp garlic granules

1. Preheat the oven to 200°C (180°C fan) mark 6 and line a small, shallow roasting tin with foil. To make the spice rub, mix all the ingredients in a small bowl with 1½ tsp fine salt.

2. Mix the butter, garlic, lemon zest and 2 tbsp of the spice rub and brush all over the mushrooms, reserving 1 tbsp. Arrange the mushrooms gill-side up in the lined tin. Roast for 20min, or until just tender. Remove from the oven and preheat the grill (if you have one) or leave the oven at the same setting.

3. Arrange the halloumi on top of the mushrooms and brush with the reserved spiced butter. Grill for 3–5min or roast for 10min, until the cheese is softened and bubbling. Arrange the rocket on a plate, top with the mushrooms and serve.

◆ GET AHEAD
Prepare to end of step 1 up to 1 day ahead (without preheating the oven), then cover and chill. Complete the recipe to serve.

Hands-on time: 10min
Cooking time: about 30min
Serves 6 as a side, or 2 as a main

PER SERVING (for 6) 225cals, 12g protein, 18g fat (12g saturates), 3g carbs (3g total sugars), 1g fibre

Chickpea and Mushroom Enchiladas

Jarred roasted peppers make a wonderfully easy sauce for these tasty vegetarian enchiladas. For extra heat, top with pickled jalapeños before cooking in the oven.

465g jar roasted peppers, drained
2 tsp vegetable oil
1 red onion, finely chopped
400g baby chestnut mushrooms, halved or quartered
    if large
2 tbsp chipotle paste
2 garlic cloves, crushed
400g tin chickpeas, drained and rinsed
Juice 1 lime, plus wedges to serve
Large handful coriander, roughly chopped
75g mature Cheddar or Red Leicester, grated
8 flour tortillas
150ml soured cream
Guacamole, to serve (optional)

1. Preheat the oven to 200°C (180°C fan) mark 6. Whizz 200g of the peppers in the small bowl of a food processor, or use a stick blender, until smooth. Slice the remaining peppers to make 8 long pieces. Set aside.

2. Heat the oil in a large, deep frying pan over low heat and fry the onion for 5min, until slightly softened. Increase the heat to medium, add the mushrooms and fry for 5min, until golden. Stir in the chipotle paste and garlic and cook for 1min. Stir in the chickpeas and pepper purée and bubble for 1min, then remove from the heat and stir in the lime juice, half the coriander, 25g grated cheese and some seasoning.

3. Lay a pepper strip in the middle of a tortilla, spread an eighth of the mushroom filling on top and roll up tightly. Repeat with remaining tortillas, peppers and filling. Arrange the rolls (seam-side down) in a single layer in a 2.5 litre ovenproof dish. Spread the soured cream on top, then scatter over the remaining cheese.

4. Cook the enchiladas in the oven for 25min, or until golden. Scatter over the remaining coriander and serve with lime wedges for squeezing over and guacamole, if you like.

Hands-on time: 25min
Cooking time: about 40min
Serves 4

PER SERVING 665cals, 24g protein, 26g fat (10g saturates), 81g carbs (10g total sugars), 5g fibre

Polenta with Cavolo Nero and Buttery Mushrooms

This quick dish looks impressive but is easy to make. Swap the cavolo nero for any dark greens. If you can't find exotic mushrooms, use chestnut mushrooms instead.

FOR THE MUSHROOMS
40g butter
400g mixed exotic mushrooms, sliced if large
2 garlic cloves, crushed
2 tsp dried Italian herb seasoning
175g cavolo nero leaves, tough stems removed, leaves finely shredded
400g tin chickpeas, drained and rinsed
50g crème fraîche

FOR THE POLENTA
2 tbsp extra virgin olive oil
250g quick-cook polenta
25g vegetarian Italian-style hard cheese, finely grated

1. To prepare the mushrooms, melt the butter in a large frying pan over a medium-high heat. Add the mushrooms and some seasoning and cook for 5min, until golden and any liquid has evaporated.

2. Add the garlic and dried herbs and cook for 1min. Stir in the cavolo nero and chickpeas and cook for 3min, or until the greens have wilted. Stir in the crème fraîche until melted, check the seasoning and set the pan aside.

3. For the polenta, bring 1 litre water to the boil in a large pan over a medium heat. Whisk in the extra virgin oil and 2 tsp fine salt. Slowly whisk in the polenta and keep whisking for 3min, or until thickened (be careful, as the mixture will bubble vigorously). Remove from the heat, then whisk in the cheese and plenty of seasoning. Loosen with some extra just-boiled water, if you like.

4. To serve, divide the polenta among 4 bowls and top with the mushroom mixture.

Hands-on time: 25min
Cooking time: about 15min
Serves 4

PER SERVING 529cals, 17g protein, 25g fat (11g saturates), 54g carbs (1g total sugars), 8g fibre

Vegetarian Chilli Bake

Gravy granules may sound like an odd addition, but they give this chilli a rich depth of flavour. Crumble in a vegetable stock cube, if you prefer.

½ tbsp olive oil
1 small red onion, finely sliced
1 red pepper, deseeded and finely sliced
1 tsp smoked paprika, sweet or hot
1 garlic clove, crushed
½ red chilli, deseeded and finely sliced
400g tin green lentils, drained and rinsed
100g kidney beans, from a tin (drained weight), rinsed
400g tin chopped tomatoes
2 tbsp onion gravy granules
100g soured cream
50g Cheddar, grated

1. Preheat the oven to 200°C (180°C fan) mark 6. Heat the oil in a small-medium casserole dish or ovenproof frying pan over a medium hob heat and fry the onion and pepper for 10min, until softened. Add the paprika, garlic and chilli and cook for 1min, until fragrant.

2. Stir in the lentils, kidney beans, tomatoes, gravy granules, 50–100ml just-boiled water from a kettle and plenty of seasoning.

3. Transfer to the oven and cook for 20min, or until bubbling and thickened slightly. In a small bowl, mix together the soured cream and cheese. Carefully remove the dish/pan from the oven and gently spread over the cheese mixture. Preheat the grill to high.

4. Grill for 5min, or until the cheese is melted. Serve.

 GH TIP
Stir any leftover kidney beans through spaghetti Bolognese or use to amp up baked beans on toast.

V

Hands-on time: 20min
Cooking time: about 35min
Serves 2

PER SERVING 528cals, 22g protein, 25g fat (14g saturates), 47g carbs (17g total sugars), 13g fibre

Puttanesca Stuffed Aubergines

Cooking the orzo in the tomato sauce gives a lovely creamy texture to the filling. Add anchovies with the garlic and chilli for an authentic puttanesca flavour.

1 large aubergine
2 tbsp olive oil
2 garlic cloves, crushed
½ tsp chilli flakes
100g cherry tomatoes, halved
100g orzo
25g pitted Kalamata olives, halved
Small handful basil, leaves picked and shredded, plus extra leaves to garnish
25g feta

1. Preheat the oven to 200°C (180°C fan) mark 6. Trim the stalk off the aubergine, then halve it lengthways and score the flesh. Arrange cut-side up in a small roasting tin and brush with 1 tbsp of the oil. Season and roast for 30min, or until the flesh is tender.

2. Meanwhile, heat the remaining 1 tbsp oil in a medium frying pan over a medium heat. Add the garlic and chilli flakes and cook for 2min, stirring, until fragrant. Add the tomatoes and cook for 8min, crushing the tomatoes with the back of the spoon to break them down.

3. Stir in the orzo, 300ml just-boiled water, the olives and basil. Simmer for 8min, stirring frequently, or until the orzo is tender.

4. Remove the aubergine from the oven and carefully scoop out the flesh with a spoon (leave the aubergine shells in the tin). Finely chop the flesh and stir into the tomato mixture. Check the seasoning, then spoon back into the shells.

5. Crumble over the feta and return to the oven for 5min. Garnish with extra basil and serve.

◆ GH TIP
Cook the aubergine up to 1 day ahead. Cool, cover and chill. Complete the recipe to serve.

Hands-on time: 15min
Cooking time: about 35min
Serves 2

PER SERVING 400cals, 11g protein, 19g fat (4g saturates), 42g carbs (7g total sugars), 9g fibre

Roasted Pepper, Halloumi and Sweet Potato Burgers

Grilling the potato and halloumi speeds up the cooking time. Omit the halloumi and use a plant-based mayo to make this vegan.

1 large sweet potato, peeled
2 tbsp oil
250g halloumi
4 ciabatta rolls, halved
3 large roasted peppers from a jar, drained and
   thickly sliced
Handful rocket

FOR THE GUACAMOLE
2 ripe avocados
1 red onion, finely chopped
1 jalapeño or large green chilli, deseeded and
   finely chopped
Juice 1 lime
1 tbsp extra virgin olive oil
Small handful coriander, roughly chopped

FOR THE CHIPOTLE MAYO
4 tbsp mayonnaise
1 tsp chipotle chilli paste

1. Preheat the grill to medium. Cut the sweet potatoes lengthways into 5mm-thick slices. Arrange the slices on a large baking sheet in a single layer and brush with 1 tbsp of the oil. Grill for 8min, turning halfway, or until tender. Set aside on a board.

2. Turn up the grill to high. Cut the halloumi into 8 slices, arrange on the baking sheet and brush with the remaining 1 tbsp oil. Grill for 6min, turning halfway, or until golden.

3. Meanwhile, make the guacamole. Halve and de-stone the avocados, then scoop the flesh into a small bowl. Mash thoroughly, then stir in the remaining guacamole ingredients and some seasoning. Set aside. Next, mix the chipotle mayo ingredients and set aside.

4. Put the ciabatta rolls on a baking sheet, cut-side up. Grill until light golden.

5. To assemble, spread the guacamole on the bases of the rolls. Divide the sweet potato slices, roasted peppers and halloumi between the bases. Top with the rocket. Spread the chipotle mayo on the cut-side of the ciabatta tops, then lay on top of the burgers. Serve.

Hands-on time: 15min
Cooking time: 15min
Makes 4 burgers

PER BURGER 752cals, 24g protein, 50g fat
(15g saturates), 46g carbs (11g total sugars), 10g fibre

Sprout Falafel with Crunchy Salad

If you don't have any leftover sprouts, these green falafel are equally delicious made with cooked kale.

FOR THE FALAFEL
400g tin chickpeas, drained and rinsed
½ onion, roughly chopped
2 garlic cloves, crushed
100g leftover cooked sprouts
Small handful coriander
Small handful parsley
1 tsp ground coriander
1 tsp ground cumin
1 tsp mild chilli powder
2 tbsp plain flour
1 tbsp oil

FOR THE SALAD
2 tbsp extra virgin olive oil
1 tbsp lemon juice
½ tsp Dijon mustard
½ tsp runny honey
½ cucumber
1 red apple, cored and finely sliced
2 celery sticks, finely sliced
100g baby spinach

FOR THE YOGURT DIP
200g Greek-style yogurt
2 tbsp tahini
Juice ½ lemon

Hands-on time: 25min
Cooking time: about 40min
Serves 4

PER SERVING 350cals, 12g protein, 21g fat
(5g saturates), 25g carbs (10g total sugars), 7g fibre

1. Preheat the oven to 200°C (180°C fan) mark 6. Line 2 baking sheets with baking parchment.

2. Roughly pat dry the chickpeas with kitchen paper. In a food processor, pulse the onion, garlic, sprouts and herbs until finely chopped. Add the chickpeas, spices, flour and some seasoning and pulse until combined.

3. Tip the mixture into a bowl, then shape into 20 small patties and arrange on the lined sheets. Brush the tops of the falafel with ½ tbsp of the oil. Cook for 20min, then carefully turn and brush with the remaining ½ tbsp oil. Cook for 20min more, until golden.

4. Meanwhile, make the salad. In the base of a large bowl, whisk the oil, lemon juice, mustard, honey and some seasoning to combine. Using a Y-shaped vegetable peeler, shave the cucumber into the dressing bowl in ribbons, discarding the seedy core. Add the apple, celery and spinach, and toss gently to combine.

5. For the yogurt dip, mix all the ingredients together in a small bowl with some seasoning. Serve the falafel with the salad and dip.

◆ GH TIP
We've oven-cooked these falafel for a lighter finish, but you can shallow-fry them if you prefer.

Pearl Barley and Bean Stew

This fresh stew is full of vegetables and flavour. You can swap the cannellini beans for any other tinned beans, or the kale for any dark green leaves you prefer.

1 tbsp olive oil
1 onion, finely chopped
2 celery sticks, finely chopped
2 carrots, finely chopped
3 garlic cloves, crushed
2 fresh or dried bay leaves
400g tin cannellini beans, drained and rinsed
100g pearl barley
1 litre vegetable stock
Finely grated zest and juice 1 lemon
300g Tenderstem broccoli, roughly chopped
150g kale, tough stems removed, finely shredded
Small handful parsley, finely chopped
50g vegetarian Italian-style hard cheese, grated

1. Heat the oil in a large pan over a medium heat and cook the onion, celery and carrots for 15min, until softened. Stir through the garlic and bay leaves and cook for 1min, until fragrant.

2. Add the beans, pearl barley, stock, lemon zest and juice and some seasoning and bring to the boil. Simmer for 20min, or until the pearl barley is tender.

3. Stir through the broccoli, kale and parsley and cook for 3min, until the greens are tender. Ladle into 4 bowls and sprinkle over the cheese. Serve.

Hands-on time: 20min
Cooking time: about 45min
Serves 4

PER SERVING 321cals, 16g protein, 9g fat (3g saturates), 39g carbs (7g total sugars), 12g fibre

Paneer Jalfrezi

Up the amount of chilli if you're in the mood for something a little spicier. Not a fan of chickpeas? Simply double the quantity of paneer.

2 tbsp vegetable oil
225g block paneer, cut into 2cm cubes
2 onions, roughly chopped
1 each red and green pepper, deseeded and sliced
1 red chilli, deseeded and finely chopped
2 garlic cloves, crushed
1 tbsp ground cumin
1 tbsp garam masala
1 tsp ground coriander
1 tsp ground turmeric
6 tomatoes, roughly chopped
400g tin chickpeas, drained and rinsed
Juice 1 lemon
Mango chutney, to serve

1. Heat 1 tbsp of the oil in large pan over a medium heat. Fry the paneer for 5min, turning regularly, until browned all over. Remove to a plate.

2. Add the remaining oil to the pan, lower the heat and fry the onions for 20min, stirring occasionally, until completely softened, adding the peppers for the final 5min. Add the chilli, garlic and spices to the pan and fry for 2min, until fragrant. Stir through three-quarters of the tomatoes, 200ml water and 1½ tsp fine salt. Bring to the boil, then simmer, stirring occasionally, for 10min, until the tomatoes have broken down.

3. Return the paneer to the pan with the remaining tomatoes and the chickpeas, and simmer for 2min. Stir through the lemon juice, check the seasoning and serve with mango chutney.

Hands-on time: 20min
Cooking time: about 45min
Serves 4

PER SERVING 381cals, 21g protein, 21g fat (9g saturates), 22g carbs (12g total sugars), 8g fibre

Courgette and Lentil Balls with Tomato Sauce

We've served this with buckwheat, a nutrient-rich grain-like seed that's low in calories but high in vitamins and minerals.

400g tin green lentils
2 medium courgettes (about 275g)
1 medium egg
1 garlic clove, crushed
40g vegetarian Italian-style hard cheese, grated, plus extra to serve
Small handful basil, shredded, plus extra leaves to garnish
60g fresh white or brown breadcrumbs
1 tbsp olive oil
Cooked buckwheat, pasta or rice, to serve

FOR THE SAUCE
1 tsp olive oil
1 onion, finely chopped
2 garlic cloves, crushed
400g tin chopped tomatoes
1 tsp dried oregano
Pinch sugar

1. Drain and rinse the lentils, then leave in the sieve to drain well again. Trim the courgettes, coarsely grate, then lift up handfuls over the sink and squeeze to remove all the excess moisture. Pat dry with kitchen paper. Add the courgettes to a bowl and mix in the egg, garlic, cheese, basil, breadcrumbs and plenty of seasoning.

2. Whizz the lentils in a food processor until fairly smooth, then add to the courgette bowl and mix well. Shape the mixture into 16 walnut-sized balls.

3. Heat the oil in a large non-stick frying pan over a medium heat and fry the balls, turning occasionally (they will be fairly soft), until golden, about 15min. Set aside (still in the pan).

4. Meanwhile, make the sauce: in a separate pan, heat the oil over a low-medium heat and gently fry the onion for 10min until softened. Add the remaining sauce ingredients with some seasoning and bring to the boil. Turn down the heat and simmer for 5min.

5. Add the sauce to the meatball pan and gently heat through. Serve with cooked buckwheat, as we have, pasta or rice, and garnish with basil and extra cheese.

Hands-on time: 30min
Cooking time: about 30min
Serves 4

PER SERVING (without buckwheat) 250cals, 15g protein, 9g fat (3g saturates), 25g carbs (8g total sugars), 6g fibre

Mushroom and Lentil Bourguignon with Oatmeal Dumplings

A hearty vegetarian version of the classic French stew.

2 tbsp olive oil
250g small shallots, halved
500g baby chestnut mushrooms
2 garlic cloves, crushed
2 tbsp tomato purée
450ml red wine
300ml vegetable stock
4 thyme sprigs, leaves picked
2 x 400g tins Puy lentils, drained and rinsed
Savoy cabbage, steamed, to serve (optional)

FOR THE DUMPLINGS
100g rolled oats
40g butter, chilled and grated
1 tsp baking powder
1 tbsp chopped parsley
1 tbsp wholegrain mustard
1 medium egg, beaten

1. Heat the oil in a large pan (that has a lid) over a medium-high heat, add the shallots and cook for 2–3min until golden. Add the mushrooms, fry for 2min, until starting to take on colour, then stir in garlic and tomato purée. Cook, stirring, for 1min.

2. Stir in the wine and bubble for 2–3min, until slightly reduced, then add the stock and thyme leaves and simmer over a medium heat for 10min.

3. Meanwhile, make the dumplings. Pulse the oats in the small bowl of a food processor to coarse crumbs, then add the remaining dumpling ingredients and some seasoning and pulse to combine. Tip into a bowl and mix in 2 tbsp cold water to bring the mixture together.

4. Stir the lentils into the mushroom pan and season. Spoon 4 rugby ball-shaped dumplings on top, cover with a lid and simmer gently for 20–25min, until the dumplings are cooked. Serve with steamed Savoy cabbage, if you like.

Hands-on time: 30min
Cooking time: about 45min
Serves 4

PER SERVING 433cals, 14g protein, 18g fat (7g saturates), 28g carbs (5g total sugars), 8g fibre

Lentil and Butternut Tagine with Courgette Couscous

The preserved lemons and tomatoes give this hearty tagine a tangy, sweet-and-sour flavour.

FOR THE TAGINE
2 tsp vegetable oil
1 red onion, thickly sliced
2 garlic cloves, crushed
2 tsp each ground cinnamon, cumin and coriander
2 x 400g tins chopped tomatoes
1 medium butternut squash (1kg), peeled, deseeded and cut into 2cm pieces
4 preserved lemons, deseeded and finely chopped
150g dried red lentils, rinsed
150g fine green beans, trimmed
1½ tbsp harissa paste

FOR THE COUSCOUS
200g couscous
2 medium courgettes, coarsely grated
300ml hot vegan vegetable stock
Juice 1 lemon
Handful mint leaves, shredded

1. To make the tagine, heat the oil in a large, wide pan (that has a lid) over a medium heat. Add the onion and a large pinch of salt, then cook for 10min, until softened. Stir in the garlic and spices and fry for 2min, until fragrant. Stir in the tomatoes, butternut squash, preserved lemons, lentils and 400ml water.

2. Bring to the boil, then reduce the heat, cover and bubble gently for 30–40min, stirring occasionally, until the squash is tender.

3. When the tagine is nearly ready, prepare the couscous. Put the couscous and grated courgette into a medium bowl, pour over the hot stock, then season, cover and leave to soak and soften for 10min.

4. Slice the green beans in half to make shorter lengths. Add to the tagine with the harissa and some seasoning. Bubble, uncovered, for 8min, or until the beans are tender.

5. Fluff up the couscous with a fork and stir in the lemon juice and mint. Divide among 4 bowls, top with the tagine and serve.

Hands-on time: 25min
Cooking time: about 1hr 5min
Serves 4

PER SERVING 532cals, 24g protein, 5g fat (1g saturates), 91g carbs (26g total sugars), 16g fibre

Lebanese Cauliflower Bowls

Spicy cauliflower pairs well with smokey baba ganoush in this sophisticated tabbouleh dish.

FOR THE CAULIFLOWER
600g cauliflower florets (about 1 large cauliflower)
1½ tbsp shawarma spice mix
½ tbsp olive oil
Juice ½ lemon

FOR THE BABA GANOUSH
2 large aubergines
½ tbsp olive oil
2 garlic cloves, crushed
1½ tbsp tahini
½ tsp chilli powder
1 tsp ground cumin
Juice 1 lemon

FOR THE TABBOULEH
100g bulgur wheat
400g tin chickpeas, drained and rinsed
3 tbsp olive oil
Juice 1½ lemons
Large handful parsley, roughly chopped
Small handful mint, roughly chopped
3 tomatoes, deseeded and finely chopped
1 cucumber, deseeded and finely chopped
2 spring onions, thinly sliced
50g pomegranate seeds

1. Preheat the oven to 200°C (180°C fan) mark 6. In a large roasting tin, toss together the cauliflower, shawarma spice mix and plenty of seasoning. Drizzle over the oil and roast for 30min, until just tender. Squeeze over the lemon juice and set aside.

2. For the baba ganoush, halve the aubergines lengthways, score the flesh in a criss-cross pattern (do not cut through the skin), and brush the cut sides with oil. Arrange cut-side up in a small roasting tin, then cover with foil and cook in the same oven as the cauliflower for 20–30min, until the flesh is soft. Carefully scoop out the flesh into a food processor (discard the skins). Whizz with the remaining baba ganoush ingredients until smooth, season, then set aside.

3. In a medium pan, bring the bulgur wheat and 200ml cold water to the boil. Cover with a lid and simmer for 8–10min, then take off the heat and set aside, covered, for 5min. Stir in the remaining tabbouleh ingredients and season. To serve, divide the tabbouleh among 4 bowls and top with the cauliflower and baba ganoush.

Hands-on time: 30min
Cooking time: about 35min
Serves 4

PER SERVING 434cals, 15g protein, 19g fat (3g saturates), 44g carbs (12g total sugars), 15g fibre

Butternut Katsu Curry

A tasty vegan twist on the ever-popular Japanese katsu curry, featuring 'escalopes' of sweet butternut squash.

500g butternut squash taken from the neck (about a 10cm length)
2 tsp vegetable oil, plus extra to shallow fry
75g panko breadcrumbs
2 tsp vegan mayonnaise
Salad leaves
Cooked sticky rice, to serve

FOR THE PICKLE
75ml rice vinegar
60g caster sugar
100g radishes, thinly sliced
½ red chilli, deseeded and thinly sliced (optional)

FOR THE CURRY SAUCE
1 tbsp sunflower oil
1 onion, grated
2.5cm piece fresh root ginger, peeled and grated
2 garlic cloves, crushed
2 tbsp mild curry powder
1 tbsp plain flour
2 tsp tomato purée
350ml vegan vegetable stock
100ml coconut milk
1 tbsp light soy sauce
2 tsp caster sugar

1. Preheat the oven to 200°C (180°C fan) mark 6 and line a baking sheet with baking parchment. Peel the squash neck and slice lengthways into 4 even slices, each about 2cm thick. Brush both sides of

Hands-on time: 30min, plus cooling
Cooking time: about 40min
Serves 4

PER SERVING 306cals, 4g protein, 19g fat (5g saturates), 28g carbs (15g total sugars), 5g fibre

each slice with oil and arrange in a single layer on the lined sheet. Season.

2. Roast for 20–25min, or until just tender – you want them to still hold their shape. Cool completely.

3. Meanwhile, make the pickle. Heat the vinegar, sugar, 75ml water and a pinch of salt in a small pan, stirring until dissolved. Put the radishes and chilli, if using, in a small bowl, then pour over the pickling liquid and set aside to cool.

4. For the sauce, heat the oil in a medium pan over a low-medium heat and fry the onion for 7–8min, until softened. Add the ginger and garlic and cook for 1min, then stir in the curry powder, flour and tomato purée. Cook for 1min, then gradually whisk in the stock and coconut milk. Add the soy sauce and sugar. Bring to the boil, whisking, then simmer for 10–15min, until thickened. Blend until smooth. Return to the pan, if needed.

5. Put the breadcrumbs in a shallow bowl. Pat dry the cooled squash slices with kitchen paper, then brush on both sides with mayonnaise. Press into the breadcrumbs to coat well. Heat a thin layer of oil in a large, non-stick frying pan over medium-high heat. Fry the butternut for 4–5min per side, or until golden, turning carefully with a fish slice. Drain briefly on kitchen paper.

6. Arrange the salad leaves on 4 plates, drizzle over some of the pickling liquid, then top with some of the drained pickles. Reheat the curry sauce, if needed, and spoon on to the plates. Top with the sliced butternut katsu. Serve with sticky rice and the remaining pickles on the side.

◆ GET AHEAD
Make the curry sauce a day ahead, then cool, cover and chill. Reheat gently to serve and complete the recipe. The pickles will keep, chilled, for up to 2 weeks in a jar or airtight container.

◆ GH TIP
If you're into pickle, this quantity of pickling liquid will pickle up to twice the amount of vegetables.

Nut and Lentil Roast

Filled with layers of colour and flavour, our easy-yet-impressive veggie roast makes a fantastic centrepiece.

2 tbsp olive oil, plus extra to grease
3 medium courgettes, trimmed
1 onion, finely chopped
2 garlic cloves, crushed
½ tbsp thyme leaves, chopped
125g mixed nuts
250g pack cooked Puy lentils
1 medium egg
100g roasted red peppers, from a jar
100g halloumi cheese, coarsely grated
75g fine asparagus
Rocket, to garnish (optional)

1. Grease a 900g loaf tin and line lengthways with a strip of baking parchment. Peel 2 of the courgettes into long ribbons using a Y-shaped vegetable peeler (avoid and discard the seedy core). Put the ribbons into a bowl and toss through 1 tbsp of the oil. Arrange the courgette widthways in the tin, tightly overlapping the slices and filling gaps to line the tin in an even layer (overhanging the sides is fine). Position more ribbons to line the ends of the tin, reserving the remaining ribbons.

2. Heat the remaining oil in a medium frying pan over a low heat and fry the onion for 5min, until softened. Meanwhile, coarsely grate the remaining courgette. Stir into the onion with the garlic, turn up the heat to medium, and fry for 5min, or until all the moisture has evaporated from the pan. Stir in the thyme and set aside.

3. Pulse the nuts in a food processor until finely chopped (or do this by hand). Empty into a large bowl, then add the courgette mixture, lentils, egg and some seasoning, and mix well to combine.

4. Preheat the oven to 180°C (160°C) mark 4. Press half the lentil mixture into the courgette-lined tin. Slice open the peppers if whole, and trim to fit in a neat layer over the lentil mixture. Top with the grated halloumi and a layer of fine asparagus, then press in the remaining lentil mixture. Fold in any overhanging courgettes, then arrange a layer of courgettes to cover the filling. Cover the tin with foil.

5. Cook in the oven for 50min. Remove from the oven and leave to rest in the tin for 10min before inverting on to a board. Garnish with rocket, if you like, and serve in slices.

Hands-on time: 30min, plus resting
Cooking time: about 1hr
Cuts into 6 slices

PER SLICE 315cals, 15g protein, 21g fat (5g saturates), 14g carbs (5g total sugars), 6g fibre

Cheesy Baked Ratatouille

Our classic mix of vegetables makes a lighter dish, but if you want a heartier meal, simply stir some drained tinned beans into the tomato and pepper sauce before cooking.

2 tbsp olive oil
1 large courgette, trimmed and thinly sliced into rounds
1 aubergine, thinly sliced into rounds
1 onion, finely chopped
3 garlic cloves, crushed
2 tsp thyme leaves, plus extra to garnish
8 large ripe tomatoes
1 tbsp balsamic vinegar
Pinch sugar
2 large roasted red peppers from a jar, drained and roughly chopped
150g goat's cheese log with rind, sliced into 0.5cm rounds

1. Heat ½ tbsp of the oil in a large, deep frying pan over a high heat. Working in batches and adding more oil as needed, fry the courgette and aubergine slices until golden. Remove to a plate.

2. Reduce the heat to medium, add the remaining 1 tbsp oil to the empty pan and fry the onion for 10min, until softened. Stir in the garlic and thyme and fry for 2min. Chop 6 of the tomatoes and add to the pan with the vinegar and sugar. Cook for 10min, until the tomatoes have broken down, then stir in the red peppers; check the seasoning. Scrape into a 2 litre ovenproof serving dish.

3. Preheat the oven to 200°C (180°C fan) mark 6. Thinly slice the remaining tomatoes; arrange on top of the sauce, alternating and overlapping with the aubergine, courgette and goat's cheese slices.

4. Season well and cook in the oven for 30min, or until golden and bubbling. Garnish with extra thyme and serve.

Hands-on time: 30min
Cooking time: about 1hr 5min
Serves 4

PER SERVING 246cals, 11g protein, 16g fat (8g saturates), 13g carbs (12g total sugars), 5g fibre

Veggie Toad in the Hole

The trick to a good toad in the hole is letting the batter rest – and choosing the best-quality sausages!

4 medium eggs
150g plain flour
300ml milk
4 thyme sprigs, leaves picked
8 vegetarian sausages (see GH Tip)
2 red onions, each cut into 8 wedges
2 tbsp vegetable oil
100g red onion chutney
Green salad and mustard, to serve (optional)

1. Preheat the oven to 220°C (200°C fan) mark 7. Make the batter by whisking together the eggs and flour until smooth. Slowly add the milk, whisking until smooth, then whisk through the thyme and plenty of seasoning. Leave to stand until needed.

2. Put the sausages, red onions and vegetable oil into a 25.5 x 35.5cm roasting tin and cook in the oven for 15min until browned.

3. Once browned, remove the tin from the oven and carefully pour in the batter. Dollop over the chutney and return to the oven for 30-35min, until deep golden and puffed up. Serve with a green salad and mustard, if you like.

◆ GH TIP
Pork sausages are equally delicious in this recipe, if you don't need the dish to be vegetarian.

Hands-on time: 20min
Cooking time: about 50min
Serves 4

PER SERVING 520cals, 29g protein, 17g fat (4g saturates), 59g carbs (24g total sugars), 8g fibre

Crispy Tofu Noodles

Gochujang paste has a complex spicy, sweet and savoury flavour, making it the ideal base for a quick and easy stir-fry.

280g firm tofu, cut into 1cm pieces
2 tbsp cornflour
1 tbsp vegetable oil
250g dried noodles
400g Tenderstem broccoli, trimmed and cut into 5cm pieces (see GH Tip)
4 tbsp gochujang paste

1. Pat dry the tofu with kitchen paper and toss with the cornflour and some seasoning to coat. Heat the oil in a large non-stick frying pan over a medium heat. Add the tofu and cook for 10min, turning regularly, until golden and crisp.

2. Meanwhile, cook the noodles in a large pan of boiling water according to the pack instructions, adding the broccoli for the final 3min. Drain and return to the pan.

3. In a small bowl, mix the gochujang paste with 4 tbsp water. Add to the noodle pan with the tofu and toss to combine. Check the seasoning, then divide between 4 bowls and serve.

◆ GH TIP
You can swap the broccoli for frozen edamame or mangetout, if you prefer.

Hands-on time: 15min
Cooking time: about 10min
Serves 4

PER SERVING 440cals, 21g protein, 9g fat (1g saturates), 64g carbs (7g total sugars), 7g fibre

Pulled Hoisin Mushroom Bao Buns

Sticky, sweet and smokey mushrooms make a wonderfully meaty filling for these vegan bao buns. Check brands to make sure they are suitable for vegans, if needed.

FOR THE PULLED MUSHROOMS
1 tbsp sesame oil
1 tbsp soy sauce
½ tbsp smoked paprika
½ tsp Chinese five spice
1 tbsp maple syrup
400g oyster mushrooms

FOR THE HOISIN SAUCE
50g dark brown soft sugar
3 tbsp black bean sauce
2 tbsp soy sauce
1 tbsp rice vinegar
4 prunes
½ tsp sesame oil
½ tsp Chinese five spice powder

TO SERVE
12 ready-made bao buns
1 cucumber, cut into matchsticks
6 spring onions, shredded

1. Preheat the oven to 220°C (200°C fan) mark 7. For the pulled mushrooms, mix the sesame oil, soy, paprika, Chinese five spice and maple syrup in a large roasting tin. Tear the mushrooms into thin strips and add to the tin, mixing gently to combine. Cook for 10min.

2. Meanwhile, make the hoisin sauce by blending all the ingredients until smooth.

3. After 10min, mix 2 tbsp of the hoisin sauce into the mushroom tin. Return to the oven for 5min.

4. To serve, heat the bao buns according to the pack instructions. Spread some of the remaining hoisin sauce inside each bun and fill with some of the pulled mushrooms, cucumber and spring onions.

Hands-on time: 10min
Cooking time: about 20min
Serves 4

PER SERVING 364cals, 10g protein, 5g fat (1g saturates), 67g carbs (32g total sugars), 4g fibre

Smokey Vegan Porcini 'Meatballs' with Creamy Mash

Flaxseed is the secret to binding these dairy-free, protein-packed black bean and mushroom balls.

FOR THE 'MEATBALLS'
25g dried porcini
3 tbsp olive oil
250g chestnut mushrooms, chopped
2 garlic cloves, crushed
1 tsp smoked paprika
400g tin black beans, drained and rinsed
1 tbsp ground/milled flaxseed
60g couscous (dried/uncooked)

FOR THE SAUCE
½ tbsp olive oil
1 red onion, finely chopped
2 rosemary sprigs
2 x 400g tins chopped tomatoes
250ml vegan red wine
150g baby leaf spinach

FOR THE MASH
900g floury potatoes, peeled and cut into even chunks
1 large garlic clove, peeled
75g dairy-free olive oil spread
4–5 tbsp cream alternative (optional)

◆ GET AHEAD
Prepare to end of step 6. Cool and freeze the components separately, for up to 1 month. Defrost overnight in the fridge. Reheat the sauce and mash separately on the hob, until piping hot. Add the 'meatballs' to the sauce (do not stir), then heat through.

Hands-on time: 45min, plus soaking and chilling
Cooking time: about 1hr
Serves 4

PER SERVING 692cals, 19g protein, 25g fat (5g saturates), 78g carbs (13g total sugars), 15g fibre

1. To make the 'meatballs', put the porcini in a small heatproof bowl, pour over 100ml just-boiled water and soak for 20min. Meanwhile, heat 1 tbsp of the oil in a large, deep frying pan over a medium heat. Add the mushrooms and fry for 6–7min, stirring occasionally, until softened and turning golden. Add the garlic, paprika and beans and cook, stirring, for 2min, until the mixture looks dry. Put the flaxseed in a small bowl with 2 tbsp cold water, stir and leave to soak for 10min.

2. Scrape the mushroom mix into the bowl of a food processor. Drain the porcini (reserving the water) and add to the processor with plenty of seasoning. Pulse to a coarse purée. Add the couscous and soaked flaxseed; pulse again briefly to combine. Roll into 20 balls with damp hands, then arrange on a plate and chill for 30min.

3. Meanwhile, make the sauce. In the same pan, heat the ½ tbsp oil over a low-medium heat and fry the onion for 8–10min, until softened. Add the rosemary, tomatoes, wine, reserved porcini soaking water and some seasoning, then bring to the boil and bubble for 20min, until reduced. Preheat the oven to 180°C (160°C fan) mark 4.

4. For the mash, put the potatoes into a large pan with the garlic and some salt, cover with cold water and bring to the boil. Bubble for 15min, or until the potatoes are tender. Drain and leave to steam dry in a colander for 10min.

5. Meanwhile, heat 2 tbsp of the oil in a separate frying pan over medium heat, add the 'meatballs' and shake carefully to coat in the oil. Fry for 10min, turning regularly, until well browned, then transfer to a baking tray and cook in the oven for 12min.

6. Return the potatoes and garlic to the empty pan, then mash well with the spread and cream

alternative (if using). Cover and keep warm. Stir the spinach into the sauce until just wilted.

7. To serve, divide the mash between 4 plates or bowls. Stir the 'meatballs' gently into the sauce, then spoon over the mash and serve.

Caramelised Onion, Squash and Ricotta Baked Terrine

With its combination of sweet squash, tangy onions and creamy ricotta, this pairs wonderfully with all the traditional roast-dinner accompaniments.

500g butternut squash taken from the neck, peeled and halved lengthways
4 tsp olive oil, plus extra to grease
1 large red onion, thinly sliced
2 tsp sugar
1 tbsp balsamic vinegar
500g ricotta
2 medium eggs
50g vegetarian Italian-style hard cheese or hard goat's cheese, finely grated
¼ tsp freshly grated nutmeg
3 thyme sprigs, plus extra to garnish (optional)

◆ GET AHEAD
Cook the butternut squash and onions 1 day ahead. Cover and chill separately. Complete the recipe to serve.

◆ GH TIP
Roast the leftover (raw) squash until tender and mash with plenty of butter for a delicious accompaniment to a Sunday roast.

Hands-on time: 25min, plus cooling
Cooking time: about 1hr 15min
Serves 8

PER SERVING 187cals, 10g protein, 12g fat
(6g saturates), 10g carbs (7g total sugars), 2g fibre

1. Preheat the oven to 190°C (170°C fan) mark 5. Line a baking tray with baking parchment. Slice the squash into 1cm-thick wedges and toss with 2 tsp of the oil and some seasoning. Arrange in a single layer on the lined tray and roast for 20–25min, until just tender. Set aside until cool enough to handle.

2. Meanwhile, heat the remaining oil in a medium frying pan over a low heat. Add the onion and fry, stirring occasionally, for 10–12min, until softened. Add the sugar, vinegar and a pinch of salt, then increase the heat to high and bubble for 1–2min, until reduced and sticky. Remove from the heat and set aside.

3. In a bowl, whisk together the ricotta, eggs, cheese, nutmeg, ¾ tsp salt and some freshly ground pepper.

4. Lightly grease and line a 900g loaf tin lengthways with a strip of baking parchment. Put the thyme sprigs in the bottom of the tin, then arrange the squash slices neatly on top in 2 layers. Spoon over the onions in an even layer, followed by the ricotta mixture, and smooth to level. Put the tin on a baking tray and cook in the oven for 45–50min, until just set firm.

5. Cool in the tin for 10min, then run a sharp knife around the inside edges of the tin to loosen. Invert the terrine on to a serving plate. Serve hot, warm or at room temperature, garnished with extra thyme sprigs, if you like.

Canapés
& Cocktails

Roasted Grape and Goat's Cheese Toasts

Orange adds a tangy note to this easy yet impressive starter. If you don't have a griddle pan, toast your bread in the toaster (without oil), then brush with oil while warm.

300g red seedless grapes
1 tsp thyme leaves, plus extra to serve
Finely grated zest 1 orange
2 tbsp red wine vinegar
3 tbsp olive oil
6 large slices sourdough bread
250g soft goat's cheese
100ml double cream
1 tsp freshly ground black pepper

1. Preheat the oven to 190°C (170°C fan) mark 5. Scatter the grapes, thyme and orange zest on a baking tray. Drizzle over the vinegar and 1 tbsp of the oil and mix to combine. Roast for 15min, until the grapes are soft but not collapsing. Leave to cool slightly.

2. Meanwhile, preheat a griddle pan over high heat and brush the sourdough on both sides with the remaining 2 tbsp oil. Griddle the bread for 2 min per side, until golden with charred lines (do this in batches if needed).

3. In a medium bowl, mix the goat's cheese, cream, pepper and ¼ tsp salt.

4. To serve, spread the goat's cheese mixture over the toasts and slice each in half. Arrange on a large serving plate and top with the grapes. Drizzle over any roasting juices and scatter over extra thyme leaves.

◆ GET AHEAD

Roast the grapes up to 2hr ahead, then cool, cover and store at room temperature. Mix the goat's cheese, cream and seasoning up to 1 day ahead, then cover and chill. To serve, complete the recipe.

Hands-on time: 15min
Cooking time: about 20min
Serves 6

PER SERVING 282cals, 4g protein, 15g fat (6g saturates), 32g carbs (9g total sugars), 2g fibre

Mini Salmon Roasties

Make sure you source mini new potatoes to keep these nibbles bite-size.

25 miniature new potatoes
½ tbsp olive oil
60g crème fraîche
½–1 tsp creamed horseradish, to taste
1 tsp finely grated lemon zest
50g smoked salmon trimmings
Small dill sprigs, to garnish

1. Preheat the oven to 200°C (180°C fan) mark 6. Toss the potatoes and oil in a small roasting tin and season. Roast for 30–35min, tossing occasionally, until golden and tender. Cool.

2. Meanwhile, in a small bowl, mix the crème fraîche, horseradish, lemon zest and some seasoning. Chill until needed.

3. Using a potato masher, very lightly crush each potato to create a flat base and top. Arrange on a serving plate. Pipe or spoon on the crème fraîche mixture. Top with the salmon and garnish with dill sprigs and pepper.

◆ GET AHEAD
Prepare to the end of step 2 up to a day ahead. Cover and chill the potatoes and sauce separately. To serve, allow the potatoes to come up to room temperature. Assemble up to 1hr ahead.

Hands-on time: 20min, plus cooling
Cooking time: 35min
Makes 25 canapés

PER CANAPÉ 45cals, 1g protein, 2g fat (1g saturates), 6g carbs (1g total sugars), 1g fibre

Pancetta Cups

Serve up breakfast for dinner with these tasty mini frittatas. Swap the brown sauce for ketchup, if you prefer.

Vegetable oil, to grease
12 pancetta rashers
3 medium eggs, beaten
50g crème fraîche
50g mature Cheddar, grated
Small handful chives, finely chopped
6 cherry tomatoes, halved
50ml brown sauce

1. Preheat the oven to 180°C (160°C fan) mark 4. Grease a 12-hole mini muffin tin with a little oil. Slice the pancetta rashers in half widthways. Lay 2 pieces into each hole of the tin, so they cover the base and come up the sides a little.

2. In a bowl, whisk the eggs, crème fraîche, Cheddar, most of the chives and some seasoning. Spoon into the lined holes. Add a tomato to each, cut-side up. Cook for 15min, or until golden brown and set. Cool slightly in the tin, then transfer to a serving plate.

3. Mix the brown sauce with 1 tbsp water to loosen. Drizzle over the cups, scatter over remaining chives and serve just warm.

◆ GET AHEAD
Make up to end of step 2 up to a day ahead, transfer to a baking tray, cover and chill. To serve, reheat in an oven preheated to 180°C (160°C fan) mark 4 for 5min. Complete the recipe.

Hands-on time: 20min
Cooking time: about 15min
Makes 12 cups

PER CUP 91cals, 4g protein, 8g fat (4g saturates), 2g carbs (1g total sugars), 0g fibre

Sesame Prawn Balls

Your takeaway favourite prawn toasts in ball form.

400g raw peeled king prawns
2 garlic cloves, crushed
2cm piece fresh root ginger, peeled and finely grated
2 spring onions, trimmed and roughly chopped
2 tsp soy sauce
3 medium eggs
100g fresh white breadcrumbs
50g plain flour
100g sesame seeds
Vegetable oil, to fry
Sweet chilli sauce, to serve

1. Whizz the prawns, garlic, ginger and spring onions in a food processor until fairly smooth. Add the soy sauce, 1 egg, 50g breadcrumbs and some seasoning, then whizz to combine. With wet hands, roll into 24 balls, put on a baking tray and loosely cover with cling film. Chill for 1hr to firm up.

2. Put the flour into a shallow bowl, and the sesame seeds and remaining breadcrumbs into another. In a third bowl, lightly beat 2 of the eggs. Roll the balls in flour, then in egg, then breadcrumbs.

3. Pour the oil into a large, heavy-based, high-sided pan until it comes a third of the way up the sides. Heat to 180°C or until a bread cube sizzles to golden in 40sec. Fry the balls in batches for 4min, turning halfway, until deep golden and cooked. Lift out on to kitchen paper with a slotted spoon. Cool slightly. Repeat with the remaining balls. Serve with sweet chilli sauce for dipping.

Hands-on time: 25min, plus chilling and cooling
Cooking time: about 20min
Makes 24 balls

PER CANAPÉ (without dip) 74cals, 5g protein, 4g fat (1g saturates), 4g carbs (0g total sugars), 1g fibre

Celeriac Rémoulade with Chorizo

If you like, set out the toasts, rémoulade and fried chorizo and let people assemble these canapés themselves.

FOR THE REMOULADE
Juice 1 lemon
300g celeriac
3 tbsp crème fraîche
3 tbsp mayonnaise
1–2tsp Dijon mustard, to taste
2 tbsp chopped parsley, plus extra to garnish

TO SERVE
Part-baked medium-size baguette (around 160g)
60g diced chorizo

1. For the rémoulade, put the lemon juice into a medium bowl. Peel the celeriac using a vegetable peeler, coarsely grate, then toss in the lemon juice. Mix in the remaining ingredients and check the seasoning. Cover and chill until needed.

2. Preheat the oven to 220°C (200°C fan) mark 7. Slice the baguette into 20 x 1cm rounds and arrange on a baking tray. Bake for 12–15min, turning halfway through, until crisp and golden. Cool.

3. Fry the chorizo in a pan over a medium heat for 4–5min until it's crisp and has released some of its oil.

4. To serve, spoon the rémoulade on toasts and transfer to a serving platter. Top with some chorizo, a drizzle of the chorizo oil and parsley.

Hands-on time: 20min, plus cooling
Cooking time: about 20min
Makes 20 canapés

PER CANAPÉ 63cals, 2g protein, 4g fat (1g saturates), 5g carbs (1g total sugars), 1g fibre

Limoncello and Cucumber Fizz

This refreshing cocktail is the perfect choice for warm summer days. Fresh mint would be a delicious alternative to basil.

75g caster sugar
1 cucumber, peeled into ribbons (discard the seedy core)
Large handful basil, leaves picked
Crushed ice
400ml limoncello
75cl bottle Prosecco or Cava, chilled

1. Heat the sugar and 75ml water in a large pan over a low heat, stirring to dissolve the sugar. Set aside to cool.

2. Divide the cucumber and basil between 8 large wine glasses and muddle briefly with a spoon. Fill each glass with crushed ice. Divide the cooled sugar syrup between the glasses, followed by the limoncello. Top up with fizz and serve.

◆ GH TIP
If you make lots of cocktails, make double the quantity of sugar syrup and store the remainder in the fridge in an airtight container for up to 1 month.

Hands-on time: 5min, plus cooling
Cooking time: about 5min
Makes 8 cocktails

PER COCKTAIL 252cals, <1g protein, 0g fat (0g saturates), 30g carbs (30g total sugars), <1g fibre

Peach Bourbon Iced Tea

A flavourful and fruity iced tea gets a boozy kick!

6 English breakfast teabags
6 tbsp caster sugar
3 peaches, de-stoned and cut into wedges
Large handful mint sprigs, plus extra to serve
150ml bourbon
750ml still lemonade, chilled
Ice cubes, to serve

1. Put the teabags and sugar into a large heatproof jug. Pour in 750ml just-boiled water and stir to dissolve the sugar. Allow to steep for 3–4min, then lift out the teabags, lightly squeeze and discard. Add the peaches and mint, then cool and chill for at least 2hr (or up to 12hr).

2. To serve, stir the bourbon and lemonade into the tea jug. Fill 8 tall glasses with ice, pour in the tea mixture and garnish with mint sprigs.

Hands-on time: 10min, plus cooling and chilling
Makes 8 cocktails

PER COCKTAIL 122cals, <1g protein, 0g fat (0g saturates), 19g carbs (19g total sugars), 1g fibre

Frozen Strawberry Daiquiri

Keep a stash of frozen berries on hand in your freezer so you can whip up this adult slushy any time you like!

400g hulled and frozen strawberries
75–100ml white rum
4 tbsp caster sugar
Zest and juice 1 lime

1. Whizz the frozen strawberries in a blender with the rum, caster sugar and the lime zest and juice until slushy but still frozen. Pour into 2 large glasses and serve immediately.

Hands-on time: 5min
Makes 2 cocktails

PER COCKTAIL 279cals, 1g protein, 1g fat (<1g saturates), 42g carbs (42g total sugars), 8g fibre

Red Wine Hot Chocolate

Pack this in an insulated flask to enjoy on a cold winter walk or while carol singing – it's guaranteed to warm you from the inside out.

250g dark chocolate, roughly chopped, plus extra, finely grated, to serve
400ml dry red wine
300ml milk
300ml single cream
1 tsp vanilla extract
Caster sugar, to taste

TO SERVE (optional)
Squirty cream
Marshmallows

1. In a medium pan, heat the chocolate, red wine, milk and single cream over a low heat, stirring constantly until the chocolate has melted and the mixture is piping hot.

2. Remove from the heat and stir in the vanilla. Add the sugar to sweeten to taste. Divide among 6 heatproof glasses and top with squirty cream and marshmallows, if using. Garnish with finely grated chocolate and serve.

Hands-on time: 10min
Cooking time: about 10min
Serves 6

PER SERVING 415cals, 6g protein, 22g fat (14g saturates), 35g carbs (35g total sugars), 1g fibre

Mini Chilli and Crab Doughnuts

You can use tinned crab instead of fresh, just make sure you drain it thoroughly. For a veggie version, substitute mashed hard-boiled eggs.

FOR THE DOUGHNUTS
100ml whole milk
25g unsalted butter
200g strong white flour
7g sachet fast-action dried yeast
2 tbsp caster sugar
1 medium egg
Vegetable oil, to grease and deep-fry

FOR THE FILLING
200g cooked white crab meat
75g mayonnaise
1 small red chilli, deseeded and finely chopped
Finely grated zest and juice ½ lemon
2 tbsp finely chopped chives

YOU'LL ALSO NEED
Cooking thermometer

◆ GET AHEAD
Cook the doughnuts up to 4hr ahead, then cool, cover and store unfilled at room temperature. Make the filling up to 4hr ahead, then cover and chill. To serve, reheat the doughnuts in an oven preheated to 190°C (170°C fan) mark 5 for 5min, before completing the recipe. Alternatively, make the dough to the end of step 2 a day ahead. Once risen, knock back to release the air, then cover and chill overnight. Complete the recipe to serve.

Hands-on time: 30min, plus cooling and rising
Cooking time: about 20min
Makes 16 doughnuts

PER DOUGHNUT 143cals, 5g protein, 9g fat (2g saturates), 12g carbs (2g total sugars), <1g fibre

1. For the doughnuts, heat the milk and butter in a small pan over a low heat to melt the butter. Cool until just warm.

2. In the bowl of a freestanding mixer fitted with a dough hook, combine the flour, yeast, sugar, egg, cooled milk mixture and ½ tsp fine salt. Knead on low-medium speed for 8–10min, until springy (the dough should be glossy and slightly sticky). Cover and leave to rise in a warm place for 1hr, until doubled in size.

3. Meanwhile, make the filling. Mix together all the ingredients, except the chives, with plenty of seasoning. Cover and chill until needed.

4. Once the dough has risen, grease a large baking sheet. Divide the dough into 16 equal pieces, then roll into balls and space apart on the greased sheet. Loosely cover with cling film and leave to rise again for 30min, until puffed.

5. Fill a large, heavy-based, deep pan with oil so that it's 5cm deep. Heat the oil to 160°C. Add 8 doughnuts at a time and cook for 2min per side, until deep golden brown and puffed. Using a slotted spoon, transfer to kitchen paper to drain. Cook the remaining doughnuts, monitoring the oil temperature as you go.

6. When ready to serve, cut into the top of each doughnut, almost all the way down. Spoon in the crab filling and garnish with chives.

Pea and Mint Croustades

Crisp croustade cases make a great base for these veggie canapés, but you could use crackers or toasted baguette slices instead. For meat lovers, garnish them with shards of crispy Parma ham.

200g frozen peas or petits pois
1 small garlic clove, crushed
Small handful mint leaves, plus extra small leaves to garnish (optional)
25g hard goat's cheese, finely grated, plus extra, shaved, to garnish
2 tbsp extra virgin olive oil
Lemon juice, to taste
24 ready-made croustade cases

◆ GET AHEAD
Make the recipe to the end of step 2 a few hours ahead. Bring to room temperature for 30min, before completing the recipe to serve.

1. Cook the peas in a pan of boiling water for 4–5min, until just cooked. Drain and cool in cold water, then drain again.

2. Tip the peas into the small bowl of a food processor with the garlic, mint, cheese and olive oil. Season with pepper, plenty of salt and a squeeze of lemon juice (about 1 tsp), then pulse briefly to a chunky texture. Scrape into a piping bag or small food bag and chill until needed.

3. To serve, pipe the pea mixture into the croustade cases and top each with a shaving of cheese or a small mint leaf, if using. Serve immediately.

Hands-on time: 10min
Cooking time: about 5min
Makes 24 croustades

PER CROUSTADE 28cals, 1g protein, 2g fat (1g saturates), 2g carbs (1g total sugars), 1g fibre

Spiced Tortilla Chips with Festive Houmous

Serve homemade tortilla chips with a sweet and spicy houmous for an easy nibble you can make ahead that is perfect for a drinks party.

FOR THE TORTILLA CHIPS
2 tbsp olive oil
½–1 tsp smoked sweet paprika, to taste
1 tsp dried oregano
4 large flour tortillas

FOR THE HOUMOUS
2 medium parsnips (about 300g), peeled and
    roughly chopped
400g tin chickpeas, drained and rinsed
2 tbsp tahini
1 tsp ground cumin
½ tsp ground cinnamon
1 garlic clove, crushed
1 tbsp white wine vinegar
Finely grated zest and juice ½ orange
3 tbsp olive oil, plus extra to drizzle

TO GARNISH (OPTIONAL)
2 tbsp pomegranate seeds
Small handful parsley, chopped

◆ GET AHEAD
Once cool, store the chips in an airtight container at room temperature for up to a week. Prepare the houmous to the end of step 4, then cover and chill for up to 5 days. To serve, allow the houmous to come to room temperature. Thin with water, if needed, before completing the recipe.

1. Preheat the oven to 190°C (170°C fan) mark 5. For the tortilla chips, mix together the oil, paprika, oregano and plenty of seasoning in a large bowl. Cut the tortillas into 7cm-long triangles. Add to the bowl and mix well, making sure all triangles are coated in the oil mixture.

2. Empty the chips on to a large baking tray, spreading them out to an even single layer. Cook for 18–20min, turning occasionally, until golden and crisp. Cool completely on the tray.

3. Cook the parsnips in boiling water for 10min, until tender. Drain, then steam dry for 5min. Empty the chickpeas into a food processor with the cooked parsnips, tahini, spices, garlic, vinegar, orange zest and juice. Pulse until combined.

4. With the motor of the food processor running, pour in the oil to make a smooth paste. Add just-boiled water to thin to your desired consistency and check the seasoning.

5. Serve the tortilla chips with the houmous, garnished with pomegranate seeds and parsley, if using, drizzled with the extra oil.

Hands-on time: 20min, plus cooling
Cooking time: about 20min
Serves 8

PER SERVING (with 2 tbsp houmous) 214cals,
6g protein, 12g fat (2g saturates), 20g carbs
(3g total sugars), 5g fibre

Meatball Dippers

Light and tangy with ricotta and lemon, these tender pork meatballs are great on their own, but even better with a choice of two deliciously different dipping sauces.

500g free-range pork mince
100g fresh white breadcrumbs
2 tbsp chopped chives, plus extra to serve
125g ricotta
1 medium egg, lightly beaten
Finely grated zest 1 lemon
40g Parmesan cheese, finely grated
3 tbsp olive oil, to fry

1. Combine all the ingredients (except the oil) in a large bowl, then season and mix thoroughly (using your hands is easiest). Scoop out level tablespoons of the mixture and roll into balls – you should have about 48. Arrange on a tray, then cover and chill for 30min.

2. Heat the oil in a large frying pan (that has a lid) over medium heat and fry the meatballs for 4–5min (in batches, if needed), turning often, until golden all over. Return all the browned meatballs to the pan, cover with a lid, then reduce the heat to low and cook, shaking the pan occasionally, for 15min or until the meatballs are cooked through.

3. Transfer to a serving dish and serve warm, sprinkled with extra chives and your choice of dip alongside (see right), if you like.

◆ GET AHEAD
Make and cook the meatballs up to 1 day ahead. Cool, cover and chill. To serve, reheat on a baking tray in an oven preheated to 200°C (180°C fan) mark 6 for 8–10min until piping hot.

Hands-on time: 25min, plus chilling
Cooking time: about 20min
Makes about 48 meatballs

PER MEATBALL (without dip) 37cals, 3g protein, 2g fat (1g saturates), 1g carbs (0g total sugars), 0g fibre

Swedish Cream Sauce

A Scandi-style cream sauce, spiked with mustard and dill.

25g butter
25g plain flour
250ml fresh beef or chicken stock
50ml double cream
½ tbsp Dijon mustard
2 tsp Worcestershire sauce
Pinch sugar
1 tbsp chopped dill

1. Melt the butter in a small pan over a low heat. Add the flour and cook, stirring, until deep golden. Gradually stir in the stock and double cream and bring to the boil, stirring regularly.

2. Bubble for a few min, stirring occasionally, until smooth and thick. Stir in the mustard, Worcestershire sauce and sugar. Season with plenty of salt and pepper and stir in the dill. Serve with the Meatball Dippers (see left).

◆ GET AHEAD
Make the sauce up to a day ahead. Cool, cover and chill. To serve, reheat gently in a pan, thinning with a little more stock if needed.

Hands-on time: 5min
Cooking time: about 10min
Makes about 25 servings

Per 1 tsp serving 14cals, 1g protein, 1g fat (1g saturates), 1g carbs (0g total sugars), 0g fibre

Spicy Pomegranate Ketchup

A speedy, sweet-and-spicy ketchup.

INGREDIENTS
3 tbsp tomato ketchup
4 tbsp pomegranate molasses
½ tbsp sriracha

1. Whisk together all the ingredients with a pinch of salt. Serve with the Meatball Dippers (see left).

◆ GET AHEAD
Make up to 2 days ahead. Cover and chill. Allow to come up to room temperature before serving.

Hands-on time: 5min
Makes about 25 servings

Per 1tsp serving 11cals, 0g protein, 0g fat (0g saturates), 3g carbs (2g total sugars), 0g fibre

Salmon Oatcakes

Our recipe makes more oatcakes than you'll need for the canapés, but they keep well for future nibbling.

FOR THE OATCAKES
25g butter
175g rolled oats
Plain flour, to dust

FOR THE HERBY CREAM CHEESE
125g cream cheese
Small handful chives, finely chopped
Small handful dill, finely chopped
Finely grated zest ½ lemon

TO SERVE
100g smoked salmon, cut into small strips

◆ GET AHEAD
Make the oatcakes up to 1 week ahead. Once cool, store in an airtight container at room temperature. Make the herby cream cheese up to 1 day ahead. Cover and chill. Complete the recipe to serve.

1. First make the oatcakes. Preheat the oven to 180°C (160°C fan) mark 4 and line 2 large baking trays with baking parchment. In a small pan, melt the butter and 150ml water. Set aside to cool slightly.

2. Pulse the oats and a pinch of salt in a food processor until fairly fine, then tip into a large bowl and mix in the cooled butter mixture to form a soft dough. Tip on to a lightly floured work surface and shape into a disc.

3. Roll out the dough to 3mm thick. Stamp out circles using a 5cm round cutter, or cut into 5cm squares, re-rolling the trimmings (you should have about 28 oatcakes). Arrange on the lined trays, spacing slightly apart, then bake for 20-25min, or until lightly golden. Transfer to a wire rack to cool completely.

4. Meanwhile, mix together all the herby cream cheese ingredients with plenty of seasoning. Cover and chill until needed.

5. To serve, spread the cream cheese mixture on to 12 of the oatcakes and top with smoked salmon and some freshly ground black pepper. Serve.

Hands-on time: 30min, plus cooling
Cooking time: about 25min
Makes 12 canapés

PER CANAPÉ 115cals, 4g protein, 6g fat (3g saturates), 10g carbs (1g total sugars), 1g fibre

Spicy Clementine Margarita

We've added a festive twist to the popular tequila cocktail. Use freshly squeezed orange rather than clementine juice, if you prefer.

FOR THE COCKTAIL
1 fresh jalapeño chilli
300ml tequila
150ml Cointreau
150ml clementine juice, freshly squeezed
50ml lime juice, freshly squeezed

TO SERVE
Ice cubes
1 fresh jalapeño chilli, sliced

1. Slice the whole chilli in half lengthways, add to a large jug and squash a few times with the end of a rolling pin.

2. Stir in the remaining cocktail ingredients. Fill 6 short tumblers with ice, then strain in the cocktail. Garnish with jalapeño slices and serve.

◆ GET AHEAD
Mix the cocktail up to 2hr ahead. Cover and chill. Complete the recipe to serve.

Hands-on time: 10min
Makes 6 cocktails

PER COCKTAIL 200cals, 0g protein, 0g fat (0g saturates), 8g carbs (8g total sugars), 0g fibre

Courgette Fritters

Topped with yogurt, these Turkish fritters are a pretty canapé. For a more informal nibble, serve them hot, with the topping alongside as a dip.

FOR THE FRITTERS
1 large courgette (about 225g), trimmed and
    coarsely grated
1 spring onion, finely chopped
50g feta, finely chopped
1 garlic clove, crushed
1½ tbsp chopped dill
20g plain flour
25g beaten egg (about ½ medium egg)
2 tbsp olive oil

FOR THE TOPPING
100g Greek yogurt
50g cucumber, finely chopped
1 tbsp chopped mint, plus extra to garnish
½ red chilli, deseeded and finely chopped

◆ GET AHEAD
Fry the fritters up to 1 day ahead. Once cool, store in an airtight container in the fridge. About 30min before serving, reheat in a single layer on a baking tray in an oven preheated to 180°C (160°C fan) mark 4 for 10min. Complete the recipe to serve.

1. For the fritters, put the grated courgette into a colander in the sink. Sprinkle over 1 tsp salt and mix. Set aside for at least 10min (or up to 30min) to draw out moisture.

2. Tip the salted courgette on to a clean tea towel, lift up the corners and squeeze over the sink to drain out as much liquid as possible.

3. Empty the courgette into a large bowl and mix in the spring onion, feta, garlic, dill, flour and some seasoning. Stir in the egg.

4. Heat 1 tbsp of the oil in a large, non-stick frying pan over a medium heat. Working in batches and adding the remaining oil as needed, add 1 tsp dollops of the courgette mixture to the pan, spacing apart and flattening slightly. Fry for 2–3min per side, until golden. Transfer on to a baking tray lined with kitchen paper and allow to cool slightly.

5. For the topping, mix the yogurt, cucumber, chopped mint and some seasoning in a small bowl. Arrange the fritters on a serving plate or board and spoon on a dollop of the topping. Garnish with mint and chilli and serve.

Hands-on time: 25min, plus salting and cooling
Cooking time: about 12min
Makes 24 fritters

PER FRITTER 73cals, 3g protein, 5g fat (2g saturates), 3g carbs (1g total sugars), 0g fibre

Tahini Caramel Squares

Not every canapé has to be savoury – serve these sweet treats in the later part of the evening.

FOR THE SHORTBREAD
150g butter, softened, plus extra to grease
75g caster sugar
175g plain flour

FOR THE TAHINI CARAMEL
100g butter
200g light brown soft sugar
150ml double cream
½ tsp flaked sea salt
100g tahini
½ tsp vanilla bean paste

FOR THE SEEDY TOPPING
1½ tbsp vegetable oil
1½ tbsp runny honey
150g mixed seeds

◆ GET AHEAD
Make up to 3 days ahead. Cover and chill.

1. Lightly grease and line the base and sides of a 20.5cm square tin with baking parchment. For the shortbread, pulse the sugar and butter in a food processor until smooth or beat in a bowl using a wooden spoon. Add the flour and a pinch of salt and whizz/stir until just clumping together.

2. Tip into the lined tin, then press to an even layer with the back of a cutlery spoon. Prick the base all over with a fork and chill for 15min.

3. Preheat the oven to 180°C (160°C fan) mark 4. Bake the shortbread for 20min, or until lightly golden. Leave to cool completely in the tin. Leave the oven on.

4. Make the tahini caramel. In a medium pan, gently heat the butter and sugar, until melted and smooth. Increase the heat to high, stir in the cream and sea salt, and bubble for 5min, until thickened.

5. Remove from the heat, add the tahini and vanilla and keep stirring until slightly thickened. Pour over the shortbread and spread to level. Leave to set sightly while you make the seedy topping.

6. Line a baking tray with baking parchment. In a small bowl, mix the oil and honey, then stir in the seeds. Tip on to the prepared baking sheet and spread out evenly. Bake for 15min, stirring every 5min, until lightly golden.

7. Tip the seed mixture on to the caramel layer and gently spread out with a spoon, then press in lightly. Leave to cool for 15min, then chill for at least 1hr to set. Transfer to a board and cut into 25 squares.

(V)

Hands-on time: 30min, plus chilling and cooling
Cooking time: about 45min
Cuts into 25 squares

PER SQUARE 231cals, 3g protein, 16g fat (8g saturates), 19g carbs (12g total sugars), 1g fibre

DIY Marshmallow Bar

This is a fun way to serve marshmallows that allows everyone to get stuck in and dip and sprinkle as they like. Try experimenting with different extracts, essences and colourings.

9 gelatine leaves
375g granulated sugar
400g golden syrup
Vegetable oil, to grease
Icing sugar, to dust and coat
1 tbsp vanilla bean paste
Few drops rosewater or orange blossom extract (optional)
Pink food colouring gel or paste

TO SERVE (OPTIONAL)
Salted caramel sauce
Chocolate, melted
Chopped roasted hazelnuts
Freeze-dried raspberries

YOU'LL ALSO NEED
Sugar thermometer

◆ GET AHEAD
Prepare to the end of step 5 up to 2 weeks ahead. Once set, cover and store at room temperature in an airtight container. Complete the recipe to serve.

1. Use scissors to cut the gelatine into small pieces and put into the bowl of a freestanding mixer fitted with a whisk attachment. Add 125ml cold water and leave to soak while you make the sugar syrup.

Hands-on time: 30min, plus soaking and overnight setting
Cooking time: about 15min
Makes about 40 marshmallows

PER MARSHMALLOW (without toppings) 69cals, 1g protein, 0g fat (0g saturates), 17g carbs (17g total sugars), 0g fibre

2. Put the sugar, syrup, a pinch of salt and 125ml water into a pan and heat over medium heat, stirring until the sugar dissolves. Turn up the heat, carefully swirling the pan occasionally, until the mixture reaches 115°C on a sugar thermometer.

3. Turn on the mixer to a low speed and gradually add the hot sugar syrup. Once it's all incorporated, increase the speed to high and continue beating until mixture is very thick and white, about 10–12min.

4. Meanwhile, grease and line a rough 20.5 x 30.5cm roasting tin with cling film (make sure some overhangs the edges to make removal easier). Grease the top of the cling film and dust with sifted icing sugar until covered.

5. When the marshmallow mixture is ready, beat in the vanilla, rosewater or orange blossom extract (if using) and enough food colouring to get your desired shade. Scrape into the tin, level with a palette knife and dust the top with more sifted icing sugar. Leave overnight at room temperature.

6. Using the overhanging cling film to help you, lift the marshmallow out of the tin and invert on to a chopping board. Cut (or snip) the marshmallow into bite-sized squares. Working a few at a time, toss the squares in a bowl of sifted icing sugar to coat.

7. Serve the marshmallows as they are or with salted caramel sauce, melted chocolate, chopped nuts and freeze-dried raspberries for customising.

Lemon Meringue Pots

These are a joy to eat. Decorate with sugar sprinkles, if you like, or, for more crunch, use gingersnaps instead of the shortbread biscuits.

2 gelatine leaves
200g lemon curd
100g shortbread biscuits
150ml double cream
2 tbsp icing sugar
1 tsp vanilla extract
2 meringue nests (about 25g)

1. Soak the gelatine in cold water until softened, about 5min.

2. Heat the lemon curd in a small pan over medium heat until it starts to bubble. Lift the gelatine out of the water and squeeze out the excess liquid, then stir into the hot curd to dissolve. Set aside to cool slightly, then pipe or spoon evenly into 12 x 70ml shot glasses. Chill for at least 1hr to set.

3. Pulse the biscuits to rough crumbs in a food processor or bash with a rolling pin in a food bag. Spoon 1 tbsp biscuit rubble into each glass.

4. Whip the cream, icing sugar and vanilla to soft peaks. Pipe or spoon on top of the biscuits. Crush the meringue nests and sprinkle over the cream, then serve.

◆ GET AHEAD
Prepare to end of step 2 up to a day ahead. Keep chilled. Complete the recipe up to 3hr ahead, but don't scatter on the meringue. Chill. Complete the recipe to serve.

Hands-on time: 20min, plus soaking, cooling and chilling
Cooking time: about 5min
Makes 12 pots

PER POT 170cals, 1g protein, 10g fat (6g saturates), 19g carbs (14g total sugars), 0g fibre

Beetroot and Walnut Blinis

Quick to assemble and a joy to eat! Look for cooked beetroot in natural juices, rather than pickled in jars, for this recipe.

25g walnut halves
12 ready-made canapé or cocktail blinis
1 cooked beetroot (about 25g)
50g natural yogurt
1 tsp Dijon mustard
½ tbsp finely chopped dill, plus extra to serve

1. Toast the walnuts in a dry frying pan over medium heat, until fragrant. Empty on to a chopping board and leave to cool.

2. Cook the blinis according to pack instructions, then set aside to cool completely (they can be a bit tough without this step).

3. Finely chop the cooled walnuts and beetroot (keep separate). Mix together the yogurt, mustard, dill and plenty of seasoning.

4. Spoon or pipe the yogurt mixture on to the blinis and top with chopped walnuts and beetroot. Garnish with dill sprigs and serve.

◆ GET AHEAD
Prepare the yogurt mixture up to 1 day ahead, then cover and chill. Complete the recipe to serve.

Hands-on time: 10min, plus cooling
Cooking time: about 10min
Makes 12 blinis

PER BLINI 38cals, 1g protein, 2g fat (<1g saturates), 4g carbs (1g total sugars), <1g fibre

Drunken Prawn and Chorizo Skewers

Sweet, salty and sticky, these are everything a cocktail party canapé should be.

200g raw peeled jumbo king prawns, defrosted if frozen
125g chorizo ring
4 tbsp bourbon whiskey
3 tbsp runny honey
1 garlic clove, crushed

YOU'LL ALSO NEED
18 cocktail sticks or small skewers

1. Butterfly the prawns: use a sharp knife to cut along the curved back of each prawn, slicing it about halfway through. Set aside. Skin the chorizo, then cut on the diagonal into 1cm-thick slices.

2. In a small bowl, whisk together the whiskey, honey, garlic and some seasoning. Set aside.

3. Heat a frying pan over a medium heat, add the chorizo and cook for 2–3min, until it releases its oil and starts to crisp. Add the whiskey mixture, then increase the heat to high and bubble for 2–3min, until reduced. Add the prawns and cook for 3–4min, stirring regularly, until the prawns are cooked through and coated in sticky glaze.

4. Remove from the heat and leave to cool for 5min (or up to 20min) before skewering and serving.

Hands-on time: 15min, plus cooling
Cooking time: about 10min
Makes 18 canapés

PER CANAPÉ 51cals, 4g protein, 2g fat (1g saturates), 2g carbs (2g total sugars), 0g fibre

Marmalade Gin Fizz

This zesty cocktail can be made with any sparkling wine you have, and the infused gin is also great mixed with tonic for a marmalade G&T.

3 tbsp marmalade
1 tbsp caster sugar
Pared zest and juice 1 orange, plus extra pared
  zest to serve
150ml gin
75cl bottle Prosecco, chilled

1. Heat the marmalade, sugar, orange zest and juice in a small pan over low heat, stirring regularly, until combined. Remove from the heat and stir in the gin, then cool. Strain through a fine sieve into a jug and chill for at least 1hr.

2. To serve, divide the gin mixture between 6 Champagne flutes, top up with Prosecco and garnish with orange zest.

◆ GET AHEAD
Make and chill the gin mixture up to 1 week ahead. Store in an airtight container or jar in the fridge.

Hands-on time: 10min, plus cooling and chilling
Cooking time: about 5min
Makes 6 cocktails

PER COCKTAIL 194cals, 0g protein, 0g fat
(0g saturates), 14g carbs (14g total sugars), 0g fibre

Merry Mojito

Use a still cider instead of the apple juice for an added kick. Alternatively, make it virgin by leaving out the rum without missing out on any of the flavour.

1 tsp brown sugar
10 mint leaves, plus a sprig to garnish
Juice 1 lime
50ml white rum
100ml fresh apple juice
50–75ml ginger beer

TO SERVE
Ice
Fresh ginger slices (optional)

1. In a cocktail shaker (or a jar with a lid) muddle/crush the sugar, mint leaves and lime juice with a spoon. Add the rum, apple juice and plenty of ice, then close and shake vigorously to combine and chill.

2. Strain into a highball glass filled with ice and top up with ginger beer. Garnish with a sprig of mint and ginger slices, if you like.

Hands-on time: 5min
Makes 1 cocktail

PER COCKTAIL 177cals, 0g protein, 0g fat
(0g saturates), 16g carbs (16g total sugars), 0g fibre

Brussels Satay

Roasting these green gems is the best way to bring out their flavour, and the sprouts are especially tasty when paired with the salty-sweet peanut sauce.

400g small Brussels sprouts, trimmed and outer leaves peeled
1 tsp vegetable oil
1 tbsp tamari (or use regular soy sauce if they don't need to be gluten-free)
1 tsp maple syrup

FOR THE PEANUT SAUCE
75g smooth peanut butter
Juice ½–1 lime, to taste
2 tbsp tamari (or use regular soy sauce if they don't need to be gluten-free)
1 garlic clove, crushed
2cm piece fresh root ginger, peeled and finely grated
1 tbsp sweet chilli sauce
Pinch dried chilli flakes (optional)

YOU'LL ALSO NEED
Cocktail sticks

◆ GET AHEAD
Prepare to end of step 2 up to 1 day ahead. Cool the sprouts, cover and chill. Cover and chill the sauce. To serve, empty the sprouts on to a baking tray, cover with foil and reheat in an oven preheated to 220°C (200°C fan) mark 7 for 5min, or until hot. Remove the sauce from the fridge 15min before serving, loosening it with warm water, if needed. Complete the recipe.

1. Preheat the oven to 220°C (200°C fan) mark 7. In a medium bowl, mix the sprouts, oil, tamari and maple syrup. Empty on to a baking tray and roast for 10–15min, until tender. Allow to cool slightly.

2. Meanwhile, make the peanut sauce. In a large bowl, whisk together the peanut butter, lime juice (to taste), tamari, garlic, ginger, sweet chilli sauce, chilli flakes (if using) and 2–4 tbsp warm water to give a good dipping consistency. Check the seasoning, adjusting with more sweet chilli or tamari, if you like.

3. Serve the sprouts with the peanut sauce alongside and cocktail sticks for dipping.

Hands-on time: 10min, plus cooling
Cooking time: about 15min
Serves 8

PER SERVING 97cals, 4g protein, 6g fat (1g saturates), 5g carbs (4g total sugars), 3g fibre

Turkey Bao Buns

A more substantial canapé and a great way to use up leftover roast turkey, chicken or pork. For a vegetarian option, try using pulled jackfruit instead of meat.

1 tsp vegetable oil
1 garlic clove, crushed
2cm piece fresh root ginger, peeled and finely grated
½ tsp Chinese five spice
200g leftover roast turkey or chicken, shredded
2 tbsp hoisin sauce, plus extra to serve
6 ready-made bao buns

TO SERVE
1 carrot, peeled and cut into matchsticks
¼ cucumber, cut into matchsticks (discard the seedy core)
2 spring onions, finely sliced
½ red chilli, deseeded and finely sliced
Small handful coriander, roughly chopped
Small handful mint, leaves picked and roughly chopped
Small handful salted peanuts, roughly chopped (optional)

1. Heat the oil in a large frying pan over medium heat and fry the garlic, ginger and five spice for 1min. Add the turkey or chicken and fry until piping hot and starting to crisp, about 5min. Stir in the hoisin sauce and 1–2 tbsp water to loosen.

2. Meanwhile, reheat the bao buns according to the pack instructions.

3. To serve, divide the turkey/chicken mixture between the bao buns and top each with some of the sliced vegetables, chilli, herbs and peanuts (if using).

Hands-on time: 15min
Cooking time: about 10min
Makes 6 buns

PER BUN 158cals, 12g protein, 4g fat (1g saturates), 18g carbs (7g total sugars), 1g fibre

16

Sides

Beetroot and Spinach Gratin

Who can resist a rich, creamy gratin? This is super simple and a deliciously different way to use beetroot and spinach.

Butter, to grease
600ml double cream
150ml vegetable stock
3 garlic cloves, crushed
Generous grating of nutmeg
100g pecorino, finely grated
200g bag spinach
750g beetroot

1. Preheat the oven to 180°C (160°C fan) mark 4 and grease a large ovenproof baking dish.

2. Heat the cream, stock, garlic, nutmeg and half the cheese in a saucepan, bring to a simmer and reduce by about one third. Remove from the heat, add the spinach and season with black pepper.

3. Meanwhile, peel the beetroot and thinly slice to about 5mm thick. Spread half over the base of the dish and pour over half the cream mixture, then repeat with the remaining beetroot and cream. Bake for 45min, scatter over the remaining cheese and return to the oven for 10–15min until golden and bubbling.

◆ GET AHEAD
Allow the cream mixture to cool and assemble the gratin up to 2 days ahead. Store tightly wrapped in the fridge and bring to room temperature before cooking.

◆ GH TIP
You can halve this recipe to feed fewer people, but cook it for the same amount of time.

Hands-on time: 15min
Cooking time: about 1hr
Serves 8

PER SERVING 466cals, 7g protein, 45g fat (27g saturates), 8g carbs (8g total sugars), 3g fibre

Roasted Carrots with Gremolata

You can replace the tarragon with extra parsley, if you like.

1.2kg carrots, we used a heritage variety
3 tbsp olive oil

FOR THE GREMOLATA
15g flat-leaf parsley, leaves picked
15g tarragon, leaves picked
1 garlic clove, crushed
Finely grated zest 2 lemons
1 tbsp olive oil

◆ GET AHEAD
Prepare the carrots (but don't roast), up to 2hr ahead. Set aside at room temperature. Make the gremolata up to 1 day ahead and chill in an airtight container. To serve, allow the gremolata to come up to room temperature and complete the recipe.

1. Preheat the oven to 200°C (180°C fan) mark 6. Peel and trim the carrots, cutting in half or in quarters lengthways if thick. Toss with the oil and some seasoning on a baking tray and roast for 45–50min, until tender.

2. Meanwhile, make the gremolata. Finely chop the herb leaves and mix in a small bowl with the garlic, lemon zest, oil and some seasoning.

3. Transfer the carrots to a serving dish and spoon through the gremolata. Serve.

Hands-on time: 15min
Cooking time: about 50min
Serves 8

PER SERVING 115cals, 1g protein, 6g fat (1g saturates), 11g carbs (10g total sugars), 6g fibre

St Clement's Potatoes

Make a change from regular roasties with these potatoes that are braised to add flavour, then roasted for crispness.

2kg medium-size floury potatoes, such as Maris Piper
6 garlic cloves, crushed
100ml each fresh orange and lemon juice
4 tbsp Dijon mustard
2 tbsp dried oregano
250ml olive oil
1 orange, cut into 8 wedges
1 large lemon, cut into 8 wedges

1. Preheat the oven to 200°C (180°C fan oven) mark 6. Peel and cut the potatoes into quarters lengthways. (If the potatoes are large, you may need to cut them in half horizontally, too.)

2. Put the potatoes into a large, deep roasting tin or an ovenproof serving dish. In a jug, whisk the garlic, orange and lemon juices, mustard, oregano and olive oil with some seasoning. Pour over the potatoes and stir to coat.

3. Cover the tin/dish tightly with foil and cook for 1hr 30min, stirring halfway.

4. Remove the foil and carefully stir the potatoes, being careful not to break them up. Add the orange and lemon wedges and return to the oven, uncovered, for 40–50min, giving them a shake halfway through to prevent the potatoes from sticking. Check the seasoning and serve.

Hands-on time: 15min
Cooking time: about 2hr 20min
Serves 8

PER SERVING 440cals, 6g protein, 24g fat (3g saturates), 49g carbs (4g total sugars), 5g fibre

Orange Blossom Greens

The flavour of orange blossom water lifts this dish, but you could use the finely grated zest of 1 orange instead, or swap the runny honey for orange blossom honey.

650g fine green beans, trimmed
300g frozen peas
75g blanched hazelnuts

FOR THE DRESSING
50g olive oil
1 tbsp runny honey
2 tsp orange blossom water
2 tsp white wine vinegar
1 tbsp lemon juice

1. Cook the beans in a large pan of boiling water for 4–5min, until just tender, adding the peas for the final few minutes. Drain well and set aside.

2. Heat a large frying pan over a medium heat and toast the hazelnuts, shaking the pan occasionally, until golden brown. Tip on to a chopping board and, when cool enough to handle, roughly chop.

3. Add the dressing ingredients to the frying pan with some seasoning and heat gently, whisking to combine.

4. Add the drained beans and peas to the frying pan, stirring to coat and reheat. Season and stir though most of the hazelnuts. Transfer to a serving dish and scatter over the remaining hazelnuts. Serve.

◆ GET AHEAD
Prepare to end of step 2 up to 1 day ahead. Once drained, cool the beans and peas under cold running water. Drain again and pat dry, then cover and chill. Store the hazelnuts in an airtight container at room temperature. To serve, remove the veg from the fridge 1hr before completing the recipe.

Hands-on time: 15min
Cooking time: about 10min
Serves 8

PER SERVING 170cals, 5g protein, 12g fat (4g saturates), 8g carbs (6g total sugars), 5g fibre

Parsley Wild Rice

This richly flavoured wild rice is a wonderful accompaniment to grilled meat or fish.

500g basmati and wild rice mix
25g butter
1 large onion, finely chopped
1 garlic clove, crushed
1 litre strong vegetable stock
Large handful parsley, roughly chopped
Juice 1 lemon, plus wedges to serve

◆ GET AHEAD
The rice can be made ahead and kept warm for up to 1 hour; complete the recipe up to the end of step 3, transfer to an ovenproof dish, then add 4 tbsp boiling water, cover with foil and put in the bottom of an oven preheated to 50°C (30°C fan) or on its lowest setting. Stir through the remaining ingredients before serving, adding a splash of hot water if it looks dry. To serve cold, leave to stand for 5min as in step 4. Spread out on a large rimmed tray to cool down quickly. Once cool, transfer to a mixing bowl, cover and chill. Remove from the fridge and stir through the remaining ingredients 30min before serving.

1. Put the rice into a large bowl and cover with cold water. Stir until the water becomes cloudy, then drain and repeat until the water is nearly clear. Soak the rice for 30min.

2. Heat the butter in a large pan. Add the onion, cover and cook over the lowest heat for about 10min until softened. Add the garlic and a generous grinding of black pepper, then cook for another 1min until fragrant.

3. Drain the rice through a sieve and rinse until the water runs clear. Add to the pan and cook for 2min, stirring. Pour in the stock and 1 tsp salt. Bring to the boil, cover and simmer for the time stated on the pack, stirring occasionally, until the rice is cooked al dente – tender, with a hint of bite at the centre – and all the liquid has been absorbed (about 12–15min).

4. Remove from the heat and fluff up the grains to separate. Cover the pan with a clean tea towel, replace the lid and allow to stand for 5min. Stir through the parsley and lemon juice and serve immediately with the extra lemon wedges.

Hands-on time: 20min, plus soaking
Cooking time: about 30min, plus 5min standing
Serves 8

PER SERVING 251cals, 6g protein, 3g fat (2g saturates), 50g carbs (1g total sugars), 1g fibre

Braised Lettuce and Peas

Lettuce isn't just for salad. Try eating it hot, too, as a light side dish.

---

3 Little Gem lettuces
50g butter
200ml vegetable stock
600g frozen peas
8 spring onions, trimmed and sliced

1. Trim off and discard the brown base of each lettuce but keep the stem in place – it will hold the leaves together while cooking. Cut the lettuces into quarters lengthways through the stem. Heat the butter in a large, wide pan. Add the lettuce and fry on the cut edges for 3min, until lightly golden.

2. Add the stock, peas and spring onions, then simmer, uncovered, for 5min, until the lettuce stems are tender.

◆ GET AHEAD
Complete up to the end of step 1 up to 3hr before serving. Reheat with the remaining ingredients just before serving.

Hands-on time: 12min
Cooking time: about 10min
Serves 8

PER SERVING 113cals, 5g protein, 6g fat (3g saturates), 7g carbs (3g total sugars), 6g fibre

Heirloom Tomato and Giant Couscous Salad

Jazz up this hearty salad with olives, capers, feta or mozzarella, if you fancy.

1 litre vegetarian stock
300g giant (Israeli) couscous
6 tbsp extra virgin olive oil
4 tbsp pomegranate molasses
5 spring onions, trimmed and chopped
500g mixed heirloom tomatoes, smaller ones halved, large ones roughly chopped
Large handful mixed soft herbs, leaves picked and roughly chopped – we used basil, parsley and mint

1. Bring the stock to the boil in a large pan, add the couscous and simmer for 6–8min, stirring occasionally, until tender. Drain, then rinse briefly under cold water (to stop the cooking). Set aside.

2. In a large bowl, whisk together the olive oil, pomegranate molasses and plenty of seasoning. Add the spring onions, tomatoes and drained couscous and toss gently to coat. Add the herbs and toss again, then serve.

Hands-on time: 10min
Cooking time: about 10min
Serves 8

PER SERVING 297cals, 6g protein, 13g fat (2g saturates), 38g carbs (8g total sugars), 3g fibre

Roasted Root Salad

A medley of roots works well with any roast meat, and the mint adds a welcome burst of freshness.

2 fennel bulbs
700g carrots, peeled and quartered lengthways
2 red onions, each cut into 8 wedges
2 tbsp olive oil
1½ tbsp maple syrup
2 tbsp pumpkin seeds

FOR THE DRESSING
2 tbsp extra virgin olive oil
1½ tbsp balsamic vinegar
1½ tsp maple syrup
Small handful mint leaves, roughly chopped

1. Preheat the oven to 200°C (180°C fan) mark 6. Slice the fennel bulbs in half lengthways, then slice each into 8 through the root. Toss in a large roasting tin with the carrots, onions, oil, maple syrup and plenty of seasoning.

2. Roast for 45–50min until golden brown and tender, turning halfway through and adding the pumpkin seeds for the final 5min of the cooking time.

3. Mix all the dressing ingredients and season, keeping half the mint aside to use as garnish.

4. Toss the warm vegetables with the dressing and transfer to a platter. Scatter over the remaining mint and serve.

Hands-on time: 20min
Cooking time: about 50min
Serves 8

PER SERVING 143cals, 2g protein, 8g fat (1g saturates), 13g carbs (11g total sugars), 6g fibre

Griddled Gems with Creamy Caesar

This recipe makes more Caesar dressing than you need for this charred lettuce salad, but it will keep well in a jar in the fridge for up to a week.

40g blanched hazelnuts
4 Little Gem lettuces, halved lengthways
Olive oil, to griddle
1 lemon, halved

FOR THE CREAMY CAESAR
150g crème fraîche
2tbsp mayonnaise
25g Parmesan, finely grated
½ garlic clove, crushed
½ tbsp fish sauce
½ tsp Worcestershire sauce

1. Toast the hazelnuts in a dry frying pan over a medium heat until golden. Remove to a board, cool, then very roughly chop. Set aside.

2. Heat a ridged griddle pan over high heat until smoking. Rub the lettuce halves all over with oil and griddle for 30sec–1min per side, until lightly charred. Remove to a plate, season generously and squeeze over the juice of half the lemon.

3. Whisk together the dressing ingredients, then season and add the juice of the remaining half lemon a little at a time, to taste. Serve the lettuce halves on a platter sprinkled with the hazelnuts and with the dressing on the side for dipping.

Hands-on time: 10min
Cooking time: about 5min
Serves 8

PER SERVING (with 1 tbsp dressing) 160cals, 3g protein, 16g fat (6g saturates), 1g carbs (1g total sugars), 1g fibre

Asparagus with Lemon and Caper Butter

To make this easy-to-prepare side dish even easier, spike rows of asparagus together with double skewers before cooking – it will make turning them a breeze.

100g butter
3 tbsp baby (non-pareille) capers, drained
Finely grated zest ½ and juice 1 lemon
900g asparagus spears, woody ends trimmed

1. Melt the butter in a pan and continue to heat until it's just starting to turn golden-brown and smell toasty. Remove from the heat and stir in the capers, lemon zest and juice and plenty of seasoning.

2. Preheat a barbecue or griddle to high heat. Brush the asparagus spears with a little of the butter mixture, then cook for 8–10min, turning occasionally, until charred and tender.

3. Remove the asparagus to a plate and pour over the remaining butter mixture. Serve hot or at room temperature.

Hands-on time: 10min
Cooking time: about 15min
Serves 8

PER SERVING 128cals, 4g protein, 11g fat (7g saturates), 3g carbs (2g total sugars), 3g fibre

Purple Slaw

This colourful slaw goes well with everything from burgers to savoury pies. If you prefer a richer coleslaw, use mayonnaise instead of yogurt.

---

2 carrots, peeled
2 raw beetroots, peeled
1 red cabbage, cored and finely shredded
½ red onion, finely sliced
300g natural yogurt
Juice 1 lemon
2 tbsp wholegrain mustard

1. Cut the carrots and beetroots into matchsticks (using a mandoline or the attachment in a food processor is easiest). Put into a large bowl and mix through the cabbage and onion.

2. In a separate bowl, mix together the yogurt, lemon juice, mustard and plenty of seasoning. Add to the vegetables and mix to combine. Chill until needed.

◆ GET AHEAD
Make up to 1 day ahead. Cover and chill.

Hands-on time: 15min
Serves 8

PER SERVING 64cals, 3g protein, 1g fat (0g saturates), 9g carbs (8g total sugars), 3g fibre

Broccoli with a Crunch

Our crisp Parmesan topping has a bite and adds interest to an everyday vegetable – and it's wonderful on other types of veg, too.

40g butter
4 thyme sprigs, leaves removed
75g fresh white breadcrumbs
550g Tenderstem broccoli, trimmed
40g Parmesan, grated

1. Melt the butter in a large frying pan and add the thyme and breadcrumbs. Fry gently for 10–12min until golden and crisp, stirring frequently. Tip on to a plate and leave to cool.

2. Meanwhile, bring a large pan of water to the boil and cook the broccoli for 3–5min until tender. Drain and let steam-dry in the colander for 1min.

3. Put the breadcrumbs into a bowl and stir in the Parmesan and some seasoning. Serve the broccoli immediately, topped with the Parmesan crumbs.

◆ GET AHEAD
Fry the crumbs up to 1 day ahead, leave to cool, then stir in the Parmesan. Keep in an airtight container in the fridge until needed. Complete the recipe to serve.

Hands-on time: 10min
Cooking time: about 12min
Serves 10

PER SERVING 81cals, 3g protein, 4g fat (2g saturates), 7g carbs (1g total sugars), 2g fibre

Roasted Broccoli and Cauliflower Cheese Bake

Quinoa adds protein and wholegrain goodness to this classic, indulgent dish.

1 head broccoli (about 250g), cut into florets
½ head cauliflower (about 350g), cut into florets
1 tbsp olive oil
50g butter
50g plain flour
600ml milk
125g Cheddar, roughly grated
50g Parmesan, finely grated
250g pouch cooked quinoa
Small bunch chives, finely chopped
50g dried breadcrumbs – we used panko
Green salad, to serve (optional)

1. Preheat the oven to 200°C (180°C fan) mark 6. In a large roasting tin, toss together the veg, oil and some seasoning. Roast for 10min, carefully shake the tray to turn, then roast for a further 10min.

2. Meanwhile, melt the butter in a medium pan. Stir in the flour, then take off the heat and gradually whisk in the milk. Return to the heat. Bring to the boil, stirring constantly, then simmer for 5min (stirring) until thick and glossy. Add most of the cheese and stir until melted. Check the seasoning.

3. Stir the quinoa, roasted veg and chives into the cheese sauce and transfer to a 1.8 litre dish. Top with the breadcrumbs and remaining cheese, then transfer the dish to the oven. Bake for 20min until heated through and golden on top. Serve immediately with a green salad, if you like.

Hands-on time: 15min
Cooking time: 40min
Serves 4

PER SERVING 645cals, 30g protein, 37g fat (20g saturates), 44g carbs (11g total sugars), 7g fibre

Roasted Jersey Royal Potatoes with Vine Tomatoes and Garlic

This tasty side dish would also make a flavour-packed light main – simply serve with some salad leaves.

750g Jersey Royal potatoes
1 tbsp olive oil
A few thyme sprigs
3 garlic cloves
½ lemon, cut into 4 wedges
25g pitted, sliced black olives
200g cherry tomatoes on the vine
50g vegetarian feta cheese, crumbled
Curly parsley, chopped, to serve

1. Preheat the oven to 190°C (170°C fan) mark 5. Put the potatoes into a roasting tin. Mix in the olive oil, thyme sprigs, garlic cloves and lemon wedges with some seasoning.

2. Roast for 45min, then add the olives, cherry tomatoes and feta. Cook for a further 15min or until the potatoes are tender. Garnish with chopped curly parsley to serve.

Hands-on time: 10min
Cooking time: about 1hr
Serves 2

PER SERVING 400cals, 12g protein, 10g fat (4g saturates), 62g carbs (9g total sugars), 8g fibre

Brussels Sprout and Cranberry Gratin

A cheesy cranberry sauce and crunchy topping give Brussels sprouts a mouthwatering makeover.

300g Brussels sprouts, trimmed and halved
50g dried cranberries
350g ready-made cheese sauce
75g mature Cheddar, grated
50g fresh breadcrumbs

1. Preheat the oven to 200°C (180°C fan) mark 6. Bring a medium pan of salted water to the boil. Carefully add the sprouts and simmer for 5min, or until just tender. Drain into a colander and leave to steam dry for 5min.

2. In a medium bowl, mix together the Brussels sprouts, cranberries, cheese sauce and some seasoning. Scrape into an ovenproof serving dish with about a 1 litre capacity.

3. Sprinkle over the grated Cheddar, breadcrumbs and some seasoning. Cook in the oven for 30min, or until bubbling and golden. Serve.

◆ GET AHEAD
Prepare to end of step 2 up to 1 day ahead (no need to preheat the oven). Cover and chill. Uncover and complete the recipe to serve.

Hands-on time: 10min, plus cooling
Cooking time: about 35min
Serves 6

PER SERVING 211cals, 9g protein, 11g fat (7g saturates), 18g carbs (8g total sugars), 4g fibre

Buttery Potato Stacks

These crispy beauties rival any roast potatoes, and are hassle-free as they don't need basting once in the oven.

1.4kg floury potatoes, peeled – we used Maris Piper
125g butter, melted
2 tsp dried thyme

1. Preheat the oven to 200°C (180°C fan) mark 6. Using a mandoline, slice the potatoes as thinly as possible. Alternatively, do this by hand or use the slicing blade on a food processor.

2. In a medium bowl, mix together the butter, thyme, potatoes and plenty of seasoning, making sure all the potatoes are coated in butter. Stack the slices (you don't need to be too neat) in the holes of a 12-hole muffin tin, pushing them down well.

3. Cook for 50min, until golden and crispy. Carefully remove each stack from the tin and serve.

◆ GET AHEAD
Prepare to the end of step 2 up to 1 day ahead (no need to preheat the oven). Cover and chill. Uncover and complete the recipe to serve.

Hands-on time: 15min
Cooking time: 50min
Makes 12 stacks

PER STACK 179cals, 2g protein, 9g fat (6g saturates), 22g carbs (1g total sugars), 2g fibre

Swede, Carrot and Apple Mash

This creamy, sweet and earthy mash is a great side to any meal.

1 small swede (about 400g), peeled and cut into
rough 2cm pieces
400g carrots, peeled and cut into rough 2cm slices
300g Granny Smith apples, peeled, cored and
roughly chopped
40g butter
1 tbsp wholegrain mustard
75ml crème fraîche
Small handful parsley, leaves picked and
roughly chopped

1. Bring a large pan of salted water to the boil.
Cook the swede and carrots for 25min, adding
the apple for the final 10min of cooking.

2. Drain into a colander and leave to steam dry
for 10min. Return the drained veg to the pan
with some seasoning. Add the butter, mustard
and crème fraîche and mash roughly.

3. Heat through the mash, if needed, until piping
hot. Stir through the parsley, check the
seasoning and serve.

◆ GET AHEAD
Prepare to the end of step 2 up to 1 day ahead.
Cool, cover and chill. Complete the recipe to serve,
making sure the mixture is piping hot.

Hands-on time: 20min, plus steam-drying
Cooking time: about 25min
Serves 6

PER SERVING 172cals, 2g protein, 12g fat (7g saturates),
13g carbs (13g total sugars), 5g fibre

White Winter Salad

Sweet pears paired with bitter chicory make for a tantalising side dish.

---

3 medium heads chicory, leaves separated
2 ripe pears, quartered lengthways, cored and
   thinly sliced
75g Stilton, crumbled

FOR THE DRESSING
2 tsp wholegrain mustard
1 tbsp runny honey
1½ tbsp cider vinegar
4 tbsp extra virgin olive oil

1. Whisk together the dressing ingredients in
   a large bowl with some seasoning.

2. Add the chicory and pears and gently toss
   to coat. Transfer to a platter and scatter over
   the Stilton. Serve.

◆ GET AHEAD
Make the dressing 1 day ahead, then cover
and chill. Complete the recipe to serve.

Hands-on time: 15min
Serves 6

PER SERVING 157cals, 3g protein, 12g fat
(4g saturates), 8g carbs (7g total sugars), 2g fibre

Roasted Herby Squash

We've left the skin on our squash to add texture to this side dish, but you can peel it, if you like.

---

1 large butternut squash, halved and deseeded
1 tbsp runny honey
4 tbsp olive oil
Small handful chopped soft herbs – we used parsley, basil
   and coriander
Juice ½ lemon

1. Preheat the oven to 200°C (180°C fan) mark 6.
   Cut the squash lengthways into rough 1cm-thick
   slices, cutting longer slices in half widthways.
   Put on a large baking tray in a single layer.
   Drizzle with honey and 2 tbsp of the oil and
   season. Roast for 45–50min, turning midway,
   until tender and charring at the edges.

2. Mix the remaining oil, herbs and lemon juice
   with some seasoning. Transfer the cooked
   squash to a serving plate and drizzle over
   the herby dressing. Serve.

◆ GET AHEAD
Prepare to end of step 1 up to 2hr ahead.
Set aside. To serve, reheat in an oven preheated
to 200°C (180°C fan) mark 6 for 10min and
complete the recipe.

Hands-on time: 15min
Cooking time: about 50min
Serves 6

PER SERVING 143cals, 2g protein, 8g fat (1g saturates),
15g carbs (9g total sugars), 4g fibre

Chilli and Garlic Romanesco

If you can't get hold of Romanesco broccoli, use regular broccoli instead.

600g Romanesco florets (about 1 medium head)
1 tbsp olive oil
1–2 garlic cloves, thinly sliced, to taste
1 red chilli, deseeded and finely chopped
2 tbsp flaked almonds, toasted

1. Put the Romanesco florets into a large frying pan (that has a lid), pour in 50ml just-boiled water, then cover with the lid and steam over a medium heat for 7–8min until the water has evaporated and the florets are just tender.

2. Uncover and add oil to the pan. Fry for 5min, tossing occasionally, until the florets have taken on some golden colour. Add the garlic, chilli and some seasoning, then fry for 1min to soften the garlic. Transfer to a warm serving dish, sprinkle over the flaked almonds and serve.

◆ GET AHEAD
Complete step 1 up to 1 day ahead. Transfer to a bowl, then cool, cover and chill. Complete the recipe to serve.

Hands-on time: 20min
Cooking time: about 15min
Serves 6

PER SERVING 83cals, 4g protein, 5g fat (1g saturates), 5g carbs (3g total sugars), 2g fibre

Fennel Gratin

For vegetarians, replace the Gruyère with Jarlsberg and use vegetable stock.

800g fennel bulbs
2 tbsp olive oil
40g fresh breadcrumbs
40g Gruyère or Comté, finely grated
300ml chicken stock
3tbsp half-fat crème fraîche

1. Preheat the oven to 200°C (180°C fan) mark 6. Cut the fennel into slim wedges (no more than 1.5cm at their thickest), removing any tough central core. Heat 1½ tbsp of the oil in a large frying pan over a medium-high heat and fry the fennel until golden and softening, about 10min.

2. Mix the breadcrumbs, Gruyère, remaining oil and some seasoning in a small bowl, then set aside.

3. Arrange the fennel in a large ovenproof serving dish. Return the pan to the heat, then add the stock and crème fraîche, whisking to combine. Bring to a simmer, season, then pour over the fennel and cover the dish with foil.

4. Cook in the oven for 45min until the fennel is tender, removing the foil and adding the crumb topping for the final 15min. Serve.

◆ GET AHEAD
Prepare the gratin to the end of step 3 up to 2hr ahead (without preheating the oven). Cover the fennel and crumb separately and set both aside. To serve, complete the recipe.

Hands-on time: 15min
Cooking time: about 1hr
Serves 6

PER SERVING 120cals, 5g protein, 8g fat (3g saturates), 6g carbs (3g total sugars), 5g fibre

Garlic Naans

Serve these light, chewy garlic naans alongside a fragrant curry.

225ml semi-skimmed milk
1 tsp fast-action dried yeast
150g natural yogurt
¼ tsp caster sugar
500g strong white bread flour
Vegetable oil, to knead and grease
50g butter
1–2 garlic cloves, crushed
Small handful parsley, roughly chopped, to sprinkle
Sea salt flakes, to sprinkle

1. Gently warm the milk in a small pan over a low heat until lukewarm. Remove from the heat and stir in the yeast, then set aside for 5min. Stir through the yogurt and sugar.

2. Mix the flour and ½ tsp fine sea salt in a large bowl, then make a well in the centre. Pour in the milk mixture and stir until combined. Tip out on to a lightly oiled surface and knead for 10min, until smooth and elastic. Transfer to a lightly oiled bowl, cover with cling film and leave to rise until doubled in size, about 1hr.

3. Divide the dough into 8 equal pieces and roll each into a rough 18cm circle.

4. Preheat the grill to high. Heat an ovenproof frying pan on the hob until very hot and carefully add a naan. Cook for 3min, until the surface begins to bubble. Transfer to the grill, setting the pan as close to the grill bars as possible. Cook until golden and bubbling, about 3min. Repeat with the remaining dough, keeping the cooked naans wrapped in a clean tea towel to keep them warm.

5. Melt the butter in a small pan, remove from the heat and stir in the crushed garlic. Brush the naans with garlic butter, then sprinkle with chopped parsley and sea salt flakes. Serve.

◆ GET AHEAD
Once the dough begins to rise, transfer the bowl to the fridge for 24hr. Bring back up to room temperature and complete the recipe to serve.

Hands-on time: 30min, plus standing and rising
Cooking time: about 25min
Makes 8 naan

PER NAAN 301cals, 10g protein, 7g fat (4g saturates), 50g carbs (3g total sugars), 2g fibre

Quick Mango Relish

This simple relish, inspired by mango chutney but much quicker and fresher tasting, will enhance any spiced dish.

2 green cardamom pods
100ml cider vinegar
75g caster sugar
1 garlic clove, crushed
1 red chilli, deseeded and finely chopped
½ tsp cumin seeds
½ tsp fenugreek seeds
½ tsp nigella seeds
2 ripe mangos, peeled, de-stoned and cut into 1cm pieces (about 400g fruit)

1. Using a pestle and mortar, bash the cardamom pods to break their husks. Peel open the husks and pick out the seeds. Discard the husks and finely grind the seeds.

2. Mix all the ingredients except the mango pieces in a medium pan with ½ tsp fine salt. Cook over a low heat, stirring until the sugar dissolves.

3. Increase the heat to high and add the mango. Bubble for 10min, stirring frequently, or until the mango starts to soften and most of the liquid has evaporated. Transfer to a bowl and leave to cool completely before serving.

◆ TO STORE
Keep in an airtight container in the fridge for up to 5 days (the relish may become a little looser on storing).

Hands-on time: 10min, plus cooling
Cooking time: about 15min
Serves 6

PER SERVING 94cals, 1g protein, <1g fat (<1g saturates), 22g carbs (22g total sugars), 2g fibre

Yogurt Raita

This fresh yogurt dish is a great accompaniment to any curry.

½ cucumber
250g Greek-style yogurt
½ tsp ground cumin
1 tbsp lemon juice
Small handful mint leaves, roughly chopped
Small handful coriander, roughly chopped

1. Coarsely grate the cucumber, then lift up over a sink and squeeze out the excess moisture. Mix in a bowl with the remaining ingredients, season and serve.

Hands-on time: 5min
Serves 6

PER SERVING 60cals, 3g protein, 4g fat (3g saturates), 2g carbs (2g total sugars), <1g fibre

17

Puddings &
Desserts

Lemon and Berry Meringue Roulade

Light and fluffy, this pretty roulade is bursting with berries. Scatter over chopped roasted hazelnuts or flaked almonds, if you like, before rolling it up.

4 medium egg whites
75g caster sugar
Finely grated zest ½ lemon
½ tsp cream of tartar
1 tbsp icing sugar, plus extra to dust

FOR THE FILLING
300g 0% fat Greek yogurt
2 tsp vanilla bean paste
15g icing sugar
250g mixed berries – we used blueberries, raspberries and blackberries

1. Preheat the oven to 180°C (160°C fan) mark 4. Line a shallow 23 x 33cm baking tin with baking parchment. For the meringue, use a handheld electric whisk to beat the egg whites in a large bowl until they hold stiff peaks. Gradually beat in the caster sugar, followed by the lemon zest. Beat for 1min more, then quickly beat in the cream of tartar.

2. Scrape into the lined tin and spread to level. Bake for 12–15min, until golden, risen and set. Meanwhile, dust a large sheet of baking parchment with 1 tbsp icing sugar. Invert the meringue on to the dusted sheet and remove the tin. Leave to cool completely (it will sink on cooling).

3. For the filling, whisk the yogurt, vanilla bean paste and icing sugar until combined. Peel the top parchment off the meringue and spread over the yogurt filling. Scatter over the berries. Using the parchment to help, roll up the meringue from one of the short sides and transfer to a serving plate. Dust lightly with icing sugar and serve.

Hands-on time: 15min, plus cooling
Cooking time: about 15min
Serves 6

PER SERVING 126cals, 8g protein, <1g fat (0g saturates), 23g carbs (23g total sugars), 1g fibre

Glazed Chocolate Mousse Tart

An unadulterated hit of rich chocolate. You could serve this topped with berries, if you wish, but we've kept our tart pure and simple.

FOR THE PASTRY
175g plain flour, plus extra to dust
20g cocoa powder
50g icing sugar
150g unsalted butter, chilled and cubed
1 medium egg

FOR THE MOUSSE FILLING
150g dark chocolate, roughly chopped
150g milk chocolate, roughly chopped
50g unsalted butter, chopped
300ml double cream
25g icing sugar, sifted

TO GLAZE
50ml double cream
50g dark chocolate, finely chopped
½ tbsp golden syrup

1. To make the pastry, pulse the flour, cocoa powder, icing sugar and a pinch of salt in a food processor to combine. Add the butter and pulse until the mixture resembles fine breadcrumbs. Alternatively, do this by hand, rubbing the butter into the flour mixture using your fingertips.

2. Add the egg and pulse/mix with a blunt-ended cutlery knife until the pastry clumps together. Tip on to a work surface and bring together into a disc, then wrap and chill for 30min.

Hands-on time: 30min, plus chilling, cooling and setting
Cooking time: about 35min
Serves 10

PER SERVING 542cals, 6g protein, 38g fat (24g saturates), 43g carbs (29g total sugars), 2g fibre

3. Lightly flour a work surface and roll out the pastry to 3mm thick. Use to line a 23cm round, deeply fluted tart tin (3.5cm deep). Trim the edges to neaten, then prick the base all over with a fork. Chill for 20min.

4. Preheat the oven to 190°C (170°C fan) mark 5. Line the pastry case with a large sheet of baking parchment and fill with baking beans. Blind bake for 15–18min, until the pastry sides are set. Carefully remove the parchment and beans. Return the pastry case (in its tin) to the oven for 5–8min, until the base is cooked through and feels sandy to the touch. Cool in the tin.

5. To make the mousse filling, melt the chocolates and butter in a heatproof bowl set over a pan of barely simmering water (try to stir it as little as possible). Once melted, set aside to cool.

6. In a separate bowl, whip the cream and icing sugar until the mixture just holds its shape. Fold into the cooled chocolate mixture, keeping in as much air as you can. Scrape into the pastry case (still in its tin) and smooth to level, making sure you get the mixture into the pastry flutes. Chill until set, about 3hr.

7. To make the glaze, heat the cream in a small pan until hot. Remove from the heat and stir in the chocolate to melt, followed by the golden syrup and 1 tbsp warm water. Scrape on to the tart and tilt the tart to cover with the glaze – don't spread it or you'll ruin the shine. Leave to set for 30min, then transfer to a cake stand or plate and serve.

◆ GET AHEAD
Prepare to end of step 6 up to 1 day ahead.
To serve, complete step 7 up to 2hr ahead.
Keep at room temperature. Chill any leftovers
for up to 3 days – the glaze will crack, but it
will still taste wonderful.

Peanut Butter and Jelly Ice Cream Lollies

Wow your friends with these indulgent but incredibly easy lollies. Made with a no-churn peanut butter ice cream rippled with raspberry purée, they're covered in a hard shell of chocolate.

FOR THE RIPPLE
75g raspberries, fresh or frozen
1 tbsp golden syrup

FOR THE ICE CREAM
125g smooth peanut butter
125g caramel, we used Carnation
250ml double cream
1 tsp vanilla bean paste

FOR THE COATING
200g milk or dark chocolate, chopped
2 tbsp coconut oil
1–2 tbsp salted peanuts, finely chopped
1 tbsp freeze-dried raspberry pieces (optional)

YOU'LL ALSO NEED
6 x 80–100ml silicone lolly moulds and sticks

◆ TO STORE
Once the chocolate has set hard, pack the lollies into a freezerproof container, separated with layers of baking parchment. Freeze for up to 1 month.

Hands-on time: 30min, plus cooling and (overnight) freezing
Cooking time: about 7min
Makes 6 lollies

PER LOLLY 597cals, 10g protein, 47g fat (26g saturates), 31g carbs (30g total sugars), 2g fibre

1. First, make the ripple. Heat the raspberries and golden syrup in a small pan over a low heat, stirring until the raspberries have broken down. Turn up the heat to medium and bubble for 2–3min, until slightly reduced and jammy. Pass through a sieve into a bowl (discard the seeds). Leave to cool.

2. For the ice cream, use a handheld electric whisk to beat the peanut butter, caramel, cream and vanilla in a large bowl until the mixture holds firm peaks.

3. Spoon half the ice cream mixture into the lolly moulds, pressing it down to avoid air holes (see GH Tips). Dot over most of the raspberry ripple, then spoon over the remaining ice cream and smooth to level. Dot over the remaining ripple and swirl gently with a cocktail stick. Insert the lolly sticks as directed and freeze for at least 8hr (ideally overnight), until solid.

4. For the coating, line a baking sheet with baking parchment. Melt the chocolate and coconut oil in a heatproof bowl over a pan of just simmering water. Remove the bowl from the heat and set aside. Pour into a jug, pint glass or similar, that is tall enough to fit a lolly vertically.

5. Remove the lollies from the moulds and dip, one at a time, into the melted chocolate to coat, tilting the jug to cover the lolly. Allow the excess chocolate to drip back into the jug, then quickly sprinkle with the chopped nuts and/or raspberry pieces, if using. Place on the lined sheet to set. Serve immediately or return to the freezer.

◆ GH TIPS
If your lolly moulds are vertical, at step 3,
fill a quarter of each mould with ice cream,
drizzle over a little purée, then repeat to fill.
Insert the sticks as directed and freeze.

Dipping to cover always requires more
chocolate than you'll use. Pour any leftover
on to a lined baking sheet, sprinkle with the
extra toppings and leave to set. Break into
shards for home-made chocolate bark.

Coconut and Raspberry Layered Jelly

Enjoy a taste of the tropics with this deliciously dairy-free dessert.

FOR THE RUM LAYER
Oil, to grease
3 sheets platinum-grade leaf gelatine
250ml coconut water
6 tbsp coconut rum, we used Malibu

FOR THE RASPBERRY LAYER
3 sheets platinum-grade leaf gelatine
200g raspberries
50g caster sugar
Juice 1 lime

FOR THE COCONUT LAYER
4 sheets platinum-grade leaf gelatine
400ml tin full-fat coconut milk
125g caster sugar
Finely grated zest 1 lime, plus extra pared zest
   to serve (optional)
100g raspberries, plus extra to serve (optional)

1. Lightly grease a 900g loaf tin and line with cling film, smoothing it as much as possible. For the rum layer, cover the gelatine with cold water, then soak for 5min. Heat the coconut water in a small pan until just hot, then remove from the heat.

2. Lift the gelatine out of the water, squeeze out the excess water, then stir into the coconut water to

Hands-on time: 15min, plus soaking, cooling and (overnight) setting
Cooking time: about 10min
Serves 8

PER SERVING 204cals, 2g protein, 9g fat (7g saturates), 29g carbs (28g total sugars), 2g fibre

dissolve. Stir in the rum, then cool to room temperature. Pour into the lined tin, then tap the tin down on the surface a few times to burst any bubbles in the mixture. Cool and chill until set, about 1hr.

3. Meanwhile, make the raspberry layer. Soak the gelatine as before. Heat the raspberries, sugar and 125ml water in a small pan until the raspberries are mushy. Lift the gelatine out of the water, squeeze out the excess water, then stir it into the raspberries to dissolve, followed by the lime juice. Push through a fine sieve (discard the seeds). Cool to room temperature, then pour into the tin on top of the set rum layer. Chill until set, about 1hr.

4. For the coconut layer, soak the gelatine as before. Heat the coconut milk and sugar in a pan, stirring until the sugar dissolves. Remove from the heat, lift the gelatine out of the water, squeeze out the excess water, then stir it into the pan to dissolve. Stir in the lime zest and set aside to cool completely.

5. Once the raspberry layer has set and the coconut mixture has cooled, pour the coconut mixture on to the raspberry layer. Scatter over whole raspberries and return to the fridge for at least 4hr (or up to 24hr).

6. To serve, invert on to a plate, remove the tin and peel off the cling film. Decorate with extra raspberries and pared lime zest, if you like.

Strawberry and Clotted Cream Mousses

Featuring a true summer pairing, these elegant layered desserts make for a great end to an alfresco feast.

FOR THE PANNA COTTA
3 sheets platinum-grade leaf gelatine
175ml semi-skimmed milk
40g caster sugar
1 tsp vanilla bean paste
225g clotted cream

FOR THE MOUSSE
1 sheet platinum-grade leaf gelatine
300g strawberries (hulled weight), plus extra to decorate
50g caster sugar
2 medium egg whites
150ml double cream

◆ GET AHEAD
Make the mousses up to 1 day ahead.
Keep chilled.

1. First, make the panna cotta layer. Cover the gelatine with cold water and leave to soak for 5min. Meanwhile, heat the milk and sugar in a pan over a low heat, whisking until the sugar dissolves.

Hands-on time: 35min, plus cooling and chilling
Cooking time: about 12min
Makes 6

PER SERVING 446cals, 5g protein, 38g fat
(24g saturates), 20g carbs (20g total sugars), 2g fibre

2. Lift out the gelatine, squeeze out excess water, and whisk it into the hot milk mixture to dissolve. Remove the pan from the heat and whisk in the vanilla and clotted cream (including any crust on the cream), until smooth. Divide among 6 glasses or small pudding bowls. Cool, then chill until set, about 2hr.

3. For the strawberry mousse layer, soak the gelatine in cold water for 5min. Roughly chop 225g of the strawberries and heat in a small pan with 1 tbsp of the sugar and 1 tbsp water, stirring and cooking until the strawberries are mushy. Lift out the gelatine, squeeze out excess water, then stir it into the strawberries to dissolve. Blend until smooth, then set aside to cool.

4. Using a handheld electric whisk, beat the egg whites in a medium bowl to stiff peaks. Gradually beat in the remaining sugar, whisking back up to stiff peaks. In a separate large bowl, beat the cream until fairly firm.

5. Strain the cooled strawberry mixture through a fine sieve into the cream bowl (discard the seeds), and fold in with a large metal spoon. Next, fold in the egg whites, being careful to keep in as much air as possible. Finely chop the remaining 75g strawberries and fold in. Divide the mousse among the glasses/bowls and return to the fridge for at least 2hr to set.

6. To serve, decorate with extra whole or chopped strawberries.

Lemon and Blueberry Ricotta Cheesecake

Ricotta gives this cheesecake lightness and texture. You can swap the blueberries for raspberries or blackberries, if you like.

FOR THE BISCUIT BASE
100g unsalted butter, melted, plus extra to grease
225g digestive biscuits

FOR THE FILLING
500g ricotta
250g caster sugar
300g full-fat cream cheese
4 medium eggs
1½ tbsp cornflour
Finely grated zest 2 lemons and juice 1 lemon,
 keep separate
100g blueberries

FOR THE TOPPING
200g blueberries
25g caster sugar
1 tsp cornflour

1. Preheat the oven to 180°C (160°C fan) mark 4. Lightly grease a 20.5cm round springform tin and line with baking parchment. Whizz the biscuits in a food processor until finely crushed (or bash in a food bag with a rolling pin). Add the melted butter and pulse/mix until combined. Tip into the prepared tin, level and press firmly with the back of a spoon. Bake for 15min.

Hands-on time: 30min, plus cooling and (overnight) chilling
Cooking time: about 2hr 15min
Serves 8

PER SERVING 611cals, 13g protein, 35g fat (20g saturates), 61g carbs (45g total sugars), 2g fibre

2. Turn down the oven to 150°C (130°C fan) mark 2. Fill a roasting tin with hot water, about 2.5cm deep, then put in the bottom of the oven to create steam. For the filling, drain the ricotta and put into a large bowl with the sugar and cream cheese. Beat using a handheld electric whisk, until combined. Beat in the eggs, one at a time, beating well after each addition.

3. In a small bowl, mix the cornflour with the lemon juice, then beat with the lemon zest into the ricotta mixture. Fold in the blueberries with a large spoon.

4. Scrape the filling into the tin and bake for 2hr, or until just set. Turn off the oven and leave the cheesecake to cool in the oven for 30min before removing it and cooling completely on a wire rack. It may crack a little, but don't worry as this will be covered by the topping. Chill overnight.

5. For the topping, cook the blueberries, sugar, cornflour and 1 tbsp water in a pan over a medium heat until the berries have softened but are still just holding their shape. Cool completely.

6. To serve, transfer the cheesecake to a cake stand or plate and spoon over the blueberry topping.

◆ GET AHEAD
Make the cheesecake and topping up to 2 days ahead, then cool, cover and chill (separately). Complete the recipe to serve.

Chocolate and Orange Soufflé

Soufflé is often seen as a dish that is tricky to get right, but these chocolate ones are surprisingly simple – just serve them immediately after they come out of the oven.

15g butter, for greasing
Brown sugar, for sprinkling
150g dark chocolate, broken into squares
3 large egg yolks
75ml double cream
Finely grated zest of ½ small orange
2 tbsp orange liqueur
½ tsp vanilla extract
5 large egg whites
40g soft light brown sugar
Icing sugar and extra orange zest, to decorate

FOR THE BOOZY CREAM
200ml double cream
2 tbsp orange liqueur
2 tbsp soft light brown sugar

1. Grease 6 x 175ml ramekins or large ovenproof coffee cups with butter. Sprinkle a little brown sugar in each and roll it around to lightly coat the inside. Set the ramekins on a baking tray, spaced well apart.

2. Put the chocolate in a heatproof bowl and set it over a pan of gently simmering water. Melt until almost smooth, then carefully remove the bowl and stir the chocolate with a wooden spoon until smooth. Beat in the egg yolks and stir in the cream, orange zest, liqueur and vanilla, then leave to cool for 10min. Preheat the oven to 220°C (200°C fan) mark 7.

3. While the chocolate mixture cools, prepare the boozy cream. Put the double cream, liqueur and sugar in a mixing bowl and whip with an electric whisk until soft peaks form. Set aside.

4. Whisk the egg whites together in a large bowl until stiff but not dry. Add the light brown sugar, a little at a time, whisking well.

5. Fold a quarter of the egg whites into the chocolate mixture to loosen it, then fold in the rest with a metal spoon. Take care not to over-stir the mixture or the eggs will lose volume. If you have some stubborn lumps of egg white, cut through the mixture a couple of times with a large metal whisk.

6. Spoon the mixture into the ramekins and bake in the centre of the oven for about 9–10min, until well risen but with a slight wobble in the centre. Dust the tops with sifted icing sugar, then set the ramekins on dessert plates and top with spoonfuls of boozy cream. Sprinkle with a little orange zest and serve immediately.

Hands-on time: 20min
Cooking time: about 15min
Makes 6 soufflés

PER SOUFFLÉ 474cals, 6g protein, 34g fat (20g saturates), 29g carbs (29g sugars), 1g fibre

Plum and Apple Crumble

Use Bramley apples, which slump down during cooking, or Braeburn or Gala to give a perky finish to this classic crumble.

6 large plums, halved, stoned and roughly chopped
3 Bramley apples (about 500g), peeled, cored and
  roughly chopped
50g light brown soft or caster sugar
1 tsp ground cinnamon
Finely grated zest 1 lemon

FOR THE CRUMBLE TOPPING
175g plain flour
125g unsalted butter, chilled and cubed
50g rolled oats
75g demerara sugar

1. Preheat the oven to 200°C (180°C fan) mark 6. Put the fruit into a large pan (one with a lid) with the sugar, cinnamon, lemon zest and 5 tbsp water. Cover and heat gently until the apples are softening, about 5min. Empty into a shallow, ovenproof serving dish and set aside.

2. For the topping, put the flour into a bowl and rub in the butter with your fingers until it resembles fine rubble. Mix in the oats and demerara sugar, then scatter the topping over the fruit.

3. Bake for 25–30min, or until golden. Serve with vanilla ice cream or Creamy Custard (see right).

Hands-on time: 30min
Cooking time: about 35min
Serves 6

PER SERVING (without custard) 438cals, 5g protein, 19g fat (11g saturates), 61g carbs (33g total sugars), 5g fibre

Creamy Custard

Serve your puddings with this deliciously thick custard, or enjoy it on its own with fresh fruit.

2 medium egg yolks
40g caster sugar
1 tbsp cornflour
1 tsp vanilla bean paste
150ml semi-skimmed milk, plus extra to loosen
250ml double cream

1. Put the egg yolks, sugar, cornflour and vanilla into a medium pan. Gradually whisk in the milk and double cream. Bring to the boil over medium heat, whisking constantly, until thickened.

2. Loosen with a little extra milk, if you like, then serve warm or at room temperature.

◆ GET AHEAD
Make up to 1 day ahead. Pour the hot custard into a heatproof bowl and lay baking parchment or cling film directly on the surface to stop a skin forming. Cool, then chill. To serve, reheat gently in the pan, or whisk briefly until smooth and serve at room temperature.

Hands-on time: 5min
Cooking time: 10min
Serves 6

PER SERVING 275cals, 2g protein, 25g fat (15g saturates), 11g carbs (9g total sugars), 0g fibre

Pistachio, Raspberry and White Chocolate Pavlova

Nutty meringue, boozy cream and seasonal fruit is a combination that's hard to beat. Swap the bourbon for Marsala, if you prefer, or leave it out altogether and add 1 tsp vanilla bean paste to the whipped cream.

FOR THE MERINGUE
60g pistachio kernels, plus extra, chopped, to decorate
4 medium egg whites
¼ tsp cream of tartar
225g caster sugar

FOR THE FILLING
500ml double cream
1 tbsp caster sugar
3 tbsp bourbon whiskey (optional)
300g raspberries
40g white chocolate, melted

1. Preheat the oven to 140°C (120°C fan) mark 1. Draw a 20cm circle on to baking parchment (using a cake tin is easiest), then flip so the ink is underneath and put on a baking sheet. For the meringue, pulse the pistachios in the small bowl of a food processor until coarsely ground (or finely chop by hand). Avoid whizzing, or the nuts will become too greasy and might collapse the meringue.

2. Using a stand mixer, or a handheld electric whisk and a large bowl, beat the egg whites, cream of tartar and a pinch of salt until they hold firm peaks. Gradually beat in the sugar, a spoonful at a time, until the meringue is thick and glossy. Using a large metal spoon, quickly fold in most of the ground pistachios.

3. Dab a little meringue on to each corner of the baking sheet to secure the parchment. Dollop on the meringue and, using the template as a guide, spread into a circle. Make a slight dip in the centre and sprinkle the reserved pistachios around the edge. Bake for 1hr until firm, then turn off the oven and leave the pavlova inside to cool completely (with the door closed).

4. For the filling, beat the cream, sugar and bourbon (if using) until the mixture holds soft peaks. Mash half the raspberries with a fork, then gently fold into the cream to give a ripple effect.

5. To serve, carefully transfer the pavlova to a serving plate or cake stand. Spoon the raspberry cream into the centre. Top with the remaining raspberries, drizzle over the melted chocolate and sprinkle over the extra chopped pistachios.

Hands-on time: 15min, plus cooling
Cooking time: about 1hr
Serves 6

PER SERVING 714cals, 7g protein, 53g fat
(30g saturates), 48g carbs (48g total sugars), 2g fibre

◆ GET AHEAD
Make and cool the meringue up to 1 day
ahead. Store in an airtight container at room
temperature. Make the cream (without the
raspberry ripple) up to 4hr ahead and chill.
Complete the recipe to serve.

Pomegranate and Coconut Panna Cottas

Low-fat coconut milk adds creaminess to these fragrant desserts, without piling on the calories.

FOR THE POMEGRANATE LAYER
Oil, to grease
3 leaves quick-dissolving gelatine
300ml pomegranate juice
2 tsp caster sugar
Few drops rosewater, to taste
40g pomegranate seeds

FOR THE COCONUT LAYER
6 leaves quick-dissolving gelatine
400ml tin reduced-fat coconut milk
175ml skimmed milk
50g caster sugar

◆ GET AHEAD
Prepare to end of step 4 up to 1 day ahead. Cover and chill the reserved juice. Complete the recipe to serve.

Hands-on time: 30min, plus soaking, cooling and chilling
Cooking time: about 10min
Makes 6 panna cottas

PER PANNA COTTA 126cals, 3g protein, 4g fat (4g saturates), 19g carbs (18g total sugars), 0.3g fibre

1. Lightly grease 6 x 125ml jelly moulds. To make the pomegranate layer, first soak the gelatine leaves in a bowl of cold water for 5min. Meanwhile, in a medium pan, gently heat the pomegranate juice and sugar, stirring until the sugar dissolves. Remove from the heat and add a few drops of rosewater to taste.

2. Pour 75ml of the warm pomegranate mixture into a small bowl and chill until needed. Lift the gelatine out of the water, squeeze out the excess water, then add to the remaining warm pomegranate mix. Stir to dissolve, then divide among the prepared jelly moulds. Chill until set, about 2hr.

3. Once set, make the coconut layer. Soak the gelatine in the water as before. In a clean medium pan, gently heat the coconut milk, milk and caster sugar, stirring until the sugar dissolves. Remove from the heat. Lift the gelatine out of the water, squeeze out excess water, then add to the warm coconut mixture. Stir to dissolve, then transfer the mixture to a large jug. Set aside to cool for 45min.

4. When cool, stir the coconut mixture, then divide it among the moulds, pouring it on top of the set pomegranate jelly. Chill for 4hr or until set.

5. To serve, briefly dip the moulds first in hot water (to just below the rim), dry the outside of the moulds, then invert on to serving plates. Stir the pomegranate seeds into the reserved juice and spoon over the jellies.

Meringue Nest Wreath with Plum

Shop-bought meringue nests speed up this eye-catching pudding.

3 plums, halved and de-stoned
1 tbsp caster sugar
Finely grated zest and juice 1 orange
175ml double cream
1 tsp icing sugar
75g mascarpone
6 meringue nests
25–50g white chocolate

1. Preheat the oven to 180°C (160°C fan) mark 4. Put the plum halves in a small roasting tin, cut-side down. Sprinkle over the sugar and orange zest and pour over the juice. Cook for 30min, or until the plums are tender. Set aside.

2. Meanwhile, whisk the cream and icing sugar in a large bowl until the mixture holds soft peaks. In a separate bowl, beat the mascarpone to break up any lumps, then add it to the cream bowl and whisk until just combined (be careful not to overbeat or the mixture will become grainy).

3. To serve, arrange the meringue nests in a circle on a serving plate or board. Spoon the mascarpone mixture on to the nests and top each with half a plum. Drizzle over the liquid from the plum tin. Using a vegetable peeler, shave over curls of white chocolate.

Hands-on time: 15min
Cooking time: about 30min
Makes 6 nests

PER NEST 300cals, 2g protein, 23g fat (14g saturates), 22g carbs (22g total sugars), 1g fibre

Strawberry Daiquiri Sorbet

Use coconut rum for a tropical twist or replace the rum with gin.

100ml white rum
Finely grated zest and juice 3 limes
125g caster sugar
Large handful mint sprigs
900g strawberries (hulled weight), chopped

1. In a small pan, heat the rum, lime zest and juice and sugar, stirring until the sugar dissolves. Remove from the heat, add the mint and cool.

2. Once cool, lift out and discard the mint. Whizz the rum mixture in a blender with the strawberries. Pass through a fine sieve into a bowl (discard the seeds).

3. Churn the mixture in an ice cream machine until frozen (see GH Tip). Empty into a freezerproof container, then cover and freeze until solid for up to 3 months.

4. Allow to soften at room temperature for 15min before serving in scoops.

◆ GH TIP
Don't have an ice cream machine? Put the mixture into a freezerproof container, then cover and freeze until solid. When solid, break up with a fork and whizz again until smooth.

Hands-on time: 20min, plus cooling, freezing and softening
Cooking time: about 5min
Makes about 1 litre

PER SCOOP 53cals, <1g protein, <1g fat (<1g saturates), 9g carbs (9g total sugars), 2g fibre

Cookie Dough Nice Cream

This also works well with almond butter.

FOR THE COOKIE DOUGH
40g cashew butter
40g plain flour
40g maple syrup
40g dairy-free chocolate chunks or chips

FOR THE NICE CREAM
450ml unsweetened almond milk
100g soft dates, roughly chopped
50g cashew butter
2 tsp vanilla bean paste

1. For the cookie dough, line a small baking tray with baking parchment, then mix together all the ingredients with a pinch of salt. Place 1 tsp portions on the lined tray; freeze until needed.

2. For the nice cream, whizz all the ingredients in a blender with a pinch of salt until smooth.

3. Empty into a 900g loaf tin or freezer-safe container and freeze for 2–3hr, until nearly solid.

4. Break the nice cream into a food processor and pulse to break up. Or scrape into a bowl and whisk with a fork to break up. Return the nice cream to the tin and mix through the frozen cookie dough pieces. Freeze until solid, ideally overnight.

5. To serve, allow to soften at room temperature for 10min before scooping.

Hands-on time: 20min, plus (overnight) freezing and softening
Makes 8 scoops

PER SCOOP 169cals, 4g protein, 8g fat (2g saturates), 20g carbs (14g total sugars), 2g fibre

Frozen Fruit Kebabs with Hot White Chocolate Sauce

A refreshing way to finish a summer meal.

About 800g mixed fruit – we used 8 strawberries, 16 grapes, 16 blueberries and 2 kiwi, 2 nectarines and ½ mango, all peeled, stoned and cut into bite-sized pieces

FOR THE SAUCE
200g white chocolate, chopped
200ml double cream
3 ripe passion fruit

YOU'LL ALSO NEED
8 wooden skewers

1. Thread the fruit (except the passion fruit) on to the skewers. Arrange on a baking tray lined with baking parchment and freeze for at least 4hr, until firm.

2. Melt the chocolate and cream in a heatproof bowl set over a pan of barely simmering water. Meanwhile, halve the passion fruit and scoop the pulp and seeds into a sieve placed over a jug. Work the pulp to extract all the juice. If you like, stir a few seeds back into the sieved juice, discarding the rest.

3. Remove the skewers from the freezer, arrange on a platter and allow them to soften at room temperature for around 10min. Drizzle over some of the chocolate sauce and all the passion fruit juice. Serve with the remaining sauce for dipping.

Hands-on time: 20min, plus freezing and softening
Cooking time: about 5min
Makes 8 kebabs

PER SERVING 313cals, 4g protein, 21g fat (13g saturates), 25g carbs (25g total sugars), 3g fibre

Bursting Berry Bake

This fruit pudding is often made with double cream, but we've substituted yogurt for a healthier version.

Butter, to grease
150g blackberries
100g blueberries
150g raspberries
15g flaked almonds
Icing sugar, to dust

FOR THE BATTER
50g caster sugar
75g plain flour
40g ground almonds
3 medium eggs, lightly beaten
200g natural yogurt
1 tbsp vanilla bean paste

1. Preheat the oven to 190°C (170°C fan) mark 5. Grease a 20.5–23cm ceramic flan or pie dish (or use a similar-sized ovenproof serving dish).

2. For the batter, whisk the sugar, flour and ground almonds to combine. Add the eggs, yogurt and vanilla and whisk until smooth (alternatively, whizz together all the batter ingredients in a blender). Scrape into the greased dish and scatter over the berries, followed by the flaked almonds.

3. Bake for 35–40min, until lightly golden and puffed. Allow to sit for 10min before lightly dusting with icing sugar and serving.

Hands-on time: 10min, plus resting
Cooking time: about 40min
Serves 6

PER SERVING 214cals, 9g protein, 8g fat (1g saturates), 25g carbs (15g total sugars), 3g fibre

Sticky Roast Bananas with Lime Yogurt

Wonderfully simple and comforting, this is a tasty, nursery-style pud that grown-ups will love too!

75g unsalted butter
75g light muscovado sugar
½ tsp Chinese five spice
4 medium-sized ripe bananas, halved lengthways
125g 0% fat Greek yogurt
1 tsp runny honey
Finely grated zest and juice 1 lime
½ tsp black or white sesame seeds, or a mix

1. Preheat the oven to 220°C (200°C fan) mark 7. Heat the butter, sugar, five spice and a pinch of fine salt in a large ovenproof frying pan over low heat, stirring, until the butter melts. Arrange the bananas, cut-side up, in the pan, breaking to fit, if needed.

2. Transfer to the oven and bake for 10–12min, carefully basting the bananas a couple of times with the butter.

3. Meanwhile, mix the yogurt, honey and lime juice in a bowl. Sprinkle the sesame seeds and lime zest over the bananas and serve with the yogurt.

Hands-on time: 15min
Cooking time: about 15min
Serves 4

PER SERVING 324cals, 5g protein, 16g fat (10g saturates), 40g carbs (38g total sugars), 2g fibre

Baked Maple, Pecan and Orange Pancakes

Ready-made pancakes are the key to this speedy pud. Add a dash of orange liqueur with the orange juice before baking for added oomph.

500g ricotta
75ml maple syrup
Finely grated zest 1 orange
50g pecans, roughly chopped
8 ready-made sweet pancakes or crêpes
125ml orange juice
25g unsalted butter, chopped
Icing sugar, to dust

1. Preheat the oven to 200°C (180°C fan) mark 6. In a medium bowl, mix the ricotta, maple syrup, half the orange zest and most of the pecans.

2. Spoon an eighth of the filling in a line down the centre of each pancake. Roll up and arrange in a single layer, seam-side down, in a rough 25 x 35cm ovenproof serving dish. Mix the remaining zest into the orange juice and pour over the pancakes. Dot over the butter and scatter over the remaining pecans.

3. Cover with foil and bake for 15–18min, or until piping hot. Dust with icing sugar and serve.

Hands-on time: 10min
Cooking time: about 18min
Serves 4

PER SERVING 654cals, 21g protein, 36g fat (14g saturates), 61g carbs (23g total sugars), 3g fibre

Pear and Chocolate Pudding

Chocolate, pears and almonds are a winning combination, and this quick and simple pudding is a delight.

---

3 medium eggs
75g light brown soft sugar
50g self-raising flour
25g cocoa powder
50g ground almonds
4 tinned pear halves in juice, drained (see GH Tip)
15g flaked almonds
Icing sugar, to dust

1. Preheat the oven to 180°C (160°C fan) mark 4. Using a handheld electric whisk, beat the eggs and brown sugar in a large bowl until very thick, about 5min. Sift over the flour and cocoa powder, then add the ground almonds and carefully fold together using a large metal spoon.

2. Scrape into a round ovenproof pie or serving dish (about 20.5cm across), and arrange the pears on top. Scatter over the flaked almonds and bake for 15min, until just set. Allow to sit for a few min, then lightly dust with icing sugar and serve.

◆ GH TIP
Using tinned pears helps to prevent the fruit from discolouring, but you can use fresh if you prefer.

Hands-on time: 10min, plus resting
Cooking time: 15min
Serves 4

PER SERVING 318cals, 12g protein, 14g fat (3g saturates), 34g carbs (24g total sugars), 4g fibre

Summer Fruit and White Chocolate Tart

Crisp, buttery pastry, filled with silky crème pâtissière and topped with your favourite soft fruit — this showstopping tart is a must-have for entertaining guests.

FOR THE PASTRY
175g plain flour, plus extra to dust
75g unsalted butter, chilled and cubed
40g icing sugar, plus extra to dust
1 medium egg, beaten

FOR THE FILLING
4 medium egg yolks
25g caster sugar
25g cornflour
25g plain flour
350ml whole milk
1 tsp vanilla bean paste
75g white chocolate, chopped, plus curls
    to decorate (optional)
150ml double cream
500g mixed summer fruits

1. For the pastry, pulse the flour and butter in a food processor until they resemble fine breadcrumbs. Pulse in the icing sugar, followed by the egg, until the pastry clumps together. Tip on to a work surface, shape into a disc, then wrap and chill for 30min.

2. Lightly flour a work surface and roll out the pastry. Use it to line a 23cm round, straight-sided, loose-bottomed tart tin (3.5cm deep), leaving the excess pastry hanging over the sides. Prick the base all over with a fork, then chill for 30min.

Hands-on time: 45min, plus chilling and cooling
Cooking time: about 35min
Serves 10

PER SERVING (without curls) 349cals, 7g protein, 21g fat (12g saturates), 32g carbs (15g total sugars), 3g fibre

3. Preheat the oven to 190°C (170°C fan) mark 5. Line the pastry with a large sheet of baking parchment and fill with baking beans. Bake for 20min. Carefully remove the parchment and beans, then return the pastry to the oven for 15min, until golden and base feels sandy. Cool in the tin for 5min, then trim the pastry overhang with a large serrated knife and leave to cool completely.

4. Meanwhile, make the filling. In a heatproof bowl, whisk the egg yolks, sugar and both flours until combined. Heat the milk in a medium pan until just steaming. Gradually whisk the hot milk into the yolk mixture, until smooth. Return the mixture to the pan and cook, whisking constantly, until very thick (it will need to boil). Remove from the heat and whisk in the vanilla and chocolate until melted (don't worry if the mixture is a little lumpy). Scrape into a bowl, then lay baking parchment or cling film directly on the surface, cool and chill.

5. To serve, whizz the white chocolate filling briefly in a food processor until smooth. In a large bowl, whip the cream until it holds firm peaks. Scrape in the white chocolate mixture and fold together.

6. Transfer the pastry case to a cake stand or serving plate, scrape in the filling and smooth to level. Top with the fruit and white chocolate curls (see GH Tip), if you like. Lightly dust with icing sugar and serve.

Raspberry Ripple and Pistachio Semifreddo

This iced treat is often presented as a sliceable loaf (see GH Tip), but we've served our version in scoops.

400g raspberries
75g caster sugar
3 medium eggs, separated
300ml double cream
1 tsp vanilla bean paste
75g pistachio kernels, roughly chopped

◆ GET AHEAD
Make and freeze up to 1 week ahead.
Complete the recipe to serve.

◆ GH TIP
If you want to serve the semifreddo in slices, line the tin with a double layer of cling film before filling it to make it easier to remove from the tin for slicing.

1. Put a 900g loaf tin in the freezer to chill. Put 300g of the raspberries in a pan and cook over a low heat until they are starting to burst. Press through a fine sieve into a bowl (discard the seeds). Set aside to cool.

2. Using a handheld electric whisk, beat the sugar and egg yolks in large bowl for 5min, until thick and pale. In a separate bowl and using clean beaters, whisk the egg whites until they hold stiff peaks. In a third bowl, whisk the double cream and vanilla bean paste until the mixture holds soft peaks.

3. Using a large metal spoon, fold the cream into the yolk mixture, followed by the egg whites, being careful not to knock out too much air.

4. Spoon half the mixture into the chilled loaf tin, ripple through half the raspberry purée, then sprinkle over half the pistachios. Repeat with the remaining cream mixture, raspberry purée and pistachios. Sprinkle the remaining 100g raspberries on top. Cover with foil or clingfilm and freeze for at least 5hr, ideally overnight, until set firm.

5. To serve, allow to soften at room temperature for around 15min before serving in scoops.

Hands-on time: 20min, plus cooling, (overnight) freezing and softening
Cooking time: about 5min
Serves 10

PER SERVING 259cals, 5g protein, 22g fat (11g saturates), 10g carbs (10g total sugars), 2g fibre

Chocolate Espresso Fondants

This is the perfect get-ahead dessert to impress guests, and it will deliver a deliciously tempting, gooey centre every time.

150g butter, chopped, plus extra to grease
Cocoa powder, to dust
150g dark chocolate (70% cocoa solids), chopped
2 tbsp instant espresso powder
50ml coffee liqueur, we used Kahlúa
3 medium eggs and 3 medium egg yolks
150g caster sugar
150g plain flour
Cream or vanilla ice cream, to serve (optional)

1. Grease 6 dariole moulds well with butter, then dust with cocoa powder to coat, tapping out the excess. Chill until needed.

2. Melt the butter, chocolate, espresso powder and coffee liqueur in a heatproof bowl set over a pan of barely simmering water, stirring occasionally, until combined. Remove the bowl from the heat and leave to cool for 10min.

3. Using a freestanding mixer or handheld electric whisk, beat the eggs, yolks and sugar in a large bowl until pale and fluffy, about 5min. Using a large metal spoon, fold in the flour and cooled chocolate mixture. Divide the mixture evenly between the prepared moulds. Chill for 1hr (or up to 24hr).

4. Preheat the oven to 200°C (180°C fan) mark 6. Put the moulds on a baking tray and bake for 10–12min, until well-risen and the tops appear baked. Remove from the oven and leave to sit for 1min, before turning out on small plates. Serve with cream or vanilla ice cream, if you like.

◆ GET AHEAD
Once filled, cover the moulds and freeze for up to 1 month. To serve, uncover and bake from frozen in an oven preheated to 200°C (180°C fan) mark 6 for 15–17min. Complete the recipe to serve.

Hands-on time: 20min, plus cooling and chilling
Cooking time: about 20min
Makes 6 fondants

PER FONDANT 445cals, 7g protein, 24g fat (14g saturates), 47g carbs (32g total sugars), 2g fibre

Gluten-free Banoffee Tarte Tatin

This boozy, banoffee treat tastes equally good with a base layer of thinly sliced apple, if you prefer.

280g ready-rolled gluten-free puff pastry (see GH Tip)
Oil, to grease
150g thick caramel, we used Carnation
3 large bananas, thinly sliced on the diagonal

FOR THE RUM CREAM
250ml double cream
1 tbsp dark rum
½ tbsp icing sugar

1. Preheat the oven to 200°C (180°C fan) mark 6. Unroll the pastry and, using an ovenproof frying pan measuring 23cm across the top, cut a rough circle the same size as the top of the pan. Prick the pastry circle all over with a fork and set aside. Grease the base and sides of the pan with a little oil.

2. Spread the caramel over the base of the greased pan and arrange the banana slices on top, overlapping them to fit, if needed. Lay the pastry over the bananas and tuck the edges down and slightly inwards. Bake for 25–30min, or until puffed and golden.

3. Meanwhile, make the rum cream by whisking all the ingredients until the mixture just holds soft peaks. Chill until needed.

4. Carefully remove the pan from the oven and wrap the handle with an oven glove or tea towel (to remind you it's hot!). Leave to cool for 5min before inverting on to a serving plate. Serve the tart in slices with the rum cream.

◆ GH TIP
Gluten-free pastry doesn't crack as much as regular puff pastry. If you are not following a gluten-free diet and decide to use the latter, let it sit at room temperature for 10min before unrolling.

Hands-on time: 10min, plus cooling
Cooking time: about 30min
Cuts into 6 slices

PER SLICE 424cals, 3g protein, 29g fat (17g saturates), 36g carbs (27g total sugars), 2g fibre

Afternoon Tea

Raspberry Lemonade Bars

With a fruity filling that tastes just like raspberry lemonade, you may find it hard to stop at just one of these bars!

FOR THE SHORTBREAD BASE
150g unsalted butter, chopped, plus extra to grease
175g plain flour
75g icing sugar, plus extra to dust
Finely grated zest 1 lemon

FOR THE FILLING
300g raspberries
Juice 1 lemon
200g caster sugar
25g plain flour
3 medium eggs, beaten

1. Grease and line a 20.5cm square tin with baking parchment. To make the shortbread base, pulse the butter and flour in a food processor until the mixture resembles fine breadcrumbs. Alternatively, rub the butter into the flour using your fingertips. Pulse/stir in the icing sugar, lemon zest and a pinch of salt. Press into the prepared tin and level with the back of a spoon. Prick the base all over with a fork and chill for 15min.

2. Preheat the oven to 180°C (160°C fan) mark 4. Bake the shortbread base for 25min, until lightly golden. Remove from the oven and turn down the temperature to 160°C (140°C fan) mark 3.

3. For the filling, put the raspberries and lemon juice in a blender or food processor and whizz until fairly smooth. Add the sugar, flour and eggs, and whizz again until combined. Pass the mixture through a fine sieve into a jug, working it well (discard the seeds).

4. Pour the filling over the base and carefully tap the tin a few times on a work surface to burst any air bubbles. Bake for 25–30min, until just set. Cool completely in the tin, then chill for at least 1hr to firm up. Remove from the tin and dust with icing sugar. Slice into 12 bars and serve.

Hands-on time: 25min, plus cooling and chilling
Cooking time: about 55min
Makes 12 bars

PER BAR 271cals, 4g protein, 12g fat (7g saturates), 37g carbs (24g total sugars), 2g fibre

Lemon Meringue Cupcakes

With a citrussy sponge, tangy curd filling and a towering meringue topping, these cupcakes have all the appeal of a classic lemon meringue pie.

FOR THE CAKES
200g caster sugar
125g butter, softened
Finely grated zest 2 lemons
4 medium eggs, beaten
200g self-raising flour
75g soured cream
4 tbsp lemon curd

FOR THE MERINGUE TOPPING
150g caster sugar
2 medium egg whites

YOU'LL ALSO NEED
Sugar thermometer

◆ TO STORE
Keep the cupcakes in an airtight container at room temperature for up to 2 days.

1. Preheat the oven to 200°C (180°C fan) mark 6. Line a 12-hole muffin tin with paper muffin cases.

2. For the cakes, put the sugar, butter and lemon zest into a large bowl and beat with a handheld electric whisk until pale and fluffy. Gradually beat in the eggs, adding a spoonful of flour if the mixture looks as if it's about to curdle.

3. Using a large metal spoon, fold in the rest of the flour followed by the soured cream. Divide the mixture between the muffin cases and bake for 12–15min, until risen and golden. Transfer to a wire rack to cool.

4. Next, make the meringue topping. In a medium pan, gently heat the sugar with 3 tbsp water, stirring to dissolve the sugar. Once fully dissolved, turn up the heat to medium-high and boil the syrup, swirling the pan occasionally instead of stirring, until the mixture reaches 120°C on a sugar thermometer. Remove the pan from the heat.

5. Meanwhile, whisk the egg whites in the bowl of a freestanding mixer (or in a large, clean bowl with a handheld electric whisk) to stiff peaks. With the motor on low, gradually trickle the hot sugar syrup on to the stiff egg whites, whisking constantly. Once all the syrup has been added, continue beating until the meringue is completely cool.

6. Transfer the meringue to a piping bag fitted with a 1cm closed star nozzle. Using a small sharp knife or an apple corer, carve a small hole into the centre of the top of each cake and fill each hole with 1 tsp lemon curd. Pipe the meringue on to the cakes and brown with a blowtorch, if you like. Serve.

(V)

Hands-on time: 35min, plus cooling
Cooking time: about 25min
Makes 12 cupcakes

PER CUPCAKE 305cals, 5g protein, 12g fat (7g saturates), 45g carbs (32g total sugars), 1g fibre

Pearly Oyster Madeleines

These pretty madeleines would be a perfect choice for a romantic tea party.

75g unsalted butter, plus extra to grease
75g plain flour, plus extra to dust
2 large eggs
¾ tsp vanilla extract
75g caster sugar
½ tsp baking powder
Zest and juice 1 lemon

TO DECORATE
100g white chocolate, chopped
1 tsp sunflower oil
Pink food colouring (optional)
Pearl hundreds and thousands

◆ GET AHEAD
The madeleine mixture can be stored in the fridge for up to 24 hours.

1. Preheat the oven to 180°C (160°C fan) mark 4. Grease the holes of a 12-mould madeleine tin with butter. Dust with a little flour and tap out the excess.

2. Melt the remaining butter and set aside to cool. In a large mixing bowl, use a handheld electric whisk to beat the eggs, vanilla and a pinch of salt until light and frothy. Add the sugar and continue whisking for 5-10min until the mixture is thick and has doubled in volume.

3. Sift the flour and baking powder over the mixture. Add the lemon zest. With a large metal spoon, fold gently until just combined, being careful to retain as much volume as possible.

4. Pour the lemon juice and melted butter around the edge of the bowl, then quickly but gently fold them in to the batter until smooth.

5. Carefully transfer the mixture to a large piping bag fitted with a 1cm nozzle. Pipe half the mixture into the prepared tin to fill each mould just below the rim. Bake for 15min until golden and springy to the touch. Leave to cool in the tin for 5min before turning out on to a wire rack to cool completely.

6. Meanwhile, store extra mixture in the piping bag in a jug in the fridge, with the nozzle upwards and the other end well twisted so no mixture leaks out. Re-butter and flour the cleaned moulds, then fill and bake as before.

7. Melt the chocolate and oil in a bowl set over a pan of barely simmering water. Add a little pink food colouring, if using. Holding a madeleine over the bowl, spoon over a little melted chocolate halfway up the fan, gently shaking off any excess. Repeat with the remaining madeleines. Sprinkle over the pearl hundreds and thousands and leave to set on a wire rack.

Hands-on time: 50min, plus cooling and setting
Cooking time: about 30min
Makes 24 madeleines

PER MADELEINE 78cals, 1g protein, 5g fat (3g saturates), 8g carbs (7g total sugars), 0g fibre

Berry Tiramisu Cake

Light-as-air sponge cakes, filled with luxurious mascarpone and fresh berries. Summer in a slice!

FOR THE CAKES
Butter, to grease
6 medium eggs, separated
200g granulated sugar
125g plain flour
1 tbsp cornflour
½ tsp baking powder

FOR THE FILLING
400ml double cream
75g icing sugar, sifted, plus extra to dust
1½ tsp vanilla bean paste
500g mascarpone
75ml sweet (pudding) wine, vin santo or
    Marsala (optional)
700g mixed berries, strawberries halved

◆ TO STORE
Keep loosely covered in the fridge for up to 3 days. The filling will thicken a bit, but it will still taste wonderful.

1. Preheat the oven to 170°C (150°C fan) mark 3. Lightly grease and line 2 x 20.5cm round cake tins, at least 4cm deep, with baking parchment.

2. For the cakes, whisk the egg whites to stiff peaks in the bowl of a freestanding mixer or use a handheld electric whisk and a large bowl. Gradually beat in the sugar, whisking back up to stiff peaks. Add the egg yolks and beat briefly to combine.

3. Sift over the flour, cornflour and baking powder and fold in with a large metal spoon, trying to keep in as much air as possible. Divide the batter between the lined tins, gently smooth to level, then bake for 20–25min, until risen and golden. Leave to cool in the tins for 5min, then transfer to a wire rack to cool completely.

4. To assemble, using a freestanding mixer or handheld electric whisk, beat the cream, icing sugar and vanilla until the mixture just holds its shape. Add the mascarpone and beat briefly until smooth (over-beating will make it grainy).

5. Slice the cakes in half horizontally and arrange cut-side up. Set one of the cake halves on a cake stand or plate and brush/drizzle over a quarter of the alcohol, if using. Spread over a quarter of the filling and dot with a quarter of the berries (making sure some of the berries are at the edges). Repeat the process twice more, stacking the layers.

6. Brush/drizzle the remaining alcohol, if using, over the cut side of the final cake half, then set it cut-side down on the stack. Spread over the remaining filling and scatter over the remaining berries. Dust lightly with icing sugar and serve in slices.

Hands-on time: 30min, plus cooling
Cooking time: about 25min
Cuts into 16 slices

PER SLICE 404cals, 5g protein, 29g fat (19g saturates), 28g carbs (21g total sugars), 2g fibre

Vanilla Mini Bundts with Cherry Icing

A miniature bundt cake is the perfect size for a teatime treat. Swap the cherry cordial in the icing for any flavour you prefer, or use lemon juice instead.

75g unsalted butter, softened, plus extra to grease
100g caster sugar
1 medium egg, beaten
75g soured cream
1 tsp vanilla bean paste
Finely grated zest 1 lemon
100g self-raising flour

TO DECORATE
75g icing sugar, sifted
1–2 tbsp cherry cordial (or flavour of your choice)
Red food colouring (optional)
Red, pink and white sprinkles (optional)

1. Preheat the oven to 180°C (160°C fan) mark 4 and thoroughly grease a 6-hole mini Bundt tin/mould (see GH Tip). In a large bowl with a handheld electric whisk, beat the butter and sugar until pale and fluffy. Add the egg and beat again until combined, then add the soured cream, vanilla, lemon zest and a pinch of salt and beat until combined.

2. Add the flour and fold in with a large metal spoon. Divide the cake mix among the holes in the tin, filling them two-thirds full. Bake for 20–25min until golden and firm to the touch (the cakes should spring back when poked). Cool in the tin/mould for 5min then carefully turn out onto a wire rack and leave to cool completely.

3. To decorate, in a small bowl combine the icing sugar and cordial and stir until smooth. Add a drop or two of food colouring, if you like. Drizzle over the cooled cakes, decorate with sprinkles, if using, and serve.

◆ TO STORE
Keep in an airtight container at room temperature for up to 2 days.

◆ GH TIP
Mini cake tins vary in capacity and are either silicone or metal, both of which work well here – just make sure to fill the moulds two-thirds full.

Hands-on time: 15min, plus cooling
Cooking time: about 25min
Makes 6 cakes

PER CAKE 315cals, 3g protein, 14g fat (8g saturates), 44g carbs (31g total sugars), 1g fibre

Deluxe Sausage Rolls

These flavourful sausage rolls are simple to make and can be enjoyed hot or cold.

1 tsp olive oil
2 shallots, finely chopped
450g pork sausage meat
3 tbsp chopped fresh sage
1 garlic clove, crushed
320g ready-rolled all-butter puff pastry
2 tbsp English mustard
1 medium egg, beaten

1. Heat the oil in a small frying pan and gently fry the shallots until softened, about 5min. Empty into a large bowl and leave to cool.

2. Add the sausage meat, sage, garlic and plenty of seasoning (it can take a fair amount) to the shallot bowl. Mix to combine.

3. Unroll the pastry sheet and brush with mustard. Shape the sausage mixture in a line lengthways down the middle of the pastry. Fold one side of the pastry over the meat and press the edges to seal, then crimp with a fork. Slice into 6 even portions and cut a few slits into the top of each. Arrange on a baking tray and chill for 1hr.

4. Preheat the oven to 200°C (180°C fan) mark 6. Brush the sausage rolls with egg and cook for 30min, or until the pastry is a deep golden brown. Allow to cool slightly before serving warm or at room temperature.

◆ GET AHEAD
Cook up to a day ahead, then cool, cover and chill. To serve, refresh in an oven preheated to 200°C (180°C fan) mark 6 for 5min.

Hands-on time: 20min, plus chilling
Cooking time: about 35min
Makes 6 rolls

PER ROLL 468cals, 14g protein, 33g fat (16g saturates), 27g carbs (3g total sugars), 3g fibre

Croque Monsieur Pinwheels

We used sliced Gruyère to give these pinwheels the classic croque-monsieur flavour, but you can substitute whatever cheese you fancy.

4 large white tortilla wraps
4 tsp Dijon mustard, plus extra to brush
16 slices ham (about 325g)
12 slices Gruyère (about 300g), at room temperature – this makes it easier to roll
50g salad leaves

1. Lay a wrap on a chopping board and cut off 2 of the opposite edges so you have 2 straight sides. Spread 1 tsp mustard evenly over the wrap, then add 4 slices of ham (tearing pieces to make them fit). Top with 3 torn cheese slices on the lower half of the wrap and cover this with a layer of salad leaves.

2. Tightly roll up the wrap, sticking down the edge with a little mustard to help hold it in place. With the seam-side down, cut into 5 pinwheels. Repeat with remaining ingredients.

◆ GET AHEAD
Wrap the filled, unsliced rolls tightly in cling film up to 8hr ahead. Unwrap and slice as in the recipe to serve.

Hands-on time: 25min
Makes 20 pinwheels

PER PINWHEEL 106cals, 8g protein, 6g fat (3g saturates), 5g carbs (0g total sugars), 0g fibre

Cucumber Finger Sandwiches

A must-have for your afternoon tea buffet. We've added a hint of mint to make our cucumber sandwiches particularly refreshing and light.

8 tbsp cream cheese
2 tbsp finely chopped mint
25g unsalted butter, softened
8 slices thick-cut white bread
1 cucumber, sliced into thin rounds

1. In a medium bowl, mix the cream cheese and mint, then season. Butter 4 slices of bread, then spread each of the remaining 4 slices with 2 tbsp of the cream cheese mixture.

2. Arrange the cucumber slices in 2 layers over the cream cheese, then top with the buttered slice of bread. With a sharp serrated knife, cut off the crusts, then cut each sandwich into 3 fingers. Keep your sandwiches wrapped in cling film until ready to serve.

Hands-on time: 15min
Makes 12 finger sandwiches

PER FINGER SANDWICH 115cals, 2g protein, 8g fat (5g saturates), 8g carbs (1g total sugars), 1g fibre

Salmon and Asparagus Triangles

These open sandwiches look very appealing. Using rye bread will help them last longer unwrapped, too.

4 tbsp crème fraîche
1 tbsp chopped dill
2 thick-stemmed asparagus spears, woody
   ends trimmed
4 slices rectangular rye bread
200g smoked salmon slices

1. In a small bowl, mix together the crème fraîche and dill with a good sprinkling of black pepper. Use a vegetable peeler to peel the asparagus into ribbons.

2. Spread 1 tbsp of the crème fraîche mixture on a piece of rye, then top with 3 slices salmon (about 50g) so the bread is covered up to the edges. Lay 4 or 5 asparagus ribbons on top in a lattice pattern. Press down and trim to neaten.

3. With a sharp serrated knife, cut the bread in half diagonally into triangles. Repeat with the remaining rye bread. Arrange the triangles on a plate and serve immediately, or cover with cling film and chill in the fridge up to a day in advance.

◆ GH TIP
To make the asparagus strips look brighter, blanch the spears in boiling water for 2min, then plunge into ice-cold water before peeling into ribbons.

Hands-on time: 15min
Makes 8 triangles

PER TRIANGLE 67cals, 5g protein, 3g fat (2g saturates), 6g carbs (0g total sugars), 1g fibre

White Chocolate and Raspberry Scones

No tea party would be complete without scones! We've paired ours with white chocolate and raspberry for a decadent version that's best eaten fresh.

225g self-raising flour, plus extra to dust
75g chilled butter, cut into cubes
50g caster sugar
75g white chocolate chips
1 large egg
2 tbsp buttermilk
Popping candy, to decorate (optional)
Raspberries, to decorate (optional)

FOR THE RASPBERRY BUTTER
50g unsalted butter, softened
75g icing sugar
3 tbsp raspberry jam

1. Preheat the oven to 220°C (200°C fan), mark 7. Sieve the flour into a large bowl, stir in a pinch of salt, then rub in the butter until it resembles breadcrumbs. Stir in the sugar and white chocolate chips. In a jug, combine the egg and buttermilk. Make a well in the dry ingredients and pour in the wet mixture. Use a cutlery knife to mix the dough until it just comes together.

2. Tip the dough onto a lightly floured surface and gently bring together with a little light kneading. Pat the scone dough out to a 3cm thickness, then use a 5cm round cutter to stamp out 8 scones. Dip the cutter into flour between each cut and press together any remaining dough to stamp out more scones.

3. Place the scones on baking trays lined with baking parchment. Bake in the oven for 10–12 min, until risen and lightly golden. Transfer to a wire rack to cool.

4. Meanwhile, make the raspberry butter. In a large bowl, beat together the butter and icing sugar, then beat in the raspberry jam. Sprinkle popping candy on to the scones and decorate with raspberries, if you like, then serve with the raspberry butter.

Hands on time: 25min
Cooking time: about 12min
Makes 8 scones

PER SCONE (with 1 tbsp raspberry butter)
369cals, 5g protein, 20g fat (12g saturates),
43g carbs (23g sugars), 1g fibre

Refreshing Tea

We've used Earl Grey, but floral teas,
Ceylon or jasmine would work well too.
Be careful not to brew the tea for too long
to avoid a tannic flavour.

75g caster sugar
3 tbsp loose-leaf Earl Grey
Juice ½ lemon
¼ cucumber, sliced to garnish

1. Boil 500ml water, pour into a large jug with the
   sugar and stir to dissolve it. Add 500ml water
   at room temperature and stir in the Earl Grey
   leaves. Leave to infuse for 3–5 minutes, then
   strain through a fine mesh sieve. Add the lemon
   juice and leave to cool completely before chilling
   in the fridge. To serve, pour into teacups and
   garnish each with a slice of cucumber.

Hands-on time: 10min, plus infusing and chilling
Serves 5

PER SERVING 61cals, 0g protein, 0g fat (0g saturates),
15g carbs (15g sugars), 0g fibre

Rainbow Funfetti Loaf Cake

Shining with all the colours of the rainbow, this loaf cake is a bright and lively choice for a celebration.

FOR THE CAKE
200g unsalted butter, softened, plus extra to grease
200g caster sugar
3 medium eggs
125g natural yogurt
2 tsp vanilla extract
225g self-raising flour
30g bake-stable rainbow sprinkles, plus extra to sprinkle (see GH Tip)

FOR THE BUTTERCREAM
125g unsalted butter, softened
250g icing sugar, sifted
1½ tbsp milk
Purple food colouring gel or paste (optional)

FOR THE GLAZE
100g white chocolate, finely chopped
50g double cream
15g golden syrup
Red, orange, yellow, green, blue, purple and pink food colouring gels or pastes

1. Preheat the oven to 180°C (160°C fan) mark 4 and lightly grease and line a 900g loaf tin with baking parchment. For the cake, beat the butter and sugar using a freestanding mixer or in a large bowl with a handheld electric whisk until pale and fluffy, about 5–8min.

2. In a jug, whisk the eggs, yogurt and vanilla to combine (it will be a bit lumpy). Gradually add the egg mixture to the butter bowl, beating well after each addition. Fold in the flour and sprinkles with a large metal spoon. Scrape into the lined tin and spread to level. Bake for 55min–1hr, or until a skewer inserted into the centre comes out clean. Cover the cake with foil after 30min to prevent too much browning. Cool in tin for 10min, then transfer to a wire rack to cool completely.

3. To make the buttercream, beat the butter until pale and fluffy. Add the icing sugar and milk and beat for 3min, until fluffy. Using a cocktail stick, add a pinprick of purple food colouring, if using, and beat it in – this will help to neutralise the yellow colour of the buttercream.

4. Slice the cooled cake in half horizontally, then use half the buttercream to sandwich the layers back together. Spread the remaining buttercream over the top, smoothing it as much as possible.

5. To make the glaze, melt the chocolate, cream and golden syrup in a heatproof bowl set over a pan of barely simmering water. Once melted, remove from the heat and split the glaze evenly into 7 small bowls/ramekins. Use your food colouring to dye each bowl a different colour of the rainbow.

6. Drizzle and spread the glaze on top of the cake in a rainbow, encouraging it to drizzle down the sides. Scatter over a few sprinkles, if you like. Allow to set before serving in slices.

Hands-on time: 30min, plus cooling and setting
Cooking time: about 1hr 5min
Cuts into 10 slices

PER SLICE 626cals, 6g protein, 34g fat (21g saturates), 73g carbs (55g total sugars), 1g fibre

◆ TO STORE
Keep in an airtight container at room temperature for up to 4 days.

◆ GH TIP
The right choice of sprinkles is vital here to avoid clumping or weeping, so make sure that you use a bake-stable variety (it will say so on the packaging).

Gluten-free Apple and Oat Fritters

We've used Granny Smith apples for these fritters, as they hold up to the frying well and balance the sweet cinnamon sugar with a bite of sharpness.

FOR THE CINNAMON SUGAR
75g caster sugar
2 tsp ground cinnamon

FOR THE BATTER
125g gluten-free porridge oats
50g rice flour
25g gluten-free cornflour
1 tbsp gluten-free baking powder
40g caster sugar
½ tsp ground cinnamon
1 medium egg
250ml club soda

TO FINISH
Vegetable oil, to fry
4 Granny Smith apples
Icing sugar, to dust (optional)

YOU'LL ALSO NEED
Cooking thermometer

Hands-on time: 30min, plus resting
Cooking time: about 25min
Makes 24 fritters

PER FRITTER 88cals, 1g protein, 4g fat (0g saturates),
12g carbs (6g total sugars), 1g fibre

1. For the cinnamon sugar, mix the sugar and cinnamon in a shallow bowl and set aside.

2. To make the batter, whizz the oats in a food processor until they are as fine as you can get them. Empty into a large bowl and mix in the rice flour, cornflour, baking powder, sugar, cinnamon and ¼ tsp fine salt. Whisk in the egg and soda to make a smooth batter. Set aside to rest for 10min (the batter will thicken on standing).

3. Meanwhile, fill a large heavy-based, high-sided pan with oil until it comes a third of the way up the sides. Heat to 180°C. Peel and core the apples using an apple corer. Cut into 1cm-thick slices to make 24 rings.

4. Working in batches, and maintaining the oil temperature, dip the apple slices in the batter to coat, then carefully drop them into the hot oil. Fry the slices until golden and crisp, about 4min, turning midway through. Using a slotted spoon, lift out on to a tray lined with kitchen paper to drain. Repeat the coating and frying with the remaining slices.

5. Turn the hot fritters in the cinnamon sugar and arrange on a platter. Dust with a little icing sugar, if you like. Serve with the No-churn Pistachio Ice Cream (see right).

Dairy-free No-churn Pistachio 'Ice Cream'

This 'ice cream' is a treat for children of all ages. It may seem odd in a dessert, but the avocado helps give a smooth, creamy texture to this dairy-free delight.

200g pistachio kernels
500ml Oatly! custard, chilled
125g icing sugar, sifted
1¼ ripe avocados, peeled and stoned
2 tbsp vegetable oil
¼ tsp almond extract

1. Put 175g of the pistachios in a medium pan and cover with cold water. Soak for 5min, then slowly bring to a gentle simmer over medium heat. Simmer for 1min, then check whether they are ready to be skinned: carefully lift one out and see if the skin will slip off. If it does, drain the pistachios, then cover with cold water and pinch off and discard the skins with your fingers. (They should come away easily, but if not, simmer for 30sec more and try again.) Chop the pistachios.

2. Roughly chop the reserved pistachios, then whizz in a high-speed blender with the remaining ingredients (except the skinned pistachios) and blend until smooth. Transfer to a freezer-safe container, folding in the chopped skinned pistachios as you go. Freeze for 8hr, or ideally overnight, until set.

3. To serve, allow to soften in the fridge (this can take up to 1hr), before scooping into balls.

Hands-on time: 35min, plus soaking, (overnight) freezing and softening
Cooking time: about 10min
Makes 10 scoops

PER SCOOP 295cals, 5g protein, 20g fat (5g saturates), 22g carbs (20g total sugars), 2g fibre

Gluten-Free Peach and Almond Crumble Loaf

This rich loaf easily doubles as a pudding, served just warm with vanilla ice cream.

FOR THE CAKE
175g unsalted butter, softened, plus extra to grease
2 peaches, destoned and cut into 1cm chunks (200g prepared weight)
2 tbsp rice flour
175g caster sugar
3 medium eggs
125g ground almonds
75g quick-cook/1-minute polenta
2 tsp gluten-free baking powder
225g natural yogurt

FOR THE CRUMBLE TOPPING
15g butter
1 tbsp demerara sugar
3 tbsp gluten-free oats
2 tbsp flaked almonds

◆ TO STORE
Keep in an airtight container at room temperature for up to 3 days.

Hands-on time: 20min, plus cooling
Cooking time: about 1hr 15min
Cuts into 10 slices

PER SLICE 413cals, 9g protein, 27g fat (11g saturates), 34g carbs (23g total sugars), 2g fibre

1. Preheat the oven to 170°C (150°C fan) mark 3 and lightly grease and line a 900g loaf tin with baking parchment.

2. For the cake, toss the peach chunks with the rice flour in a small bowl to coat, then set aside. Using a freestanding mixer or handheld electric whisk, beat the butter and sugar until pale and fluffy. Gradually beat in the eggs, one at a time, adding 1 tbsp of ground almonds with each egg.

3. Beat in the polenta, baking powder, yogurt and the rest of the ground almonds until combined. Using a large metal spoon, fold in the peach chunks. Scrape into the lined tin and spread to level. Bake for 45min.

4. Meanwhile, make the crumble topping. Melt the butter in a small pan, then set aside to cool for 10min. Stir through the sugar, oats and almonds.

5. Once the cake has been in the oven for 45min, sprinkle over the crumble topping. Return to the oven for 30min, or until a skewer inserted into the centre comes out clean. Cool in the tin for 10min, then transfer to a wire rack to continue cooling. Slice and serve just warm or at room temperature.

Cherry Cheesecake Blondies

We've added a decadent cheesecake layer to these chewy blondies. Raspberries would make a great alternative to cherries.

FOR THE COMPOTE
½ tbsp cornflour
400g tin cherries in syrup, drained and 1 tbsp syrup reserved
2 tbsp caster sugar

FOR THE CHEESECAKE LAYER
175g full-fat cream cheese
2 tbsp caster sugar
1 medium egg
1 tsp vanilla bean paste
1 tbsp plain flour

FOR THE BLONDIE
250g unsalted butter, melted, plus extra to grease
150g light brown soft sugar
100g caster sugar
3 medium eggs, beaten
1 tsp vanilla bean paste
175g plain flour
½ tsp baking powder
150g white chocolate, roughly chopped

◆ **TO STORE**
Keep in an airtight container in the fridge for up to 5 days.

1. To make the compote, mix the cornflour and reserved syrup in a small pan. Add the cherries and sugar and bring to the boil, stirring occasionally, over high heat. Bubble for 5min, until reduced and slightly thickened. Set aside to cool.

2. In a medium bowl, whisk the cheesecake layer ingredients together until combined. Set aside.

3. Preheat the oven to 180°C (160°C fan) mark 4. Grease and line a 20.5cm square tin with baking parchment. For the blondie, mix the sugars and melted butter in a large bowl. Mix in the eggs and vanilla, followed by the flour, baking powder and white chocolate, until combined. Scrape into the prepared tin and smooth to level.

4. Dollop the cheesecake mixture on to the blondie base and swirl it into the batter with a skewer. Dot over the cherry compote. Bake for 50min, or until golden and set. Cool completely in the tin, then chill for at least 2hr.

5. Slice into 16 squares and serve.

Hands-on time: 20min, plus cooling and chilling
Cooking time: about 1hr
Makes 16 squares

PER SQUARE 341cals, 4g protein, 20g fat (12g saturates), 36g carbs (27g total sugars), 1g fibre

Mini Earl Grey Loaf Cakes

These pretty individual cakes are delicately fragranced with Earl Grey tea.

FOR THE CAKES
100ml whole milk
3 tbsp loose-leaf Earl Grey tea
175g unsalted butter, softened
175g light brown soft sugar
3 medium eggs, beaten
175g self-raising flour
½ tsp baking powder
½ tsp ground ginger

TO DECORATE
1 tbsp whole milk
1 tsp loose-leaf Earl Grey tea
75g icing sugar
Small handful edible dried rose petals (optional)

YOU WILL ALSO NEED
8 mini loaf cases, available from baking stores

◆ TO STORE
Keep in an airtight container at room temperature for up to 3 days.

◆ GH TIP
If you don't have loose-leaf tea, you can swap it for 3 Earl Grey tea bags when infusing the milk for the cakes and leave it out of the icing.

Hands-on time: 20min, plus infusing, cooling and setting
Cooking time: about 25min
Makes 8 cakes

PER CAKE 404cals, 6g protein, 21g fat (12g saturates), 48g carbs (31g total sugars), 1g fibre

1. Preheat the oven to 180°C (160°C fan) mark 4 and arrange 8 mini loaf cases on a large baking tray. For the cakes, in a small pan, heat the milk and tea until steaming. Remove from the heat and leave to infuse for 20min.

2. In a large bowl using a handheld electric whisk, beat the butter and sugar until pale and fluffy, about 4min. Gradually beat in the eggs. Next, strain in the infused milk, pressing the tea leaves against the sieve with a spoon to extract as much flavour and liquid as possible. Discard the leaves. Add the flour, baking powder, ginger and a pinch of fine salt, then gently beat until just combined.

3. Divide the batter evenly among the loaf cases, filling each no more than halfway. Bake for 20–25min, or until a skewer inserted into the centre comes out clean. Transfer to a wire rack (still in the cases) to cool completely.

4. To decorate, heat the milk and tea in a small pan until steaming. Set aside to infuse for 10min. Sift the icing sugar into a medium bowl, then strain in the infused milk, pressing and discarding the tea leaves as before. Mix to make a smooth icing, then pipe, spoon or spread the icing over the cooled cakes. Scatter over the rose petals, if using. Allow the icing to set before serving.

Vegan Macarons

There's no denying it takes practice to make macarons well, but if you make sure the consistency is right before piping and your oven is at the correct temperature (an oven thermometer is best for this), you'll be on to a winner.

FOR THE MACARONS
100g icing sugar
150g almond flour, or very finely ground almonds
100g aquafaba (measure liquid from a tin of chickpeas)
¼ tsp cream of tartar
125g granulated sugar
½ tsp vanilla extract
Vegan sugar sprinkles (optional)

FOR THE FILLING
60g vegan spread
150g vegan icing sugar, sifted
1 tsp vanilla extract
Vegan food colouring paste, we used pink and blue (optional)

1. For the macarons, start by sifting the icing sugar into a bowl. Add the almond flour/finely ground almonds, then set aside. Line 2 large baking sheets with baking parchment. Draw 4cm circles on the parchment, spacing them about 2.5cm apart, then flip the parchment so the ink is underneath.

2. Using a handheld electric whisk, beat the aquafaba and cream of tartar on a low speed for 1min. Turn up the speed to medium and beat for 2min, then turn up the speed to high and beat until the mixture holds very stiff

Hands-on time: 45min, plus resting and cooling
Cooking time: about 20min
Makes 22

PER MACARON 126cals, 2g protein, 5g fat (1g saturates), 18g carbs (17g total sugars), 1g fibre

peaks, about 5min. Gradually beat in the granulated sugar, whisking all the time. Beat back up to thick, glossy peaks – this can take a few min (it's vital the mixture is very thick). Beat in the vanilla extract.

3. Add the icing sugar mixture and, using a stiff spatula, fold it in confidently, knocking out the air as you go. You can also smear the mixture on to the insides of the bowl to knock out the air. Keep going until your mixture moves like lava (slowly settling into itself). Test it by lifting a full spatula above the bowl – the mixture should continue to ooze off slowly.

4. Transfer half the mixture to a piping bag with a 1cm plain nozzle and, holding the piping bag vertically, pipe the mixture inside the drawn circles. Repeat with the remaining mixture. Bang the baking sheets down hard against your counter 4 or 5 times to burst any air bubbles. If you have any peaks on your macarons, smooth them down carefully with a toothpick. Scatter some sprinkles, if using, over half the macarons.

5. Set the trays aside at room temperature for about 1hr 30min, or until the macarons have formed a dry skin. If you touch them gently, no mixture should come off on your finger.

6. Preheat the oven to 140°C (120°C fan) mark 1. Bake the macarons in the bottom half of the oven for 5min. Open the oven and carefully rotate the trays. Bake for a further 15min, or until they feel as if they would peel off the parchment. Allow to cool completely on the trays.

7. To make the filling, beat together all the ingredients, apart from the food colouring, with a handheld electric whisk (this may take a while). If you like, split the filling among 3 bowls, and dye the filling in 2 of the bowls to your desired shade. Spoon alternate teaspoonfuls of the filling into a piping bag fitted with a 1cm nozzle. Use the filling to sandwich the macarons together, using a plain base and sprinkled top (if you used sprinkles). Serve.

◆ TO STORE

Keep in an airtight container at room temperature for up to 4 days (or in the fridge for up to a week).

19

Cakes
& Bakes

Blueberry Coffee Cake

A crumb cake flavoured with blueberries and pecans that's perfect with an afternoon cup of coffee.

FOR THE CRUMB TOPPING
40g unsalted butter, chilled and chopped, plus
    extra to grease
50g plain flour
40g demerara sugar
50g pecans, roughly chopped

FOR THE CAKE
200g plain flour
125g granulated sugar
1½ tsp baking powder
150g blueberries
125ml milk
1 medium egg
75ml vegetable oil
Finely grated zest and juice 1 lemon

1. Preheat the oven to 180°C (160°C fan) mark 4. Grease and line a 900g loaf tin with baking parchment. To make the crumb topping, use your fingers to rub the butter into the flour until the mixture resembles large breadcrumbs. Stir through the sugar and pecans. Set aside.

2. To make the cake, mix the flour, sugar and baking powder in a large bowl. Gently mix in the blueberries. In a jug mix the milk, egg, oil, lemon zest and juice (it will curdle, but this is fine). Add to the dry ingredients and stir until just combined. Scrape into prepared tin and level.

3. Sprinkle over the crumb topping, squeezing it into larger clumps. Bake for 1hr, or until a skewer inserted into the cake comes out clean. Allow to cool for 10min in the tin, then transfer to a wire rack. Serve just warm or at room temperature.

◆ TO STORE
Once cool, store the cake in an airtight container at room temperature for up to 2 days.

Hands-on time: 15min, plus cooling
Cooking time: about 1hr
Serves 8

PER SERVING 365cals, 5g protein, 17g fat (4g saturates), 47g carbs (23g total sugars), 2g fibre

Blackberry, Polenta and Orange Upside-Down Cake

Polenta adds a little crunch to this moist cake. Try serving it warm, with crème fraîche or some custard spiked with orange zest.

250g unsalted butter, softened, plus extra to grease
2–3 oranges (see step 1)
300g blackberries
275g caster sugar
4 medium eggs
175g plain flour
200g natural yogurt
1 tbsp vanilla bean paste
50g quick-cook/1-minute polenta
2 tsp baking powder

◆ TO STORE
Cool completely before turning out. Store in an airtight container at room temperature for up to 3 days.

1. Grease a 20.5cm round cake tin, at least 4cm deep, and line the base and sides with one large sheet of baking parchment, smoothing it out as best you can. Finely grate the zest of 2 oranges and set aside. Halve and juice the zested oranges and pour into a measuring jug – you should have 150ml juice. If not, top up with extra juice from the third orange.

2. In a medium pan over medium heat, cook the blackberries, 25g sugar and half the orange zest for 5min, until bubbling and the blackberries have broken down a little. Scrape into the lined tin and spread to level.

3. Preheat the oven to 190°C (170°C fan) mark 5. In a large bowl using a handheld electric whisk, beat the butter and remaining sugar until pale and fluffy, about 5min. Gradually beat in the eggs, adding a little of the flour if the mixture looks as if it might curdle. Beat in the yogurt and vanilla until just combined. With a large metal spoon, fold in the rest of the flour, the polenta, baking powder, orange juice and remaining zest.

4. Scrape the mixture into the tin and smooth to level. Bake for 1hr, or until deep golden. If serving warm, leave to cool in the tin for 15min before carefully inverting on to a cake stand or plate. If serving at room temperature, leave to cool completely in the tin before turning out.

Hands-on time: 25min, plus cooling
Cooking time: about 1hr 5min
Serves 10

PER SERVING 431cals, 6g protein, 23g fat (14g saturates), 49g carbs (32g total sugars), 2g fibre

Tarta de Santiago

Originating from Galicia in north-west Spain, this simple, gluten-free cake is said to date back to medieval times. It is traditionally decorated with the Cross of St James.

Unsalted butter, to grease
4 medium eggs
200g golden caster sugar
200g ground almonds
Finely grated zest 1 small lemon
Finely grated zest 1 small orange
½ tsp ground cinnamon
¼ tsp almond extract
Icing sugar, to dust

1. Preheat the oven to 180°C (160°C fan) mark 4. Grease and line a 20.5cm round, 7cm deep cake tin with baking parchment. Using a handheld electric whisk, beat the eggs and sugar in a large bowl for 2–3min, until pale, light and airy.

2. Using a large metal spoon, fold in the ground almonds, lemon and orange zests, cinnamon, almond extract and a pinch of salt, until just combined. Scrape into the cake tin and smooth to level. Bake for about 30min, or until risen and golden, or when gently pressed in the centre the cake springs back.

3. Cool in the tin for 30min, then transfer to a wire rack to cool completely. Put on a serving plate or cake stand, dust with icing sugar and serve.

◆ TO STORE
Keep in an airtight container at room temperature for up to 3 days.

◆ GH TIP
There are many variations on this cake. Some use only lemon zest and some no cinnamon, so adjust the flavourings according to your taste. You can find cross stencils online – print and cut them out, set on top of the cake, then dust with the icing sugar to leave an imprint

Hands-on time: 15min, plus cooling
Cooking time: about 30min
Serves 10

PER SERVING 235cals, 8g protein, 13g fat (1g saturates), 21g carbs (21g total sugars), 2g fibre

Cinnamon Monkey Bread

This sweetly spiced American pull-apart bread is perfect as part of an indulgent brunch – or even for pudding!

FOR THE DOUGH
200ml whole milk
75g unsalted butter, chopped, plus extra to grease
600g strong white bread flour
2 x 7g sachets fast-action dried yeast
75g caster sugar
3 medium eggs

TO ASSEMBLE
125g unsalted butter, chopped
175g light brown soft sugar
1½ tbsp ground cinnamon
1 tsp ground ginger
50g pecans, roughly chopped

FOR THE GLAZE
60g icing sugar, sifted
1 tbsp whole milk, at room temperature
15g butter, melted and cooled
1 tsp vanilla bean paste

1. For the dough, heat the milk and butter in a small pan until the butter melts. Cool until just warm.

2. Mix the flour, yeast, sugar and 1½ tsp fine salt in a freestanding mixer fitted with a dough hook, until combined. Or do this in a large bowl with a wooden spoon. Whisk the eggs into the cooled milk mixture, then add to the flour bowl and mix to combine. Knead by machine or hand for 5–10min, until the dough is springy and elastic.

Hands-on time: 50min, plus rising, proving and cooling
Cooking time: about 45min
Serves 12

PER SERVING 476cals, 9g protein, 20g fat (11g saturates), 64g carbs (27g total sugars), 2g fibre

3. Return the dough to a greased bowl if kneaded by hand. Cover the bowl with cling film and leave to rise in a warm place for 1hr, until risen and doubled in volume.

4. Grease a 2.5 litre bundt tin with butter. To assemble, melt the butter in a small pan, then spoon 2 tbsp into the base of the tin. In a medium bowl, mix the sugar and spices. Scatter 3 tbsp of the sugar mixture into the base of the tin, followed by a third of the pecans.

5. Punch down the dough in the bowl, then roll into rough 20g balls. Roll each ball in the melted butter, followed by the spiced sugar. Arrange in the base of the tin in an even layer, pressing them gently together. When you have one layer, scatter over a few more pecans (if your tin is quite squat, you may only have room for 2 layers, in which case, scatter over all the remaining pecans). Repeat until all the balls are in the tin, aiming for a flattish surface.

6. If any butter and sugar are left, mix them together and drizzle over the dough. Cover the bread with greased cling film, butter-side down, and leave to rise again for 30min, until visibly puffed.

7. Preheat the oven to 180°C (160°C fan) mark 4. Uncover the tin and bake for 40min, until risen and golden. Cool for 5min in the tin, then invert on to a board and leave to cool, until just warm.

8. For the glaze, mix the icing sugar, milk, butter and vanilla. Drizzle the icing over the bread, allow to set for 5min, then serve.

Strawberry and Prosecco Celebration Cake

This spectacular centrepiece is easier to make than you might think. Decorate the cake as you like – we added white chocolate shards, strawberries and meringue kisses.

FOR THE MERINGUE KISSES
2 large egg whites
100g caster sugar
½ tsp vanilla extract
Red food colouring gel

FOR THE CAKE
275g unsalted butter, softened, plus extra to grease
275g caster sugar
4 large eggs
275g self-raising flour
2 tsp vanilla extract
1 tsp baking powder
2 tbsp milk

FOR THE WHITE CHOCOLATE SHARDS
300g white chocolate, roughly chopped
Red food colouring gel
1 tsp freeze-dried strawberries (optional)

FOR THE PROSECCO SYRUP, ICING AND FILLING
200ml Prosecco
75g caster sugar
200g unsalted butter, softened
350g icing sugar, sifted
½ tsp vanilla extract
400g strawberries
4 heaped tbsp good-quality strawberry jam

Hands-on time: 1hr, plus cooling and chilling
Cooking time: about 1hr 40min
Serves 16

PER SERVING (including 1 meringue kiss and a small piece of chocolate shard) 645cals, 6g protein, 32g fat (19g saturates), 81g carb (68g sugars), 2g fibre

1. First make the meringue kisses. Preheat the oven to 120°C (100°C fan) mark ½ and line a large baking sheet with baking parchment. Beat the egg whites in a large clean bowl until stiff, then gradually whisk in the sugar a little at a time until thick and glossy. Finally, whisk in the vanilla extract.

2. Paint 3 stripes of red food colouring on the inside of a piping bag fitted with a 1cm plain nozzle (or snip off the end to this width if you don't have a nozzle). Fill with the meringue and pipe little kisses on to the baking sheet, lifting the piping bag up sharply to create peaks. Bake in the oven for 1hr, or until firm, then remove and leave to cool on the tray.

3. Increase the oven temperature to 180°C (160°C fan) mark 4. Grease and line the bases of 2 x 20.5cm round cake tins. In a large bowl, beat the butter and sugar together until light and creamy, about 5min. Whisk in the eggs, one at a time, beating well between each addition and adding a little of the flour if the mixture begins to curdle. Beat in the vanilla. Sift the rest of the flour and baking powder over the mixture with a pinch of salt and fold in with a large metal spoon until combined. Finally, fold in the milk to loosen. Divide the batter between the tins and level. Bake for about 30min, or until risen and golden. Leave to cool for 10min in the tins, then transfer to a wire rack to cool completely.

4. For the white chocolate shards, melt the chocolate in a bowl over a pan of barely simmering water. Once melted, remove about 3 tbsp to a small bowl and stir in enough red food colouring to colour the chocolate pink. Pour the melted white chocolate into a baking tin (about 20.5cm square) lined with baking parchment, tilting the tin to spread it in an even layer. Add spoonfuls of the pink chocolate and use the tip of a knife to marble it through. Scatter over freeze-dried strawberries (if using), then leave to set in a cool place.

5. Meanwhile, make the syrup: gently heat the Prosecco and sugar in a pan until the sugar dissolves. Increase the heat and bubble for about 3min until it's just beginning to turn syrupy. Leave to cool.

6. Cut each cooled cake in half horizontally to make 4 even layers. Arrange the layers cut-side up, then drizzle each layer with 1 tsp Prosecco syrup.

7. For the icing, beat the butter until light and creamy, then beat in the icing sugar in stages until just combined. Add the remaining Prosecco syrup (about 3 tbsp) and the vanilla extract and beat for 2min until smooth and creamy.

8. When ready to assemble the cake, set aside about 5 of the prettiest strawberries for decoration. Hull and finely slice the remaining berries. Set the first cake layer on a serving plate or cake stand, spread with a thin layer of icing, add 1 tbsp jam, spreading it out to the edges, then top with a single layer of strawberry slices. Repeat twice more, finishing with the final cake layer. Thinly cover the top of the cake with icing, then spread the rest of the icing around the sides of the cake, leaving the layers partially visible to create a 'naked cake' look. Chill for 30min.

9. To decorate, cut the white chocolate into shards and arrange with the reserved strawberries and meringue kisses on top of and around the cake. Slice and serve.

◆ GET AHEAD
Make the meringue kisses and white chocolate shards up to 2 days ahead. Once cool, store in an airtight container in a cool place. Bake the sponges up to a day ahead, then store in an airtight container. The assembled cake is best eaten on the day it is made.

◆ GH TIP
For an extra hit of fizz, soak the sliced strawberries for the filling in 100ml Prosecco for 15min. Strain before using to assemble the cake.

Cherry Ripple Baked Alaska Cake

Although it takes some time to make, this stunning dessert will reward you with oohs and ahhs from your guests.

FOR THE CAKE
250g unsalted butter, softened, plus extra to grease
200g dark brown soft sugar
100g cocoa powder, sifted
2 tsp vanilla bean paste
250g caster sugar
4 large eggs
400g plain flour
1 tsp baking powder
1 tsp bicarbonate of soda

FOR THE CHERRY ICE CREAM LAYER
300g fresh cherries, pitted
50g caster sugar
1 litre good-quality vanilla ice cream slightly softened
(see GH Tip)

FOR THE MERINGUE
4 large egg whites
200g caster sugar
1 tsp cornflour

**Hands-on time: 1hr, plus cooling, (overnight) freezing
and softening
Cooking time: about 1hr
Serves 18**

PER SERVING 474cals, 8g protein, 20g fat
(12g saturates), 65g carbs (47g total sugars), 2g fibre

1. Preheat the oven to 180°C (160°C fan) mark 4 and grease and line 2 x 20.5cm round springform cake tins. For the cake, whisk together the brown sugar, cocoa powder and vanilla paste with 300ml boiling water in a medium bowl, until smooth. Set aside to cool slightly.

2. Using a freestanding mixer or handheld electric whisk and large bowl, beat the butter and sugar until pale and fluffy. Gradually beat in the eggs. Sift in the flour, baking powder and bicarbonate of soda and beat again until just combined, then beat in the cooled cocoa mixture.

3. Divide the batter equally between the tins and smooth to level. Bake for 45min, or until a skewer inserted into the centre comes out clean. Leave to cool completely in the tins.

4. Meanwhile, make the cherry ice cream layer. In a medium pan, heat the cherries, sugar and 1 tbsp water over low heat, stirring occasionally, until the sugar dissolves. Turn up the heat to medium and bubble for 10min, or until the liquid around the cherries is syrupy. Set aside to cool.

5. Remove the cooled cakes from the tins. Clean the tins and line both with a double layer of cling film, leaving the excess hanging over the sides. Slice the sponges in half horizontally. Scoop the softened ice cream into a bowl and ripple through the cooled cherry compote.

6. Put a sponge layer (cut-side up) in the base of the first tin and spread over a third of the ice cream. Top with another layer of sponge (cut-side down) and spread over another third of the ice cream, smoothing to level. Repeat the layering once more in the second tin, sandwiching the remaining ice cream between the 2 sponges. Wrap the tins individually in cling film and freeze for at least 5hr, or ideally overnight, until the ice cream is solid.

7. To serve, preheat the oven to 220°C (200°C fan) mark 7 and put a rack on the bottom shelf (with nothing above it). Line a large baking tray with baking parchment. To make the meringue, use a handheld electric whisk to beat the egg whites until they hold stiff peaks. Gradually beat in the caster sugar, whisking back to stiff peaks after each addition. The meringue should be thick and glossy. Add the cornflour and briefly whisk to combine.

8. Remove the frozen cakes from their tins and peel off the cling film. Put the ice cream-topped cake on the prepared baking tray and press the second cake on top. Spread the meringue over the top and sides of the whole cake, swirling it into peaks. Make sure there are no gaps in the meringue and that it comes right down to the baking tray.

9. Bake for 4–5min, or until lightly browned all over. Transfer to a serving plate and leave to soften for 10–15min before slicing and serving.

◆ GET AHEAD
You can prepare to the end of step 6 up to a week ahead. Complete the recipe to serve.

◆ GH TIP
For this recipe, do not use ice creams that are scoopable straight from the freezer as they will melt too quickly on softening at step 9. The ice cream needs to be only just soft when rippling through the cherries, to avoid it leaking down the sides of the cake.

'99 Ice Cream' Cupcakes

Adding the traditional chocolate flake to these fun cupcakes in cones makes them look all the more like their ice-cream counterparts.

FOR THE CUPCAKES
150g light muscovado sugar
150g unsalted butter, softened
2 large eggs, lightly beaten
100g self-raising flour
40g cocoa powder, sifted
1½ tsp vanilla extract
12 flat-bottomed ice cream cup cones

FOR THE ICING AND DECORATION
100g white chocolate, chopped
150g unsalted butter, softened
150g icing sugar, sifted
75ml double cream
2 tsp vanilla extract
3 x 20g Cadbury flakes

◆ TO STORE
The iced cupcakes are best eaten on the day,
but can be stored in an airtight container
in the fridge for up to 2 days. Allow to come
to room temperature before serving (the cones
will soften slightly).

◆ GH TIP
You could also top these with hundreds and
thousands, chopped nuts, grated chocolate
or a drizzle of strawberry sauce.

Hands-on time: 30min, plus cooling
Cooking time: about 35min
Makes 12 cupcakes

PER CUPCAKE 457cals, 5g protein, 30g fat
(18g saturates), 42g carbs (32g total sugars), 1g fibre

1. Preheat the oven to 180°C (160°C fan) mark 4. Put all the cupcake ingredients (except the cones) into a large bowl, pour in 50ml just-boiled water and beat with a handheld electric whisk for 1min, until smooth. Divide evenly between the ice cream cones, then arrange the cones in a large roasting tin, spaced apart.

2. Bake for 25–30min, or until a skewer inserted into the centre of the cakes comes out clean. Leave them to cool completely in the tin.

3. When the cakes have cooled, make the icing. Melt the white chocolate in a small heatproof bowl set over a small pan of barely simmering water (don't allow the bottom of the bowl to touch the water). Remove from the heat and set aside to cool for 5min, until just room temperature but still melted.

4. In a large bowl using a handheld electric whisk, beat the butter, icing sugar, double cream and vanilla extract, until smooth and combined. Add the cooled chocolate and beat for 1min, until pale and silky.

5. Scrape the icing into a piping bag fitted with a large star-shaped nozzle and pipe swirls to resemble a '99 ice cream' on to the cooled cakes.

6. Halve the flakes to make 2 short pieces, then cut each half lengthways to make 12 strips. Push a flake into the icing on each cupcake and serve.

Raspberry Muffins with Passion Fruit Drizzle

You don't need to be coeliac to enjoy these fruity, zesty muffins — they'll be a hit with everyone, whether as a lunchbox treat or with afternoon tea.

225g gluten-free white/plain flour blend
125g ground almonds
1½ tsp gluten-free baking powder
½ tsp xanthan gum
250g caster sugar
225g Greek-style yogurt
150g butter, melted and cooled
2 medium eggs
Finely grated zest 1 lemon
150g raspberries

FOR THE PASSION FRUIT DRIZZLE
3 passion fruit, halved
75g granulated sugar

◆ TO STORE
Keep in an airtight container at room temperature for up to 2 days.

1. Preheat the oven to 200°C (180°C fan) mark 6. Line a 12-hole muffin tin with paper muffin cases.

2. In a large bowl, combine the flour, almonds, baking powder, xanthan gum, caster sugar and a pinch of salt. In a jug, whisk together the yogurt, butter, eggs and lemon zest (it will look curdled, but this is fine).

3. Pour the wet ingredients into the dry bowl and mix together until just combined. Add the raspberries and fold through with a large metal spoon. Divide the mixture among the muffin cases (an ice-cream scoop is useful for this) and bake for 25–30min until risen and a skewer inserted in the centre comes out clean.

4. Meanwhile, make the drizzle. Scoop the pulp from the passion fruit and pass it through a sieve, rubbing well to extract as much juice as possible. Stir the granulated sugar into the passion fruit juice and add a few of the passion fruit seeds, if you like.

5. Once cooked, remove the muffins from the oven and poke holes all over the tops with a skewer or cocktail stick. Spoon over the passion fruit drizzle, then leave to cool in the tin. Serve.

Hands-on time: 20min, plus cooling
Cooking time: about 30min
Makes 12 muffins

PER MUFFIN 382cals, 7g protein, 19g fat (9g saturates), 44g carbs (29g total sugars), 1g fibre

Courgette and Pistachio Loaf Cake

Expand your repertoire of bakes with this moist, unusual cake, which gets its fresh green tone from courgettes and pistachio kernels.

◆ TO STORE
Keep in an airtight container in the fridge for up to 3 days. Allow to come to room temperature before serving.

FOR THE CAKE
200ml vegetable oil, plus extra to grease
100g pistachio kernels, plus extra to decorate
200g caster sugar
3 medium eggs
75g natural yogurt
1 tsp vanilla bean paste
200g self-raising flour
1 large courgette (about 200g), coarsely grated
Finely grated zest 1 lemon

FOR THE ICING
50g unsalted butter, softened
40g icing sugar, sifted
180g tub full-fat cream cheese, at room temperature
Finely grated zest 1 lemon

1. Preheat the oven to 150°C (130°C fan) mark 2. Grease and line a 900g loaf tin with baking parchment. Pulse the pistachios in a food processor until finely ground (or chop by hand). Set aside.

2. In a large bowl, whisk the oil, sugar, eggs, yogurt and vanilla, until combined. Next, whisk in the flour, courgette, lemon zest and ground pistachios. Scrape into the prepared tin. Bake for 1hr 30min without opening the oven door, then check whether a skewer inserted into the centre of the cake comes out clean (if not, return to the oven for 5min). Allow to cool completely in the tin.

3. Once the cake is cool, make the icing. Using a handheld electric whisk, beat the butter and icing sugar until smooth and fluffy. Beat in the cream cheese and lemon zest, until combined. Spread the icing on top of the cooled cake and decorate with the chopped pistachios. Serve in slices.

Hands-on time: 30min, plus cooling
Cooking time: about 1hr 30min
Serves 10

PER SERVING 473cals, 8g protein, 30g fat (8g saturates), 41g carbs (26g total sugars), 2g fibre

Gingerbread Latte Bundt Cake with Caramel Drizzle

This seasonally inspired cake works equally well as a dessert or as a special afternoon treat. You can buy mini gingerbread men sprinkles online, or in supermarkets at Christmas.

FOR THE CAKE
225g unsalted butter, softened, plus extra to grease
150g caster sugar
75g light brown soft sugar
4 large eggs
225g self-raising flour
1 tsp ground mixed spice
2 tsp ground ginger
½ tsp ground cinnamon
40g skimmed milk powder
50g ground almonds
2 tbsp instant coffee, mixed with 3 tbsp just-boiled water

FOR THE CARAMEL DRIZZLE
125g light brown soft sugar
75ml double cream
25g unsalted butter

FOR THE DECORATION (OPTIONAL)
Edible gold spray
Edible gold pearls and mini gingerbread men sprinkles
Mini gingerbread men biscuits

1. Preheat the oven to 180°C (160°C fan) mark 4. Thoroughly grease a 2 litre bundt tin with butter. For the cake, using a freestanding mixer or handheld electric whisk and a large bowl, beat the butter and both sugars until pale and fluffy. Gradually beat in the eggs, one at a time, beating

Hands-on time: 40min, plus cooling
Cooking time: about 50min
Serves 10

PER SERVING (without extra decorations) 520cals, 8g protein, 30g fat (17g saturates), 54g carbs (37g total sugars), 1g fibre

well after each addition. Sift over the flour and spices and fold in with a large metal spoon, until just combined.

2. In a small bowl, mix the milk powder and ground almonds, then fold into the cake mixture, followed by the coffee. Scrape into the greased tin and smooth to level.

3. Cover the top of the tin with a piece of baking parchment or foil, scrunching it at the edges. Bake in the centre of the oven for 35–40min, or until a skewer inserted into the centre of the cake comes out clean. Leave to cool in the tin for 10min, then invert on to a wire rack, remove the tin and cool until just warm.

4. Meanwhile, make the caramel drizzle. Heat the sugar and 1 tbsp water in a medium pan over a medium heat, swirling the pan until the sugar dissolves and the mixture starts to bubble. Remove the pan from the heat, then gradually whisk in the cream (careful, it may splutter), followed by the butter. Pour into a heatproof jug or bowl. Set aside to cool.

5. To serve, transfer the cake to a serving plate or cake stand. Spray with edible gold, if using. Stir the caramel (see GH Tip), then drizzle some over the cake. Scatter over the gold pearls and gingerbread men sprinkles, if using. Position the mini gingerbread men biscuits on top, if using. Slice and serve with the extra caramel drizzle on the side.

◆ TO STORE
Keep in an airtight container at room temperature for up to 3 days.

◆ GH TIP
The caramel drizzle will continue to thicken as it cools. If it's too thick to pour, warm it in the microwave on medium power for 10sec, or stir in 1–2 tsp just-boiled water, to thin it a little.

Classic Blueberry Muffins

They're a classic for a reason! Cooking really brings out the best in blueberries, and the hint of lemon and tanginess from the yogurt in the batter accentuates their sweetness.

350g plain flour
1½ tsp baking powder
200g caster sugar, plus extra to sprinkle
Finely grated zest 1 lemon
250g Greek-style yoghurt
125g butter, melted and cooled
2 medium eggs
2 tsp vanilla extract
150g blueberries
1½ tbsp milk

1. Preheat the oven to 200°C (180°C fan) mark 6. Line a 12-hole muffin tin with paper muffin cases.

2. In a large bowl, combine the flour, baking powder, caster sugar, lemon zest and a pinch of salt. In a jug, whisk together the yogurt, butter, eggs and vanilla extract (it will look curdled, but this is fine).

3. Pour the wet ingredients into the dry bowl and mix together until just combined. Add the blueberries and fold through with a large metal spoon.

4. Divide the mixture between the muffin cases (an ice-cream scoop is useful for this) and bake for 25min until risen and a skewer inserted in the centre comes out clean. Remove from the oven and immediately brush the tops with milk and sprinkle with a little extra caster sugar. Transfer to a wire rack before serving warm or at room temperature.

◆ TO STORE
Store in an airtight container at room temperature for up to 2 days.

Hands-on time: 10min, plus cooling
Cooking time: about 25min
Makes 12 muffins

PER MUFFIN 300cals, 6g protein, 12g fat
(7g saturates), 41g carbs (19g total sugars), 1g fibre

Flourless Chocolate and Chestnut Torte

Earthy chestnuts and rich chocolate combine to make a delicious, dense pudding cake.

200g unsalted butter, chopped, plus extra to grease
100g cooked chestnuts
200g caster sugar
200g dark chocolate, chopped
200g ground almonds
6 medium eggs, separated

TO DECORATE
300ml double cream
1 tsp vanilla bean paste
1 tbsp icing sugar, sifted
1 tsp cocoa powder, to dust

1. Preheat the oven to 180°C (160°C fan) mark 4. Grease and line a 23cm round springform tin with baking parchment.

2. In a food processor, whizz the chestnuts and 25g of the sugar to a smooth paste, then set aside. Melt the butter and chocolate in a large pan over a low heat. Cool slightly before stirring through the chestnut mixture and ground almonds.

3. Beat the remaining sugar and egg yolks in a large bowl with a handheld electric whisk until pale and fluffy, about 5min. Add the chocolate mixture, folding it in with a large metal spoon.

4. Using clean beaters and a separate bowl, beat the egg whites to stiff peaks. Fold the whites through the chocolate mixture. Scrape the mixture into the lined tin, level gently and bake for 40min, or until the cake has risen and is firm to the touch. Leave to cool completely in the tin.

5. To serve, whip the cream, vanilla and icing sugar to soft peaks with a handheld electric whisk. Transfer the cake to a cake stand or plate and peel off the baking parchment. Spoon on the cream, dust with cocoa and serve in slices.

Hands-on time: 30min, plus cooling
Cooking time: about 45min
Serves 12

PER SERVING 563cals, 9g protein, 44g fat
(21g saturates), 32g carbs (30g total sugars), 2g fibre

Chocolate, Peanut Butter and Jam Cake

What happens when you combine a beloved sandwich with chocolate cake? We've taken this to the next level by topping it with peanut praline crumble and raspberries.

250g unsalted butter, softened, plus extra to grease
100g cocoa powder, sifted
2 tsp vanilla extract
200g dark brown soft sugar
250g caster sugar
4 large eggs
400g plain flour
1 tsp baking powder
1 tsp bicarbonate of soda

FOR THE PRALINE CRUMBLE TOPPING
50g caster sugar
25g salted peanuts
2 Oreo biscuits (or similar)
25g dark chocolate, roughly chopped

FOR THE PEANUT BUTTER FROSTING
300g cream cheese, at room temperature
200g smooth peanut butter
700g icing sugar, sifted

FOR THE FILLING AND DECORATION
125g raspberry jam
Fresh raspberries

◆ TO STORE
Keep the cake covered in the fridge for up to 2 days.

Hands-on time: 1hr, plus cooling
Cooking time: about 45min
Serves 16

PER SERVING 708cals, 11g protein, 29g fat (15g saturates), 101g carbs (79g total sugars), 3g fibre

1. Preheat the oven to 180°C (160°C fan) mark 4. Grease and line 2 deep 20.5cm round cake tins with baking parchment.

2. In a medium bowl, whisk together the cocoa powder, vanilla, dark brown soft sugar and 300ml just-boiled water from the kettle. Set aside to cool slightly.

3. Using a freestanding mixer (fitted with a paddle attachment) or a handheld electric whisk, beat the butter and caster sugar until pale and fluffy. Beat in the eggs one at a time. Sift over the flour, baking powder and bicarbonate of soda and briefly mix to combine. Fold through the slightly cooled chocolate mixture.

4. Divide the mixture between the prepared tins and bake for 45min or until a skewer inserted into the centre comes out clean. Leave to cool completely in the tins.

5. Meanwhile, make the praline crumble. Line a baking tray with baking parchment. In a heavy-based pan, gently heat the sugar and 50ml water, stirring to dissolve the sugar. Turn up the heat to high and bubble until the caramel turns golden – do not stir, swirl the pan instead. Take the pan off the heat and stir in the peanuts. Scrape onto the prepared baking tray and leave to cool completely.

6. Once the praline is cool, pulse it in a food processor with the biscuits to break into smaller pieces. Tip into a bowl, stir through the chocolate and set aside.

7. To make the peanut butter frosting, using a freestanding mixer (fitted with a paddle attachment) or a handheld electric whisk, beat the cream cheese and peanut butter until very pale and fluffy. Add the icing sugar and, starting slowly to avoid an icing-sugar cloud, beat until well combined. Cover and chill until needed.

8. Slice the cooled cakes in half. Sandwich the layers back together with a thin layer of raspberry jam topped with a more generous layer of the frosting. Spread the top with the remaining frosting. Sprinkle a ring of praline crumble around the top of the cake, then fill the centre of the crumble ring with raspberries. Serve in slices.

Pick 'n' Mix Cupcakes

These cupcakes bring out the kid in everyone. With a rainbow sprinkled sponge and fluffy custard buttercream, they're fabulous even without the scattering of sweets on top.

FOR THE CAKES
200g caster sugar
125g butter, softened
1 tsp vanilla extract
4 medium eggs
200g self-raising flour
1 tbsp milk
3 tbsp bake-stable rainbow sprinkles (see GH Tip)

FOR THE CUSTARD BUTTERCREAM
125g butter, softened
250g icing sugar
2 tbsp custard powder
1 tsp vanilla extract
1–2 tbsp milk
A selection of pick 'n' mix sweets – we used flying saucers, bubblegum and cola bottles, hearts, fried eggs, bears and rings (optional)

◆ TO STORE
Store in an airtight container at cool room temperature for up to 3 days.

◆ GH TIP
Check the description on your sprinkles label to make sure that they are bake-stable, as those that are not may lose their colour or bleed into the sponge when baked.

1. Preheat the oven to 200°C (180°C fan) mark 6. Line a 12-hole muffin tin with paper muffin cases.

2. For the cakes, put the sugar, butter, vanilla and a pinch of salt into a large bowl and beat with a handheld electric whisk, until pale and fluffy. Gradually beat in the eggs, one at a time, adding a small spoonful of flour with each egg to help stop the mixture curdling.

3. Using a large metal spoon, fold in the rest of the flour followed by the milk, mixing until just combined. Mix in the sprinkles, then divide the mixture between the cases. Bake for 12–15min, until risen and golden. Transfer to a wire rack to cool.

4. Make the buttercream. Put the butter in a large bowl and sift over the icing sugar and custard powder. Beat with a handheld electric whisk until light and fluffy. Add the vanilla and milk and beat until smooth. Pipe or spread on top of the cupcakes and decorate with the pick 'n' mix, if using. Serve.

Hands-on time: 25min, plus cooling
Cooking time: about 15min
Makes 12 cupcakes

PER CUPCAKE 418cals, 4g protein, 20g fat (12g saturates), 56g carbs (40g total sugars), 1g fibre

Apple Streusel Cake

Known as *apfelstreuselkuchen* in Germany, this traditional cake has a base of yeasted dough, a layer of sliced fruit and a streusel topping to give crunch.

FOR THE DOUGH
100g unsalted butter, chopped, plus extra to grease
200ml whole milk
100g caster sugar, plus 1 tbsp
7g sachet fast-action dried yeast
500g plain flour, plus extra to dust
2 medium eggs, beaten
1 tsp vanilla bean paste

FOR THE STREUSEL TOPPING
125g plain flour
125g granulated sugar
100g unsalted butter, chilled and cubed
70g pecans, roughly chopped

FOR THE APPLE FILLING
800g apples, we used Granny Smiths, peeled, halved, cored and thickly sliced
1 heaped tsp ground cinnamon
1 heaped tbsp dark brown soft sugar
Juice ½ lemon

◆ TO STORE
Leftovers will keep in an airtight container at room temperature for 1 day.

◆ GH TIP
Next time, try adding blackberries to the apples or swapping them for plums or peaches. If you don't like pecans, flaked almonds also work well.

Hands-on time: 40min, plus standing, rising and cooling
Cooking time about 50min
Serves 12

PER SERVING 498cals, 8g protein, 20g fat (10g saturates), 70g carbs (30g total sugars), 3g fibre

1. Grease and line a 23 x 33cm, 7cm deep tin and line it with baking parchment. For the dough, warm the milk in a small pan over low heat until just steaming. Pour 50ml of the milk into a small bowl, stir in the 1 tbsp sugar and sprinkle over the yeast. Set aside until bubbling, about 5min. Meanwhile, stir the butter into the remaining milk in the pan to melt.

2. Mix the flour, 100g sugar and ½ tsp fine salt in a large bowl. Tip in the warm milk and butter, the yeast mixture, eggs and vanilla. Mix with a spatula until combined. Cover with a clean tea towel and leave to rise in a warm place for 1hr.

3. Preheat the oven to 180°C (160°C fan) mark 4. Tip the dough on to a work surface. Lightly flour your hands and knead the dough for 3–4min, until smooth. Using your fingers, spread the dough evenly into the base of the lined tin. Cover with the tea towel and leave to rise again for 30min.

4. For the streusel topping, put the flour, sugar, butter and a pinch of salt into a bowl and rub together with your fingertips, until the mixture resembles clumpy breadcrumbs. Mix in the chopped pecans.

5. For the apple filing, toss the apples in the cinnamon, sugar and lemon juice. Scatter or arrange the apples over the risen dough and gently press them in. Sprinkle over the streusel topping and bake for 45min, until golden. Cool completely in the tin, then transfer to a board and serve.

Carrot Cake Loaf

A loaf cake version of the family favourite. Swap the walnuts for pecans, if you prefer.

FOR THE CAKE
200ml sunflower oil, plus extra to grease
3 medium eggs
200g light brown soft sugar
200g self-raising flour
1 tsp bicarbonate of soda
2 tsp mixed spice
1 tsp ground cinnamon
¼ tsp freshly grated nutmeg
175g carrots, peeled and grated
75g walnuts, roughly chopped

FOR THE ICING
75g unsalted butter, softened
75g full-fat cream cheese
350g icing sugar, sifted
2 tbsp apricot jam

1. Preheat the oven to 180°C (160°C fan) mark 4. Lightly grease and line a 900g loaf tin with baking parchment.

2. For the cake, whisk together the oil, eggs and sugar in a large bowl until combined. Whisk in the flour, bicarbonate of soda and spices, then fold through the carrots and walnuts. Scrape into the prepared tin. Level and bake for 1hr, or until a skewer inserted in the centre comes out clean. Leave to cool completely in the tin.

3. For the icing, use a handheld electric whisk to beat all the ingredients in a large bowl until smooth and fluffy. Pipe or spread over the top of the cooled cake. Serve in slices.

◆ GH TIP
We used a wide petal nozzle to create piped ruffles on top of our cake.

Hands-on time: 20min, plus cooling
Cooking time: about 1hr
Serves 8

PER SERVING 731cals, 7g protein, 37g fat (10g saturates), 92g carbs (72g total sugars), 2g fibre

◆ TO STORE
Keep in an airtight container in the fridge for up to 3 days. Allow to come to room temperature before serving.

Bottom of the Chocolate Box Cookies

Rye flour adds a wonderful nutty flavour to these crisp-on-the-outside, chewy-in-the-middle cookies.

125g unsalted butter, chopped
125g light brown soft sugar
60g caster sugar
1 medium egg, plus 1 egg yolk
1 tsp vanilla extract
100g plain flour
100g wholemeal rye flour
½ tsp bicarbonate of soda
125g milk, dark or white chocolate, chopped
40g pecans or salted peanuts, roughly chopped (optional)
14 whole chocolates or truffles (optional)

1. In a small pan, melt the butter. Tip into a large bowl and leave to cool for 10min. Using a wooden spoon, mix in the sugars, egg, egg yolk and vanilla.

2. Add the flours and bicarbonate of soda and mix until combined. Stir in the chopped chocolate and nuts, if using. Chill for at least 1hr, or up to 24hr (see GH Tip).

3. Preheat the oven to 180°C (160°C fan) mark 4 and line 2 large baking sheets with baking parchment. Scoop out rough heaped 1½ tbsp of the mixture (it will be stiff) and arrange on the lined sheets (no need to flatten). Top each with a whole chocolate or truffle, if using, or shape each ball of cookie dough around a chocolate/truffle, if using, and return to the sheets.

4. Bake for 13–15min, or until lightly golden at the edges. Leave to cool on the sheets for 3min, then transfer to a wire rack to cool completely. Serve.

◆ TO STORE
Keep in an airtight container at room temperature for up to 5 days.

◆ GH TIP
Chilling the dough allows the flours to hydrate and stops the cookies spreading too much.

Hands-on time: 15min, plus chilling and cooling
Cooking time: about 17min
Makes 14 cookies

PER COOKIE 293cals, 4g protein, 15g fat (8g saturates), 34g carbs (24g total sugars), 2g fibre

Special Occasions

BONFIRE NIGHT

Korean Hot Wings

Sweet, sticky, smokey and spicy, Korean wings get their flavour from a fermented hot pepper paste called gochujang, which you can find in larger supermarkets. The ginger soured cream is a delicious creamy contrast to the heat of the wings.

1kg chicken wings, jointed
1 tbsp black or white sesame seeds

FOR THE SAUCE
6 tbsp gochujang
2 tbsp rice vinegar
1½ tbsp soy sauce
4 tbsp runny honey
1 large garlic clove, crushed

FOR THE GINGER SOURED CREAM
100g soured cream
30g sushi ginger, drained and roughly chopped,
    plus 1 tsp pickling liquid
1 tbsp finely chopped chives, plus extra to sprinkle

1. Preheat the oven to 140°C (120°C fan) mark 1, and line 2 baking trays with baking parchment. Thoroughly pat dry the wings with kitchen paper and put on the lined trays. Sprinkle generously with salt, toss to coat, then arrange in a single layer (skin-side up). Cook for 30min.

2. Turn up the oven temperature to 240°C (220°C fan) mark 9. Continue cooking the wings for 20–25min, turning after 10min, until deep golden and crisp.

3. Meanwhile, in a small pan, whisk all the sauce ingredients to combine. Warm through over low heat. Set aside. In a small serving bowl, mix all the ginger soured cream ingredients with a pinch of salt.

4. Tip the cooked wings into a large bowl and mix through the sauce. Tip on to a platter, garnish with sesame seeds and extra chives. Serve with the ginger soured cream for dipping.

Hands-on time: 10min
Cooking time: about 55min
Serves 4

PER SERVING 481cals, 52g protein, 19g fat (7g saturates), 25g carbs (16g total sugars), 1g fibre

Flammkuchen

Also known as flammekueche or tarte flambée, this is essentially a type of pizza hailing from the Alsace region of France.

300g strong white bread flour
1 tsp fast-action dried yeast
3 tbsp olive oil, plus extra to grease
100g chunky smoked pancetta lardons
25g butter
1 large onion, finely sliced
100g crème fraîche
¼ tsp freshly grated nutmeg
1 tbsp chopped chives

◆ GH TIPS
This is a very elastic dough, so rolling it on an un-floured work surface will help you stretch it thinly, but check while rolling that it's not sticking to the surface.

For a crisper, more biscuity base, you can skip the yeast and rising at step 1.

1. In a large bowl, mix the flour, yeast and 1 tsp fine salt. In one go, add the olive oil and 150ml tepid water and mix to a rough dough. Tip on to a lightly greased work surface and knead for 5min, until smooth and elastic. Return the dough to the bowl, cover and leave to rise in a warm place for 1hr, or until risen and puffed.

2. Meanwhile, heat a large frying pan over medium heat. Add the pancetta and fry for 2–3min, until just cooked but not coloured. Using a slotted spoon, remove to a plate. Add the butter and onion to the pan with a pinch of salt, then reduce the heat to low and cook gently, stirring occasionally, until softened and pale gold, about 20–25min. Set the pan aside to cool slightly.

3. Preheat the oven to 240°C (220°C fan) mark 9 and put a large baking sheet into the oven to preheat. In a bowl, mix the crème fraîche with half the onions, the nutmeg and some seasoning.

4. Tip the dough on to a clean work surface, knead briefly, then roll out to a large rectangle about 35 x 24cm, or as thin as you can make it (see GH Tips). Transfer to a sheet of baking parchment and prick all over with a fork. Spread the crème fraîche mixture over the dough base, leaving a rough 1cm border. Top with the remaining onions and lardons.

5. Working carefully, take the preheated baking sheet out of the oven and slide the flammkuchen, still on the baking parchment, on to it. Cook for 10–12min, or until the base is cooked and golden at the edges. Season with freshly ground black pepper, sprinkle over the chives and serve.

Hands-on time: 30min, plus rising and cooling
Cooking time: about 40min
Serves 4

PER SERVING 601cals, 15g protein, 33g fat (16g saturates), 60g carbs (3g total sugars), 3g fibre

Vegan Smokey Mushroom Tacos

The spicy mushroom filling and creamy avocado topping work equally well in soft mini tortillas or crisp shells, so use whichever you prefer.

FOR THE TOPPINGS
½ red onion, finely sliced
Juice 2 limes
1 avocado, peeled, de-stoned and roughly chopped
2 tbsp vegan crème fraîche
Handful coriander, leaves and stalks separated

FOR THE TACOS
1 tbsp vegetable oil
300g mini portabello (portabellini) mushrooms, thickly sliced
50g walnuts, finely chopped
1 garlic clove, crushed
2½ tbsp chipotle chilli paste
1½ tsp ground cumin
1 tsp sweet smoked paprika
60g sweetcorn (tinned or frozen, defrosted if frozen)
8 mini soft tortillas or crunchy taco shells

1. First make the toppings. In a small bowl, mix the onion, half the lime juice and a pinch of salt. Set aside to quick-pickle until needed.

2. For the lime cream, whizz the avocado, crème fraîche alternative, remaining lime juice, coriander stalks and some salt in the small bowl of a food processor or blender until smooth and thick. Scrape into a serving bowl, cover and chill until needed.

3. For the tacos, heat the oil in a large frying pan over a high heat and cook the mushrooms for 2–3min, stirring occasionally, until slightly softened. Add the walnuts and garlic and fry for 1min, then stir in the chipotle paste, cumin, paprika and 2 tbsp water. Bubble for 1–2min, then remove from the heat and stir in the sweetcorn.

4. To serve, warm the tortillas or taco shells following the pack instructions and drain the onions. Divide the mushrooms between the tortillas/tacos, then spoon over a little of the lime cream and finish with the pickled onions and coriander leaves. Serve with the remaining lime cream for spooning over.

Hands-on time: 20min
Cooking time: about 10min
Makes 8 tacos

PER TACO 196cals, 5g protein, 12g fat (2g saturates), 16g carbs (3g total sugars), 3g fibre

Lentil, Chickpea and Cauliflower Dahl

Warming, full of flavour and deeply moreish. The trick is to cook the lentils until they're mushy. We've used vegan coconut yogurt, but use a dairy yogurt if you like.

1 tbsp vegetable oil
1 onion, finely sliced
2 garlic cloves, crushed
5cm piece fresh root ginger, peeled and grated
1 tsp each ground coriander, turmeric and garam masala
2 tsp ground cumin
1–2 green chillies, to taste, deseeded and finely chopped
150g red lentils, well washed
3 tomatoes, chopped
250g cauliflower florets
400g tin chickpeas, drained and rinsed
100g baby leaf spinach

TO SERVE (OPTIONAL)
Handful coriander, chopped
Dairy-free coconut yogurt

1. Heat the oil in a large pan and gently fry the onion for 10min until completely softened. Stir in the garlic, ginger, spices and chilli(es), and cook for 1min until very aromatic.

2. Add the lentils, tomatoes and 600ml water and bring to the boil. Turn down the heat and simmer for 35min, adding the cauliflower for the final 10min of cooking. The lentils should be fairly mushy.

3. Stir in the chickpeas and spinach to wilt. Check the seasoning (it will take a fair amount of salt) and serve sprinkled with coriander and a dollop of yogurt, if you like.

Hands-on time: 15min
Cooking time: about 50min
Serves 4

PER SERVING 262cals, 16g protein, 4g fat (0g saturates), 37g carbs (7g total sugars), 9g fibre

Rosemary-infused Sausage and Apple Traybake

The woody, resinous taste of rosemary pairs well with the sweet flavours in this simple recipe.

600g sweet potato (unpeeled), cut into 2.5cm pieces
2 red onions, each cut through the root into 8 wedges
8 rosemary sprigs
2 tbsp olive oil
2 tbsp balsamic vinegar
2 red-skinned apples
8 pork sausages

1. Preheat the oven to 200°C (180°C fan) mark 6. In a large roasting tin, mix the sweet potatoes, red onions, rosemary, olive oil, vinegar and some seasoning. Spread into a single layer and roast for 15min.

2. Meanwhile, halve and core the apples, then slice each half into 4 wedges. Carefully mix the apples and sausages with the veg in the roasting tin and return to the oven for 45–50min, turning halfway, until the sausages are cooked through and the sweet potatoes are tender. Serve.

Hands-on time: 15min
Cooking time: about 1hr 5min
Serves 4

PER SERVING 604cals, 16g protein, 34g fat (11g saturates), 53g carbs (22g total sugars), 10g fibre

Chicken Chilli Masala

Sometimes only a properly hot chicken curry will do. Frying the curry leaves and spices at the last minute adds an intense aromatic flavour that's integral to the dish.

2 tbsp ghee or vegetable oil (see GH Tip)
8 boneless, skinless chicken thighs (about 750g), each cut into 6–8 pieces
1 large onion, finely chopped
3cm piece fresh root ginger, peeled and grated
3 garlic cloves, crushed
4 small red birdseye chillies, pierced with a sharp knife but left whole
1½ tsp mild chilli powder
2 tsp cumin seeds
4 tsp garam masala
2 x 400g tins plum tomatoes
125g frozen peas
Small handful fresh or dried curry leaves

◆ GET AHEAD
Prepare the curry to the end of step 3 up to a day ahead, then cool, cover and chill. To serve, reheat until piping hot and complete the recipe.

◆ GH TIP
Ghee is clarified butter, and is often used in Indian cookery. It adds wonderful flavour and richness to dishes, especially when added at the end of cooking.

1. Heat 1 tbsp of the ghee/oil in a wide pan (that has a lid) over medium-high heat. Add the chicken and brown, in batches if necessary, for 5–6min. Remove to a plate and set aside.

2. Lower the heat and add the onion to the pan. Fry gently for 8–10min, stirring occasionally, until softened. Stir in the ginger, garlic, chillies, chilli powder and half each of the cumin seeds and garam masala, then fry for 2min, until fragrant. Add the tomatoes to the pan, then rinse out the tins with 100ml water and add the water to the pan with a pinch of salt.

3. Bring the sauce to the boil and bubble vigorously for 10min, stirring occasionally to help break up the tomatoes. Lower the heat to medium, return the chicken to the pan (along with any juices), partially cover with a lid and cook, stirring occasionally, for 25–30min, or until the sauce is reduced and concentrated and the chicken is tender.

4. Stir in the peas and cook, uncovered, for 5min more. Meanwhile, heat the remaining ghee/oil in a small frying pan over a medium heat. Add the reserved spices and curry leaves (be careful, they may splutter) and fry for 30sec, until aromatic. Quickly pour the spice mixture over the curry and serve.

Hands-on time: 25min
Cooking time: about 1hr
Serves 4

PER SERVING 450cals, 38g protein, 26g fat
(9g saturates), 14g carbs (11g total sugars), 4g fibre

Skinny Sausage Cassoulet

This lighter version of the French classic is made with reduced-fat sausages and hearty haricot beans.

1 tbsp olive oil
8 reduced-fat sausages
200g bacon lardons
1 onion, finely chopped
1 celery stick, finely chopped
2 large garlic cloves, crushed
1 bay leaf
2–3 sprigs thyme
400g tin chopped tomatoes
200ml passata
400g tin haricot beans, drained and rinsed
Small handful parsley, chopped
Crusty bread, to serve (optional)

1. Heat the oil in a large heavy based pan over a medium heat. Add the sausages, fry for a few min on each side until browned, then remove and set aside.

2. Add the lardons to the hot pan and cook for 5min until crispy, then set aside with the sausages. Add the onion and celery to the pan for 5–6min until beginning to soften. Stir through the garlic, bay and thyme for 2min, then return the sausages and lardons to the pan.

3. Pour over the chopped tomatoes, passata and beans. Stir well and bring to the boil, cover with a lid and simmer for 20–25min, until the sausages are cooked through and the sauce has thickened. Sprinkle with parsley, season to taste and serve with crusty bread, if you like.

Hands-on time: 10min
Cooking time: about 45min
Serves 4

PER SERVING 479cals, 33g protein, 23g fat (8g saturates), 30g carbs (13g total sugars), 11g fibre

Stromboli

The whole family will enjoy these rolled pizza breads, packed full of flavour and oozing with cheesiness. If you're cooking for vegetarians, omit the mortadella and pepperoni and make sure that you use vegetarian mozzarella.

225g strong white flour, plus extra to dust
7g sachet fast-action dried yeast
1 tsp caster sugar
1 tbsp olive oil, plus extra to grease
50g tomato purée
50g passata
75g mortadella, sliced
40g pepperoni, sliced
150g mozzarella, drained and torn
25g ready-roasted mixed peppers, drained and roughly chopped
25g pitted black olives, halved
1 egg, lightly beaten
1 tsp sesame seeds (optional)
Flaked sea salt, to sprinkle (optional)
Green salad, to serve (optional)

◆ GET AHEAD
Assemble and cook the stromboli, then leave to cool completely. Wrap them well individually and freeze for up to 1 month. To serve, reheat in an oven preheated to 220°C (200°C fan) mark 7 for 20–25min, until piping hot.

1. In a large bowl, mix the flour, yeast, sugar and 1 tsp fine salt. Make a well in the centre and pour in 125ml lukewarm water and the olive oil. Mix with a wooden spoon to combine, then bring together with your hands to make a soft dough (add more water if the mixture looks dry).

Hands-on time: 30min, plus rising
Cooking time: about 30min
Serves 4

PER SERVING 475cals, 21g protein, 22g fat (10g saturates), 46g carbs (4g total sugars), 3g fibre

2. Tip on to a lightly floured work surface and knead for 5min, until smooth and elastic. Transfer to a large, lightly greased bowl, cover with cling film and leave to rise in a warm place for 1hr, or until doubled in size.

3. Tip the dough out on to a lightly floured surface and divide in half. Roll each half into a neat 18 x 28cm rectangle.

4. Spread tomato purée evenly over the top of each base, leaving a 3cm border around the edge. Next, spread on the passata. Arrange the mortadella and pepperoni evenly over the passata, then top with the mozzarella, peppers and olives.

5. Working with one base at a time, slightly fold in the short sides over the filling. Then, working from the long side closest to you, roll up the pizza in a tight cylinder, pinching the seam to seal. Repeat with the second base.

6. Line a large baking tray with baking parchment. Put the rolled stromboli on the lined tray (sealed edge down), spacing them apart, and cover with a clean tea towel. Leave to rise for 30min.

7. Preheat the oven to 220°C (200°C fan) mark 7 and put in a large baking tray to heat up. Brush the stromboli all over with beaten egg and sprinkle with sesame seeds and sea salt flakes, if using. Slide the stromboli, still on their baking parchment, on to the preheated tray and cook in oven for 30min, until golden.

8. Transfer to a large board and slice each stromboli in half. Serve with a green salad, if you like.

Banoffee Dutch Baby

An American treat, a Dutch baby is a cross between a sweet Yorkshire pudding and a thick pancake. We've filled ours with an indulgent, classic combination of bananas and toffee.

100g plain flour
25g light brown soft sugar
3 large eggs, plus 1 large egg white
150ml semi-skimmed milk
1 tsp vanilla extract
15g unsalted butter

FOR THE FILLING
50g pecans, roughly chopped
175g light brown soft sugar
75ml double cream
75g unsalted butter
3 ripe bananas, sliced
Vanilla ice cream, to serve (optional)

1. Sift the flour into a medium bowl, then whisk in the sugar and a pinch of salt. In a large jug, whisk together the eggs, egg white, milk and vanilla extract. Make a well in the flour mixture and gradually whisk in the wet ingredients until smooth. Cover the bowl with cling film and leave to rest for 45min.

2. Preheat the oven to 220°C (200°C fan) mark 7, and put an ovenproof sauté or deep frying pan (or a fixed-base, 23cm-diameter cake tin) into the oven to heat up, about 10min.

3. Carefully add the butter to the pan and swirl to coat the bottom and sides. Immediately pour in the batter and return the pan to the oven. Bake for 20–25min until puffed and golden (don't worry if it puffs up in the middle – it will sink once it's out of the oven).

4. While the pancake is cooking, make the filling. Firstly, toast the pecans in a dry frying pan over a medium heat until fragrant. Tip into a bowl and set aside, then return the pan to the heat.

5. To make the caramel, add 125g sugar and 2 tbsp water to the pan. Heat until the sugar has dissolved (but is not simmering), then turn up the heat and boil for about 5min, until it turns an amber colour. Stir in the cream and 25g butter. Pour the caramel into a jug and set aside. Return the pan to the heat and melt the remaining butter and sugar, heating until combined. Add the sliced bananas, turn up the heat and fry for 3–5min until the bananas are caramelised, turning once.

6. Remove the pancake from the oven, fill with the caramelised bananas, then drizzle over some of the caramel sauce and scatter over the toasted pecans. Serve with ice cream and a drizzle of extra caramel sauce, if you like.

Hands-on time: 15min, plus resting
Cooking time: about 25min
Serves 6

PER SERVING (without ice cream) 528cals, 9g protein, 28g fat (14g saturates), 59g carbs (44g total sugars), 2g fibre

Pumpkin Spiced Latte Cheesecake

Everyone's favourite autumn coffee-order is transformed into a beautiful baked cheesecake. Magic!

FOR THE BASE
60g unsalted butter, melted, plus extra to grease
200g gingernut biscuits
1½ tsp instant coffee granules

FOR THE FILLING
350g full-fat cream cheese
150g caster sugar
425g tin pumpkin purée
225ml soured cream
2 tsp vanilla bean paste
1½ tsp ground cinnamon
¾ tsp ground ginger
½ tsp ground nutmeg
3 medium eggs, at room temperature

TO SERVE
200ml double cream
25g icing sugar, sifted
60ml coffee liqueur, we used Tia Maria
Ground coffee or cinnamon, to sprinkle

◆ GH TIP
Keep any leftover cheesecake loosely covered in the fridge for up to 3 days.

Hands-on time: 25min, plus cooling and (overnight) chilling
Cooking time: about 2hr
Serves 10

PER SERVING 492cals, 7g protein, 33g fat (20g saturates), 39g carbs (29g total sugars), 2g fibre

1. Preheat the oven to 180°C (160°C fan) mark 4. Lightly grease a 20.5cm round springform tin and line the base and sides with baking parchment. For the base, whizz the biscuits and coffee in a food processor, until finely crushed (or bash in a food bag with a rolling pin). Add the melted butter and pulse/mix until combined. Tip into the prepared tin, level and press firmly with the back of a spoon. Bake for 15min, then set aside. Turn down the oven to 150°C (130°C fan) mark 2.

2. For the filling, use a freestanding mixer fitted with a paddle attachment or a handheld electric whisk to beat the cream cheese until smooth. Add the sugar, pumpkin purée, soured cream, vanilla and spices, and beat again until combined. With the motor running, beat in the eggs, one at a time, making sure you scrape down the sides occasionally.

3. Pour the cheesecake mixture into the tin and smooth to level. Put on a baking tray (as you might have a little leakage) and bake for 1hr 45min, or until there is only a gentle wobble in the centre when the tin is tapped. Allow to cool completely at room temperature, then chill for a few hours, or ideally overnight.

4. To serve, whip the cream, icing sugar and coffee liqueur until the mixture just holds its shape. Transfer the cheesecake to a cake stand or plate, spoon on the flavoured cream, sprinkle with ground coffee or cinnamon and serve in slices.

Toffee Apple Profiteroles

Kids and adults alike will love these profiteroles with a tangy apple custard filling smothered in rich toffee sauce.

FOR THE FILLING
500g Bramley apples, peeled, cored and chopped
50g caster sugar
2 tbsp cornflour
350g fresh vanilla custard

FOR THE PROFITEROLES
100g unsalted butter, chopped
125g plain flour
3 medium eggs, beaten

FOR THE TOFFEE SAUCE
60g unsalted butter
175g light brown soft sugar
125ml double cream
Pinch sea salt flakes (optional)

1. First, make the filling. In a medium pan over low-medium heat, mix the apples, sugar and 2 tbsp water, stirring occasionally, until the apples are broken down and pulpy. Remove from the heat and mash thoroughly or whizz with a stick blender until smooth.

2. Remove 3 tbsp of the apple purée to a small bowl and mix in the cornflour to make a smooth paste. Stir the cornflour mixture into the apple pan and cook over medium-high heat for a couple of min, or until bubbling. Pour into a large bowl and stir in the custard. Cover and chill.

Hands-on time: 55min, plus chilling and cooling
Cooking time: about 45min
Makes 28 profiteroles

PER PROFITEROLE 145cals, 2g protein, 9g fat (5g saturates), 15g carbs (10g total sugars), 1g fibre

3. Next, make the profiteroles. Preheat the oven to 200°C (180°C fan) mark 6 and line 2 large baking sheets with baking parchment. Melt the butter and 225ml water in a medium pan over a low heat. Turn up the heat to high and bring to the boil. As soon as it's boiling, take the pan off the heat and quickly beat in the flour with a wooden spoon. Keep beating until the mixture is shiny and comes away from the sides of the pan. Empty into a large bowl and leave to cool until just warm to the touch.

4. Using a handheld electric whisk, gradually beat the eggs into the cooled flour mixture until smooth and glossy. Spoon into a piping bag fitted with a 1cm plain nozzle. Pipe 28 mounds on to lined sheets, spacing them apart, with each mound about 3cm wide and 3cm tall. With a damp finger, gently pat down any peaks. Bake for 25min, or until puffed and golden.

5. Remove from the oven and, when cool enough to handle, pierce a central 5mm hole in the base of each bun with a skewer, to allow steam to escape. Return to the oven, holes uppermost, for 5min. Cool completely on wire rack.

6. Meanwhile, make the toffee sauce. Heat the butter and sugar in a medium pan over a low heat, stirring, until melted. Turn up the heat to medium-high and bubble for 2–3min, swirling the pan rather than stirring, until darkened and caramelised. Remove from the heat and whisk in the cream (careful, it will splutter). Return to the heat and stir until smooth. Add a pinch of sea salt, if using, and set aside to cool.

7. To serve, spoon the chilled filling into a piping bag fitted with a 5mm nozzle. Pipe the mixture into the skewered holes, filling each bun. Dip the top of each bun in the toffee sauce, then arrange, toffee-side up, on a cake stand or serving plate. Serve with the remaining toffee sauce alongside.

◆ GET AHEAD

Make the profiterole buns up to a day ahead. Cool, then store in an airtight container at room temperature. To re-crisp (up to 2hr before filling), arrange the buns on a baking sheet and return to an oven preheated to 200°C (180°C fan) mark 6 for 3–5min. Complete the recipe up to 3hr ahead, then cover loosely and keep at cool room temperature.

EASTER

Butterflied Moroccan Lamb

Sliced, arranged on a platter and scattered with pomegranate jewels, this simple-to-serve lamb joint looks gorgeously impressive. Get a butcher to butterfly the meat for you for maximum ease.

FOR THE LAMB
25g tomato purée
2 tbsp Greek yogurt
1 tsp ground cinnamon
1 tbsp ground cumin
1 tbsp ground coriander
½ tsp chilli powder
4 garlic cloves, crushed
Finely grated zest and juice 1 lemon
2.5kg (whole bone-in weight) lamb leg, boned and butterflied
40g pomegranate seeds
15g flaked almonds

FOR THE CHERMOULA DRESSING
2 tsp whole cumin seeds
2 tsp whole coriander seeds
30g coriander
30g parsley
4 tbsp olive oil
Finely grated zest and juice 1 lemon

Hands-on time: 30min, plus (overnight) marinating and resting
Cooking time: about 35min
Serves 8

PER SERVING 603cals, 55g protein, 42g fat (16g saturates), 1g carbs (1g total sugars), 1g fibre

1. For the lamb, in a small bowl, mix the tomato purée, yogurt, spices, garlic, lemon zest and juice and some seasoning. Put the lamb in a large roasting tin or ovenproof dish and rub the marinade over both sides. Arrange skin-side up, cover with cling film and leave to marinate in the fridge for at least 2hr (or overnight).

2. Preheat the grill to high and preheat the oven to 200°C (180°C fan) mark 6. Uncover the lamb and grill for 5min, until lightly golden. Transfer the lamb to the oven and roast for about 30min for pink meat (this may take a little longer if parts of your lamb are very thick). A meat thermometer should reach 60°C when inserted into the thickest part. Cover with foil and leave to rest for 20–30min.

3. Meanwhile, make the chermoula dressing. Heat a small frying pan over low-medium heat, then fry the cumin and coriander seeds for 1–2min, until fragrant. Empty into the small bowl of a food processor and add the remaining dressing ingredients and some seasoning. Whizz until finely chopped with a loose consistency, adding a little water if needed.

4. Slice the rested lamb and arrange on a platter. Drizzle over some of the juices from the tin and scatter over the pomegranate seeds and flaked almonds. Serve with the chermoula dressing.

Spiced Whole-roasted Cauliflower

Filled with a nutty pumpkin seed and houmous stuffing and served with a Syrian-inspired sauce, this flavoursome dish is sure to wow.

FOR THE CAULIFLOWER
75g houmous
1 tbsp plain flour
25g pumpkin seeds, roughly chopped
½ tsp ground cumin
1 tbsp chopped coriander, plus extra to garnish
2 garlic cloves, crushed
1 whole cauliflower (about 800g), leaves trimmed
1½ tbsp coriander seeds
1 tbsp cumin seeds
1 tsp ground cinnamon
½ tsp turmeric
Juice ½ lemon
2 tbsp olive oil
2 tbsp pomegranate seeds
1 tbsp flaked almonds

FOR THE MUHAMMARA SAUCE
25g blanched almonds
75g roasted red peppers from a jar (drained weight)
1 tbsp dried breadcrumbs
1 garlic clove
1 tbsp olive oil

1. For the cauliflower, in a small bowl, mix the houmous, flour, pumpkin seeds, cumin, fresh coriander and half the garlic. Set aside. Lay a large sheet of baking parchment into a deep casserole dish (that has a lid) large enough to hold the cauliflower.

Hands-on time: 30min, plus (overnight) marinating
Cooking time: about 50min
Serves 4

PER SERVING 365cals, 13g protein, 25g fat (2g saturates), 19g carbs (8g total sugars), 8g fibre

2. Using a pestle and mortar, roughly crush the coriander and cumin seeds. Heat a small frying pan over low-medium heat and fry the crushed seeds for 1min, until fragrant. Remove from the heat and mix in the cinnamon, turmeric, lemon juice, olive oil, remaining garlic and ½ tsp salt. Set aside.

3. Gently pull apart the cauliflower florets to loosen them slightly. Trim the base and, using a small sharp knife, remove the core to make a cavity (making sure you keep the florets attached).

4. Press the houmous mixture into the cavity and around the base of the cauliflower. Set the cauliflower stuffing-side down in the lined dish. Brush/rub over the crushed seed mixture, working it into the gaps between the florets. Cover with a lid and leave to marinate for 1hr at room temperature, or overnight in the fridge.

5. Preheat the oven to 200°C (180°C fan) mark 6. Roast the cauliflower (covered) for 50min, or until tender. Meanwhile, make the muhammara sauce. In the small bowl of a food processor, pulse the almonds to finely chop. Add the remaining ingredients, 1 tbsp water and some seasoning, and whizz until creamy.

6. Using the parchment to help, carefully transfer the cauliflower on to a serving plate or board. Garnish with pomegranate seeds, flaked almonds and chopped coriander. Serve with the muhammara sauce.

Herb-crumbed Leg of Lamb

Elevate your roast lamb with a delicious nutty, herby crust. It looks attractive, and the crumb also serves as a stuffing alongside the meat.

2kg whole leg of lamb (on the bone)
2 onions, each cut into 8 wedges through the root
1 tbsp olive oil

FOR THE CRUMB
125g white bread or fresh breadcrumbs
2 garlic cloves, peeled
100g pistachio kernels
25g walnuts
30g bunch flat-leaf parsley
30g bunch mint, leaves picked
Finely grated zest 1 orange
100ml olive oil
2 tbsp Dijon mustard

FOR THE GRAVY
3 tbsp plain flour
200ml white wine
400ml lamb or chicken stock

1. Take the lamb out of the fridge 30min before roasting. Pat dry with kitchen paper.

2. Preheat the oven to 200°C (180°C fan) mark 6. Put the lamb in a roasting tin just large enough to hold it, then arrange the onions around it. Season and drizzle over the 1 tbsp oil. Roast for 1hr 30min for pink meat. If your leg of lamb is larger/smaller, allow 18min per 500g, plus 15min for medium-rare or 20-22min per 500g, plus 15min for well done.

3. Meanwhile, make the crumb: whizz the breadcrumbs, garlic and nuts to crumbs in a food processor. Add the parsley (stalks and all), mint leaves and orange zest and whizz again until finely chopped. Alternatively, finely chop by hand. Scrape the mixture into a bowl and mix in the oil and plenty of seasoning – it should hold together when pressed (you may need more oil if chopped by hand).

4. Remove the lamb from the oven 20min before the end of the cooking time. Brush the mustard over the top and sides and carefully spoon on the crumb and pat down (don't worry if some falls into the tin). Return to the oven for the remaining cooking time – a meat thermometer pushed into the thickest part of the meat should read about 60°C (for pink meat). Lift the lamb on to a board (reserve the tin), cover loosely with foil and leave to rest in a warm place for 30-45min.

5. Meanwhile, make the gravy. Spoon all but 2 tbsp fat out of the tin (leaving onions and any crumb mixture in the tin). Stir in the flour and cook on the hob over medium heat for 1min. Gradually stir in the wine and simmer for a few min. Stir in the stock and simmer, stirring occasionally, until thickened. Strain and check the seasoning. Serve alongside the lamb, reheated if needed.

Hands-on time: 20min, plus coming up to room temperature and resting
Cooking time: about 1hr 40min
Serves 8

PER SERVING 679cals, 44g protein, 48g fat (12g saturates), 14g carbs (2g total sugars), 2g fibre

◆ GET AHEAD
Make the herb crumb up to 2hr ahead. Cover
and store at room temperature. Complete
the recipe to serve.

Roasted Onion and Sage Yorkshire Pudding

A classic accompaniment to any roast, and the onion and sage flavours complement lamb beautifully.

50g beef dripping or 50ml vegetable oil
225g plain flour
1 tsp English mustard powder
4 medium eggs
250ml milk
1 large red onion
Small handful sage leaves, about 12

1. Preheat the oven to 200°C (180°C fan) mark 6. Heat the beef dripping/oil in the oven in a heavy-based, ovenproof frying pan (roughly 25cm diameter), for 10min.

2. Meanwhile, in a large jug or mixing bowl, whisk the flour, mustard powder, eggs and half the milk to a thick paste. Gradually whisk in the remaining milk to make a smooth batter. Season generously.

3. Cut the onion into 12 slim wedges through the root. Carefully remove the pan from the oven and add the onion, turning to coat in the fat. Return to the oven for 5min.

4. Scatter the sage into the pan, pour in the batter and cook for 30–35min, until the pudding is puffed and golden. Serve.

Hands-on time: 10min
Cooking time: about 50min
Serves 6

PER SERVING 290cals, 10g protein, 13g fat
(6g saturates), 33g carbs (4g total sugars), 2g fibre

Dairy-free Cod and Chorizo Pie with Cannellini Mash

Chorizo and sherry pair wonderfully with meaty cod in this dairy-free twist on fish pie. Cannellini beans make a great alternative to mash, but you could top this with regular or even sweet potato mash.

7 tbsp extra virgin olive oil
150g cooking chorizo, sliced into 5mm rings
50g plain flour
75ml dry sherry
200ml chicken or vegetable stock
600g skinless boneless cod loin, cut into large chunks
3 spring onions, sliced

FOR THE TOPPING
100g fresh breadcrumbs
Finely grated zest 1 lemon
3 tbsp finely chopped parsley
2 garlic cloves, crushed
2 x 400g tins cannellini beans, drained and rinsed

1. Preheat the oven to 200°C (180°C fan) mark 6. Heat 2 tbsp of the oil in a medium pan and fry the chorizo over medium heat until golden. Remove with a slotted spoon to a plate. Add the flour to the pan and stir until combined. Gradually stir in the sherry and stock to make a smooth paste. Simmer for 2min until very thick, then season and set aside.

2. For the topping, heat 2 tbsp of the oil in a medium frying pan, add the breadcrumbs and cook until lightly toasted. Stir in the lemon zest and parsley, then remove to a separate plate. Wipe out the pan with kitchen paper and add the final 3 tbsp oil. Add the garlic and drained beans and fry gently for 2–3min until warmed through. Mash roughly and season.

3. Arrange the cod, chorizo and spring onions in a 1.7 litre pie dish and dollop over the sauce (the fish will release a lot of liquid to thin the sauce). Cover with the bean mash and breadcrumbs.

4. Cook in the oven for 30min until piping hot and the breadcrumbs are deep golden. Serve.

Hands-on time: 30min
Cooking time: about 50min
Serves 4

PER SERVING 553cals, 41g protein, 22g fat (3g saturates), 39g carbs (1g total sugars), 10g fibre

Lemon, Pancetta and Tarragon Roast Chicken

The crispy pancetta topping will make this simple roast chicken a summer favourite.

750g small waxy potatoes, halved
20g fresh tarragon, roughly chopped
2 tbsp olive oil
50g butter, softened
2 garlic cloves, crushed
1 lemon
1.4kg free-range chicken
12 pancetta slices
400g cherry tomatoes on the vine

1. Preheat the oven to 200°C (180°C fan) mark 6. Toss the potatoes with half the tarragon, the oil and some seasoning in a roasting tin large enough to hold the chicken with some space around it. Set aside.

2. In a small bowl, mix the butter, garlic, remaining tarragon, some seasoning and the finely grated zest of the lemon. Put the chicken on a board, remove any trussing and pat dry with kitchen paper. Halve the zested lemon and squeeze the juice into the chicken cavity, then tuck the squeezed lemon halves inside the bird. Lift up the neck flap and use your fingers to gently ease the skin away from the flesh along the length of the breast.

3. Spread half the flavoured butter mixture under the skin, all over the breast. Rub the remaining butter all over the bird. Sit the chicken, breast-side up, in the roasting tin, moving the potatoes to the sides. Lay the pancetta over the breast of the chicken and tie the legs together with kitchen string.

4. Roast for 40min, or until the legs are golden and the pancetta is starting to crisp. Turn down the oven to 180°C (160°C fan) mark 4 and pour 100ml water into the tin. Roast for a further 40–45min, adding the tomatoes to the tin for the final 20min. When cooked, a meat thermometer inserted into the thickest part of the thigh should read at least 75°C.

5. Loosely cover the tin with foil and set aside to rest in a warm place for 20min, before serving with the juices from the tin.

Hands-on time: 20min, plus resting
Cooking time: about 1hr 25min
Serves 4

PER SERVING 869cals, 52g protein, 58g fat
(20g saturates), 33g carbs (6g total sugars), 5g fibre

Easter Egg Tiffin

Making tiffin is good way to use up dried fruit, nuts and biscuits. Try experimenting with different combinations.

FOR THE TIFFIN
100g unsalted butter, chopped, plus extra to grease
50g sunflower seeds
100g cashew nuts
300g dark chocolate (about 55% cocoa solids), chopped
100g milk chocolate, chopped
50g golden syrup
100g raisins
200g digestives, roughly broken

FOR THE TOPPING
100g dark chocolate (about 55% cocoa solids), chopped
100g milk chocolate, chopped
30g white chocolate, finely chopped
75g chocolate mini eggs

1. Preheat the oven to 180°C (160°C fan) mark 4. Lightly grease and line a 20.5cm square tin with baking parchment. For the tiffin, spread the sunflower seeds and cashews on a separate baking tray, then toast in oven for 8min, or until golden. Cool completely.

2. Meanwhile, melt the chocolates, butter, syrup and a pinch of salt in a heatproof bowl set over a pan of barely simmering water, stirring occasionally. Set the bowl aside to cool for 5min, then stir in the raisins, digestives and toasted sunflower seeds and cashews. Tip into the lined tin and roughly flatten with the back of a spoon. Chill for 30min.

3. For the topping, melt the dark and milk chocolates together as before, followed by the white chocolate in a separate bowl. Spread the dark chocolate mixture evenly over the tiffin. Using a teaspoon, dollop on small blobs of melted white chocolate, then use the tip of a cutlery knife or a skewer to marble them in.

4. Arrange the mini eggs over the top and chill until set. Soften at room temperature for 10min, then cut into 16 squares. Serve.

Hands-on time: 20min, plus cooling, chilling and softening
Cooking time: about 20min
Makes 16 squares

PER SQUARE 418cals, 6g protein, 25g fat (13g saturates), 42g carbs (35g total sugars), 2g fibre

Orange Blossom Baklava Cheesecake

Delicate floral notes and warm sweet spices perfume this silky cheesecake and crunchy topping.

FOR THE CHEESECAKE
100g unsalted butter, melted, plus extra to grease
250g shortbread biscuits
50g pistachio kernels
3 cardamom pods, bashed open
500g mascarpone, at room temperature
125g icing sugar, sifted
1 tbsp runny honey
2 tbsp orange blossom water
300ml double cream

FOR THE BAKLAVA TOPPING
50g pistachio kernels, finely chopped
50g blanched almonds, finely chopped
1 tsp ground cinnamon
100g runny honey
2 tbsp caster sugar
1 tbsp rosewater
Red/pink food colouring (optional)
2 filo pastry sheets
25g unsalted butter, melted

TO DECORATE (OPTIONAL)
Crystallised rose petal pieces
Gold leaf

Hands-on time: 35min, plus (overnight) chilling and cooling
Cooking time: about 10min
Serves 12

PER SERVING 657cals, 7g protein, 52g fat (29g saturates), 39g carbs (27g total sugars), 1g fibre

1. For the cheesecake, lightly grease and line the base and sides of a 20.5cm round springform tin with baking parchment (see GH Tips). In a food processor, whizz the shortbread, pistachios and seeds from the cardamom pods (discard the husks) until finely crushed. Add 50g melted butter and pulse to combine.

2. Empty into the lined tin and press firmly with the back of a spoon to level. Chill until needed.

3. In a large bowl, using a handheld electric whisk, beat the mascarpone, icing sugar, honey, orange blossom water and remaining 50g melted butter until smooth. In a separate bowl, whip the cream until it just holds its shape. Using a large metal spoon, fold the cream into the mascarpone mixture until just combined.

4. Scrape into the tin and spread to level. Cover loosely and chill for at least 6hr, ideally overnight.

5. For the baklava topping, mix the chopped pistachios and almonds in a medium bowl. Set aside 2 tbsp of the nuts for decoration, then mix the cinnamon into the remaining nuts.

6. In a small pan, heat the honey, sugar and rosewater over low heat, stirring until the sugar dissolves. Remove from the heat and mix 2½ tbsp of the honey syrup into the cinnamon and nut bowl. If you like, stir a drop of food colouring into the remaining syrup to dye it pink. Set aside.

7. Preheat the oven to 200°C (180°C fan) mark 6. Lay the filo sheets side by side and brush the top of each sheet with melted butter. Slice each sheet into 8 and spoon the nut mixture into the centre of each piece. Working one piece at a time, lift the corners and loosely scrunch so the pastry stands upright. Repeat with remaining pieces.

8. Arrange on a baking tray and bake for 5-8min, until the pastry is golden. Cool completely.

9. To serve, transfer the cheesecake to a cake stand or plate. Arrange the baklava pastries on top. If needed, mix a few drops of water into the honey syrup to loosen, then drizzle most of it over the cheesecake. Scatter over the reserved nuts and crystallised rose petal pieces and gold leaf, if using. Serve with the remaining syrup.

◆ GET AHEAD

Prepare to end of step 8 up to 2 days ahead. Chill the cheesecake and store the cooled baklava pastries and syrup in separate airtight containers at room temperature. Assemble up to 1hr before serving.

◆ TO STORE

Keep loosely covered in the fridge for up to 3 days. The pastries will soften over time.

◆ GH TIPS

To line the tin, flip the base upside down, then lay a sheet of baking parchment over it. Clip the base back into the tin, making sure the parchment is

stretched, then trim the parchment outside the tin. This will make the cheesecake easier to remove.

To slice the cheesecake neatly, lift off the baklava topping first.

Apricot and Cardamom Hot Cross Buns

For a new twist on the old favourite, these buns are scented with cardamom and studded with dried apricots.

FOR THE BUNS
8 cardamom pods
275ml whole milk
75g caster sugar
7g sachet fast-action dried yeast
1 tsp vanilla bean paste
60g unsalted butter, chopped
500g strong white flour, plus extra to dust
1 tsp ground cinnamon
1 medium egg, beaten
200g soft dried apricots, finely chopped
Butter, to serve (optional)

FOR THE GLAZE AND CROSSES
1 medium egg, beaten
75g plain flour
3 tbsp apricot jam

1. For the buns, using a pestle and mortar, bash open the cardamom pods. Pick out the seeds (reserve the husks) and finely grind. Set aside. Pour the milk into a small pan, add the cardamom husks and heat until just steaming.

2. Spoon 3 tbsp of the warm milk (avoid the husks) into a small bowl and mix in 1 tbsp sugar and all the yeast. Set aside for 5min, until bubbling. Stir the vanilla and butter into the milk pan to melt.

Hands-on time: 40min, plus rising and cooling
Cooking time: about 30min
Makes 12 buns

PER BUN 314cals, 9g protein, 7g fat (4g saturates), 53g carbs (17g total sugars), 3g fibre

3. In a freestanding mixer fitted with a dough hook, or in a large bowl with a wooden spoon, mix the flour, remaining sugar, ground cardamom, cinnamon and 1 tsp fine salt. Strain in the rest of the warm milk (discard the husks), then add the yeast mixture and egg. Mix to combine, then knead (in the machine or on a work surface by hand) for 8-10min, until smooth and elastic. Lightly flour your hands if the dough is sticky.

4. Knead in the apricots until evenly distributed. Return to a clean bowl (if needed), cover and leave to rise in a warm place for 1-1hr 30min, or until doubled in size.

5. Line a large baking tray with baking parchment. Divide the dough into 12 equal pieces (weigh for best results) and roll into balls, tucking the dough under at the base to create smooth, taut tops. Arrange the buns on the lined tray, spacing slightly apart. Loosely cover and leave to rise again until visibly puffed, about 45min.

6. Preheat the oven to 190°C (170°C fan) mark 5. To glaze, brush the buns with beaten egg. For the crosses, mix the flour with 4-5 tbsp water in a small bowl to make a smooth, thick paste. Transfer to a small piping bag (or use a disposable food bag and snip off a corner) and pipe crosses over the buns. Bake for 20-25min, or until golden.

7. In a small pan, warm the jam with 1 tbsp water. Strain through a sieve, if needed, then brush over the warm buns. Leave to cool. Serve just warm or at room temperature with butter, if you like.

◆ TO STORE
Keep in an airtight container at
room temperature for up to 3 days.

◆ GH TIP
Rising times can vary greatly. On
a chillier day it will take the dough
much longer to double in size, so
try to leave it in a nice warm spot.

Plaited Easter Bread

Wonderful served in thick slices with jam, this enriched, slightly sweetened loaf also toasts and freezes well. And the plaiting is much easier than it looks!

250ml double cream, plus 1 tbsp to glaze
750g strong white bread flour
2 x 7g sachets fast-action dried yeast
75g caster sugar
2 tsp vanilla extract
Finely grated zest 1 lemon
4 medium eggs
Oil, to grease
15g flaked almonds
1 tbsp pearl sugar, optional

1. Heat 250ml cream and 75ml water in a small pan until steaming. Remove from the heat and cool until just warm.

2. Mix the flour, yeast, sugar and 1½ tsp fine salt in a freestanding mixer fitted with a dough hook. (This bread is best not attempted by hand as it's a heavy knead.) Add the vanilla, lemon zest, cooled cream, 3 whole eggs and 1 egg white (reserve the remaining egg yolk for glazing). Knead for 5–10min on medium speed, until the dough is springy and elastic.

3. Cover the bowl with cling film and leave to rise in a warm place for 1hr 30min–2hr, until well risen and doubled in volume.

4. Line a large baking sheet with baking parchment. Punch the dough down in the bowl and divide into 4 equal portions (weigh for best results). Roll out each portion on a clean work surface to an even 45cm length.

5. Arrange the lengths vertically in front of you and squeeze the ends furthest away from you together. Number the lengths 1 to 4, from left to right, and plait the bread as follows: place length 4 over length 3, under length 2 and over length 1. Repeat this pattern, always starting from the right side, until the full length of the bread has been plaited. Squeeze the ends together and tuck under.

6. Transfer the loaf to a lined baking sheet, then cover with greased cling film (oil-side down) and leave to rise again (prove) for 45min, until noticeably puffed.

7. Preheat the oven to 190°C (170°C fan) mark 5. Mix the remaining egg yolk and the 1 tbsp cream to combine. Brush over the plaited bread, then scatter over the almonds and pearl sugar, if using. Bake for 30min, until deep golden and the loaf sounds hollow when you tap the base. Cool completely on a wire rack before serving in slices.

(V)

Hands-on time: 45min, plus rising and cooling
Cooking time: about 35min
Serves 10

PER SERVING 472cals, 13g protein, 17g fat (9g saturates), 66g carbs (10g total sugars), 3g fibre

◆ GET AHEAD
Once cool, wrap the loaf in cling film, either whole or in slices (separated by baking parchment). Freeze for up to 3 months. To serve, defrost at room temperature before toasting or serving.

◆ GH TIP
Even though it's slightly sweetened, this bread works well with both sweet and savoury toppings.

CHRISTMAS
The Ultimate Festive Feast

The tree is twinkling, the carols are on and the fizz is chilled, so it's time to treat your family to the most anticipated meal of the year, lovingly created by the GH cookery team.

Menu for 8

COCKTAILS AND CANAPÉS
Spiced Apple Ginger
Knickerbocker
Italicus Spritz
Prosecco and Maple-glazed Pigs in Blankets
Whipped Blue Cheese and Pear Crostini
Fried Stuffed Olives

A STUNNING STARTER
Clementine and Crab Tartlets

THE MAIN EVENT
Dry-brined Turkey with Ultimate
Get-ahead Gravy

A VEGETARIAN CENTREPIECE
Beetroot and Goat's Cheese Roulade V

THE STUFFINGS
Clementine, Sage and Onion Stuffing Loaf
Apple and Chestnut Stuffing Muffins V

DELICIOUS SIDE DISHES
Shredded Sprouts with Brown Butter
and Cheese GF
Duck Fat Roast Potatoes GF DF
Lemon, Honey and Thyme Roasted Onions V GF
Camembert and Root Veg Gratin
Za'atar Roasted Carrots VN GF
Pomegranate Braised Red Cabbage

PERFECT ACCOMPANIMENTS
Spiced Cranberry Margarita Sauce V GF
Garlic Bread Sauce V

THE GRAND FINALE
Chocolate Orange Christmas Pudding V
Chilled Orange Crème Anglaise V

Spiced Apple Ginger

This is also lovely as a mocktail — just leave out the vodka and make sure your ginger beer is booze-free. The sugar-dipped rims make these look extra special.

125ml vodka
400ml ginger beer
200ml cloudy apple juice
Ice cubes
Apple slices and cinnamon sticks, to garnish

FOR THE DIPPED RIMS
1 tbsp cloudy apple juice
¼ tsp ground cinnamon
1 tbsp demerara sugar

1. Start by dipping the rims of the glasses. Pour the 1 tbsp apple juice into a small saucer. In a ramekin, mix the cinnamon and demerara sugar. Dip the rims of 4 highball glasses first into the juice, then into the cinnamon sugar (you can use any remaining cinnamon sugar in coffees or on porridge). Set aside.

2. In a large jug, mix the vodka, ginger beer and 200ml cloudy apple juice. Fill the glasses with ice cubes and pour in the cocktail. Garnish with apple slices and cinnamon sticks and serve.

◆ GET AHEAD
Prepare the rims of the highball glasses up to 1hr ahead. Complete the recipe to serve.

Hands-on time: 10 min
Serves 4

PER SERVING 113cals, 0g protein, 0g fat (0g saturates), 11g carbs (11g total sugars), 0g fibre

COCKTAILS AND CANAPÉS
'Always a must for me, drinks and nibbles set the tone for the rest of the festivities. Take your pick from a warming long cocktail, a fruity tipple and a new spritz idea, accompanied by awesome bites to get the excitement flowing for the main event.'
Meike Beck, cookery director

Knickerbocker

Refreshing yet boozily warming, a fruity cocktail is a great way to start off any winter celebration.

150g caster sugar
200g fresh or frozen raspberries
250ml golden rum
100ml fresh lime juice
75ml Cointreau
Crushed ice
Fresh raspberries, to decorate

1. In a medium pan, heat the sugar with 150ml water, stirring to dissolve the sugar. Add the raspberries and bubble for 8–10min, stirring occasionally, until starting to turn a bit jammy. Strain through a fine sieve, working the pulp well (you should have about 250ml syrup), then allow to cool.

2. In a large jug, mix together the rum, all the raspberry syrup, the lime juice and Cointreau. Fill 8 short tumblers with crushed ice and pour in the cocktail. Decorate with raspberries and serve.

◆ GET AHEAD
Make in a jug up to a day ahead and chill. Complete the recipe to serve.

Hands-on time: 10min
Cooking time: about 10min
Serves 8

PER SERVING 183cals, 0g protein, 0g fat (0g saturates), 22g carbs (22g total sugars), 0g fibre

Italicus Spritz

Rosolio is an Italian liqueur often flavoured with bergamot, rose petals and aromatic herbs. Italicus, a modern rosolio with a balance of honeyed sweetness and bitterness, is great in a spritz.

Ice cubes
50ml Italicus Rosolio di Bergamotto (widely available online)
Prosecco, to taste
Green olives, to serve

1. Half fill a wine glass with ice and pour in the liqueur. Top up with Prosecco and decorate with a skewer of green olives, then serve.

Hands-on time: 5min
Serves 1

PER SERVING 195cals, 0g protein, 0g fat (0g saturates), 19g carbs (19g total sugars), 0g fibre

Prosecco and Maple-glazed Pigs in Blankets

These sticky sausages are always so popular – people seem to hover near the oven when they know they're almost ready!

---

24 ready-made pigs in blankets

FOR THE GLAZE
250ml Prosecco
25ml runny honey
25g dark brown soft sugar
1 tbsp Dijon mustard

1. Preheat the oven to 190°C (170°C fan) mark 5. To make the glaze, bubble the Prosecco in a small pan over a high heat, until reduced to 50ml. Whisk in the remaining glaze ingredients and some seasoning, and bubble for a few minutes more, stirring occasionally.

2. Empty the pigs in blankets into a medium roasting tin. Pour in the glaze and mix to coat. Cook in the oven for 25–30min, tossing halfway through. Allow to cool for 5min before serving.

◆ GET AHEAD
Make the glaze up to 1 day ahead. Cool, cover and chill. Complete the recipe to serve.

Hands-on time: 5min, plus cooling
Cooking time: about 45min
Makes 24 sausages

PER CANAPÉ 150cals, 5g protein, 7g fat (2g saturates), 11g carbs (7g total sugars), 0g fibre

Whipped Blue Cheese and Pear Crostini

For extra crunch, sprinkle with chopped walnuts at the end.

---

1 small part-baked baguette
1½ tbsp olive oil
60g cream cheese
60g soft blue cheese, we used Dolcelatte
1 pear
1 tbsp runny honey

1. Preheat the oven to 190°C (170°C fan) mark 5. Slice the baguette into 16 x 5mm-thick slices, on a diagonal. Discard the ends. Brush the slices with oil on both sides and arrange on a baking tray. Sprinkle over some salt.

2. Cook for 5min, then turn and cook for 5–7min more, until golden and crisp. Cool completely. Meanwhile, using a handheld electric whisk, beat the cheeses in a medium bowl until smooth.

3. Halve, core and finely slice the pear. Spread the whipped cheese mixture on to the crostini and top with slices of the pear. Arrange on a board or platter. Drizzle over the honey and serve.

◆ GET AHEAD
Prepare to end of step 2 up to 1 day ahead. Store the crostini in an airtight container at room temperature. Cover and chill the cheese mixture. Complete the recipe to serve.

Hands-on time: 15min, plus cooling
Cooking time: about 12min
Makes 16 canapés

PER CANAPÉ 115cals, 3g protein, 7g fat (3g saturates), 10g carbs (4g total sugars), 1g fibre

Fried Stuffed Olives

These salty, crunchy morsels are stuffed with either anchovies or sun-dried tomatoes, but you can use a mix, if you prefer. Halloumi also works well as an alternative filling.

250g pitted large green olives, we used Gordal
Vegetable oil, to fry

FOR THE STUFFING (CHOOSE ONE)
4 sun-dried tomatoes
8 marinated anchovies

FOR THE COATING
15g plain flour
1 medium egg, beaten
75g fresh white breadcrumbs

YOU'LL ALSO NEED
Cooking thermometer

◆ GET AHEAD
Prepare to end of step 2 up to 1 day ahead. Loosely cover and chill. Complete the recipe to serve. Alternatively, fry up to 6hr ahead. Once cool, loosely cover and keep at room temperature. To serve, reheat in an oven preheated to 190°C (170°C fan) mark 5 for 10min.

1. Dry the olives using kitchen paper. If stuffing with sun-dried tomatoes, cut each tomato in half widthways, then cut each half into 3. If using anchovies, cut each into 3 to make shorter pieces. Stuff either a piece of anchovy or sun-dried tomato into each olive.

2. To coat, put the flour, egg and breadcrumbs into 3 small bowls. Season the flour with some freshly ground black pepper. Roll a handful of olives in the flour to coat. Lift out (shake off the excess flour) and lower into the egg bowl. Turn in the egg, lift out (let the excess egg drip off) and lower into the breadcrumb bowl. Turn to coat in the crumbs, rolling between your palms to stick them on. Lift on to a plate. Repeat to coat the remaining olives.

3. Pour enough oil into a small-medium, heavy-based, high-sided pan so it's about 3cm deep. Heat the oil to 180°C.

4. Using a slotted spoon, lower half the coated olives into the hot oil and fry until golden and crisp, about 2min. Lift on to kitchen paper to drain. Fry the remaining olives, monitoring the oil temperature as you go. Allow to cool for a few minutes before serving.

Hands-on time: 15min, plus cooling
Cooking time: about 5min
Makes about 24 canapés

PER CANAPÉ 146cals, 3g protein, 11g fat (1g saturates), 9g carbs (1g total sugars), 1g fibre

Clementine and Crab Tartlets

These tartlets are filled with a mix of brown and white crab meat for flavour, but you can just use the white for a more delicate finish, if you prefer.

FOR THE TARTLETS
3 medium eggs, lightly beaten
200ml double cream
Finely grated zest 3 clementines
200g mix fresh white and brown crab meat
2 sprigs tarragon, leaves picked and roughly chopped
40g butter, melted
4 sheets filo pastry
15g Parmesan, finely grated

FOR THE DRESSING
1 tbsp wholegrain mustard
1 tbsp red wine vinegar
1 tsp caster sugar
4 tbsp extra virgin olive oil

TO SERVE
Radicchio leaves
24 clementine segments

◆ GET AHEAD
Prepare to end of step 1 up to 6hr ahead, then cover and chill. Complete the recipe to serve.

1. Preheat the oven to 180°C (160°C fan) mark 4. For the tartlets, whisk the eggs and cream in a medium bowl until combined. Add the clementine zest, 150g of the crab meat and most of the tarragon. Season well and whisk to combine, then chill until needed.

2. Brush 8 x 10cm loose-bottomed tart tins with some of the butter. Brush a filo sheet with butter, then top with a second sheet. Brush with more butter, then fold in half widthways. Slice into 4 equal pieces. Press each quarter into a tart tin and trim the filo edges with scissors. Arrange the tins on a baking tray. Repeat the lining process with the remaining filo and butter.

3. Divide the cream mixture between the tins, then sprinkle over the Parmesan, the remaining 50g crab and the tarragon. Cook for 30–35min, until the filo is golden.

4. Leave to rest in the tins for 10min. Meanwhile, whisk together the dressing ingredients and season. Transfer the tartlets on to 8 plates. Arrange the radicchio and clementine segments on the side of each tartlet and drizzle over the dressing. Serve.

Hands-on time: 25min, plus cooling
Cooking time: about 35min
Makes 8 tartlets

PER TARTLET 338cals, 11g protein, 27g fat (13g saturates), 12g carbs (2g total sugars), 0g fibre

Dry-brined Turkey with Ultimate Get-ahead Gravy

As well as adding flavour, brining, or marinating in a salt rub, results in a beautifully moist roast. Don't let the long cooking time worry you – most of that is the gravy, which can be done weeks or even months ahead.

5kg turkey, with giblets (see GH Tips)
1 tsp black peppercorns
2 fresh or dried bay leaves, shredded
3 tbsp flaked sea salt
75g butter, softened
2 tbsp runny honey

FOR THE GRAVY
900g chicken wings
2 large onions, quartered
2 large carrots, roughly chopped
1 tbsp vegetable oil
2 bay leaves, fresh or dried, plus extra fresh
   to garnish (optional)
200ml rosé vermouth or dry sherry
2 tbsp cornflour

◆ GET AHEAD
Brine the turkey up to 2 days ahead. Prepare the gravy to the end of step 4 up to 3 months ahead, cool, then freeze. Defrost and complete the recipe to serve.

**Hands-on time: 30min, plus brining, cooling, coming
   up to room temperature and resting
Cooking time: about 6hr 50min
Serves 8, with leftovers**

**PER SERVING (125g meat and 100ml gravy)
372cals, 39g protein, 18g fat (7g saturates),
7g carbs (4g total sugars), 0g fibre**

1. At least 24hr ahead, prepare the turkey. Remove the giblets (keep chilled for use in the gravy) and any trussing. Pat dry with kitchen paper and pull out any stray feathers with tweezers. Using a pestle and mortar, coarsely grind the peppercorns and shredded bay leaves. Add the salt and grind until fine.

2. Put the turkey into a large roasting tin and rub with the salt mixture, including a little inside the cavity and under the neck flap. Cover with cling film, chill and leave to brine for up to 2 days.

3. Meanwhile, make the stock for the gravy. Preheat the oven to 220°C (200°C fan) mark 7. Toss the chicken wings, vegetables and ½ tbsp oil in a medium roasting tin. Roast for 45min, tossing halfway through.

4. Tip the wings and vegetables into a large pan (that has a lid). Add a splash of hot water to the empty tin and scrape the base with a wooden spoon to dissolve caramelised bits. Pour the mixture into the wing pan and add 1.25 litres water, or enough to just cover everything. Bring to the boil, then reduce the heat to very low. Cover and simmer for 3hr, stirring occasionally, removing the lid for the final hour. Strain through a fine sieve into a jug (discard the meat and veg). You should have about 750ml stock. Cool, skim off the fat and chill or freeze the stock until needed.

Recipe continues overleaf

IT'S THE MAIN EVENT!
'Turkey is traditional, of course, but especially so in my household, where it's completely non-negotiable! This recipe heroes two outstanding Essex ingredients that are integral to my family festivities: bronze turkey and sea salt.'
Emma Franklin, cookery editor

5. One hour before you are ready to cook, remove the turkey from the fridge. Using kitchen paper, thoroughly brush off the salt mixture from the outside. Weigh the turkey and calculate the cooking time, allowing 30–35min per kg. Clean the roasting tin, return the turkey to it (breast-side up) and allow it to come to room temperature for 45min.

6. Preheat the oven to 190°C (170°C fan) mark 5. Rub 50g butter all over the turkey and loosely cover the tin with foil. Roast for the calculated time.

7. With 45min left before the turkey is due to be ready, heat the remaining 25g butter, the honey and ½ tsp freshly ground black pepper in a small pan until melted. Brush all over the turkey. Return to the oven (without the foil) for the remaining cooking time.

8. Meanwhile, heat the remaining ½ tbsp oil in a medium pan over medium-high heat and brown the turkey giblets all over. Add 750ml chicken-wing stock and the bay leaves, bring to the boil, then simmer for 30–45min. Strain (discard the giblets) and return the stock to the pan.

9. To check if the turkey is cooked, insert a fork into the thickest part of the breast and see that the juices run golden and clear. If not, return to the oven and keep checking every 10min. Alternatively, use a meat thermometer – the temperature needs to be at least 72°C when inserted into the thickest part of the breast.

10. Transfer the turkey to a board, cover well with foil and lay on a couple of clean tea towels to help keep in the heat. Leave to rest in a warm place for at least 30min or up to 1hr 15min. Spoon off the excess fat from the turkey tin and pour the remaining tin juices and the vermouth or sherry into the gravy pan. In a small bowl, mix the cornflour and 2 tbsp water to a smooth paste. Add to the pan and cook, whisking, until the gravy thickens (it will need to boil). Transfer to a jug.

11. To serve, unwrap the turkey and transfer to a board or platter. Garnish with bay leaves, if you like, and serve with the gravy and sides.

◆ GH TIPS
You'll need to start brining at least 24hr before you want to roast your turkey. If you don't have time for this stage, just start from step 3, omitting the salt rub, and instead season generously with salt at step 6.

Giblets add a delicious depth of flavour to gravy, but if your turkey comes without them, dissolve 1 tsp Marmite into the hot chicken wing stock instead.

Beetroot and Goat's Cheese Roulade

The colour of this roulade is so enticing, and makes it a perfect centrepiece for the festive table. If you're not a fan of goat's cheese, cream cheese works well, too.

300g cooked beetroot, in natural juices, drained
5 medium eggs, separated
1 tsp Dijon mustard
1 tsp white wine vinegar
50g plain flour
1 tsp baking powder
150g spinach
150g soft goat's cheese
300g ricotta
50g toasted walnuts, finely chopped, plus extra, chopped, to garnish
1 tbsp chopped thyme leaves, plus sprigs to garnish
Oil, to grease

1. Preheat the oven to 190°C (170°C fan) mark 5; line a 23 x 33cm swiss roll tin with baking parchment.

2. In a blender or food processor, whizz together the beetroot, egg yolks, mustard, white wine vinegar, flour, baking powder and plenty of seasoning until smooth. Tip into a bowl.

3. In a separate large bowl, whisk the egg whites until they hold stiff peaks. Using a metal spoon, mix a spoonful of the whites into the beetroot mixture to loosen, then fold in the remaining whites, keeping in as much air as possible.

4. Scrape into the lined tin and gently smooth to level. Cook for 15–18min, or until firm to the touch and lightly golden. Cool in the tin.

5. Put the spinach into a colander in the sink and pour over a full kettle of just-boiled water to wilt. When cool enough to handle, lift up handfuls and firmly squeeze out the excess moisture.

A VEGETARIAN CENTREPIECE
'There are lots of vegetarians at our Christmas table, and this beautiful roulade ensures no one feels left out. Swap the thyme for any herbs that take your fancy. Leftovers will keep well in the fridge – simply enjoy them chilled with a glass of fizz.'
Alice Shields, cookery writer

Roughly chop, then mix with the cheeses, walnuts, thyme and plenty of seasoning.

6. Lightly grease a sheet of baking parchment and invert the roulade on to it. Peel off the lining parchment, then spread over the filling. With the help of the base parchment, roll up the roulade from a short edge. Transfer to a serving plate or board, seam-side down. Garnish with extra walnuts and thyme sprigs, then serve.

Hands-on time: 30min, plus cooling
Cooking time: about 18min
Serves 8

PER SERVING 248cals, 15g protein, 17g fat (7g saturates), 8g carbs (3g total sugars), 2g fibre

Clementine, Sage and Onion Stuffing Loaf

A sliceable stuffing loaf that the whole family will enjoy. If you can't get clementines, use the finely grated zest of half a small orange in the stuffing.

FOR THE LOAF
1 tbsp olive oil, plus extra to grease
2 large onions, finely sliced
Small handful sage, leaves picked and finely chopped
Finely grated zest 1 clementine
150g fresh breadcrumbs
350g sausage meat
1 medium egg
18 smoked streaky bacon rashers

TO GARNISH (OPTIONAL)
1 tsp olive oil
1 clementine, sliced
Few whole sage leaves

◆ GET AHEAD
Prepare to end of step 3 up to a day ahead (do not preheat oven). Chill. Complete recipe to serve.

1. Preheat the oven to 190°C (170°C fan) mark 5. For the loaf, heat the oil in a pan over a medium heat and cook the onions for 10min, until softened. Tip into a large bowl and allow to cool.

2. Mix the sage, clementine zest, breadcrumbs, sausage meat, egg and plenty of freshly ground black pepper into the onion bowl.

3. Lightly grease a 900g loaf tin. Line the base and sides with bacon (you may have to stretch the rashers slightly to fit), leaving a little overhanging the sides. Spoon in the onion mixture, pressing down and smoothing to level. Fold in any overhanging bacon, then cover the tin with foil.

4. Cook for 1hr, removing the foil for the final 15min.

5. Meanwhile, make the garnish, if using. Heat the oil in a frying pan over a high heat. Fry the clementine slices until caramelised, then lift on to a plate lined with kitchen paper. Next, fry the sage leaves until crisp, then add to the plate.

6. Remove the loaf from the oven. If there is a lot of liquid in the tin, carefully pour it out and discard responsibly. Invert the loaf on to a baking tray. Remove the tin and return the loaf to the oven for 10min, or until the bacon is crispy.

7. Leave to rest for 10min, then transfer to a serving plate. Top with the clementine slices and sage and serve.

Hands-on time: 30min, plus cooling
Cooking time: about 1hr 20min
Serves 8

PER SERVING 378cals, 20g protein, 24g fat (8g saturates), 20g carbs (4g total sugars), 2g fibre

Apple and Chestnut Stuffing Muffins

The apple makes these deliciously moist and fruity, and the satisfying texture is thanks to the chestnuts.

50g butter, plus extra to grease
1 large onion, finely chopped
2 celery sticks, finely chopped
2 apples, coarsely grated, we used Braeburn
Small handful sage, leaves picked and finely sliced
100g ready-cooked chestnuts, roughly chopped
Large handful parsley, finely chopped
150g fresh breadcrumbs
1 medium egg, beaten

1. Preheat the oven to 190°C (170°C) mark 5 and grease 8 holes of a muffin tin, or line with paper cases (we made our own using baking parchment). Melt the butter in a medium pan over a low heat and cook the onion and celery for 10min, until softened.

2. Stir in the apples and sage and fry for 2–3min, to evaporate some of the moisture. Empty into a large bowl and leave to cool. Mix in the chestnuts, parsley, breadcrumbs, egg, ½ tsp fine salt and plenty of freshly ground pepper.

3. Divide the stuffing among the muffin holes/cases, pressing down lightly. Cook in the oven for 25–30min, or until golden and crisp on top. Serve.

◆ GET AHEAD
Prepare to end of step 2 up to 3hr ahead, then cover and chill. Complete the recipe to serve. Alternatively, cook the muffins up to 3hr ahead. To serve, warm through in an oven preheated to 190°C (170°C fan) mark 5 for 5–10min.

Hands-on time: 15min, plus cooling
Cooking time: about 40min
Makes 8

PER MUFFIN 167cals, 4g protein, 7g fat (4g saturates), 22g carbs (6g total sugars), 2g fibre

Shredded Sprouts with Brown Butter and Cheese

Pecorino would also work well here. To save time, shred your sprouts in a food processor using the slicing attachment.

75g butter
400g Brussels sprouts, shredded
Finely grated zest 1 lemon
25g Parmesan or Italian-style vegetarian hard cheese, finely grated

◆ GET AHEAD
Shred the sprouts up to 1 day ahead. Cover with damp kitchen paper and chill. Complete the recipe.

Hands-on time: 20min
Cooking time: about 15min
Serves 8

PER SERVING 109cals, 3g protein, 9g fat (6g saturates), 2g carbs (2g total sugars), 3g fibre

1. Melt the butter in a large frying pan over a low heat. Once melted, turn up the heat to medium and cook until the butter is golden brown and smells nutty.

2. Add the sprouts, turn up the heat slightly and fry for 5min, stirring regularly, until the sprouts are golden and tender. Stir through the lemon zest and some seasoning.

3. Transfer to a warmed serving dish and sprinkle over the cheese. Serve.

Duck Fat Roast Potatoes

We've kept our roasties simple with just a hint of garlic and thyme. Use olive oil if you want a veggie side.

2kg floury potatoes, we used Maris Piper
6 tbsp duck fat
10 thyme sprigs
5 garlic cloves, skin on and lightly crushed

◆ GET AHEAD
Complete steps 1 and 3 up to 1 day ahead. Cool, cover and chill. Complete the recipe to serve.

Hands-on time: 15min, plus steam-drying
Cooking time: about 1hr 50min
Serves 8

PER SERVING 290cals, 5g protein, 8g fat (2g saturates), 47g carbs (2g total sugars), 5g fibre

1. Preheat the oven to 190°C (170°C fan) mark 5. Peel the potatoes and cut into large, even chunks. Put into a large pan, cover with cold water and bring to the boil. Simmer for 8–10min.

2. Meanwhile, spoon the fat into a large roasting tin that will hold the potatoes in a single layer. Heat in the oven for 15min.

3. Drain the potatoes well and leave to steam-dry in a colander for 5min. Return the potatoes to the empty pan and shake well to rough up the edges.

4. Carefully add the potatoes, thyme, garlic and some seasoning to the hot fat, turning to coat. Roast for 1hr 30min, until golden, basting and turning occasionally. Season well and empty into a warmed serving dish. Serve.

Lemon, Honey and Thyme Roasted Onions

This simple and delectable side lets the main event shine. Use red onions for a splash of colour.

4 medium onions (about 600g), peeled
Juice 2 lemons
Handful thyme sprigs, leaves picked
1 tbsp light brown soft sugar
40g butter

1. Preheat the oven to 190°C (170°C fan) mark 5. Trim the tops and bottoms off the onions, then halve through the circumference. Arrange, cut-side up, in a roasting tin or ovenproof serving dish in which they fit snugly.

2. Pour over the lemon juice, then sprinkle in the thyme leaves, sugar and plenty of seasoning. Cut the butter into 8 slices and place a slice on top of each onion half.

3. Pour in 100ml water (avoiding the tops of the onions). Roast for 1hr, basting the onions with the juices occasionally, or until tender and golden. Serve.

Hands-on time: 20min
Cooking time: about 1hr
Serves 8

PER SERVING 74cals, 1g protein, 4g fat (3g saturates), 8g carbs (6g total sugars), 2g fibre

Camembert and Root Veg Gratin

Sliced beetroot would be tasty here, too.

4 medium parsnips, peeled
2 medium sweet potatoes, peeled
500g swede, peeled
2 tbsp olive oil
3 tbsp plain flour
1 tsp Dijon mustard
500ml vegetable stock
100ml double cream
250g Camembert, sliced
50g fresh breadcrumbs
1 tbsp thyme leaves, roughly chopped

1. Preheat the oven to 190°C (170°C fan) mark 5. Bring a large pan of salted water to the boil. Finely slice the veg – a mandoline is ideal – and cook in the boiling water, in batches if needed, until just tender, about 2min. Drain and steam-dry in a colander.

2. Heat 1 tbsp of the oil in a pan over medium heat. Stir in the flour and mustard, and cook for 1min. Remove the pan from the heat, stir in the stock, then return to heat and cook, stirring, until thickened. Remove from the heat, stir through the cream and season.

3. Arrange half the veg in a 25 x 32cm ovenproof serving dish. Lay over half the cheese slices. Repeat the layering once more, then pour over the sauce.

4. In a small bowl, mix the breadcrumbs, the remaining 1 tbsp oil, the thyme and a little seasoning. Scatter over the dish and cook for 50min, or until golden and bubbling. Serve.

Hands-on time: 20min, plus steam-drying
Cooking time: about 1hr
Serves 8

PER SERVING 357cals, 11g protein, 18g fat (9g saturates), 34g carbs (11g total sugars), 7g fibre

Za'atar Roasted Carrots

This recipe would also work well with parsnips.

1.5kg carrots, we used mixed heritage varieties
3 tbsp olive oil
1 tbsp za'atar
½ tbsp sesame seeds, toasted

1. Preheat the oven to 190°C (170°C fan) mark 5. Peel and trim the carrots, then slice in half or into quarters lengthways if thick. Put on a large baking tray and mix with the oil, za'atar and plenty of seasoning.

2. Roast for 45–50min, turning halfway through, until tender. Empty into a warmed serving dish, sprinkle over the sesame seeds and serve.

◆ GET AHEAD
Prepare to end of step 1 up to 2hr ahead.
Cover and chill. Complete the recipe to serve.

Hands-on time: 10min
Cooking time: about 50min
Serves 8

PER SERVING 120cals, 2g protein, 6g fat (1g saturates), 11g carbs (10g total sugars), 7g fibre

Pomegranate Braised Red Cabbage

Much of the work here is done by the hob, with only the occasional stir needed. A great side for Boxing Day meals, too.

50g butter
1 large red cabbage (about 1kg), core removed, finely shredded
500ml pomegranate juice
150ml vegetable stock
1½ tbsp sugar
1 tbsp apple cider or red wine vinegar
125g pomegranate seeds
Large handful parsley, roughly chopped

1. Melt the butter in a large, heavy-based pan over a medium heat. Add the cabbage and cook for 10min, stirring occasionally, until softening.

2. Add the pomegranate juice, stock, sugar, vinegar and plenty of seasoning. Bring to the boil, then simmer for 1hr 30min, stirring occasionally, until the cabbage is tender and any liquid in the pan has evaporated.

3. Check the seasoning and stir through the pomegranate seeds and parsley. Transfer to a warmed serving dish. Serve.

◆ GET AHEAD
Prepare to the end of step 2 up to 1 day ahead. Cool, cover and chill. To serve, reheat gently in a pan with 1 tbsp water until piping hot. Complete the recipe to serve.

Hands-on time: 15min
Cooking time: about 1hr 40min
Serves 8

PER SERVING 125cals, 1g protein, 6g fat (3g saturates), 15g carbs (15g total sugars), 4g fibre

Spiced Cranberry Margarita Sauce

Swap the tequila for water or apple juice for a family-friendly version.

500g cranberries, fresh or frozen
75ml tequila, or use water or apple juice
Finely grated zest and juice 1 lime
Finely grated zest 1 orange
150g caster sugar
2 cinnamon sticks

1. Mix all the ingredients with a pinch of salt in a medium pan over a low heat. Stir until the sugar dissolves. Turn up the heat and bubble for 10min, or until most of the berries have burst and the liquid has thickened slightly.

2. Discard the cinnamon sticks, empty into a heatproof serving bowl and leave to cool completely – the sauce will continue to thicken on cooling.

3. Chill until needed. Serve.

◆ GET AHEAD
Make, cool, cover and chill up to 3 days ahead. Alternatively, freeze in an airtight container for up to 1 month. To serve, defrost in the fridge (if frozen).

Hands-on time: 10min, plus cooling
Cooking time: about 15min
Serves 8

PER SERVING 110cals, 0g protein, 0g fat (0g saturates), 21g carbs (21g total sugars), 2g fibre

Garlic Bread Sauce

We all know how moreish a shop-bought garlic bread can be, so we've turned it into the most flavourful bread sauce.

225g garlic bread baguette
25g butter
2 shallots, finely chopped
750ml whole milk
2 tbsp double cream
Freshly grated nutmeg, to taste, plus extra to garnish
Small handful parsley, finely chopped

1. Cook the garlic bread according to the pack instructions. Cool completely, then whizz in a food processor to make fine breadcrumbs.

2. Melt the butter in a pan over a low heat and cook the shallots for 5min. Add the milk, breadcrumbs and plenty of seasoning. Bring up to a simmer and cook, stirring, for 2–3min, until thickened.

3. Stir through the cream, nutmeg and parsley. Check the seasoning. Transfer to a warmed serving dish, grate over some extra nutmeg and serve.

◆ GET AHEAD
Prepare to the end of step 2 up to 1 day ahead. Pour into a container and lay baking parchment or cling film on the surface. Cover and chill. Or freeze for up to 1 month. To serve, defrost overnight in the fridge, then warm through in a pan and complete the recipe, loosening with extra milk, if needed.

Hands-on time: 15min, plus cooling
Cooking time: about 20min
Serves 8

PER SERVING 203cals, 5g protein, 13g fat (8g saturates), 17g carbs (5g total sugars), 1g fibre

Chocolate Orange Christmas Pudding

A zesty pudding with added richness from the chocolatey twist. Swap the dark chocolate for milk if you prefer a sweeter pudding. Serve with Chilled Orange Crème Anglaise (see right) if you like.

100g sultanas
75g raisins
75g currants
175g chopped mixed peel
Finely grated zest 2 oranges, plus 50ml orange juice
100ml Cointreau
Butter, to grease
1 tbsp mixed spice
2 tbsp cocoa powder
150g dark chocolate (70% cocoa solids), chopped
2 tsp orange blossom water (optional)
125g dark brown soft sugar
50g plain flour
50g fresh white breadcrumbs
2 medium eggs, beaten
25g vegetarian suet

◆ GH TIP
To flame the pudding, heat 50ml fresh Cointreau or brandy in a small pan. Warm gently, then carefully light the alcohol using a gas lighter or long match and slowly pour over the pudding.

1. Mix the dried fruit, mixed peel, orange zest, orange juice and Cointreau in a large non-metallic bowl. Cover and leave to soak overnight at room temperature.

Hands-on time: 25min, plus overnight soaking, cooling and (optional) maturing
Cooking time: 4hr 30min
Serves 8

PER SERVING 463cals, 6g protein, 11g fat (6g saturates), 76g carbs (61g total sugars), 3g fibre

2. Lightly grease a 900ml pudding basin and line the base with a disc of baking parchment. Put a 35.5cm square of foil on top of a square of baking parchment the same size. Fold a 4cm pleat across the centre. Set aside.

3. Add the remaining ingredients to the soaked fruit and mix well. Spoon into the prepared basin, pressing down to level. Put the pleated foil and parchment square (foil-side up) on top of the basin and smooth down to cover. Using a long piece of string, tie securely under the lip of the basin and loop over the top and tie to make a handle.

4. To cook, put a heatproof saucer in the base of a large, deep pan that has a tight-fitting lid. Lower in the prepared pudding and pour in enough water to come halfway up the sides of the basin, taking care not to get any on top of the pudding. Cover the pan with the lid, bring to the boil, then simmer gently for 4hr 30min, checking the water level and topping up as necessary.

5. If not serving immediately, carefully remove the pudding from the pan and cool completely. Wrap the basin, still with foil lid, in several layers of cling film, followed by a layer of foil. Store in a cool, dark place to mature for up to 2 months.

6. To reheat, remove the foil, cling film and lid. Re-cover as per the instructions in steps 2 and 3. Following the method in step 4, reheat for 2hr, or until piping hot in the centre when pierced with a skewer. To serve, remove from the pan and allow to sit for 5min. Carefully remove the lid and invert on to a cake stand or serving plate. Peel off the baking parchment and serve.

Chilled Orange Crème Anglaise

The ideal accompaniment to our Chocolate Orange Christmas Pudding.

300ml whole milk
150ml double cream
2 medium egg yolks
2 tsp cornflour
1 tsp vanilla bean paste
3 tbsp caster sugar
Finely grated zest 1 orange

1. Heat the milk and cream in a medium pan over a medium heat until steaming, but not boiling. Meanwhile, in a heatproof bowl, whisk the egg yolks, cornflour, vanilla and sugar until smooth.

2. Gradually whisk in the hot milk mixture, then pour back into the pan. Return to a medium heat and cook, whisking constantly, until slightly thickened, about 1–2min.

3. Remove from the heat and whisk through the orange zest. Pour into a jug, then lay baking parchment or cling film directly on the surface to stop a skin from forming. Cool and then chill until needed. Serve.

◆ GET AHEAD
Make, cool and chill up to 2 days ahead.

Hands-on time: 10min, plus cooling and chilling
Cooking time: about 10min
Serves 8

PER SERVING 159cals, 2g protein, 13g fat (8g saturates), 9g carbs (8g total sugars), 0g fibre

NOW THE GRAND FINALE!
'A chocolate orange is a big thing in our family, since Father Christmas always put one in the bottom of our stockings. That's why I incorporated those flavours into this glorious pudding – the perfect end to our feast.'
Georgie D'Arcy Coles, cookery assistant

Index